CONTENTS

THE EM
NEGLEC

THE EMOTIONALLY ABUSED AND NEGLECTED CHILD

Identification, Assessment and Intervention
A Practice Handbook
Second Edition

Dorota Iwaniec

John Wiley & Sons, Ltd

Designations used by companies to distinguish their products are often claimed as trademarks. All brand names and product names used in this book are trade names, service marks, trademarks or registered trademarks of their respective owners. The Publisher is not associated with any product or vendor mentioned in this book.

This publication is designed to provide accurate and authoritative information in regard to the subject matter covered. It is sold on the understanding that the Publisher is not engaged in rendering professional services. If professional advice or other expert assistance is required, the services of a competent professional should be sought.

Other Wiley Editorial Offices

John Wiley & Sons Inc., 111 River Street, Hoboken, NJ 07030, USA

Jossey-Bass, 989 Market Street, San Francisco, CA 94103-1741, USA

Wiley-VCH Verlag GmbH, Boschstr. 12, D-69469 Weinheim, Germany

John Wiley & Sons Australia Ltd, 42 McDougall Street, Milton, Queensland 4064, Australia

John Wiley & Sons (Asia) Pte Ltd, 2 Clementi Loop #02-01, Jin Xing Distripark, Singapore 129809

John Wiley & Sons Canada Ltd, 22 Worcester Road, Etobicoke, Ontario, Canada M9W 1L1

Wiley also publishes its books in a variety of electronic formats. Some content that appears in print may not be available in electronic books.

Library of Congress Cataloging in Publication Data

The emotionally abused and neglected child : identification, assessment and intervention : a practice handbook / Dorota Iwaniec. — 2nd ed.
    p. cm.
Includes bibliographical references and index.
ISBN-13: 978-0-470-01100-3 (cloth : alk. paper)
ISBN-10: 0-470-01100-9 (cloth : alk. paper)
ISBN-13: 978-0-470-01101-0 (pbk. : alk. paper)
ISBN-10: 0-470-01101-7 (pbk. : alk. paper)
1. Psychologically abused children—Mental health. 2. Child psychotherapy. I. Title.
RJ507.A29I93 2006
618.92'89—dc22   2005029096

British Library Cataloguing in Publication Data

A catalogue record for this book is available from the British Library

ISBN-13 978-0-470-01100-3 (hbk)   978-0-470-01101-0 (pbk)
ISBN-10 0-470-01100-9 (hbk)   0-470-01101-7 (pbk)

Typeset in 10/12pt Palatino by Integra Software Services Pvt. Ltd, Pondicherry, India
Printed and bound in Great Britain by Antony Rowe Ltd, Chippenham, Wiltshire
This book is printed on acid-free paper responsibly manufactured from sustainable forestry in which at least two trees are planted for each one used for paper production.

*Non ignara mali miseris succurrere disco**

[Not a stranger to misfortune, I learn
to succour those who are unhappy]

for my husband
James,
with love

---

* Publius Vergilius Maro (70–19 BC): *Æneid*, Book 1, Line 630

ABOUT THE AUTHOR

Dorota Iwaniec is Emeritus Professor of Social Work and former Director of the Institute of Child Care Research at Queen's University Belfast (she retired in 2005). Professor Iwaniec is well-known for her extensive research and writing in the areas of emotional abuse and neglect and failure to thrive in children. She is the author of nearly a hundred scientific and practice papers and many chapters in edited books. She has written several books on the subject of child care and child protection and some books have been translated into different languages. Her writing is influenced by continuous practice and empirical evidence.

PREFACE

The first edition of *The Emotionally Abused and Neglected Child: Identification, Assessment and Intervention* was published 11 years ago. It focused very much on children who, due to neglect and emotional maltreatment, were insufficiently fed and nurtured, and therefore failed to thrive. Since then, our understanding of what constitutes emotional abuse and neglect and of how a child's growth, development, behaviour, and well-being can be affected, has considerably increased. Public awareness of the problem and the professional skills in dealing with such cases have also improved.

The second edition is virtually a new book: it goes well beyond an update of the literature, and has been expanded to include much new material (e.g. emotional abuse outside the family, covering abuse of children in care, in schools, in remand centres for young offenders, and peer bullying), and a further chapter has been written on emotional abuse at home, including domestic violence, substance misuse, emotional neglect, and the effect of divorce on children. A study of children with disabilities is also an addition to the book, as is mention of risk and resilience. There is an extensive chapter on assessment based on the ecological model on children-in-need, covering parental capacity, children's development and behaviour, and family and environmental factors. Many check-lists, questionnaires, and suggestions on how to identify and assess emotional abuse and neglect are also included.

Intervention and treatment of emotional abuse are covered in five extensive chapters, ranging from levels of intervention and service provision at different stages of presenting problems to individual work with children and families. Therapeutic methods include: behavioural/cognitive work with parents and children; family therapy; counselling; group work; attachment-work; play therapy; building resilience; social skills and assertiveness training; problem-solving; and many other techniques designed to deal with the effects of emotional abuse on children and emotionally abusive behaviour of parents and carers.

Service provision to help these children is described, elaborated upon, and discussed (e.g. day-nurseries, family centres, foster-placements, home-visitation, case-monitoring, and accommodation of children whose carers experience parenting problems). The last chapter looks at the legal aspects and the difficulties of taking emotional-abuse cases through the courts.

Issues of social workers' professional credibility and confidence when dealing with emotional maltreatment of children are discussed. Attention is drawn to different roles and responsibilities of legal and social work professionals, and the necessity of receiving joint training is highlighted.

The primary sources for the first and second editions of *The Emotionally Abused and Neglected Child: Identification, Assessment and Intervention* have been a personal, lifelong interest in the subject, and experience gained in working in the field for over 40 years. Growing up after the 1939–45 war in Poland (which was devastated not only in an economic and physical sense, but also psychologically and emotionally) provided many unforgettable and painful images of orphaned and abandoned children who, at times, had no one to turn to for emotional support, comfort, reassurance, and protection. The images of very sad, detached, and devastated children are still with me to this day. There were many children whose mothers became so completely depressed (as the result of losses, cruelty, and war atrocities) that they could not provide a nurturing environment for their traumatised children. These children were often brought up in children's homes or by relatives who cared for them because it was expected of them to do so and not because they wanted to. The lives of such children, as can be imagined, were grim, sad, devoid of affection and hope for the future, and often led to emotional breakdown and mental-health problems.

Later on in my adult life my social work experience gave me the opportunity to work with many such children, and prompted extensive research work, the development of helping strategies, and evaluation of the effectiveness of intervention. I saw many very unhappy children living with families, which, for one reason or another, could not provide the basic ingredients for the child's sense of security and feelings of being loved. Many of these children succumbed to parental ill-treatment, at times with devastating results. The last ten years or so brought me back in touch with these children again through expert-witness work for the courts.

While the literature on what constitutes emotional abuse and how to identify it increases yearly, there is little written on how to help these children and how to evaluate the results of intervention and treatment. The second edition provides an extended section on intervention which, I hope, will help overburdened practitioners to choose methods, techniques, and services which will match the needs of those in need of care or protection. I also hope that this book will provide teaching material for students preparing for professional life and who, through their work, may come into contact with children such as those described within.

ACKNOWLEDGEMENTS

I acknowledge, most warmly and with gratitude, the support and guidance given by my husband, Professor James Stevens Curl, during the writing of this book. I am also very grateful and indebted to Mrs Maura Dunn for her unfailing assistance and help during the production of the book and her continuous loyal support and good humour in writing and rewriting the text. A big 'thank you' goes to Mrs Alice Sluckin who provided me with much interesting material. I am also very grateful to Dr Siobhan Higgins and Ms Siobhan McAlister for helping with the preparation of the text and literature review. Warm thanks also go to Dr Emma Larkin. My thanks go to my colleagues at Queen's University Belfast for their encouragement and interest in my work and, in particular, my staff at the Institute of Child Care Research.

Dorota Iwaniec
Holywood, Co Down

SECTION 1

THE PROBLEM

CHAPTER 1

INTRODUCTION TO EMOTIONAL ABUSE AND NEGLECT

CONTENTS

INTRODUCTION

Children, young people, or adults who suffered some form of abuse in the past, always refer to emotional hurt and psychological pain before mentioning physical pain. Almost without exception, victims of abuse will talk about fear, anxiety, loneliness, emotional lack of support, and being ignored, degraded and humiliated, feeling unloved and unwanted, and being powerless when terrorised or tormented by parents or carers. The popular slogan 'words can hit as hard as fists' is true when hurtful words are often used, and they mean to hurt. Gestures, tones of voice, manner, and frequency and intensity of these within the context of poor relationships will convey negative messages of not being loved, wanted, or appreciated to a child. Psychological unavailability of parents or carers to children, and hostile, rejecting, low-on-warmth, and high-on-criticism parental behaviour are identified as emotional abuse and neglect. But, in spite of recognised problems pointing to emotional abuse, this is the most difficult area of child maltreatment to measure with reasonable accuracy because parental behaviour and the effects on the child (including probable long-term development, competence, and social adjustment) have to be taken into account.

Unlike sexual and physical abuse and neglect, the emotional-abuse concept has been much slower to gain acceptance as a part of child protection, requiring conferencing, registration, assessment, and intervention including (in severe cases) court proceedings; such tardiness is not surprising, as emotional abuse is a dynamic and changeable social construct. What is considered today as emotionally abusive, requiring some form of intervention, was not the case a quarter of a century ago in the UK, and is not seen as abuse in many other countries even now. The very private and highly nebulous qualities of emotional abuse make it a difficult concept to define in a useful operational sense (see Chapter 2 for further discussion.)

However, there is now a general consensus that emotional abuse is more prevalent than realised: it is at the core of all major forms of abuse and neglect, is more damaging in its impact than acts of physical and sexual abuse alone, and requires special attention to disentangle it from physical and sexual acts of maltreatment. Much work has been done on both sides of the Atlantic in the last decade or so to provide empirical evidence and to expand theoretical knowledge on emotional abuse and neglect. Practice, although still somewhat problematic in resource allocation and protection, has become more explicit and better informed (Brassard, Germain, & Hart, 1987; Doyle, 1997; Glaser & Prior, 2002; Iwaniec, 1995).

There is also growing recognition that emotional abuse happens not only within the walls of the family home. Some children who are looked after, either by foster-parents or who reside in children's homes, are also sometimes emotionally abused and neglected. Equally, young people in secure units or other penal systems are terrorised, degraded, humiliated, and threatened by staff and by older inmates. Given their vulnerability and problems, which led them to these institutions in the first place, it is not surprising that they cannot cope, and often are driven, out of despair, to take their own lives (see Chapter 4 for further discussion). It is believed that emotional abuse is quite widespread, but suffered in silence.

Services to help these children are rarely offered, as emotional abuse is still considered not serious enough to warrant prompt intervention. Taking into consideration the financial cost of child-protection work it is not surprising that decisions are made on what is 'seen' (physical injury) or what is morally unacceptable 'sexual abuse', leaving little resources and time for equally damaging emotional-abuse and neglect cases. In the United Kingdom the total cost for child protection per annum has been estimated at £735 million and in the United States at US $12 410 (World Health Organisation, 1999). Much discussion has taken place in recent years to work out policies and procedures to reduce cost, but at the same time to protect children. It would appear that much more should be done at a universal level as prevention. It is too late to step in when the damage is done and, subsequently, intervention required at such times is very costly, of long duration, and quite often ineffective.

Binggeli, Hart, & Brassard (2001), after reviewing literature on emotional abuse (occurring either alone or in combination with other forms of maltreatment), estimated that psychological maltreatment may have been significantly present in the childhood histories of more than one-third of the general adult population of the United States. In addition, they estimated that approximately 10–15% of all people have experienced severe and chronic forms of emotional abuse. In spite of using conservative definitions, their figures for such experiences nevertheless were high.

HISTORY OF THE CONCEPT

It would be fair to say that emotional abuse has been brought back to the public's attention as a result of growing awareness and well-publicised cases of physical and sexual abuse and neglect. Yet emotional abuse is by no means a new phenomenon: Klosinski (1993) pointed out that emotional abuse (or the concept of emotional abuse) was an area of interest and research in the fields of psychoanalysis and developmental psychology in the early part of the twentieth century, and that the early literature on insecure attachment was clearly related to hostile, rejective, and cruel parenting, which forms the basis of contemporary understanding of emotional abuse. Of course, literature, paintings, and historical accounts are full of descriptions and depictions of emotionally maltreated children and young people: the novelist Charles Dickens (1812–70) alone brought to public attention the plight of abandoned, terrorised, corrupted, rejected, and destitute children (what we would now call 'street children') in nineteenth-century England.

Rudyard Kipling (1865–1936), writer and poet, vividly described in a short story the emotionally traumatising experiences he and his sister Trix had as children, when their parents left them in England with a completely strange and rather cruel woman before returning to India. This was by no means unusual for families serving the Raj, as many children whose parents worked and lived in India were boarded out in England. However, in Kipling's case it was disastrous. In the short story entitled *Baa Baa, Black Sheep*, republished in 1995 by the Penguin Group, he described how the woman (and her family) treated them. She had always referred to him as 'Black Sheep', which left an emotional scar on him for life. Quoting the well-known nursery rhyme to express his own feelings, he saw himself in it:

> Baa, baa, black sheep
> Have you any wool?
> Yes, Sir, yes, Sir,

> Three bags full:
> One for the master,
> And one for the dame,
> None for the little boy
> Who cries down the lane.

Rudyard and Trix were boarded with Mrs Pryse Agar Holloway in Southsea, Hampshire, where they stayed for several years. Neither child was prepared for this, nor was anything explained to them beforehand. Trix wrote that it was 'like a double death, or rather, like an avalanche that had swept away everything happy and familiar' (Fleming, 1939, p. 171).

When Kipling and his sister found their mother had gone, they went to the sea-shore to try to find her, but could not do so (Kipling, 1995, p. 11). Soon 'Aunty Rosa' (Mrs Holloway), according to Kipling, set sister against brother, humiliated the 'Black Sheep' (as she called him), and permitted (even egged on) her son to terrorise and torment the boy, both mentally and physically, while she denied him simple things. On top of these horrors, the youngster was introduced to a fearsome Calvinistic hell (Kipling, 1990, Ch. 1), and forced to read religious books and tracts, thus acquiring biblical knowledge and imagery. For Rudyard it was terrifying teaching as he had grown up, while in India with his parents, in a relaxed and undemanding way.

After a few years 'Punch' (as Kipling was called by his parents) began to show manifestations of clumsiness, banging into things, breaking objects, becoming frightened of simple things, and terrified all the time, as his sister became more and more estranged. One day, a 'visitor...who knew their parents came to see the children, looked deep down in the "Black Sheep's" eyes for half a minute, and then said suddenly: "Good God, the little chap's nearly blind"'. The 'visitor' was none other than Edward Burne-Jones (1833–98), the distinguished painter (married to Alice Kipling's sister Georgiana [1840–1920]), who immediately informed Alice Kipling of her son's condition. When Alice arrived at what Kipling called the 'House of Desolation' her children, unsurprisingly, had difficulty adjusting to her, and the 'Black Sheep' referred to her as 'that woman'. Nevertheless, Alice noticed that the cold, repressive, loveless regime at Southsea had distressed the boy 'with a system of small deceptions' which 'Aunty Rosa' then magnified into 'deadly sins'. The 'Fear of the Lord was so often the beginning of falsehood' (Kipling, 1995, p. 38). Having

> drunk deep of the bitter waters of Hate, Suspicion, and Despair, all the love in the world will not wholly take away that knowledge; though it may turn darkened eyes for a while to the light, and teach Faith where no Faith was'
> (Kipling, 1995, p. 39).

Kipling was to write later that his experiences in the 'House of Desolation' bred in him a 'constant wariness, the habit of observation, and attendance on moods and tempers' (Kipling, 1990, Ch. 1), but that he was saved and compensated by the annual visit to his aunt Georgiana at her house in Fulham, London, which he described as a 'paradise' of 'love and affection' (Kipling, 1990, Ch. 1), and where he saw his uncle at work and heard him conversing with friends in an easy, humorous manner.

However, Kipling had some sort of nervous collapse as a result of his experiences in Southsea, and Trix, who at first seemed less affected by the 'House of Desolation', suffered from a series of mental breakdowns for the greater part of her subsequent life, obliging her mother to care for her until *she* died in 1910. Kipling himself suffered from pain and chronic ill health. He claimed that his experiences in Southsea had 'drained' him of 'any capacity for real, personal hate' for the rest of his days (Kipling, 1990, Ch. 1).

Sometimes excessive parental pressure for a child to achieve what its parents want them to achieve without due consideration for what the youngster is able to do, and overcorrection of the child's interests, may, unwittingly, result in emotional abuse. No one could have expressed this better than the novelist Franz Kafka (1883–1924) in the *Letter to his father* (1919):

> What I would have needed was a little encouragement, a little friendliness, a little keeping open of my road, instead of which you blocked it for me, though, of course, with the good intention of making me go another road. But I was not fit for that.

It is important to remember that there are elements of psychological abuse in all parenting, with most parents saying and doing thoughtless or inappropriate things to their children on occasions but, in general, they are caring and loving. Trowell (1983) suggested that 'adversity in manageable doses that comes in digestible packages' is essential for normal development. Children cannot be brought up wrapped up in cotton wool, devoid of painful experiences, but we would not label that as emotional abuse. In contrast, emotional abuse is a persistent, chronic pattern of parental behaviour, often towards a particularly vulnerable child, which over the years becomes internalised and gives rise to the feeling that the child alone is to blame. Laing (1976) quotes a poem of an emotionally confused and hurting child:

> My mother does not love me, I feel bad,
> I feel bad because she does not love me,
> I am bad because I feel bad,
> I am bad because she does not love me,
> She does not love me because I am bad.

Children who have been emotionally abused consistently give up trying to progress in their development and succumb to 'learned helplessness' (Suligman, 1975), a state of mind which is characterised by the belief that one has no control over the outcome of adverse events. Once established, such an attitude is very difficult to reverse or eradicate. There is much evidence from follow-up studies that unless something is done to help them, emotionally abused children may, as adults, be unable to form warm, intimate relationships, and have difficulty with the management of hostility and aggression which, it is claimed, may give rise to depression in later life (Rutter, 1995b).

EARLY STUDIES

Some of the best documentations of early emotional abuse, neglect, and absence of nurturing (resulting in poor growth, problematic psychosocial development, and emotionally disturbed behaviour) were those of Spitz (1945, 1946) and Widdowson (1951). A significant aetiological factor was gleaned from Spitz's study of infants cared for by their mothers, whom Spitz compared with another group raised in virtual isolation from other infants and adults. Children who were given physical and medical care, but no emotional care, contracted more infections, suffered from intellectual deficit and developed a condition called anaclitic depression manifesting itself in withdrawal, retardation in cognitive development, failure to thrive, insomnia, and sadness, and 37% of them died by the age of two.

Widdowson (1951) replicated Spitz's findings and proved that provision of adequate nutrition in an unfavourable emotional environment (due to harsh and unsympathetic handling) may seriously curtail growth rate and produce emotional and educational problems. Widdowson studied children in two German orphanages just after the Second World War. A dietary supplement, which was expected to produce faster weight-gain, was introduced as an experiment in one orphanage, using the other as a control. Contrary to expectations, it was the control group which gained weight and grew a little faster during the experimental period of six months. What was also observed was that the children in the experimental group began to show emotionally disturbed behaviour (e.g. weeping, irritability, frustration, sadness, sleeping problems, and quarrelsome behaviours). When analysing these fascinating and worrying findings, it was discovered that the matrons of the two orphanages had swapped over at about the time of the start of the dietary supplement. The matron of the first orphanage had been warm, kind, and attentive to the children's emotional needs, but the matron of the control group (who had transferred to the experimental group) was emotionally unavailable, critical, demanding, distant, harsh, not interested in emotional needs, and unsupportive. Her regime and treatment of children was emotionally abusive and harmful and, due to her anxiety- and fear-provoking behaviour, the children lost their appetites: even if they took food the calories were wasted and consumed by constant stress.

It is now a cliché that a child needs close, confident and warm physical and emotional contact (mother, father, or other carer) in order to grow and develop healthily and happily. The absence of such continuing nurturance and physically gentle intimacy can bring about anxiety and confusion in the child (e.g. fretting and disruption of biological functions). Montague (1978), in his chapter on 'Tender loving care', describes the effects of emotionally available care for very sick, hospitalised children, and relates an interesting anecdote. In a German hospital before the Second World War, a visiting American doctor, while being shown over the wards in one of the hospitals, noticed an old woman who was carrying a very undernourished infant. He enquired of the director who the old woman was and was told that she was 'Old Anna': when the staff at the hospital had done everything they could medically for the baby and it still did not make much progress, they handed it over to 'Old Anna', who succeeded in getting the child into a better psychological state and physical health. She rocked the baby, held it closely to her, carried it, talked to it in a gentle, reassuring way, giving caring and tender attention as well as the close physical contact which every baby needs. It is not surprising that babies passed to her, who had been near death's door (despite all the physical treatment then available to doctors) did better with her unsophisticated but essentially nurturing tender care.

Both popular writing and research literature have drawn attention to the importance, over many centuries, of emotional nurturing, and to the detrimental effects that severe and prolonged emotional deprivation (what we call these days 'emotional abuse') can have on children and young people (and for that matter on all people generally).

THE CONCEPT OF EMOTIONAL ABUSE

It was not until the 1980s that emotional abuse was fully recognised as a distinct form of child maltreatment with its own causalities, manifestations, and consequences, appearing independently on the child-protection register and being dealt with in its own right. However, decision-making on when, how, and why to intervene in such cases proved to be more problematic.

Lack of confidence among practitioners dealing with child-protection cases, especially with emotional abuse and neglect, was mostly due (and still is) to lack of certainty about at what point emotionally harsh treatment becomes emotional abuse, and how bad emotional abuse has to become to warrant classification of significant harm requiring child-protection action. These difficulties are not easy to overcome or to be simplified, as signs of emotional abuse are not universal to all emotionally abused children. Some are straightforward and speak for themselves once identified (e.g. severe failure to thrive): others, however, are far more subtle and open to misinterpretation.

Because of difficulties in substantiating emotional abuse and proving its harmful nature, both researchers and child-protection agencies have tended to keep a low profile, resulting in slow progress in academic and practice arenas: this is clearly illustrated in the work of Behl, Conyngham, and May (2003). The authors undertook a review of the child-maltreatment articles of six journals specialising in this subject. Examining four types of child abuse (physical abuse, sexual abuse, neglect, and emotional abuse), they found that articles specific to emotional abuse were very few. Despite the fact that in the 1980s studies began to separate different forms of abuse, recognising that outcomes of each type may be different, child emotional abuse and neglect was not part of this 'great leap forward'. While the number of research articles on the issues of child maltreatment increased from 54 in 1977 to 344 in 1998, a total of only 15 of these were dedicated solely to the issue of child emotional abuse and neglect. This represented 4.2% of all the articles on child maltreatment over a 22-year period. In addition to this impoverished interest in researching and writing about emotional abuse, much of the writing was concerned with the issue of definition.

It is believed that lack of interest in and focus on child emotional abuse may be due to the perception that it has fewer negative consequences than other forms of child maltreatment. As far as research on emotional abuse is concerned, it is also far more difficult to design rigorous investigations in the absence of validated measures specifically developed for this purpose. Equally, very little is written on how to help abused and abusers, and little evaluative research is available to tell us what works in helping emotionally abused children and their abusive carers. The review of the current literature would suggest that this trend has changed for the better as far as registration is concerned (Doyle, 1997; Glaser & Prior, 1997), but problems with definition still exist, as do the difficulties in accepting that persistent emotional abuse and neglect can lead to significant harm with serious consequences. What can be more serious than a child being driven to take its own life because of severe emotional abuse; or a child's growth being arrested and psychosocial development delayed and disturbed because of rejection and neglect; or a child being prevented from learning various life-skills and to be socialised because of crippling overprotection; or a child being paralysed by fear and anxiety because of living in a violent home? The sheer unhappiness, constant distress, and psychological pain experienced by some children have to be taken into consideration if there is a sincere desire to help them and to improve the quality of life and prospects for a healthy and happy childhood. There is no better way to introduce the reader to emotional abuse and neglect of children and young people than to share a few case studies describing various forms of emotional abuse and neglect of different severity.

CASE STUDIES

Chris's Case (from Iwaniec, 2004)

Chris was adopted by a middle-class, childless couple when he was two years old. Prior to adoption he spent 18 months in two different foster-homes. He was an attractive boy, developmentally within the lower average range, active, and curious. Both parents were pleased in securing adoption and having a child they longed to have. When Chris was four years old the mother became unexpectedly pregnant (which surprised the couple as they had been told they could not have any children). She gave birth to a girl and a year later to a boy.

After the birth of the first child attention was switched from Chris, and interaction became limited to care and control, and only occasionally was he played with. After the birth of a second child the relationships worsened sharply, not only between Chris and the mother, but also between Chris and the father. The more distant and preoccupied the parents became with the babies the more attention-seeking, disruptive, and demanding Chris became. They increasingly found him hard work, unrewarding, and difficult to enjoy. At the same time they invested energy and affection in their younger children, leaving little time and attention for Chris. Most of the little activities and treats from their early life together were gradually eliminated. He could not come to the parents' bed anymore, his father would not play football with him in the garden or the park, he was not read a story regularly at night, but above all he was not cuddled and was not given attention, praise, and encouragement. He became a very lonely and confused child. His weight dropped from the 75th to 2nd percentile within a few months, and he became stunted in height. He started wandering around the house at night, making bizarre animal noises and searching for food. His eating behaviour changed dramatically from being fussy and taking a rather long time to eat to becoming greedy, eating fast, and gulping food. He consumed large amounts and was constantly asking for more.

As his behaviour worsened, the parents became more rejective, hostile, and uncom- promising. They felt embarrassed and, as they said, they were let down by Chris and requested to have a break from him, so that 'he gets the necessary treatment for his incontinence and disturbed behaviour'. They stated that they did not love him, but attributed this to Chris's changed behaviour, not theirs. However, they said that they had a moral obligation to care for him. Chris was admitted to hospital for observa- tion and testing, although nobody believed that there was anything wrong with him. While in hospital he interacted well with nurses, but in a possessive and attention- seeking way. He was jealous when they played with or attended to other children, and he tended to be aggressive towards these children, but only when the nurses or doctors interacted with them and not with him.

Chris returned home and within days his disturbed behaviour again returned. In three weeks' time he lost 5.5 kg (12 lbs 2 ozs). Parental rejection was so strong and Chris's pain and disturbance so high that the only solution available was to place him in a different home to give him another chance. Chris was fostered out but never recovered from the emotional rejection. He was killed while joy-riding when he was 16 years old.

Sonia's Case

Sonia, a nine-year-old girl, had been cared for by her grandmother. As a result of a hostile and rejecting relationship with her parents, Sonia's mother abandoned her when she was three years old. The mother was simply thrown out of the house when she wanted to take Sonia with her. The grandparents separated soon after the disappearance of Sonia's mother, and the grandmother became extremely overprotective to the point of developmental paralysis in all areas of Sonia's life. At the age of nine Sonia did not know how to dress herself, how to wash, clean, bathe, eat on her own, or make decisions as to what to wear and what to do. The grandmother had done everything for her for years so she had not acquired any skills in doing things for herself (e.g. she would sit in a bath waiting to be bathed, washed, and dried). In the morning she would not know what to do (i.e. dressing, washing, brushing her teeth) as these things were always done for her.

At school she did not know how to relate to and interact with peers, seldom spoke, and was unable to stand up for herself. Children shied away from her and considered her as odd and different. Because she was unhappy at school the grandmother assumed that she was being bullied and stopped sending her to school. She was not allowed to play with the children in the neighbourhood to avoid being hurt by them. She could only play in the corridor or stairs. The curtains were drawn all the time to prevent people looking at what they were doing. The grandmother would not allow anyone in, and would not answer letters or telephone calls. Because of Sonia's failure to attend school and the grandmother's prohibition on permitting any outside contact with Sonia, an interim care order was granted by the court, and Sonia was placed in the foster-home. She did not show distress at being separated from her grandmother and asked only occasionally when she would see her grandmother again. The foster-parents were amazed that she could not do anything for herself and that she would not make even the easiest of decisions. Her social interaction was even more striking, as even a four-year-old was bossing her, and she passively did what she was asked to do. She did not know (and appeared apprehensive of) how to play with children of her own age. She just stood by the window watching them. Quite often she did not follow conversations within the family, and did not understand what was going on. She appeared to have a serious deficit in understanding basic everyday functioning, and many common activities were alien to her. She was very polite, responsive to requests, and unquestioningly obedient.

This type of crippling overprotection is emotionally abusive for several reasons: first, such children are very unhappy as they are restricted in all actions and activities; second, their socialisation is seriously impaired as they are prevented from doing things for themselves; third, their abilities to interact with peers and to build meaningful and appropriate relationships are affected by the lack of exposure to other children; and fourth, their self-esteem and self-confidence are low because of being laughed at, criticised and not accepted by peers, so they are socially isolated. Overprotected children are not prepared for independent living, not only in the physical sense but also emotionally and cognitively. They are unable to make decisions, or experience success or failure and act accordingly. Their behaviour seems to be passive, accepting everything, agreeing with everything and everybody, and waiting for things to be done for them and to them. Emotionally they seem to be flat, neither sad nor happy, and find it difficult to show appropriate emotions.

Richard's Case

Richard, 10 years of age, was the eldest in a family of 3 children. Due to the mother's depression and inability to cope with the children's demanding behaviour they were voluntarily placed in the care of the local authority – Richard in the children's home, and the younger ones in a foster-home.

Richard presented himself as an extremely anxious, emotionally distraught, and unhappy child, who suffered acute separation-anxiety from his mother. He worried about her safety, health, and well-being. He would not go to sleep until he spoke to his mother on the telephone to reassure himself that she was safe. He tended to wake up at night in a panic, feeling that something bad had happened to her. Bringing him back after spending a weekend at home with his mother was extremely distressing as he clung to her, begged to stay, cried, and usually became very panicky.

Careful assessment revealed that the mother talked to Richard about her problems, feeling sad and anxious about her health and life generally, saying that she often thought about taking an overdose again, that she could not cope, she was very unhappy, and that the only person she had to support and understand her was Richard. She often said to him that he might find her dead one of these days. Additionally, she told him time and time again that Richard's (and his siblings') behaviour triggered clinical depression, which led to her taking an overdose and her subsequent admission to hospital. Richard felt guilty and responsible for his mother's mental-health problems and for his and his siblings being taken into care. He blamed himself that it was his difficult behaviour which brought so much distress to his mother that she became ill. Additionally, he felt it was his duty to look after her, to make sure that she did not take an overdose or did not cut her wrists. The acute panic attacks, nightmares, and inability to relax were the result of constant worry about his mother and the fact that he was prevented from being with her all the time. He felt that he was letting her down as she relied on his support and companionship. Feelings of insecurity that he might lose his mother's love if he did not look after her led to numerous behavioural and emotional problems at the children's home and at school. Richard was asked to become a carer and protector at the age of 10, and to carry the burden of guilt and responsibility for his mother's mental health.

Jackie's Case

After attending a conference on emotional abuse and neglect, a policewoman in her late thirties asked for help to come to terms with her abusive past and to be helped in rebuilding her life. She said that a talk brought back very painful memories from her childhood and of a lifelong frightening relationship with her mother, which was still evident today.

She described her early years as extremely tense, unhappy, and riddled with constant fear and apprehension. She could never satisfy her mother, and whatever she did was not good enough. The mother constantly complained about her difficult behaviour and regularly told her father, when he returned from work, how bad she was. At the same time she was not allowed to defend herself and tell her father her story or to go to her father for comfort, a cuddle or support. She felt that her domineering mother was perhaps jealous of the father's affection for his daughter. Jackie spent a lot of time in her room on her own – as the mother used to send her there for minor misbehaviour. She remembered hugging her teddy-bear for comfort and for being her friend and companion. Her mother used to scream at her, call her names, and threaten her if she did not do things the way she wanted her to do them. She was so frightened of her mother that she would 'freeze' when she approached her. Although the mother seldom smacked her, she punished Jackie in a most cruel way. The child had to eat everything her mother put in front of her and, if she did not, the same food would be given to her for the next meal, and then the next, until it was eaten. She described how her mother kept giving her horsemeat which she did not like but she insisted that she ate it even if it took two or three days to do so. Jackie used to kneel in front of her mother begging her not to make her eat that meal and in spite of Jackie being sick and extremely distressed she had to eat it. The mother shamed her in front of her peers and neighbours on a regular basis, and that hurt her most of all, making her feel deeply ashamed, embarrassed, and useless. It came to a point when she started to avoid people, hide behind buildings when someone she knew appeared, or run to the other side of the road.

After her father's death she left home, joined the police force, married the first man who showed her affection and attention and had two children by him. The marriage did not work out as she did not know how to show feelings and how to negotiate her position within the marital union. She said that she did not really know how to behave as a wife and mother with equal rights and responsibilities, as she had not had a good model of family functioning from her parents. Jackie's memory of her parents' relationship was one of quarrels, long silent days, her mother not speaking to her father, or even to Jackie, and lack of warmth and support for each other.

In her marriage she lacked confidence and found it extremely difficult to make any decisions, exert authority, and stand up for herself. She also used to lie regarding minor, unimportant things to prevent criticism (e.g. when dinner was a bit late, she would make untrue and unnecessary excuses). She tended to be on the defensive all the time, which created a lot of tension and disharmony in the family. As a result, her husband started spending more time away from home, and eventually left for good. Jackie became convinced that there was something wrong with her and that her mother was right in what she said and the way she treated her.

After the break-up of the marriage Jackie's mother wanted to take over looking after the children and running the house, saying that Jackie would ruin her children and herself completely as she was a complete disaster. Although she did not move to live with them she dictated every move and made decisions for Jackie and the grandchildren, as Jackie continued to be extremely frightened of her and unable to stand up for herself and say no. Low self-esteem and a sense of worthlessness has prevailed in her private life in spite of her quite satisfactory work as a policewoman.

Ann and Simon's Case

Ann (12 years) and Simon (14 years), currently in residential care, had a history of serious emotional abuse, rejection, and physical and emotional neglect. Both their parents abused alcohol on a regular basis, and family violence was a frequent fixture in their daily lives. Ann's and Simon's school attendance was infrequent as they were not sent to school due to their parents being intoxicated and unable to get up on time. They frequently witnessed violent quarrels and fights between their parents and their drinking companions. On several occasions the police were involved when Ann and Simon ran out of the house in the middle of the night crying and knocking on the neighbours' doors. Quite often they would hide in the wardrobe to protect themselves out of fear that they might be attacked as well, or sexually interfered with. Simon used to keep a stick to protect himself and his sister in case of being attacked. The parents separated as a result of family violence, but the mother continued to drink excessively, either on her own (consuming 2 litres of vodka a day), or having drinking parties at home. As a rule Simon, at the age of 7 years, would take over caring responsibilities to look after his mother and his sister. He would take his mother to bed, prepare food, do shopping, and often protected her from her drinking companions.

After one particularly violent weekend, Simon was placed with quite old maternal grandparents and Ann with the maternal aunt and uncle. Simon became calmer once removed from constant fear and anxiety, but he missed his mother and worried about her safety and welfare. Ann's life, however, in the aunt's house was far from satisfactory: because of her bed-wetting, lying, and attention-seeking behaviour, she was rejected by her cousins and then by her uncle and aunt, and was asked to leave. Ann was then placed in a short-term foster-home with an elderly couple: the foster-parents found it excessively difficult to deal with Ann's bed-wetting, the constant washing of sheets and the smell in the house. Although they liked Ann, they asked for termination of the placement. Ann was devastated by their decision and felt very hurt as she thought they liked her and she was doing her best to please them. The second foster-placement broke down very quickly as the family found Ann's problems too difficult to cope with (especially the bed-wetting), and their children did not find Ann rewarding to be with. Ann was then placed in residential care, very confused, emotionally disturbed, and feeling rejected and unwanted by everybody. Her self-esteem and confidence were at rock-bottom with a prevailing sense of helplessness regarding her enuresis, and increasingly feelings of depression. Ann became withdrawn, seldom spoke, avoided adults and peers, and used to burst into tears when spoken to. Additionally, she started having nightmares, slept little and lost a lot of weight. She needed urgent therapeutic attention to help her cope with the devastating feelings of being rejected, and to deal with her bed-wetting in an informed way.

Simon, on the other hand, became too difficult for the grandparents to control and care for. He used to spend a lot of time out of the house, hanging around with other boys and behaving in an antisocial way. As a result he was placed in residential care for teenagers. Simon's behaviour in the children's home and at school deteriorated to the point of being expelled on several occasions, running away, being aggressive towards staff and peers, and defiance. At 15 years old he was placed in a secure unit as he was beyond control.

Dean's Case

Dean was six-and-a-half years old at the time of referral. He looked very thin, small, unhealthy, and unhappy. He presented various and, at times, puzzling problems. Being aggressive and attacking siblings and peers for no apparent reason was quite common, as was self-harming and destructive behaviour. Dean cut his new trousers, shirt, and jumper to pieces, and occasionally would tear bedding and curtains and strip wallpaper from the walls. He set fire to things in the middle of the room on several occasions. He never destroyed anything belonging to other members of the family, or children at school. Quite often, after his mother punished him for hitting his sisters (e.g. sending him to his bedroom or telling him off), he would scratch or cut himself. He never cried, never asked for anything, and never complained. Occasionally, when particularly stressed, he would revert to baby talk, which disturbed and frightened his mother.

This extremely disturbed behaviour was a result of Dean being terrorised by his stepfather when he was about four-and-a-half years old. There was also a history of severe family violence. He was interfered with sexually when his mother was at work during the evenings, and when his mother became suspicious because of Dean's sudden change in behaviour (e.g. in sleeping and eating patterns, screaming and shouting, acute defiance, and lack of communication), the stepfather killed his puppy and threatened to kill him if he disclosed sexual abuse. Eventually, the mother discovered what was happening, and secretly left home with her three children. She found a place in the women's refuge in the neighbouring town, but her partner pursued them there so they moved to another refuge in another town. Eventually, a house was allocated and they began to rebuild their lives, but not Dean.

Dean's behaviour remained problematic, which his mother found difficult to understand and cope with. Frequent outbursts of aggression – tormenting his sisters, defiance, stealing, lying, and disruptive and attention-seeking behaviour at school – brought about deterioration of the mother–child relationship and a visibly growing love–hate relationship. Dean was referred for help by the school with his mother's agreement. The assessment revealed that Dean was a very frightened and confused child, carrying enormous baggage of unresolved problems that needed therapeutic attention.

CONSEQUENCES OF EMOTIONAL ABUSE

The consequences of emotional abuse and neglect in respect of all individuals described in the case studies speak for themselves.

Simon and Ann reached adolescence as extremely disturbed young people: Simon ended up in a secure unit as his behaviour became beyond control. He felt let down, abandoned by his parents and grandparents, and unsupported when he needed help, love, and attention. Ann's emotionally disturbed behaviour, because of emotional abuse, led to numerous experiences of rejection by carers and the development of a serious sense of helplessness, hopelessness, and depression. By the age of 13 years she strongly believed that she was useless, bad, and unworthy of love.

Chris was brutally rejected by his adoptive parents, which he could not understand and cope with. The pain of being rejected brought about various

Case studies

severe emotional problems
development. He never reco\
abandoned, and, as stated, wa:

Richard, at the age of 10 years,
mental-health problems, and v
take an overdose, or cut her v
anxiety, guilt and panic attac
unwittingly inflicted by his m

Sonia, at the age of nine year:
think and make the smallest
crippling overprotection. She was denied development or individuality,
socialisation, and preparation for independent functioning.

Jackie, in spite of being successful as a policewoman, remained ineffective as
a wife and mother as she was made to believe by her mother that she was
useless, bad, and stupid. The model of family life she experienced as a child
ill-prepared her for life as a wife and mother. In spite of being over 30 years
old she was still petrified of her mother's criticism and denigration.

Dean was sexually abused, and then terrorised and threatened by his
stepfather to prevent disclosure. Being made to watch the killing of his
much-loved pet, and often being exposed to family violence, made him
believe that he would be killed as well if he talked of being abused. The
mother assumed that being rescued from the cruelty of the stepfather would
solve the problems. However, Dean needed intensive therapy to come to
terms with his ordeal.

Individuals presented in the above cases have several things in common:

- they are all unhappy;
- they have poor emotional and social support, and appear to be lonely and
  isolated;
- their disturbed behaviour reflects inner turmoil, distress, and confusion;
- their development is delayed and problematic;
- their attachments to primary caregivers are insecure;
- carers' relationships with these children are hostile, neglectful, rejective, dismissive, or paralysing of development of individuality and
  independence;
- they suffer from low self-esteem, believing that they are not worthy of
  being loved, wanted, or able to achieve anything in life;
- they seem to be in a never-ending state of stress, anxiety, and uncertainty;
- their relationships with peers lack assertiveness and personal appeal;
- their educational attainments are poor.

The problem profile of these people is of considerable concern, and shows negative consequences persisting for a long time (as seen in Jackie's case), and tragic outcome (as seen in Chris's case), or seriously damaged childhood (Ann and Simon). All of them have crossed a line of significant harm, raising the question as to why they were left for so long in an emotionally harmful environment which resulted in devastating outcomes, one way or another, for all of them. The author recently reviewed 72 cases of emotional abuse (see Chapter 2) and found that the 'wait-and-see approach' was prominent in decision-making, probably due to poor understanding of the harmful effects it can have on children's lives, and in the difficulties of measuring such effects at the onset of a warring parent–child relationship, emotional unavailability, and problematic parental behaviour.

PURPOSE AND OVERVIEW OF THE BOOK

This book is an effort to rise to the challenge before us, to identify, assess, protect, and help emotionally abused and neglected children. It aims to produce an easy-to-follow model of assessment and various intervention and treatment strategies (which have been tested and tried over the years for the efficacy in helping children and their carers). Additionally, it reviews what is currently known about emotional abuse inside and outside the family. It is written for practitioners from different disciplines who are charged with protecting children from harm, and helping families to parent their children in a rewarding and responsible way. It is hoped that managers, supervisors of practice, and academics (whose task is to teach students and prepare them for professional life) will find this book informative and useful.

TERMINOLOGY

Emotional abuse and psychological maltreatment are used interchangeably, meaning the same thing. As in the United States researchers and writers use the term psychological maltreatment, and in the United Kingdom emotional abuse is used, the author applies psychological maltreatment only when it seems necessary, but mostly uses emotional abuse as a concept. Again, labels, such as parents and carers, are used, according to what seems to be more appropriate and accurate when referring to people who have parenting responsibilities.

Cases presented in this book are real, but names, and often places, are disguised to protect the identity of children and families.

THE ORGANISATION OF THE BOOK

The book is organised into four sections:
Section 1 The Problem
Section 2 Assessment of Emotional Abuse and Neglect
Section 3 Treatment and Intervention of Emotional Abuse and Neglect
Section 4 The Burden of Proof: Legal and Social Work Difficulties in Dealing
          with Emotional Abuse and Neglect Cases

Section 1 The Problem

This section consists of nine chapters. *Chapter 1* discusses the concept of
emotional abuse, historical factors, and reasons for concern, and provides five
cases, with illustrations, of different forms of emotional abuse and neglect.

Chapter 2 deals with issues of definition, categorisation, and prevalence based on
literature review. Caregivers' emotionally harmful behaviour, as well as abused
children's behavioural and developmental characteristics, are discussed.
Check-lists of caregivers' emotionally abusive behaviours, and children and
young people's emotionally disturbed behaviour, are provided. The check-lists
have been developed by the author based on empirical evidence.

Chapter 3 looks at specific emotionally abusive behaviour within the family,
such as family violence and the effects on children within western and Asian
families and communities. It examines acrimonious divorce cases and issues
of contact visits with non-resident parents. Chapter 3 also explores growing
concerns of alcohol and drug abuse and the quality of childcare in such
families. The association of substance misuse, family violence, and neglect
are discussed and illustrated by case studies.

Chapter 4 explores emotional abuse and neglect outside the family settings –
inflicted by carers other than natural parents. Children in residential homes
or other group-care settings are often abused emotionally by teachers when
they are at school or by residential staff in children's homes. However,
seldom is public attention drawn to the plight of these children. Growing
concerns of suicides among young people in the penal system, as a result of
emotional abuse, are drawn to the reader's attention, as well as issues of
widespread bullying in schools.

Chapter 5 deals with children's emotional well-being and sense of security by
exploring attachment of children. Insecure attachment features widely with
emotionally abused and neglected children, as do poor relationships with other
caregivers. Attachment and bonding theories are discussed. The mechanisms

controlling and maintaining insecure and secure reattachments are elaborated upon, and links between attachment and emotional abuse are examined.

Chapter 6 explains that some children presenting severe failure to thrive are unwanted, rejected, or physically and emotionally neglected. All children of psychosocial short stature, without exception, are emotionally abused to the point of growth-hormone arrest and retardation of psychosocial development. The effects of emotional abuse on children's growth and development will be presented and illustrated by case studies.

Chapter 7 deals with children with disabilities as they are at great risk of being emotionally abused and neglected. The plight of these children who (more often than not) cannot protect themselves or alert others to their maltreatment will be shared with readers. Assessment, prevention, and intervention are discussed.

Chapter 8 looks at children's developmental tasks from birth to adolescence, and examines the effects of emotional abuse and neglect on such children's physical, cognitive, emotional, social, intellectual, and language development.

Chapter 9 explores risk and resilience in cases of emotional abuse, and illustrates how vulnerability increases risks in children, and how resilience is strengthened by protective factors. A discussion on how resilience can be built on, and how risk-factors can be addressed, is dealt with and illustrated by three cases.

Section 2 Assessment of Emotional Abuse and Neglect

Chapter 10 covers the schedule of comprehensive assessment, based on modified *Department of Health 2000 Framework of Assessment of Children in Need*, exploring: children's developmental needs, parental capacity, and environmental factors. Numerous assessment tools, mostly developed and evaluated by the author, are provided. The assessment schedule is based on ecological theory, which is briefly discussed.

Section 3 Treatment and Intervention of Emotional Abuse and Neglect

Emotionally abusive parents and carers need help on many different levels, not least to understand that their hostile and insensitive behaviour is harmful and painful. The type and level of intervention or treatment must be based on assessment outcomes. Different families will need different help as they have different needs and present different problems. Tailor-made intervention and treatment for each family are essential in order to provide workable, achievable, and agreed problem-solving strategies.

The models of intervention presented in this book are multifactorial and multidimensional, based on psychodynamic, cognitive-behavioural, and ecological theories. Most of the approaches and methods presented in this book have been used and evaluated by the author or independent assessors in relation to evaluative research.

Chapter 11 describes four levels of intervention and service provision: *universal level* – available to all children and families; *selected level* – available to children in need and those who may be at risk if family support is not provided; *targeted level* or *registration level* – applied to children who are at recognised risk of abuse and neglect, and whose names are put on the Child Protection List following a multidisciplinary case conference; and *civil court intervention* – for those who are suffering or may suffer significant harm.

Chapter 12 describes and discusses behavioural-cognitive approaches to helping emotionally abused and neglected children. Practical applications of methods and techniques are illustrated and supported by case studies. Theory, research, and practice are reviewed.

Chapter 13 discusses ways of improving parent–child relationships and children's attachment to parents. Psychotherapeutic methods such as video-recording and feedback are mentioned, including; Watch, Wait, and Wonder; parent–child interaction therapy; recalling early-childhood memories; and working with foster-parents to build new relationships and attachments are demonstrated. Methods discussed in this chapter are based on psychodynamic theories and approaches.

Chapter 14 deals with direct work with children and young people – such as: play therapy, promoting resilience at all ages, social skills and assertiveness training for adolescents – and gives an example of therapeutic work with older children entitled 'the jug of loving water'. A case study is provided to illustrate the use of the technique.

Chapter 15 discusses 'how to help parents and their families'. Family therapy, counselling, marital work, psychoeducation, and other forms of helping families experiencing difficulties in their mutual relationships are demonstrated, and helping strategies are illustrated.

Section 4 The Burden of Proof: Legal and Social Work Difficulties in Dealing with Emotional Abuse and Neglect Cases

Chapter 16 debates the difficulties of taking a case to court as evidence of significant harm may not be clear at the time of proceedings. Problems of gathering relevant information and decision-making, both by the court and social services, are discussed. The need for multidisciplinary training, including legal people, is advocated.

SUMMARY

The existence of emotional cruelty and ill-treatment has been known for centuries and was demonstrated by writers, painters, philosophers, and poets. Children, however, were seen, in every sense of the word, as the property and responsibility of parents, and interference in the way parents treated their children was discouraged. The State stepped in only when there was proof that the child was killed, starved to death, or seriously injured. In the 1960s and 1970s, after wide publicity of the battered-child syndrome by Henry Kemper and his colleagues, child abuse was taken seriously and appeared on the statute book as a criminal offence. However, emotional abuse was not recognised until the 1980s and, although it is accepted as a distinct child-abuse category, it is often not seen as serious enough to warrant intervention of the same kind as do physical and sexual abuse. This chapter aims to set up a context for the following chapters, including examples of early research describing emotional abuse and effects on children, illustration of emotional ill-treatment in popular literature, and case studies describing current concerns.

DEFINITION, PREVALENCE, AND CHARACTERISTICS OF EMOTIONALLY ABUSED CHILDREN AND THEIR CARERS

CONTENTS

INTRODUCTION

Of the four main types of maltreatment discussed in the literature – physical abuse, sexual abuse, neglect, and emotional maltreatment – the hardest to define and, hence, the most difficult to formulate for reporting and then intervention, is emotional abuse. It has been viewed as both central to all types of abuse and as occurring as a distinct problem. Emotionally abusive acts are ones that are psychologically damaging to the behavioural, cognitive, affective, or physical functioning of a child (Brassard *et al.*, 1987; Iwaniec, Herbert, & Sluckin, 2002; Glaser & Prior, 2002).

Research evidence and practice wisdom strongly suggest that the most lasting effects of physical and sexual abuse and neglect are reported to be psychological rather than physical, carrying equally if not more serious consequences for the child immediately and later in life (Iwaniec, 2004;

Doyle, 1997; Hart, Binggeli, & Brassard, 1998; Erickson & Egeland, 2002; Claussen & Crittenden, 1991). Since the 1980s there have been growing concerns and interest in emotional abuse among researchers, child-welfare activists, practitioners, and legislators. In most western countries emotional abuse (as a separate form of child maltreatment) was added to the statute book on child protection in recent years. However, emotional abuse was only recognised in England and Wales by legislators in the 1980s, although in the United States it has been part of the child-abuse statutes in several States since 1977. Despite the fact that the number of referrals has grown on both sides of the Atlantic, reports of emotional abuse either by professionals or the public at large are still problematic and rather few.

Emotional abuse is not a new phenomenon, as was discussed in Chapter 1. Despite the fact that there is now much agreement among theorists, researchers, and practitioners that emotional abuse and neglect are the most pervasive forms of child maltreatment, they remain the most under-researched and least well-understood. It is fair to say that researchers and practitioners often shy away from dealing with emotional abuse because physical signs of its occurrence are not immediately visible, and developmental impairments or emotional and behavioural disturbances may be attributable to other causes. Emotional abuse has been linked to difficulties in forming secure attachment (Egeland, Sroufe, & Erickson, 1983): it has also been associated with increased aggression (Spillane-Grieco, 2000), and it may be connected with the development of eating disorders (Rorty, Yager, & Rossotto, 1994), low self-esteem (Mullen, Martin, Anderson, Romans, & Herbison, 1996), stunted physical growth, and self-harming behaviour (Iwaniec, 1995). Yet emotional abuse is still perceived by many as the least serious form of child maltreatment. State intervention in the protection of children is fraught with many difficulties, as there are conflicting requirements. On the one hand the rights of children have to be considered, but on the other the rights of parents as defined in the European Court of Human Rights have also to be observed. Family privacy must be protected from interference by the State (or by agents of the State) unless circumstances dictate otherwise. Nevertheless, the number of recorded cases of emotional abuse has grown significantly in the last decade, and dealing with them in effective and appropriate ways remains problematic, from both the legal and professional perspectives.

This chapter aims to highlight some of the difficulties surrounding the concept and occurrence of emotional abuse, noting the increase in research and practice in recent years. Prevalence and identification will be discussed as well as continued definitional issues surrounding emotional abuse; attempts will also be made to provide the reader with guidance as to what constitutes emotional abuse and neglect in childhood and adolescence. Emotionally harmful parenting or caregiving will be described, and the profiles and characteristics of children who have suffered emotional abuse will be discussed, together with some of the consequences of such abuse and neglect.

DEFINITION

Considerable efforts have been expended on attempts to arrive at acceptable definitions of emotional abuse and neglect, but there remain many problems associated with numerous philosophical, scientific, legal, political, and cultural issues (Hart, Brassard, Binggeli, & Davidson, 2002). Much is still unresolved which continues to plague attempts at finding one consensual definition of emotional abuse and neglect; many terms describing such abuse have been employed, often interchangeably, with little precision or justification. These have included psychological abuse (Burnett, 1993; O'Hagan, 1995), psychological battering (Garbarino, Guttmann, & Seeley, 1986), mental injury (Kavanagh, 1982), mental cruelty (Navarre, 1987), and soul murder (Shengold, 1989). O'Hagan (1995) argued that often these terms were used to mean one and the same thing, but in fact they can vary. Furthermore, some writers have separated the concepts of emotional abuse from those of emotional neglect, noting differing experiences of the children involved (Whiting, 1976). These matters of definition are actually extremely important in both practice and research to avoid confusion: clarity and precision are essential. For some working in this field the most important aspects are 'perpetrator acts' (acts of omission and commission), while for others they concern what happens to the children (English, 1998; Evans, 2002; Glaser, 2002; Iwaniec, 1995). Disturbed behaviour in a child may not become overt until some time has elapsed, making an assessment of its development difficult, and complicating any process of intervention let alone prevention. Few writers address a child's or young person's imme- diate pain and never-ending states of tension, anxiety, fear, and loneliness, with no prospect of escape. Thus definitions associated with outcomes may be possible only after the damage is done.

Although the generic terms of psychological maltreatment and emotional abuse are used more generally today (psychological maltreatment in the United States and emotional abuse in the United Kingdom), some continue to argue that these have different nuances or even meanings. Tomison and Tucci (1997) suggest that the emphasis in psychological-maltreatment literature tends to be on how the 'mental abilities' of the child (e.g. intellect, attention-span, cognition, etc.) are affected, while that in emotional-abuse literature is more concerned with emotional development (e.g. ability to form attachments and meaningful relationships, and to express and differentiate feelings, etc.). Glaser (2002), among others, would take a line similar to that of Iwaniec (1995), stating that emotional and psychological effects are so intrinsically linked that examining one without the other is nearly impossible and therefore pointless. For example, parents who always rebuke and criticise, and who are never satisfied with their child's performance, will inhibit the child's curiosity to explore and to learn but, at the same time, will curtail its ability to form close and warm relationships with the parents, and slow or damage the growth of its self-esteem. Therefore it is perhaps unnecessary to compartmentalise, because, in real life, many things are interconnected: preoccupations with precise definitions, though of some longevity, have had limited success in arriving at unified, global, acceptable standards. The very fact that emotional abuse is a social construct, dynamic in nature, prevents the formation of such definition as different cultures perceive emotionally hurtful acts in different ways. Some, in fact (e.g. China, South East Asia, etc.), see criticism, shaming, and threatening behaviour as appropriate in order to make children believe and achieve at school. What is important, however, is to recognise emotional abuse and be able to differentiate between abusive behaviour and emotionally undemonstrative behaviour of the carers.

DEFINING CHARACTERISTICS

The major characteristics of emotional abuse and neglect are shown in the nature and quality of relationship and interaction between the emotionally abused child and its abusive parent or carer. If interactions between the child and the caregiver are continually hostile, dismissive, critical, or indifferent, then the caregiver–child relationship will become persistently unfriendly, lacking warmth, security, and a sense of belonging and, on the whole, will be negative in nature. Emotional harm comes as a result of an accumulation of painful, anxiety-provoking, degrading, and confusing experiences inflicted on a child by a caregiver on a frequent basis in the absence of a compensatory protective relationship with (a) significant other person(s): it includes omission and commission aspects of carers' behaviour and feelings and, therefore, is referred to as emotional abuse and neglect.

There is general agreement and recognition that emotional abuse exists on a continuum, in that some acts or behaviours can be relatively mild and occur from time to time, while others can be severe and extremely damaging. It needs to be remembered that isolated incidents, or a series of incidents of inappropriate behaviour, do not in themselves constitute an emotionally abusive relationship. In order to classify behaviour as emotionally abusive, such actions must be repetitive and sustained over time in that they characterise or pervade the relationship as a whole, and not only in specific circumstances.

Additionally, emotional abuse must be considered within the cultural context of the time. Community standards about appropriate and inappropriate caregiver behaviour are constantly changing and are not homogenous or easily identifiable. As is shown in Daniel's case (Chapter 5), it was community dissatisfaction with the way the mother treated Daniel emotionally that led to the referral: the public actually requested intervention in order to stop emotional maltreatment. On the other hand, as noted above, shaming, criticising, or belittling can be seen in some communities as appropriate and acceptable, and are used as forms of discipline to make children adhere to standards and expectations. Added to this is the acknowledgement that emotional abuse (incorporating emotional neglect) includes both acts of commission and acts of omission, in that it can be active or passive and, therefore, physical contact is not needed for it to occur.

The other main feature of all definitions of emotional abuse is the understanding that motivation to harm the child is not necessary: in fact it is well recognised that some parents may not realise that their behaviour is harmful at all. When taking preventive or protective action, evidence of intent to harm is not required. Overprotection or unrealistic expectations are good examples of parental unawareness that what they are doing is harmful to the child, as illustrated in Sonia's case in Chapter 1.

Emotional abuse can take the form of hostile words, angry gestures, prolonged ignoring, and negative attitudes. Parents and carers who persistently criticise, shame, rebuke, threaten, ridicule, humiliate, put down, and induce fear and anxiety, and who are never satisfied with the child's behaviour and performance, are emotionally abusive. Their verbal expressions and interactions are insensitive and often hostile, which builds emotional barriers between carer and child, preventing the development of a warm, affectionate relationship and a sense of security (Iwaniec, 1995). Equally, encouraging children to pursue socially unacceptable behaviour (such as drinking, drug abuse, or stealing) is corrupting and, therefore, emotionally abusive, and so is family violence and exposure of children to fearful, anxiety-provoking situations. Some children are forced to watch a sadistic carer's behaviour to keep them frightened and quiet (as demonstrated in Dean's case [Chapter 1]). If, in order to stop a child disclosing the carer's offending behaviour, their child is forced to watch the killing of a beloved pet or the destruction of a favourite toy, this may be classed as profoundly abusive and terrorising behaviour.

DEFINITION AND TYPOLOGY OF EMOTIONALLY ABUSIVE BEHAVIOUR

The most influential typology of *emotional abuse* was produced by Garbarino *et al.* (1986) and Hart, Germain and Brassard (1987): it has been subsequently adopted and adapted by a host of researchers and practitioners in the field and constitutes most of the official definitions and guidelines today, not only in the USA but also in other countries. The United States' definition varies from State to State, but the most widely used and approved is stated in the *Guidelines for the Psychosocial Evaluation of Suspected Psychological Maltreatment in Children and Adolescence* of the American Professional Society on Abuse of Children (APSAC, 1995).

> Psychological maltreatment means a repeated pattern of care-giver behaviour or extreme incident(s) that convey to children that they are worthless, flawed, unloved, unwanted, endangered, or only of value in meeting another's needs. It includes: (1) spurning; (2) terrorising; (3) isolating; (4) exploiting/corrupting; (5) denying emotional responsiveness; and (6) mental health, medical, and educational neglect.

Some terms require definition:

(1) *Spurning* – may involve verbal and non-verbal behaviours, such as belittling children, shaming or ridiculing them, and general degrading or rejecting or abandoning them.

(2) *Terrorising* – refers to acts of placing children in danger, threatening them, someone, or something they care for, or generally creating a climate of fear.

(3) *Isolating* – imposing severe restrictions on a child, preventing developmentally appropriate social interaction, and separating a child from the rest of the family.

(4) *Exploiting/corrupting* – encouraging children to develop inappropriate and/or antisocial behaviours or values, such as stealing, abusing others verbally, breaking into houses, and hurting older people or younger children.

(5) *Denying emotional responsiveness* – being emotional unavailable, ignoring the child, failing to express affection, becoming distant physically and emotionally, and being dismissive of children's needs for warmth and affection.

(6) *Mental health, medical and educational neglect* – failing to provide and attend to the psychological, medical, and cognitive and developmental needs of the child.

Interestingly, rejection in Hart *et al*. (2002) has no category of its own, but is included in spurning (act of commission) and denying emotional responsiveness (act of omission). It is also argued that rejection is evident in all categories. Rejection, however, is so obvious and singular, in some cases, that it seems necessary to have a separate category for it (e.g. children rejected at birth because of disability, deformation, or when they were conceived as a result of rape, or when they are rejected because of acute behavioural problems, e.g. autism). Rejection in the above-mentioned situation does not have to go hand in hand with spurning, but will include denying positive emotional responsiveness. The emotions shown to such children will always be negative (either hostile or, at best, indifferent). Additional parenting behaviours that could be termed emotionally abusive include: constant criticism; parenting indifference; inconsistent parenting; unrealistic expectations; discrimination in comparison to siblings (the Cinderella syndrome); and stimulus deprivation (Glaser, 2002; Iwaniec, 1995; Kairys, Johnson, & the Committee on Child Abuse, 2002; Schorr, 2002).

It needs to be noted that the experience of one or more ill-treatment categories will have different effects depending on the child's developmental stage. For example, understimulation in infancy is likely to result in a slowing down of intellectual, language, and social development, but in middle childhood or adolescence it will be less important. However, depriving a teenager from possibilities of forming close relationships with peers, and not allowing him or her to mix with the peer group, would be developmentally harmful and emotionally abusive. In terms of more general effects of emotional ill-treatment, the messages received by the child convey that it is worthless, a burden, flawed, unloved, unwanted, endangered, or valued only in meeting someone else's needs.

However, categories of psychological maltreatment, as proposed by Hart *et al.*, are not universally accepted as they stand. Glaser and Prior (2002) for example, advocated an alternative perspective on definitions of emotional abuse. Responding to the limitations of definitions which focused on carer behaviours, they proposed a conceptual framework, concentrating on the child's psychosocial well-being. They argued that concentrating on the child's needs would account for carers' actions that are indeed emotionally abusive, relevant to the individual child, but which would be omitted by systems of classification relying exclusively on parental behaviour.

Glaser and Prior (2002) proposed the following categories of ill-treatment:

(1) emotional unavailability, unresponsiveness, and neglect (addressing issues of omission);
(2) negative attributions and misattributions to the child (such as rejection, denigration, and hostility, making the child believe it is unworthy of love);
(3) developmentally inappropriate or inconsistent interactions with the child (including unrealistic expectations, overprotection, and exposure to traumatic events);
(4) failure to recognise or acknowledge the child's individuality and psychological boundaries (such as using the child to fulfil parental psychological needs, failure to see the child's predicament, and establish what are the adult's beliefs);
(5) failure to promote the child's social adaptation (such as mis-socialising, corrupting, and failure to provide cognitive stimulation and experiential learning, as well as involving children in criminal activities).

Despite differential frameworks, these models addressing parental behaviours and the child's psychosocial needs for healthy development raise the same areas of concern, and a merging of both would be advantageous. It is clear that the fundamental components of both parental behaviour and a child's psychosocial need are embedded in the Department of Health (1999) definition of emotional abuse:

> Emotional abuse is the persistent emotional ill-treatment of a child such as to cause severe and persistent adverse effects on the child's emotional development. It may involve conveying to children that they are worthless or unloved, inadequate, or valued only insofar as they meet the needs of another person. It may feature age or developmentally inappropriate expectations being imposed on children. It may involve causing children frequently to feel frightened or in danger, or the exploitation or corruption of children. Some level of emotional abuse is involved in all types of ill-treatment of a child, though it may occur alone.

EMOTIONALLY ABUSIVE PARENTING

Emotional damage to a child can be caused by verbal hostility; denigration; unrealistic expectations; induced fear and anxiety of threats of abandonment; rejection; witnessing domestic violence; deprivation of love, attention, and stimulation; and having excessive power over the child (including overprotection).

The overwhelming majority of parents identified as emotionally abusive showed persistent negative attitudes towards the child, perceived it as unrewarding, difficult to enjoy and socialise, and associated their negative feelings with the child's difficult behaviour and troublesome reactions to their child-rearing methods. Parental attitudes towards the child in abusive homes generally (but in particular in cases of emotional abuse) are negative in nature. Parental perceptions (the way they view the child and the way they justify their feelings towards it) are at best indifferent and, at worst, hostile and rejective. Parents often perceive a child as wicked, deliberately behaving in a difficult way to hurt or to annoy them, so they lash out verbally at the child, using degrading and hurtful language and anxiety- and fear-provoking threats, and distance themselves physically and emotionally from the child, thus creating an emotional vacuum, social isolation, and loneliness, which, in turn, has a devastating effect on the child's growth, development, and well-being. Parents who persistently behave in such a manner towards a child will invariably damage the child's self-esteem, degrade a sense of achievement and social competence, diminish a sense of belonging and security, prevent healthy and vigorous development, and generally make the child's life miserable and painful (Iwaniec, 1995; Iwaniec & Herbert, 1999).

In order to understand why some parents find it difficult to establish an emotional bond and rewarding relationship with their children it is necessary to examine some research findings and practice experiences. The most consistent findings across the breadth of literature on child maltreatment are that parents who abuse have often been abused themselves as children. Parents who were emotionally abused and neglected during their childhood brought to their parenting a model of child-rearing which tended to be cold, distant, undemonstrative, and lacking sensitivity and appropriate supportive responsiveness in all areas of their children's lives. The quality of parenting is often a mirror of the experiences parents had as children. Such parents often lack sufficient knowledge of children's developmental needs and skills to make their offsprings' lives happy and satisfying. They tend to adopt the same model of behaviour as their parents or other people in the communities in which they lived. Some of them simply have not been able to observe or to learn an emotionally supportive pattern of parenting. Of course, this is not to suggest that all emotionally maltreated children will become maltreating parents; many survivors of emotional abuse bear witness to the resilience that can be experienced, determination to change their lives, and to make their parenting and functioning better (Clarke & Clarke, 2000; Doyle, 2001 – see Chapter 9 for further discussion).

Two particular experiences in the family backgrounds of emotionally abusive mothers have been found as significant within research. In their examination of Dutch children who had been admitted to hospital, Lesnik-Oberstein, Koers, & Cohen (1995) found that abusive mothers reported their relationships with their own mothers and fathers as less caring than non-abusive mothers, and that they experienced more lack of affection and being overcontrolled by their fathers. The work of Hemenway, Solnick, & Carter (1994), looking at verbal aggression experienced by parents as children and their level of verbal aggression towards their own children, revealed that parents who were yelled at daily by their own parents yelled at their own children more often than those who reported being yelled at less often as children.

Iwaniec (2004), in her study of severe failure-to-thrive children, found that many mothers were hostile when interacting with them, and found little pleasure being in their children's company. Hostility took the form of screaming, dismissing needs, and punishing in a cruel way (e.g. locking the child in the bedroom, depriving it of treats and referring to it in a derogatory way). Additionally, 70% of parents showed emotional unavailability to their children and made them feel unworthy to have contact with their parents and to be loved. It was interesting to note that 60% of these mothers reported having had a very poor relationship with their parents (but specifically mothers) all their lives, and they felt unloved, ignored, unsupported by their mothers, and some by fathers, when they were children, as illustrated by Jackie's case in Chapter 1. The relationship between parents themselves was reported to be problematic, lacking warmth, unity and affection. In 60% of cases, father–child relationship and interaction was much better and in some instances compensated for the emotional unavailability of mothers to their children.

Erickson, Egeland, & Pianta (1989), in the perspective longitudinal study of 250 children, found that parents identified as *at risk* experienced parenting problems resulting in all types of maltreatment. It was pointed out that emotionally neglected children had parents who were emotionally unavailable, and their mothers were found to be detached and unresponsive to the children's emotional needs and signals of distress. The mother–child interaction lacked pleasure and satisfaction, and was described as mechanical and perfunctory. Emotionally unavailable mothers were more tense, depressed, angry, and confused. The attachment pattern of two-thirds of neglected children was classified as anxious at the age of 1 year. At the age of 2, they additionally showed low enthusiasm, low levels of frustration, increased anger, and no compliance. At the age of 54 months these children showed further problems such as poor impulse control, acute dependence on their teachers, attention-seeking, and disruptive behaviour. The final analysis showed that developmental deficit of these children, as examined between 9 and 24 months, was substantial.

Several other parental behaviours or attributes have been found, somewhat consistently, in the lives of parents (mainly mothers) who emotionally abuse and neglect their children. Individual factors such as poor impulse-control, low self-esteem, social isolation, family violence, substance misuse, and mental-health problems can play important roles. Within the last, anxiety, depression, suicide attempts and stress have been noted (Black, Smith Slep, & Heyman, 2001; English, 1998; Evans, 2002; Kairys *et al.*, 2002; Tomison & Tucci, 1997). Schorr (2002) highlights further family factors and situations which can place the child at an increased risk of emotional abuse or neglect (e.g. parents being involved in a contentious divorce, or unplanned or unwanted pregnancies). Glaser and Prior (1997), in their research with 53 families whose children were on the Child Protection Register for emotional abuse, found that 63% of these families presented a variety of parental attributes mentioned above, which was believed to contribute to emotional maltreatment of children reaching criteria of significant harm. Family violence, substance misuse, and effects of contentious divorce on children will be fully discussed in the next chapter.

The author investigated 72 registered cases of emotional abuse (between 2000 and 2003) which had reached significant harm criteria and were considered for court hearings. Of these, 30% of the cases were registered as sole emotional abuse and neglect, 40% as a significant part of the physical abuse, and 30% as a major part of physical neglect. Painstaking interviews with the abusive parents, with key professionals involved in the cases (social workers, guardians, teachers, health visitors, foster-parents, family-centre workers, and others), together with careful observation of parent–child interaction, helped to identify emotionally harmful behaviours of the parents and emotionally disturbed behaviour of the children. The emotionally abusive behaviours listed in Table 2.1 were identified, and can be rated in frequency, duration, and intensity by the caregivers, by an independent assessor and by older children themselves.

Table 2.1   Checklist: Carers' emotionally abusive behaviour

	Often	Seldom	Almost never	Intensity strong/weak	Length of abuse
Negative attitudes towards the child (can't find anything good and pleasing about the child, always finding faults, excessive criticism, etc.)					
Lack of interest in the child (seldom interacts, shows no concern or wanting to know anything about the child's activities and feelings, lack of interest in school work)					
Failure to remember child's birthday – does not give present, card, or organise party					
Failure to attend events at school where child is taking part (e.g. Christmas play, sports day, parents' evenings)					
Failure to provide sensitive supervision and guidance					
Either rigid, iron rules and routines, or complete lack of them					
No response and sympathy when child is upset, worried or sad					
Little physical contact or closeness					
Social isolation of the child within the family – scapegoating					
Lack of praise and acknowledgement of child's pro-social behaviour					
Ignoring child's presence and overlooking emotional needs					

Table 2.1   (Continued)

	Often	Seldom	Almost never	Intensity strong/weak	Length of abuse
Lack of sensitivity in response to child's signals of distress					
Emotional unavailability to the child					
Using child in marital disputes – divorce					
Overprotecting a child to the point of developmental paralysis, where child is prevented from making the simplest decisions and doing things for him/herself					
Encouraging or allowing a child to use alcohol; involving a child in drug-dealing on behalf of parents; or other antisocial behaviour, e.g. stealing, shoplifting, hurting other people					
Telling a child that it is unwanted, unloved, and is an intruder in the family					
Encouraging racism and sectarianism, thus promoting attitudinal corruption					
Threatening a child with abandonment – given away, killed, severely punished if it does not do what parents or carers want it to do					
Killing a pet, destroying a favourite toy, banishing a child to an empty room (cellar, dark cupboards) as a punishment for not doing what was asked					
Depriving a child of food, treats, and privileges for minor misbehaviour on a regular basis					
Having unrealistic expectations for the child's age and level of cognitive ability. Exerting pressure and making demands which child is unable to meet					

Table 2.1   (Continued)

	Often	Seldom	Almost never	Intensity strong/weak	Length of abuse
Exposing a child to parental quarrels, fights, and violence – leaving a child frightened, anxious, stressed, and overwhelmed with fear that the violent parent will kill or badly hurt the victim's parent					
Ignoring child's illness – child is not taken to see the doctor, or given medication to relieve pain, so child suffers unattended and alone					
Child might be exposed to fabricated illnesses or induced illness, thus suffering physical and emotional pain					
Parents expecting a child to take parenting role and overburdening a child with their problems, using a child as a counsellor and confidant					
Parental (usually mother's) self-harming behaviour (e.g. wrist-cutting, overdose) in the children's presence. Suicide or attempted suicide					
Multiple rejection by parents, extended family, and foster-parents					
Children left with complete strangers not known to the parent or children in order to go out, e.g. drinking					
Children exposed to drunk and violent parental companions, until late at night, who at times give them alcohol					
Contact visit for accommodated children not attended by the parents, or attended irregularly, causing upsets and disappointments					
Leaving children for several days or weeks with strange people and not telling them where parent is going and for how long					

'ROFILE OF EMOTIONALLY ABUSED AND
' CHILDREN

..ect of emotional abuse on a baby, child, or young person will show itself in different ways. Babies who are emotionally neglected or rejected will often fail to thrive; pre-school children will show developmental delays and emotional/behavioural problems; in middle childhood they will present school adjustment problems and poor educational attainments; and in adolescence a range of antisocial behaviours, identity problems, and relationship difficulties will be observed (see Chapter 8). For those who work with emotionally abused children and adolescents, the profiles of these individuals are disturbing and worrying, especially those who are rejected, threatened, denigrated, and terrorised.

As a result of persistent anxiety and fear, many of these children show various psychosomatic disorders, such as: sleep disturbance, pains and aches, vomiting and diarrhoea, eating problems, and generally feeling sick and unwell. Those exposed to frequent family violence and those who are terrorised and threatened often show these symptoms. A considerable number of emotionally ill-treated children suffer from soiling, bed-wetting, and disturbed toileting behaviour, e.g. deliberate urination and smearing of faeces over the bed, walls, furniture, and toys, and soiling and wetting at school. Such behaviour indicates a high level of unhappiness, inner turmoil, and distress. It may be that an aggressive retaliation is directed at those who inflict hurt in their daily lives. It may also indicate developmental delay due to emotional upheaval: punitive toilet-training by parents may perhaps be a factor. Soiling at school presents particularly difficult problems for these children, as they are perceived by peers as dirty and disgusting, and by teachers as rather unpleasant to have in the classroom. Such children tend to be isolated, as peers avoid sitting next to them or playing with them outside the classroom (Iwaniec, 2004; Skuse, 1989). Emotionally abused children tend to be destructive, disruptive, and attention-seeking, have short attention-spans, or are withdrawn, detached, nervous, and depressed. Elective mutism is seen from time to time, especially among rejected and humiliated children (Sluckin, 2000).

Due to low self-esteem and feelings of unworthiness, possession of objects may be problematic: toys, books, and clothing are often destroyed, and because of profound unhappiness and confusion such children harm themselves. Cutting, scratching, and head-banging are not uncommon among ill-treated children: running away from home, glue-sniffing, or other substance abuse are not unknown among those in middle childhood or in adolescence. Frequent lies and denials of behaviour (even when not serious) are common to avoid punishment or presumed punishment or telling off, and being humiliated. Stealing from parents, peers at school, and shops, even of things which are useless and meaningless to the child (e.g. clothes pegs, tea towels, etc.) indicates a cry for attention and help. The child, by behaving in such a manner, tries to solve a problem but has no confidence or trust in adults, and often no cognitive ability to do so in an appropriate way. Small numbers of emotionally abused children regress into babyish behaviour such as thumb-sucking, rocking, or reverting to infantile speech. Seeing an eight- or nine-year-old child who is very stressed and unhappy (because of continuous lack of attention and affection from parents) regressing to infantilism is very disturbing to observe and with which to deal. As a rule such behaviour generates even more anger and resentment from the carers as they see it as manipulative attention-seeking, but not as attention-needing.

In some children, emotional upheaval tends to demonstrate itself in a bizarre eating pattern such as: overeating, hoarding food, getting up at night in search of food, scavenging food from waste-bins, eating non-food items, begging food from strangers, and showing constant preoccupation with food. Such children eat for comfort but physically do not benefit from eating. It can be argued that calories are wasted and absorbed by stress. Some children, however, lose their appetite because of emotional stress and will show anorexic-like tendencies (see Chapter 7 for full discussion).

REJECTED CHILDREN

Rejection can be expressed in many ways and can take many forms. For some children, rejection means callousness and indifference, neglect, hostility, and even cruelty: for others it may be more subtle and covert, with even more complicated emotional convolutions (Rohner, 1986).

A rejected child is likely to be more dependent, more clinging, more intensely possessive, and more seeking of parental approval, nurturance, attention, and physical contact than the accepted child. All human beings have a basic need for positive responses in others, but if a child's 'significant others' are rejecting, and if its needs for warmth and affection are unfulfilled, the child will, up to a point, increase its efforts to attract love and attention. In other words, it will become dependent. Beyond a certain point the dependency responses may be extinguished. The point here is that the seriously rejected child has not learned how to give love because it has never known a loving parent after whom it can model its own behaviour, and even though it may crave affection, it has difficulty in accepting it when it is offered. In order to protect itself from more emotional hurt, it tends to insulate its emotions, and ultimately stops trying to get affection from the people from whom it craves emotional warmth. Thus the emotionally abused child becomes emotionally isolated, unable freely and openly to form warm, lasting, and intimate relationships with others. Its attachments tend to be troubled by emotional constriction or defensiveness; in addition, as a result of the psychological damage brought about by maltreatment, the child will have less tolerance of stress. Such children are apt to become resentful of or angry with their parents, as well as being fearful of more rejection, and thereby evolve a 'defensive' independence of or emotional withdrawal from the parents. Such a pattern of behaviour by the child may be initiating a process of counter-rejection in the parents. Behind a child's defensive independence or emotional detachment can often be an unrecognised longing to re-establish a warm, nurturant relationship with the parents. The child is especially likely to be hostile, aggressive, or passively aggressive if rejection takes the form of parental hostility. Under these conditions the child is provided with an aggressive model to emulate, and thus its own aggressive responses may intensify. Ineffectual and rejecting parenting is likely to show up in disturbance of eating and sleeping patterns, toilet-training, and general compliance, as these are the first tasks of every child's socialisation. So, if the child is unloved, it will become unloving, and the parents and child will become mutually antagonistic.

The author's investigation of 72 registered cases of emotional abuse awaiting court hearing revealed the problems manifested by these children shown in Table 2.2. Frequency, duration, intensity, and attached meaning of such behaviour can be rated by older children, by carers, and an independent assessor.

Table 2.2   Checklist: Disturbed behaviours manifested by emotionally abused children

	Often	Seldom	Almost never	Intensity strong/weak	Length of abuse
Over-activity – inability to concentrate, focus attention, settle down, be calm, feel at peace, and apply itself to a specific task					
Restlessness in all activities					
Poor impulse control					
Anxiety and general nervousness					
Poor sleeping – waking up, wandering around the house, or lying motionless in bed					
Overeating for comfort – hoarding food					
Undereating, no appetite					
Failure to thrive					

Table 2.2   (Continued)

	Often	Seldom	Almost never	Intensity strong/weak	Length of abuse
Destructiveness – tearing things, breaking toys, destroying personal belongings, pulling off wallpaper, etc.					
Lacking self-confidence – frequent self-doubts, apprehension, getting no satisfaction from tasks well done					
Low self-esteem – feeling of not being worthy of getting things, of being loved and appreciated, feeling incapable of change and undeserving					
Stealing from parents, peers, or shops					
Bed-wetting and soiling					
Looking sad and withdrawn					
Bursting into tears when even mildly criticised					
Passive obedience					
Non-compliance – stubborn defiance					
Lack of assertiveness					
Avoiding social interaction					
Suicide or attempted suicides					
Aggression					
Fire-setting – in the middle of the room, curtains, bedding, furniture, or personal clothing and toys					
Self-harming – self-cutting, scratching, biting, throwing oneself down the stairs, stealing to attract attention to the hurt and helplessness the child is experiencing					
Lying to avoid criticism and punishment					
Putting blame on others – false accusations – to make others suffer as he/she is suffering					
Inability/inhibition to communicate – elective mutism					
Prostitution					
Running away					
Being guarded – careful in what to say					

Table 2.2   (Continued)

	Often	Seldom	Almost never	Intensity strong/weak	Length of abuse
Glue-sniffing or drug misuse					
Difficulties in forming meaningful/in-depth relationships with other people and peers					
Insecurely attached to mothers/caregivers					
Being eager to help and assist, e.g. schoolteachers, foster-parents, or other people outside the home					
Inability to foresee the consequences of behaviour					
Lack of trust in other people					
Difficulties in identifying their own feelings and the feelings of other people					
Not showing guilt or remorse after hurting somebody or breaking rules					
Difficulty in thinking ahead and in recognising basic cause and effect					
Negativism. Seeing things and people in a fatalistic and negative way and anticipating failure					
Underachievement at school					
Difficulties in decision-making					
Alcohol abuse					

Factor analysis revealed that rejection was present in 72% of the cases, degrading and humiliating behaviour in 85%, terrorising in 63%, isolating in 70%, exploiting and corrupting in 45%, denying emotional responsiveness in 93%, overprotection in 25%, Münchausen's syndrome by proxy in two cases, and educational neglect in 50% of the sample. Emotional abuse was multiple in all cases.

CONSEQUENCES OF EMOTIONALLY HARMFUL PARENTING – MESSAGES FROM RESEARCH AND PRACTICE

Emotional abuse is not regarded as a short-term crisis in a child's life. A number of immediate non-specific psychological, physical and behavioural sequelae have been observed in childhood responses to emotional abuse which appear to provide the basis for dysfunctional cognitive and emotive processing and, consequently, maladaptive developmental pathways.

Historically, it has been difficult to reach a clear consensus on the effects of emotional maltreatment as few studies have differentiated the individual effects of this form of abuse. There is also a tendency for researchers to address specific incomplete components of the problem (Malo, Moreau, Chamberland, Leveille, & Roy, 2004). In addition, emotional maltreatment is more elusive than other forms of abuse. It is often under-reported, hidden behind other types of abuse, and investigated less often by child-protection agencies (Gracia, 1995). However, research has recently begun to examine the impact of emotional maltreatment relative to other types of harm (e.g. Ney, Fung, & Wickett, 1994; Rodgers et al., 2004).

All forms of abuse have an element of emotional harm (Lynch & Browne, 1997). However, research has indicated that emotional maltreatment in isolation is particularly harmful (Hart et al., 1998). Indeed, Egeland and colleagues found that psychologically unavailable parenting was the most harmful form of abuse of the multiple types of abuse examined (Egeland et al., 1983; Egeland & Erickson, 1987). This form of abuse can seriously compromise a child's development by punishing positive normal behaviours such as smiling or exploration, discouraging early attachment, damaging self-esteem, and inhibiting the development of interpersonal skills necessary for adequate performance outside of the family environment (Garbarino, Eckenrode, & Bolger, 1997).

A number of research projects have highlighted the potential negative short- and long-term consequences of emotional maltreatment for later functioning (e.g. Brassard, Germain, & Hart, 1987; Doyle, 1997; Iwaniec, Herbert, & Sluckin, 2002; Glaser & Prior, 2002; Thoburn, Wilding, & Watson, 2000). This form of harm is particularly destructive for a child's competence in a number of areas including verbal and non-verbal communication skills, patience, and goal-setting, and ego development in terms of basic confidence and security (Garbarino et al., 1997). Effects have been found to include withdrawal, academic underachievement, and emotional instability (Hart, Brassard, & Karlson, 1996); social adjustment and interpersonal problems and difficulties in forming secure attachment (Farber & Egeland, 1987; Egeland et al., 1983), stunted physical growth, and self-harming behaviour (Iwaniec, 1995).

Research has indicated that emotional maltreatment is particularly damaging to a child's self-esteem (Mullen et al., 1996). This is likely to be as a result of the belittling nature of this form of harm and the fact that it directly targets a child's worth through internalisation of sustained negative criticism (Briere & Runtz, 1990; Gross & Keller, 1992; Morimoto & Sharma, 2004). Low self-esteem has, in turn, been seen as a key factor in the development of a

Consequences of emotional abuse

), for example, found that long-term
a strong sense of shame, feelings of
action, and disempowerment, and
ne low self-esteem, aggression, self-
future.

und to play a key role in the
y *et al.*, 1994). For example, Kent,
notional abuse was the only type of
ysical and sexual abuse) to have a
attitudes in young women. Mullen
altreatment was more likely to result
buse. Self-esteem is believed to play
a significant role in this relationship. For example, Kent and Waller (2000) reviewed the literature on emotional maltreatment and eating disorders and found evidence of a link between childhood emotional maltreatment and eating psychopathology that might be particularly linked to the damage that this form of abuse exerts upon self-esteem.

The effect of emotional maltreatment has now been examined across multiple developmental stages. Emotionally maltreated children have been found to have higher levels of aggression, anger, frustration, and ego under control, and lower levels of ego resilience than non-maltreated children (Farber & Egeland, 1987; Manly, Kim, Rogosch, & Cicchetti, 2001). Problems among older children and adolescents who have been emotionally maltreated have been found to include social rejection, dependency, school difficulties, problems in concentrating, behaviour problems, and delinquency (Gagné, 1995; Solomon & Serres, 1999). College students who have experienced emotional maltreatment have been found to be significantly more likely to experience clinical distress and psychological disturbance (obsessive compulsiveness, depression, anxiety, and distress) and to perceive themselves as being more depressed, more aggressive, less worthy, and to be more overwhelmed in interpersonal relationships than controls (Rich, Gingersich, & Rosen, 1997; Morimoto & Sharma, 2004). Adults who have been emotionally maltreated have been found to have problems such as depression, somatisation, eating disorders, suicidal ideation, anxiety, low self-esteem, interpersonal and sexual problems, increased levels of substance abuse, eating disorders, and psychiatric symptoms (Gross & Keller, 1992; Gagné, 1995; Hoglund & Nicholas, 1995; Mullen *et al.*, 1996; Briere & Runtz, 1990; Moran, Vuchinich, & Hall, 2004).

Cognitive and Educational Outcomes

The detrimental effects of emotional maltreatment on cognitive and school performance are the most robust findings in the research literature. Difficulties in the acquisition of basic skills (specifically deficits in reading, language, and maths) are observed. Teachers often report that these children struggle in their efforts to adapt to the demands of the school environment to attend to tasks requiring cognitive skills (Kurtz, Gaudin, Wodarski, & Howing, 1993; Oates, 1996). Emotionally and physically neglected children, if they survive physically, often fail to develop the confidence, concentration, and social skills that would enable them to succeed in school and in relationships. The behaviour they bring to the classroom sets them up for a continuing cycle of failure and disappointment unless something happens to make a difference.

Teenagers with a history of emotional maltreatment report low educational and vocational attainments and aspirations and are more likely to be disruptive, display discipline problems, and have to repeat the year grades (Kelly, Thornberry, & Smith, 1997; Malinosky-Rummell & Hansen, 1993): they are also more likely to be suspended and finish school without any qualifications, thus limiting employment and economic opportunities and prospects for financial security (Kendall-Tackett & Eckenrode, 1996).

On the whole, the impact of neglect on children's development is noticeable but, in particular, the consequences of emotional neglect are striking and show long-lasting impact on children's adaptation within the family, with peers and teachers, and with regard to learning and problem-solving. Emotionally neglected children have been shown to have behavioural problems and conduct disorders, problems in social relationships, and display less competent behaviour. They stand out among their peers for their diminished self-esteem, lack of confidence, general unhappiness, low school achievement, and insecure attachment to their parents or carers (Erickson *et al.*, 1989). They tend to be passive and exhibit some of the characteristics of learned helplessness, although angry outbursts and non-compliance are also characteristic of emotionally neglected children. Some have suggested that neglect is more likely to victimise younger children than adolescents because older children are less exclusively dependent on their caregivers for emotional nurturing and positive attention. However, older children who are abandoned and adolescents who are literally thrown out of their homes constitute an increasing concern among the population of emotionally abused and neglected children. Emotional neglect, especially among young children, often goes unnoticed as it occurs in private, away from the public eye, and because children are too young to speak about their unhappiness and often do not know what constitutes nurturing care and attention.

Social and Behavioural Outcomes

Emotional maltreatment can have a serious negative effect on an individual's ability to manage emotional difficulties, cope with stressful situations and develop problem-solving skills (Shields, Cicchetti, & Ryan, 1994). A host of social and behavioural difficulties are associated with the experience of psychological abuse in childhood, some of which become more apparent throughout development, particularly in the teenage years. During adolescence, self-reported drug and alcohol use is significantly higher in samples who have been victimised by psychological abuse (Dembo, Getreu, Williams, Berry, & La Voie, 1990; Widom & White, 1997). Children who have experienced maltreatment are also at higher risk of truancy and running away from home (Manion & Wilson, 1995), and consistently display higher levels of a variety of delinquent behaviours, from minor delinquency to violent antisocial behaviour, involving arrests and convictions (Kelly *et al.*, 1997). Teenage pregnancy rates are particularly high for adolescent girls with a prevalence rate of 52% compared to 34% in non-maltreated controls. Much problematic behaviour is often a manifestation or a direct symptom of the history or current experience of maltreatment, and may function as a coping mechanism to manage the trauma or deleterious effects of the abuse on self-esteem and self-confidence (Agnew, 1992; Harter & Marold, 1994; Iwaniec, 2004).

Interpersonal and Mental Health Difficulties

Several studies have reported that a history of psychological maltreatment in childhood is strongly predictive of mental-health problems, particularly low mood, hopelessness, and low self-esteem (e.g. Brown, Cohen, Johnson, & Smailes, 1999; Kaufman, 1991; Kelly *et al.*, 1997; Toth, Manly, & Cicchetti, 1992). Emotional abuse, in the form of parental criticism and verbal hostility, appears to be particularly significant in the development of adjustment difficulties. Children and young people appear to internalise the critical voice of the abusive caregiver and come to believe that they are 'bad' and 'worthless', which lays the foundation for low self-esteem and mood disorders in adulthood. They often present with poor relationship skills, are isolated from peers, and are more passive and withdrawn (Camras & Rappaport, 1993). In comparison to other types of maltreatment (e.g. sexual and/or physical abuse) the experience of emotional abuse appears to have a more deleterious effect on adjustment, and is a stronger predictor of psychological difficulties (Crittenden, Claussen, & Sugarman, 1994), particularly for females (McGee, Wolfe, & Wilson, 1997).

Children and young people who have experienced emotional abuse lose confidence in their carers' availability and responsiveness, and may subsequently adopt insecure attachment styles as a strategy to cope with their emotional and relationship needs (Bowlby, 1973). A child's cognitive and emotional capacities are often insufficiently developed to cope with contradictory models of caregiving, which are sources of both protection and harm (Crittenden, 1988; Tomison & Tucci, 1997; Crittenden & Ainsworth,

1989). The carer, and by extension other adults, are believed to be lovable, but also rejecting and untrustworthy. Relationships with others are considered as both a source of pleasure and of emotional pain (Bowlby, 1973; Doyle, 2001). Experiencing such paradoxical and unpredictable parenting renders a child less confident, inhibits capacity for emotional expression, and undermines its capacity to manage its emotions, address stressful situations and understand the environment (O'Hagan, 1995).

Emotional abuse also places children at considerable risk in terms of their ability to develop positive relationships with others. The abused individual tends to select relationships and social situations which replicate and confirm the abusive experience (Bowlby, 1973). Adults with a childhood history of psychological maltreatment are frequently observed to present difficulties in relationships with peers and partners, inadequate and often inappropriate parenting skills, and limited capacity to empathise with others (Bronfenbrenner, 1979; Briggs & Hawkins, 1996; Crittenden & Ainsworth, 1989). These subsequent difficulties appear to perpetuate the cycle of risk and maladaptive outcomes for the victims of emotional abuse.

Timing, Chronicity, and Severity of Emotional Abuse

The extent to which emotional abuse affects a child's development is linked to the timing, chronicity, and severity of the maltreatment (Cicchetti & Toth, 1995a). For example, Thornberry, Ireland, and Smith, 2001 found that when the maltreatment ceased for children who experienced neglect in early childhood, the risk of psychological maladjustment, substance abuse, and trouble with the law faded with time. However, for adolescents who were continuously subjected to psychological maltreatment in their teenage years, the vulnerability to multiple difficulties remained. Such findings have particular implications for care planning and interventions affecting children and young people. For adolescents who are taken into care, although the attachment problems can remain pronounced (Daniel, Wassell, & Gilligan, 1999), there appears to be some evidence that placing the child in a more supportive environment has a beneficial effect on adjustment, lower rates of teen pregnancy, and delinquent behaviour.

Physical and Health Outcomes

Although physical contact does not normally occur in emotional abuse and neglect, there can be several significant physical and medical outcomes which adversely affect the child's development. Children who are victims of emotional maltreatment are likely to be smaller in stature, weight less than same-age peers, and often fail to meet expected developmental milestones (Cleaver, Unell, & Aldgate, 1999; Iwaniec, 2004). There also appears to be a significant neurological component to psychological abuse which has been linked to presentations of hyperactivity, sleep-disturbance, anxiety, and learning and memory problems as well as a vulnerability to mood-swings throughout adulthood (Perry, 2001b; Dallam, 2001).

Although many of the child's difficulties remit when the child is removed from the abusive system (Keiley, Howe, Dodge, Bates, & Petit, 2001; Skuse, Albanese, Stanhope, Gilmore, & Voss, 1996; Iwaniec, 2004), many children still show signs of dysfunction years after the abuse has terminated, particularly if they remain exposed to a number of risk-factors and if emotional support and other protective measures are unavailable (Widom, 1999a).

IDENTIFICATION AND INCIDENCE

> Emotional abuse scars the heart and damages the soul. Like cancer, it does its most deadly work internally. And like cancer, it can metastasize if untreated
>
> (Vachss, 1994)

Emotional abuse is often referred to as the 'hidden form of maltreatment' or an 'elusive crime' in that it is the most underestimated and difficult form of maltreatment to identify. As previously stated, emotional maltreatment leaves no visible signs or scars and there is often no clear intention to harm the child. Added to this, it is suggested that children lack knowledge of what constitutes good parenting and become accustomed to their treatment, rarely telling others of their unhappiness (Iwaniec, 1995, 2003). The physical signs of emotional maltreatment, other than non-organic failure to thrive, are also difficult to ascertain, and further evidence in terms of social, emotional, and cognitive developmental delays may not become apparent until later stages in the child's development (Department of Health and Human Service, 1999). Not only do these issues make estimating the prevalence of emotional abuse difficult but they also pose serious issues for practitioners in terms of intervention. Delays in identification also mean that 'children are exposed to more prolonged abuse and neglect, and that interactional patterns become more entrenched and difficult to change' (Glaser, 2002).

Tomison and Tucci (1997) note that estimates of the prevalence of emotional abuse range from 0.69 to 25.7% of children, depending on the definition and measurement used. In England at the end of March 2002, 18% of children and young people on the Child Protection Register, and 14% in Northern Ireland, were registered under the emotional abuse only category (www.statistics.gov.uk). Although these statistics are thought to hugely underestimate the scale of the problem, as only a small number of cases will ever come to official attention, this category of child maltreatment has been increasing while others have recently declined. While some would argue that the relatively low levels of referrals may signal a reluctance to label behaviour as emotionally abusive due to problems in operationalising the concept (Evans, 2002; Stevenson, 1999), these figures may suggest that this trend is beginning to change in the UK. It should also be noted that while many now believe that emotional abuse is present in all forms of child maltreatment, it is recorded in this category only when it is the *sole* reason for referral. This is despite the fact that Claussen and Crittenden (1991) found experiences of psychological maltreatment in 90% of children who had been physically abused or neglected.

Needless to say, incidence rates vary from place to place, and indeed according to the definition of emotional abuse employed and the methods used to assess and measure it. From a glance at the US national incident rates on child maltreatment, it would seem that a smaller proportion of children appears for emotional abuse only. Figures from 1999 show that 51% of maltreated children were neglected, 26% were physically abused, 10% were the victims of sexual abuse and only 4% were emotionally abused (cited in Behl *et al.*, 2003). Although this figure appears low, it should not in itself be taken as evidence that emotional abuse is a relatively small-scale problem in the USA. Different states and child-protection departments will employ different operational definitions and practices and this may in part be reflected in these relatively low incident rates. This point is further substantiated by Binggeli *et al.* (2001) whose extensive review of the literature estimating the scale of psychological maltreatment in the USA concluded that it may feature in the child histories of more than one-third of the American adult population.

The work of Tomison and Tucci (1997) provides an illuminating breakdown of reports of child emotional abuse across the various state territories in Australia from 1991 to 1996. This clearly highlights huge disparities in the levels of substantiated cases of emotional abuse over this time period (and before), disparities which simply do not exist to the same degree across states with regard to other forms of child maltreatment. As a result, these authors, among others, suggest that this is an indication of the continued implications of the use of different definitions across the country. National data from Australia shows that, in 1995–1996, 31% of all substantiated cases of child maltreatment were emotional-abuse ones. They suggest that the now 'expanded definition' of emotional abuse in some states, which includes exposure to domestic violence and parental mental-health problems, may in part be responsible for the higher proportion of emotional abuse cases within national statistics.

Several studies of the incidence of emotional abuse break this down by the various 'types' of abuse/neglect experienced, allowing an insight (if nothing else) into those behaviours which are most likely to bring families to the attention of child-protection services. The Canadian Incidence Study of Reported Abuse and Neglect (2001) provides an overview of children referred to child-welfare services over a three-month period in 1998. Of these cases, 40% involved investigations of neglect, 31% involved investigations of physical abuse, 19% investigated emotional maltreatment, and the remaining 10% of investigations were for sexual abuse. As would be expected, some children experienced multiple forms of emotional maltreatment: the most prevalent form found to be substantiated was exposure to family violence (58%). This was followed by emotional abuse (34%) and emotional neglect (16%). It was reported that non-organic failure to thrive occurred too infrequently to allow for analysis (Trocme & Wolfe, 2001).

A recent retrospective study carried out by the NSPCC in the UK examined experiences of child abuse and neglect among a sample of 2 869 of 18- to 24-year-olds, and also provided data on the most commonly reported forms of emotional abuse. It revealed that 6% of all respondents could be defined as having suffered emotional abuse as children (based on measures of severity and frequency). The most common form of abuse reported was 'terrorising' (34%), which included threats of harm to the child or a loved one, and threatening to send the child away. This was followed by 'psychological domination and control', which included behaviours such as isolation and attempts to control the child's thinking. Further to this, 18% of respondents reported acts of humiliation and attacks on self-esteem, and 17% reported experiencing what is referred to as 'psycho/physical abuse'. This refers to physical acts which cause emotional rather than physical pain (Cawson *et al.*, 2001 cited in Evans, 2002). Glaser and Prior (1997) also found high levels of reported child neglect in the form of rejection and emotionally unavailable parenting in their analysis of the histories of 94 children on Child Protection Registers for emotional abuse. They observed that a substantial proportion of children were experiencing more than one form of emotional abuse (41%).

Findings reported by Doyle (1997) highlighted that fear-inducing behaviour (such as terrorising) was the most prevalent form of emotional abuse, experienced by 95% of children in her sample drawn from the Child Protection Register. The following emotionally abusive behaviours were identified: giving children inappropriate roles (92%); rejection (86%); isolation (54%); degrading (53%); ignoring (28%).

A similar analysis of children on Child Protection Registers today may reveal high levels of children exposed to family violence in the emotional-abuse category (as was found in the Canadian Incident Study), due to increased recognition among professionals of the effects domestic violence can have upon children's well-being. As can be seen, emotional abuse can clearly take many forms, and some children (as revealed in the NSPCC study) will experience multiple forms of such abuse leading to significant harm on a short- and long-term basis. Available evidence points to the fact that children exposed to emotional abuse and neglect experience maltreatment in multiple forms and ways.

SUMMARY

Despite recognition that the consequences of emotional abuse/neglect are as severe and long-lasting as other forms of maltreatment, if not more so, it still remains 'on the margins of child abuse' (Tomison & Tucci, 1997). Problems with assessment, identification, and estimation have continued due to the very nature of this form of maltreatment and differential operational definitions of the concept. It is clear to see, from incidence rates around the globe and indeed within countries, that different operational definitions and child-protection practices are in place. Indeed, an analysis of how definitions of emotional abuse are operationalised across various trusts and agencies would reveal and further highlight the very real practice issues surrounding these definitional problems. Tomison and Tucci (1997) suggest that an in-depth examination of the full range of emotionally abusive and neglectful interactions that a child may face, both inside and outside the home, would provide child-protection workers with baseline information with which to work. Indeed, the more recent move (among some in the field of emotional abuse) of recognising the various forms it can take beyond the home (e.g. in community and institutional settings), can only add to the growing recognition and knowledge surrounding this form of child maltreatment. Yet there remains much work to be done on these issues, as will be discussed at length in a later chapter.

In sum, the subject of the emotional abuse of children has grown and moved forward in the last decade or so, yet it would appear that the same issues and concerns that have always plagued the concept continue to exist. It would not seem unfair or overdramatic to suggest that until a clear and consensual definition is achieved and implemented these problems will continue to impact upon research and practice.

CHAPTER 3

EMOTIONAL ABUSE AND NEGLECT WITHIN THE FAMILY

CONTENTS

INTRODUCTION

This chapter focuses on those inter-family issues/relationships which have recently begun to receive more attention in literature concerning child maltreatment: for example, exposure of children to family violence; the experience of parental divorce/separation; and parental substance misuse. The aim of the chapter is to highlight that such experiences can be emotionally damaging to children, exposing them to possible negative outcomes. Despite this, it will be demonstrated that research in these areas has been dogged by methodological problems, and that more work is needed to fully understand the complexities of the issues involved to better inform policy and practice.

FAMILY VIOLENCE

Children who are exposed to family violence are often referred to as the 'forgotten', 'invisible', or 'accidental' victims of abuse: if they are not directly victimised they have often been overlooked in research and intervention (Hughes & Graham-Bermann, 1998; Somer & Braunstein, 1999; Tomison, 2000). It was not until the late 1980s that research on the effects of family violence upon children first began to emerge: previous invisibility in research literature was in part due to the lack of adequate data on the nature and scale of the problem (Fantuzzo & Mohr, 1999).

Perhaps one of the biggest issues with which research in this area has had to grapple has been that of definition. Research studies use a range of differing definitions: they vary from children 'witnessing' (i.e. actually seeing) family violence, to being 'exposed' to (i.e. overhearing, being aware of and/or coping with) violence and its aftermath. Some studies focus only on physical violence, while others include verbally aggressive behaviour in their analyses. Yet there may be confusion concerning what actually constitutes family violence or domestic violence. Some studies use the label 'wife abuse', others focus on 'spouse/marital abuse', while others still employ definitions such as 'intimate partner violence'. Despite the litany of problems, however, there has been some forward movement in that the term 'child exposure' has taken over from 'child witnessing' in the last decade or so, thus including various ways in which children may be affected by 'family violence' (a term preferable to others in that it embraces the totality of violence [Tomison, 2000]). Whatever definition is employed, there appears to be consensual agreement that children living in households experiencing interparental/partner violence run a considerable risk of maladjustment and social and mental problems (Butler-Sloss, 2001). Furthermore, there is growing recognition that exposure of children to family violence constitutes a form of psychological/emotional abuse (Graham-Bermann, 2002; Hughes & Graham-Bermann, 1998; Jellen, McCarroll, & Thayer, 2001; Kairys *et al.*, 2002; Kerig & Fedorowicz, 1999; Somer & Braunstein, 1999; Tomison, 2000).

Scale and Incidence

The extent to which children are exposed to interparental/partner violence is difficult to estimate: indeed, from a review of the literature it would appear that there are few prevalent studies concerning exposure of children to family violence, but some reports appear to suggest that such exposure 'may range from a fleeting moment of abusive language to homicide' (James, 1994, p. 3). In his paper given at the Barbican Centre, London (22 March 2004) Lord Falconer of Thoroton has quoted shocking statistics regarding the scale of domestic violence in the United Kingdom. Most victims in domestic violence are women, but it must be remembered that there is significant violence committed by some women against men. The differences between gender speak for themselves. One in four women will be a victim of domestic violence some time in their lives; for men, the figure is one in six; domestic violence accounts for nearly one quarter of all recorded crime. On average, 120 women and 30 men are killed every year by a present or former partner, and there are an estimated 600 000 incidents of domestic violence each year, yet it is estimated that there are only 7 000 criminal prosecutions. Women, on average, are attacked

35 times before they seek help against the perpetrators of domestic violence, but only 19 000 victims of domestic violence seek non-molestation orders through the civil courts.

From US national surveys of family violence it has been estimated that between 3.3 and 10 million children are at risk of witnessing verbal or physical violence between parents/carers (Graham-Bermann, 2002; Tomison, 2000). These estimates are based on reports where violence is known to have occurred, yet little is known regarding frequency, duration, and intensity. Further research in the USA has estimated that children were present in 40% to 80% of households where there were reports of family violence (Jaffe *et al.*, 1980 cited in Tomison, 2000). Several US studies, however, agree that interparental/partner violence occurs disproportionately in households where there are children under the age of five years, and that these are most likely to be exposed to multiple incidents of it (Fantuzzo & Mohr, 1999; Graham-Bermann, 2002). Australian studies of family violence have also attempted to estimate exposure of children to such violence. In Queensland it was found that 88% of respondents who reported experiencing family violence stated that children were present in the household. Of these children, 90% witnessed domestic violence incidents (James, 1994). Also, rather shockingly, in Victoria it was revealed that in 65% of domestic disputes that involved a gun, children under five years of age were present. This was also true of 79% of incidents that involved the use of another weapon (Tomison, 2000).

Estimating the extent of child exposure to family violence is further confounded by the fact that this often co-occurs with other forms of child abuse/neglect. Indeed, in a number of studies each form of child maltreatment is not fully identified when examining outcomes. It is well established, however, that much child abuse/neglect occurs in homes where there is also a history of domestic violence. It has been suggested that children living in homes where there is such violence comprise 15% of the national average of those neglected (Osofsky, 1999; Tomison, 2000). By the very nature of household dynamics it is clear that children may be at more risk of physical harm, particularly when they try to intervene in disputes (Kerig & Fedorowicz, 1999). Apart from physical abuse/neglect, the co-occurrence of domestic violence and all forms of child maltreatment, particularly emotional abuse, have been highlighted in many studies (Cousins, Monteith, Larkin, & Percy, 2003; Fantuzzo & Mohr, 1999; Graham-Bermann, 2002; McGuigan & Platt, 2001). Establishing causality and temporal order, however, is far from clear-cut. With regard to emotional abuse in particular, it is important to note that this may not necessarily signal co-morbidity, but an increased recognition among child-protection workers that exposure to family violence is in itself emotionally abusive, and is therefore recorded as such. The next section will discuss in more detail how exposure to family violence is inherently emotionally abusive to children.

Exposure to Family Violence as Child Emotional Maltreatment

Incidents in which exposure to family violence can be emotionally abusive to the child are numerous, and clearly fall within one or more of the categories of child psychological maltreatment outlined by Hart *et al.* (2002; see Chapter 1). Tomison (2000, p. 8) provides an insightful if incomplete list of what 'witnessing domestic violence' can mean: it includes having a violent partner hit or threaten a child while in its mother's arms, using the child as a 'hostage' to make the mother stay, using the child as a physical weapon, making a child watch/participate, making a child spy on a parent, and attempting to break the mother–child bond. In addition, research has documented that children can be traumatised by overhearing as well as seeing disputes (Graham-Bermann, 2002; Holzworth-Munroe, Smutzler, & Sandin, 1997). Dealing with the aftermath of a violent incident (verbal or physical) can also be traumatic for the child as can dealing with a parent whose mood periodically swings from violent to intimate. Depending on the level of violence, children may also have to deal with the experience of police involvement, injury to the mother, removal of the father from the home, and/or placement in a shelter. It is clear that any of these incidents, especially when exposure is prolonged, are emotionally abusive to the child. Somer and Braunstein (1999, p. 3) go as far as to suggest that children exposed to family violence are 'psychologically maltreated by the offending parent, who failed to shield the observing child from the traumatising sight'.

In addition to the fact that the situation is emotionally traumatising for the child, research suggests that parents living in violent households can become emotionally/psychologically unavailable to children. Parents (particularly the victim), can become emotionally numb, uncommunicative, and frightened; thus so unable to cope with their own trauma that they are emotionally unresponsive to children (Hughes & Graham-Bermann, 1998; James, 1994; McGuigan & Platt, 2001; Osofsky, 1999). Indeed, Osofsky (1999, p. 40) states that it is 'crucial' to understand that, when 'experiencing trauma', a parent's ability to play a 'stable, consistent role' in a child's life (and, therefore, to support a child's resilience) may be severely compromised.

The consequences of emotionally unavailable parenting are known to include withdrawal in children, disorganised behaviours, and attachment difficulties in relationships in later life (Egeland & Erickson, 1987; Osofsky, 1999). The variety of other possible negative outcomes associated with exposure of children to family violence is discussed in detail in the next section.

CASE STUDY

A case of two sisters presented below illustrates the plight of children living in a violent home.

Two sisters – four and six years old respectively – frequently witnessed their drunk father beating and kicking their mother. He swore at her and called her degrading names. He told them that she was a slut, a useless bitch, and good for nothing. The mother was often hospitalised because of inflicted injuries. The mother made all sorts of excuses for her injuries: that she walked into a cupboard in the dark, that she fell down, that something dropped on her, etc. Even when she admitted to her husband's violence she did not want to take action, fearing that one way or another he would make their lives miserable, e.g. wailing at the corner of the street and begging for forgiveness, giving the children expensive presents, etc. On two occasions when the mother and children stayed with relatives he either promised to change or threatened them and the extended family.

When under the influence of alcohol, the father often told his daughters that he would kill them one day. They used to cry and hide during beating episodes, and were not allowed to go to their mother when the beatings were over. The six-year-old cuddled and comforted her petrified sister who could not sleep and had recurring nightmares. The six-year-old refused to go to school and showed symptoms of school-phobic behaviour, as she thought her mother would be killed when she was at school. The symptoms included: feeling sick or actually being sick; sweating; feeling faint; trembling; having tummy-ache and diarrhoea; and occasionally running a temperature. At school neither child could concentrate; they looked tense and sad, and their school attainments were poor. When approached by the teachers and when told that their work must improve they tended to burst into tears. The older girl stopped talking and showed symptoms of elective mutism. Both of them looked permanently frightened and anxious. At home they did not speak: they whispered, afraid to annoy their father.

Domestic Violence in Black and Asian Communities

Domestic violence is also widespread in ethnic families. Unfortunately, there are few available statistics, as these events are hidden within the families and communities. Ali Jan Haider, in his paper, 'Tackling domestic violence within the Asian Community' delivered at the Cardiff conference in September 2003, described the range and extent of domestic violence within Asian–Muslim communities, arguing that it is culture, not religion, that allows maltreatment of women and, as a consequence, of children. He stated that current statistics regarding domestic violence suggest that Muslim communities (in particular their religious leaders and elders) may not advocate what is good, eradicate what is wrong, or help rather than chide. He argued that this is contrary to what the Koran teaches. Recent figures of domestic violence from Bradford make disturbing reading. The statistics indicate that out of 8 607 incidents reported to police from April 2002 to

March 2003, 1 025 involved Asian victims. Taking into consideration unreported cases of domestic violence, which is estimated at 25%, the final
number comes to over 4 000 cases. The picture is even more alarming when
we take into consideration that children are present in at least 42% of cases
(British Crime Survey, 2003).

The Crown Prosecution Service (CPS), in consultation with the Black and
Asian voluntary sector, issued the Policy and Internal Guidance for
Prosecutors in November 2001. The CPS made a strong statement that it
respects cultural beliefs, but also that cultural difference is not a reason for
failing to protect a minority ethnic community victim of domestic violence.
The assumption that cultural practices must be respected, however, can lead
to refusal or failure by professional agencies to intervene. For example, the
Female Genital Mutilation Act 2003 came into operation on 3 March 2004,
making it an offence to perform the mutilation of girls or assist in it, either in
the UK or abroad. The Crown Prosecution Service's view is that domestic
violence is domestic violence and, where it amounts to a criminal offence,
regardless of cultural differences, there is no excuse for failing to protect
victims from any community.

There is strong belief among different practitioners that cultural differences
within black and minority ethnic communities act as barriers (to reporting
offences and intervening in the same way as with other groups of people.
These can include pressures from within the family and the wider Asian
community. Family pressure to uphold the family honour (*izzat*) and fear of
bringing shame (*sharam*) are additional barriers to dealing with family
violence. Additionally, experiences of racism and lack of confidence in the
criminal justice system can also play a role in failing to report observable
offences.

It is recognised that, apart from recognised physical, emotional, sexual, and
financial abuse in all sections of society, domestic violence can take different
forms within black and ethnic minority communities: for example, forced
marriage (as opposed to arranged marriage based on consent), dowry-
related violence, or the above-mentioned genital mutilation of girls.

The community, extended family, and religious leaders' pressure on abused
women not to leave an abusive home or report violence is enormous (to avoid
shame and disrespect), so they stay, suffering abuse, not only from the
husband, but also his family. More often than not the emotional abuse
continues, even when women leave the house, as people from the
community reject them.

Attention should be drawn to the plight of refugee women and their
children. The lack of independent immigration status can create yet another

barrier, preventing women from leaving an abusive relationship. They may fear being deported, so they suffer quietly, as do their children. Hostility towards refugees, often shown by the media, also deters women from finding courage and confidence to get help for themselves and their children from the appropriate agencies (as they fear being reported and deported).

Decisions as to how to prevent domestic violence are not only in the legal domain: they are in the social, cultural, and community avenues as well. Intervention may provoke ostracism, harassment, or violence on women for bringing shame on their family and community, and pressure can be exerted on women through threats to her parents or name-calling of her children. Honour-killing exists even today and may be more widespread than is realised. Additionally, the fear of no respectable Asian family wishing their son to marry her daughters through transferring dishonour to her child is so strong among Asian women that they would rather put up with the abuse than expose loved children to misfortune and rejection.

Children exposed to domestic violence are harmed in many ways, as discussed earlier in this chapter. Children from Asian communities, however, can face additional problems. They are often asked to act as protectors for their mother as well as facing racist name-calling and violence outside the home, even at school. They often have the additional burden of having to function as translators and reporters on behalf of their mothers. It needs to be remembered that the safety, physical and emotional well-being of children and the victim are pivotal issues when making decisions about their future in cases of domestic violence.

The Consequences of Child Exposure to Family Violence

It is well established that exposure to family violence can seriously threaten the health and well-being of children and has both short- and long-term negative consequences. Most studies, however, show that it can have different developmental outcomes at different stages in life. With regard to infants, toddlers, and pre-school children (that is those under the age of five years), it is suggested that exposure to family violence is particularly traumatic and psychologically abusive. This is due to the helplessness, confusion, and terror experienced by the child (Kerig & Fedorowicz, 1999). Jaffe *et al.* (1980 cited in James 1994), in their research with infants exposed to domestic violence, reported that those infants had poorer health and sleep habits than their counterparts, and often indulged in excessive screaming. Additionally, in their reviews of the research literature, Osofsky (1999) and James (1994) found that children and toddlers exposed to family violence were reported as displaying excessive irritability, a fear of being alone, immature behaviours, severe shyness, lower self-esteem, increased behavioural problems, and regression in toileting and language. Hughes & Graham-Bermann (1988) also found more behavioural problems in pre-school children exposed to domestic violence and higher levels of depression and anxiety than among those living in non-violent households. Exposure to family violence among this age-group has also been found to impact upon social-cognitive development. These children have been reported to be more socially isolated than their peers, and have problems in relating to age-appropriate activities (Hughes & Graham-Bermann, 1988). Related to this, Graham-Bermann and Levendensky (1998) found these children to be more aggressive in play and less able to regulate negative emotions than were other children (cited in Graham-Bermann, 2002).

As children under five years of age have fewer coping mechanisms, and parental attachment can be affected by exposure to family violence (as outlined in the previous section), this very young age-group can be placed at increased risk of developing attachment problems throughout their lives. In terms of long-term consequences, Perry (2001a) suggests that early exposure to violence can affect brain development in ways that are maladaptive in the long term. He states that this can lead to a child developing chronic fear responses and hypersensitivity to threat.

Similar negative outcomes have been found in school-age children exposed to family violence. Various reviews of the salient research literature report that this age-group exhibits high levels of internalising and externalising behavioural problems including withdrawal, anxiety, low self-esteem, aggressiveness, and delinquency. Further difficulties include problems in interpersonal relationships (such as establishing and maintaining friendships), and school-related problems such as poorer academic performance, poorer problem-solving abilities, more difficulties in concentrating, and more school avoidance (Graham-Bermann, 2002; Kernic et al., 2003; Hughes & Graham-Bermann, 1998; Holzworth-Monroe et al., 1997; James, 1994; Osofsky, 1999). Sternberg et al. (1993), in their study of children aged between 8 and 12, found more behavioural problems and higher depression scores among children who had witnessed family violence: in particular, they found that depression was most problematic among girls of this age. Furthermore, the children involved in this study themselves acknowledged that they often behaved in ways likely to get them into trouble. Through their reports it was found that they felt more sad and unwanted and less healthy than their peers (who did not witness family violence).

More recently, Baldry (2003) has suggested an association between exposure to domestic violence and school bullying. Controlling for a number of other factors (including other forms of child abuse), this study of 1 059 Italian school children found that 61% of all children who had been exposed to domestic violence were bullies, compared to 46% who were not so exposed. Startlingly, girls exposed to domestic violence were three times more likely to be bullies than those girls who lived in non-violent households. Baldry suggests that, because parents in violent relationships may show less care and consideration for children's feelings, their children, in turn, may lack empathy. In this view, aggression and violence are seen as 'learned behaviours'. Conversely, this study also found that 71% of all children exposed to domestic violence were bully victims in school compared to 46% of those not exposed to domestic violence. In the light of these findings Baldry suggests that 'Exposure to interparental violence may reduce a child's capacity of being assertive when victimized at school; the vicious cycle of victimization starts at home and continues in school' (2003, p. 12).

Although there appears to be less research on the effects of exposure to family violence among adolescents, a recent study of Arab adolescents does provide some useful information, particularly as it is one of the few studies which examines the effects of mother-to-father and father-to-mother physical and verbal violence, and takes the frequency of exposure into account in its analysis. This study revealed that the more adolescents witnessed either physical or verbal aggression, in either direction, the higher their levels of hopelessness and psychological adjustment problems, and the lower their levels of self-esteem.

Those studies that either follow children exposed to family violence longitudinally, or examine outcomes in a retrospective manner in young adulthood, also report a range of long-term negative outcomes. In their 12-year longitudinal study, for example, McNeal and Amato (1998) found that exposure to interparental violence was associated with less close child–parent relationships and lower levels of psychological well-being. They also report that interparental violence increased the odds of offspring relationship violence by 189%. These findings held true after controlling for factors such as harsh parenting and parental substance misuse. Other suggested long-term negative outcomes associated with child exposure to family violence include an increased risk of suicidal thoughts, mental-health problems, offending behaviour, and substance misuse (Fantuzzo & Mohr, 1999; Jellen *et al.*, 2001; Somer & Braunstein, 1999).

Finally, it is worth noting that where samples relating to child research have been drawn from shelters for battered women, negative outcomes have been found to be particularly telling. Often, children of these women are reported to suffer from post-traumatic stress disorder (PTSD), including experiences such as repeated nightmares, intrusive thoughts, and inability to focus attention. It should be noted, however, that other factors may contribute to the intensity of these experiences; these might include being uprooted from their homes, separated from family members and witnessing mothers in a state of extreme stress (Fantuzzo & Mohr, 1999; Graham-Bermann, 2002; Haj-Yahia, 2001; Kernic *et al.*, 2003). Additionally, some argue that the effects of being exposed to interparental/partner violence vary in intensity depending on whether the violence is physical or verbal (McNeal & Amato, 1998). There are factors which can mediate negative outcomes such as a mother's ability to provide adequate parenting, the child's level of intelligence, environmental factors, and levels of social/legal interventions. Despite this, in their review of the literature, Kolbo, Blakey, & Engelmann (1996) concluded that the evidence was unequivocal that exposure to family violence has a negative impact on child behavioural and emotional functioning (cited in Hughes & Graham-Bermann, 1998). Tomison (2000, p. 10) also suggests that 'even when not the target of violence, children who witness domestic violence often exhibit the same constellation of symptoms as other abused or neglected children'. Yet Tomison maintains that this remains an issue which is not fully understood and largely unaddressed.

In light of the findings outlined above, it is clear that child-protection workers and others who work closely with children should be made more aware of the effects of exposure to family violence and the potential risks it poses to children. This is particularly important as even if a parent in an abusive relationship is worried about his or her child's well-being, he or she often feels unable to seek help for fear that the child will be removed from the home. Additionally, given the high levels of other forms of child maltreatment occurring in homes where domestic violence is also present, McGuigan and Platt (2001) suggest that addressing both concerns in interventions can be beneficial. With regard to advances in research in this field, standardised measures for assessing child functioning in the context of domestic violence are urgently needed, as are more longitudinal analyses which separate exposure to family violence from other forms of child maltreatment, and which examine mediating factors in order to further inform intervention practices.

PARENTAL DIVORCE/SEPARATION

It has been argued for some time that divorce rates in England and Wales are among the highest in Europe, with an estimated quarter (28%) of children experiencing their parents' divorce by the age of 16 (Bream & Buchanan, 2003; Butler, Scanlan, Robinson, Douglas, & Murch, 2003; Rodgers & Pryor, 1998). In the USA it is estimated that around 45% of marriages end in divorce and that in 1996 over a million children were involved in parental divorce (Hetherington & Stanley-Hagan, 1999). The level of separation among cohabiting couples with children may also be high, but estimates are, to date, unavailable.

Although divorce and separation are more frequent today, the impact upon families is no less traumatic (Schmidt Neven, 1996). In fact, divorce has been rated as one of the most stressful life events by parents and children alike. As such, divorce/separation has been defined by some as a 'traumatic event' or a 'crisis' in the lives of children (Butler *et al.*, 2003), in that the short-term emotional pain and distress and its effect on psychological functioning is recognised, as are the potential long-term consequences on child development. In short, Butler *et al.* (2003, pp. 33–34) state that with divorce the 'practical and emotional infrastructure of their [children's] lives is about to change decisively'.

In the short-term it is reported that children experience unhappiness, anxiety, depression, anger, low self-esteem, behavioural problems, a drop in school performance, problems with peers, and a loss of contact with a significant number of their extended family (Hetherington & Stanley-Hagan, 1999; Rodgers & Pryor, 1998). Yet it is well recognised that most of the immediate distress fades with time, that most children's outcomes are resiliency rather than dysfunctionality, and that negative long-term outcomes depend on a number of child, parent, and situational factors (Bream & Buchanan, 2003; Butler *et al.*, 2003; Hetherington & Stanley-Hagan, 1999; Rogers & Pryor, 1998). Those factors which have been suggested to place children at risk of poor adjustment and negative long-term outcomes include 'erratic, hostile, or depressed parenting in the custodial residence' (Bream & Buchanan, 2003, p. 229), mental-health problems in the resident parent, and continued parental conflict. With regard to child characteristics, Hetherington and Stanley-Hagan (1999, p. 136) state that the 'psychologically rich get richer and the poor get poorer in dealing with the challenges of divorce'.

A number of these issues will be explored in more detail shortly when illustrating the ways in which divorce/separation can be emotionally abusive/neglectful to the children. At this point, however, it is important to state that there is no clear or direct relationship between parental separation/divorce and children's adjustment or poor outcomes. Having said this, available research would tend to suggest that children of divorced families are twice as likely to experience poorer outcomes than children in intact families. These include greater levels of poverty, lower educational attainment, poorer health, higher rates of behavioural problems, higher levels of depressive symptoms, and higher levels of smoking, alcohol consumption, drug abuse, and teenage pregnancy (Butler *et al.*, 2003; Rodgers & Pryor, 1998). That is, they are less socially, emotionally, and academically adjusted than children of non-divorced parents. Hetherington and Stanley-Hagan (1999) also state that children and adults from divorced families are two to three times more likely to receive psychological treatment than non-divorced families. The degree to which these may or may not be experienced will depend on some of the risk-factors previously outlined.

Before moving on to examine some of the factors which place children at an increased risk of poor outcomes it is also worth mentioning that the effects of divorce/separation are not always negative. Many authors point out that for those children living in families characterised by high levels of conflict, abuse and/or neglect, their problems often diminish after divorce. Additionally, although most of what will be discussed here refers to married couples, it is suggested that children of cohabiting parents who separate will have much the same experiences.

Lack of Communication and Emotionally Unavailable Parenting

As previously stated, the experience and process of separation/divorce are emotionally traumatic for all involved. In addition to the emotional distress of effectively losing a life-partner, and the legal formalities of separation/divorce, the custodial parent has the added material and emotional stress of becoming a single parent. In the midst of this, parents often become very self-involved. Consequently, they may not take time to discuss processes or decisions with children, or they may become emotionally unavailable to them as they get wrapped up in the problems with which they are faced. Parents may become depressed, anxious, angry, irritable, and/or impulsive, which may affect their parenting ability. As such they may fail to be responsive, supportive, and sensitive to the emotional needs of their children at a time when the latter are in most need of consistent support. If parents fail to recover significantly from these feelings of distress this can affect the child's ability to adjust and may affect its long-term development (Hawthorne *et al.*, 2003; Maclean, 2004; Rodgers & Pryor, 1998).

On the other hand, children may end up effectively tending to the emotional needs of the resident parent in terms of undertaking what Butler *et al.* (2003) define as 'emotional maintenance work'. Klosinski (1993) refers to this form of treatment and level of expectation on the child as 'unconscious child abuse': when this behaviour becomes prolonged, the child may become 'parentified'. Parentification refers to the process whereby a child takes on many of the roles and responsibilities of a parent when they are not developmentally ready to fulfil such roles (Barnett & Parker, 1998; Klosinski, 1993; Mayselless, Bartholomew, Henderson, & Trinke, 2004). Research has found that the long-term costs of severe parentification of young girls after parental divorce are high. They tend to display high levels of depressive symptoms, low levels of self-worth, get involved in 'needy relationships', and provide 'inappropriate caring' in later life (Hetherington & Stanley-Hagan, 1999).

Several research studies also suggest that the lack of communication between parents and children at such a distressing time can cause children additional confusion and pain, and impact upon their long-term relationships with parents. Parents often find it difficult or inappropriate to discuss issues surrounding the separation/divorce with children, generally due to the belief that not involving them is protecting them from further harm and distress (Hawthorne *et al.*, 2003). In turn, this has led children to feel unable to talk to parents about their feelings for fear of hurting them further. For some children, this may ultimately lead to the suppression of feelings, in particular feelings of being rejected by one parent and/or of blaming themselves for the marital breakdown. Effective and sensitive communication with children is important because as Butler *et al.* (2003, p. 58) state:

> From the moment that children become aware of their parents' separation they become 'involved', at least emotionally, in the process of their parents' divorce. This can be a confused, isolated and exceptionally sad experience, especially if children are not told what is going on around them.

Contact, Conflict, and the Courts

That aspect of separation/divorce which appears to pose most challenges for the family is in relation to contact arrangements and visits with the non-custodial parent. Contact can be a confusing business in its own right, in that arrangements have to be made around both parents and child/ren, but when there is continued conflict between parents, this makes it even more difficult for the child to adjust. Indeed Rodgers and Pryor (1998) report conflict to be the main factor in detrimental outcomes. Although the level of parental conflict most often declines with time, Hetherington and Stanley-Hagan (1999) report that around one quarter of parents still have relationships which are characterised by high levels of conflict in which children are often caught in the middle. In these circumstances children often attempt to manage contact and parental conflict themselves in an attempt to maintain a meaningful relationship with both parents. Not only does this place a huge emotional burden on the child, but it also means that children often compromise their own needs in an attempt to keep both parents happy (Butler *et al.*, 2003; Klosinski, 1993).

Parental conflict is emotionally abusive to the child in a variety of ways in that children are often used as 'go-betweens', passing messages from one parent to the other. They may also experience 'divided loyalties', feeling emotionally torn between parents. Additionally, children may witness parents 'bad-mouthing' each other, they may be asked detailed questions about the other parent's personal life, asked to keep 'secrets' from the other parent, and witness parents openly arguing in front of them. In their research with 61 divorced families, Trinder, Beek, and Connolly (2002) found that in all families where there was continued parental conflict, all of the children were well aware of this. Indeed Butler *et al.* (2003) found that children often blamed themselves for the conflict, believing it was essentially about them and any contact arrangements. The effects of parental divorce on children can be serious in terms of emotional disturbances and feelings of insecurity in everyday life.

The case described below illustrates some of the problems discussed above.

POST-DIVORCE PARENTAL CONFLICT AND THE EFFECT ON CHILDREN

A professional couple, both married before, ended their eight-year marriage acrimoniously with accusations and counter-accusations and many court appearances regarding custody of the children. Finally, they got joint custody, with the children spending weekdays with the mother and weekends with the father. The father, because of his high-profile job, wanted to portray himself as an innocent party, accused his wife of stealing, laziness, extramarital affairs, and neglect of their two children. The wife (who ended the marriage), fearing his reaction, took the children and flew to another city to start a new life there, assuming that the ex-husband could not interfere because of the geographical distance. He traced them, however, and got a court order to bring the children back.

Both parties talked to their children, portraying each other in a most negative way. The children were always asked what their mother or their father were doing and saying, and who was coming into the house. If they did not want to talk about it, they were emotionally blackmailed and told that they were ungrateful children and did not deserved to be loved, and would not get a pony or bicycle, etc. They were accused of not loving the father who cared for them so much and thanks to him they had everything they needed. Quite often the father would say that their lazy and bad mother thought only about herself. The mother, on the other hand, would cry, telling them that it was their father who made life miserable for them all and that he was a wicked person. If they misbehaved she would say that they were as bad as their father.

Instead of getting better for the children's psychosocial adjustment, the post-divorce situation got worse, and emotional disturbances began to manifest themselves in both children. The five-year-old started to wet herself both at night and during the day, and developed severe encopresis. She became very withdrawn, weepy, and uncommunicative. Quite often she would burst into tears if a teacher asked her to do something or reprimanded her. The older boy became stubborn, aggressive, oppositional, and disobedient. His schoolwork deteriorated and his behaviour became difficult to manage, especially his outbursts of aggression. Both children received individual intensive play therapy which lasted about eight months, and revealed how confused, frightened, insecure, and trapped in a no-win situation they had become. Eventually, the parents agreed to have some counselling regarding their behaviour towards each other, what they said to the children and the effect it had on them. A formal, negotiated contract was written and signed by both of them, obliging them to stop making derogatory remarks about each other and putting pressure on the children by blackmailing, withdrawing affection, or denying treats.

The penalty for not sticking to the terms of contract was possible removal of the children from their care by applying for a care order in respect of both of them.

In some cases issues around contact and residency are so full of conflict that parents have to resort to the family courts to help resolve them. Bream and Buchannan (2003) recently examined the emotional costs to children when the family was subjected to court welfare reports following separation/divorce. They found in the first wave of data collection, shortly after the conclusion of court proceedings, that 52% of boys and 48% of girls had adjustment problems. One year later, 62% of boys and 32% of girls were found to have borderline or abnormal scores on measures of childhood distress. They also detected a particularly high increase in distress among children under 7 years of age, with 80% of these having high scores at the next follow-up. They note this is 4 times that which would be expected in the general population. In fact, the authors suggest that some of these children could be defined as having suffered 'prolonged psychological abuse' as a result of continuing conflict between separated/divorced parents (p. 232). Both parents and children alike reported that the actual court process was highly stressful, and the authors suggest that the stress of this may impact upon parenting ability at a crucial time in children's lives. In the light of their findings, the authors concluded that 'it may be that the adversarial judicial system designed to reduce the conflict might actually be adding further fuel to the flames' (p. 235). Similarly, Trinder *et al.* (2002) concluded, from their research regarding contact issues following separation/divorce, that court involvement could serve to exacerbate rather than resolve parental disputes.

Continued parental conflict, particularly when the child is caught in the middle, is damaging and harmful, and those children who feel caught in parental conflict are more likely to have poor outcomes. These children have been found to experience more stress and anxiety, to be more withdrawn and aggressive, and to have less positive relationships with parents. Additionally, it is suggested that conflict is a contributory factor in other adverse outcomes such as behavioural problems (Rodgers & Pryor, 1998). Where contact was stressful for children and adults, Tinder *et al.* (2002) reported that the emotional costs far outweighed the reported benefits. Yet the impact of parental separation/divorce upon children's well-being has been found to be mediated by good parent–child relationships and a high quality of parenting at this difficult time.

Hawthorne *et al.* (2003) suggest that parents are supported and helped in reducing the stresses which often come with separation/divorce, and encouraged to provide warmth and nurturing to children. With regard to contact, children themselves report how helpful it is when parents can at least communicate in a civil manner when making contact arrangements. Indeed Tinder *et al.* (2002, p. 3) found that 'active facilitation was vital in ensuring that children had the emotional permission to enjoy contact' and that contact tended to work best in cases where there was no legal intervention. The case below illustrates some post-divorce disputes and accusations.

CONTACT DISPUTE CASE

A couple with two children (a boy and a girl aged eight and six years respectively), divorced after the gradual deterioration of their relationship. The mother had custody of the children and the father had unsupervised access twice a week.

After two months, contact with the children suddenly stopped, and the mother claimed that they refused to see the father because they were frightened of him, and it was boring being in his company. The mother claimed that they were physically abused by the father while living together and they remembered it well. He apparently used to smack, kick, twist their wrists, and pinch them. He sat on his son to prevent him running around and making a noise while he was watching cricket on the television. The father denied being cruel to the children, was surprised that all of a sudden they claimed being mistreated by him, and tried to talk to them on the telephone, but was told by his ex-wife that they did not want to speak to him.

The case was heard in the court and new arrangements issued to facilitate the father's access to the children. He agreed to supervised contact, if the children wished it, and in a place chosen by them and their mother. Once-a-week contact – lasting two hours – was arranged. Two weeks later the children did not turn up, in spite of apparently having an enjoyable time during the two previous contact visits. Again the mother said they refused to come, and that they hid upstairs. The case went to court again, as the father did not believe his wife's story. An independent expert assessment was ordered by the court. Independent assessment of the children revealed that, in order to break up the children's contact with the father, the mother kept telling them that he was very cruel to them when they were small and that, although they did not remember it, it was true. Additionally, she was indicating that he might hurt them during an access visit, abduct them, and they might never see their house and her again and, therefore, they should not see him. She was telling them that he was mean, never gave her much money to feed and clothe them, and although they had a lovely house and went to an expensive public school, it was thanks to her good management of money rather than the father's contribution. His son began to tell friends that his father was a 'monster' and that everyone should keep away from him. If his younger sister wanted to see her father, because she was missing him, he would shout at her, saying that he would kill her if she saw him.

Both children developed negative attitudes towards their father and genuinely began to fear him. The younger one began to present sleeping problems and fear of being left alone as she thought that her father might come while she was asleep to kidnap or kill her. The older child became angry, confused, and aggressive, feeling that he had to protect his mother and sister. His school work deteriorated due to the lack of concentration and constant worry about his mother's and sister's safety.

This case demonstrates emotional abuse, inflicted by the mother, by fabricating untrue stories about her husband as a means of punishing him for leaving her. She knew that depriving him of seeing his much-loved children would hurt him. The fact that such behaviour was damaging to the children was not taken into consideration.

PARENTAL SUBSTANCE MISUSE

At least since the 1990s there have been growing recognition and concern about the effects of parental substance misuse on the well-being of children (Alison, 2000). Although it is generally acknowledged that child maltreatment is multifaceted and cannot be attributed to any single factor, it is now agreed that parental substance misuse (both in terms of alcohol and drugs), is a risk and contributory factor to child abuse and/or neglect (Ammerman, Kolko, Kirisci, Blackson, & Dawes, 1999; US Department of Health & Human Services, 1999; Graham-Bermann, 2002; Keen & Alison, 2001; Kelley, 2002; McNeal & Amato, 1998; Tomison, 1996b). Parental substance misuse is now known to affect family functioning (Wolock & Magura, 1996), to be one of the leading factors in children being taken into care, and to have long-term and devastating consequences for children (Ammerman *et al.*, 1999; Keen & Alison, 2001).

Substance misuse, as described in the many studies that will be referred to shortly, is a 'global term which may encompass the use or abuse of a range of substances, such as alcohol, illicit drugs, and prescribed drugs'. Yet it should be noted at this point that not all substance abusers will maltreat their children, and that there are factors which often mediate the effect of parental substance misuse. In sum, and as will be demonstrated, the association between parental substance misuse and child maltreatment is far from clear-cut. However, evidence will be presented of the various ways in which it may negatively impact upon the emotional well-being of the child.

Scale and Incidence

To date, and as alluded to earlier, the primary focus of the literature relating to substance misuse and child maltreatment is with regards to family violence (Tomison, 1996b) and prenatal drug-exposure (Kelley, 2002). In addition to this, few studies have specifically examined the relationship, if any, between substance misuse and child emotional abuse and neglect. Indeed researchers tend either to focus on one particular type of child maltreatment, such as physical abuse or family violence, or to examine the various types of abuse and neglect under the overarching heading of child maltreatment. Further to this, Alison (2000) points out that the majority of studies in this field are US-based, and that the literature in the UK is surprisingly scarce. While important lessons can be gleaned from US and other international studies, she reminds us that there are significant differences in drug-taking cultures and habits and the legal and welfare systems of these countries. As a consequence, findings may not be immediately transferable to a UK context.

Large-scale national surveys give us some idea of the numbers of children living in families with parental substance misuse problems. The US National Household Survey of Drug Abuse (1996), for example, revealed that 8.3 million children (that is, 11% of all children in the US) lived in a family where at least one parent had an alcohol or drug-use problem (US Department of Health and Human Services, 1999). The majority of these cases, however, will never come to the attention of child-protection agencies. With regard to the prevalence of substance misuse in known abusive and/or neglectful families, there has been growing research in this area. However, the fact that definitions of child maltreatment and substance misuse vary across studies as do methodologies and time orders, estimating the nature and scale of the association is fraught with difficulties, as is comparing findings across studies. With regard to alcohol abuse, for example, Black (1981) noted that the rate to which this has been identified in maltreating families in the USA varies from between 25% and 84% due to differing definitions and methodologies (cited in Tomison, 1996b). With regard to general substance-use problems in maltreating families, Mugura and Laudet (1996) found that retrospective studies suggest that it has been identified in between 13% to 70% of the research populations (cited in Ammerman *et al.*, 1999). In cases of domestic abuse, which has already been shown to be emotionally abusive to those children exposed to it, the SAMHSA study (1997) found that in up to 70% of all incidents either the perpetrator, the victim or both had consumed alcohol (US Department of Health and Human Services, 1999).

Examining the incidence of drug misuse across the various categories of child maltreatment, few, as previously stated, look at emotional abuse or neglect in isolation. In reviewing previous studies of the possible association between child maltreatment and substance misuse, the US Department of Health and Human Services (1999) suggest that between one-third and two-thirds of all cases of child abuse and neglect had a parent with a substance-abuse problem. This was found to be most prominent in neglect cases. Alison's (2000) overview of international literature found the same. A recent examination of the care careers of 388 looked-after children under the age of 5 in Northern Ireland, however, found that a history of family alcohol abuse was most prominent in the backgrounds of emotionally abused children. Alcohol abuse had been identified as a problem in 100% of all emotional-abuse cases and family drug abuse was identified in 43% of cases (Cousins *et al.*, 2003). The National Clinical Evaluation Study (1988) in the USA also found high levels of substance misuse in emotional-abuse cases. In this, family substance misuse was identified as a factor in 61% of emotional-abuse cases, 58% of physical-abuse cases, 53% of neglect cases and 50% of sexual-abuse cases (cited in Tomison, 1996b). Additionally, there are several Australian studies which have examined the incidence of substance misuse in families known to child protection for emotional abuse. An analysis of 1994–95 national child-maltreatment statistics revealed that 22% of all substantiated cases of emotional abuse in New South Wales were reported as a result of a parent's substance misuse problems (Tomison, 1996b). Additionally, Tomison, in his own analysis of cases in the Victoria region, found that alcohol abuse had been identified in 40% of physical-abuse cases, 31% of emotional-abuse cases, 28% of neglect cases and 17% of sexual-abuse cases. Contradictory findings were revealed by Clarke & Stephenson (1994) who concluded from an investigation of a random sample of 75 child-maltreatment cases in Victoria that substance misuse did not feature prominently in cases of emotional abuse.

In sum, the research, particularly with regard to emotional abuse and neglect of children, is fairly inconclusive. It does appear clear, however, that a significant proportion of the maltreated children known to child-protection agencies do live within families where parental substance use has been identified as a problem. It is unlikely, however, that in the majority of cases this is the only reason for abuse/neglect. The National Council of the Institute of Medicine (1993, p. 19) notes that in the case of both substance misuse and child maltreatment they 'are often complicated by the presence of other social and economic variables . . . that confound the analysis of the contributing role of drugs themselves' (cited in US Department of Health and Human Services, 1999, part 5, p. 1). Despite this, however, there are some research studies which, if not deliberately focused on parental substance misuse and child emotional abuse/neglect, do make some relevant observations. It is to a review of these that we now turn.

The Impact of Parental Substance Abuse on Child Emotional Abuse/Neglect

Due to the very nature of substance use and misuse in terms of the physical and psychological effects of drugs/alcohol and the culture and lifestyle that often surrounds it, it is clear that it can impact upon parenting and family functioning. Being under the influence of substances, the time and resources often dedicated to acquiring them and the after-effects of their use, can all impact upon a parent's ability to care for a child (Iwaniec, Herbert, & Sluckin, 2002). Alison (2000), Ammerman et al. (1999), Kelley (2002) and Pemmaraju Rao (2001) have noted some of the effects of substance use/abuse upon users. These include irritability, inconsistent moods, impulsiveness, low frustration tolerance, selfishness, impaired judgement, lack of ability to monitor behaviour, drowsiness, and unconsciousness. These factors can lead to a child being emotionally abused or neglected in various ways. At a general level, however, substance misuse can affect a parent's ability to tend to the emotional needs of a child (e.g. ignoring and rejecting), and a parent's actions, or lack of them, can be emotionally abusive (e.g. verbal assaults and inappropriate expectations).

Alison (2000) also reports that it has been found that some drug users do not provide a stimulating environment for children, engaging in less family play and other activities with the children. Conversely, it has been reported that parents on methadone treatment programmes show substantial increases in the time they spent with their families. In addition to this, the effort often spent acquiring substances means that the child may spend a substantial amount of time alone or in the care of various, often inappropriate, others. Not only may this place the child at risk of further abuse, but it inevitably means that parent–child attachment may be affected. This is important, as we know that if attachment is impaired at an early age, this can influence the ability to form meaningful bonds in later life (Bowlby, 1969). Parent–child attachment may also be affected by the fact that substance-abusing parents are more likely to be separated from children due to time spent in hospital and/or prison (Alison, 2000; Tomison, 1996b).

Due to the parent's addiction and the various factors related to it, such as increased likelihood of physical/mental illness, the child is often expected to take on many parenting roles. It is well established in the literature that parental substance misusers are often socially isolated, living without a great deal of family/community support. Not only does this increase parental stress, but it can also lead to the 'parentification' of children within the family (Barnett & Parker, 1998; Kelley, 2002; Pemmanaju Rao, 2002; Tomison, 1996b). This can involve physically and emotionally caring for parents (role reversal) and/or siblings, and can, therefore, also entail undertaking inappropriate household duties (Barnett & Parker, 1998; Glaser & Prior, 2002; Mayseless *et al.*, 2004). Not only is this emotionally abusive to the child in the short term in that it essentially 'steals the magic of childhood' (Pemmaraju Rao, 2001, p. 1), but also in the long term as it can impact upon a child's development (Mayseless *et al.*, 2004). Additionally, parentification, as seen in Chapter 1 (Ann and Simon's case), especially in the case of role reversal (which is often reported in families of substance misusers), can be emotionally abusive when it leads to 'profound and pervasive disturbances in the child's feelings of safety and security', which can in effect result in attachment disorders. Of parentified children Pemmaraju Rao (2001, p. 1) states, 'they are very mature and responsible on the outside, but on the inside feel rage, fear and resentment about disrupted boundaries, and inappropriate expectations'. In addition to this, children of substance-misusing parents often live in fear and suffer panic, anxiety, and dread as there is little stability in their lives and they never know when something can go wrong. Alison (2000) also points out that children living with substance-misusing parents are at an increased risk of witnessing traumatic events such as parental overdoses, arrest, violence or murder, and self-harm.

One of the main outcomes reported with regard to children living with substance-misusing parents has been that they perform less well academically than other children. Many researchers found that, among older children whose parents misused substances, they had poor developmental progress in school, truancy problems, and behavioural difficulties. Not dissimilarly, Onroy (1996, cited in Alison, 2000) examined the outcomes of children of heroin-dependent mothers who were adopted at a young age and those who stayed in the family home. This revealed that those who stayed in the family home had lower IQ levels, higher levels of hyperactivity, poorer attention-spans, and more behavioural problems. High levels of anxiety, depression, and mental health problems have also been reported among these children most often as a result of isolation and parentification (Cousins *et al.*, 2003; Mayseless *et al.*, 2004; Pemmaraju Rao, 2001; Wolock & Magura, 1996).

Although it is difficult to assess the extent to which poor child outcomes are a direct result of parental substance misuse (as such families often suffer a number of related problems), there is no denying that substance misuse is a growing factor being identified in the case files of maltreated children (Cousins *et al.*, 2003). Additionally, although several factors have been found to mediate the negative effects of parental substance misuse (such as voluntary involvement in treatment programmes and a parent's previous ability to care for other children), this remains an area which is in need of further investigation (Alison, 2000; Tomison, 1996b). Further to this and of great relevance to treatment and intervention is that Wolock and Magura (1996), in their examination of re-reported cases of child maltreatment (that is those cases which were previously closed and later re-reported), found a direct link between substance-misusing families and re-reporting. From this they conclude that these families either did not get enough support the first time around or were not adequately monitored once the case was closed. As such, these children are 'falling between the cracks' in the system (p. 1191). Clearly, parental substance misuse has important implications for treatment and intervention, yet it would appear that these have not yet been fully recognised and implemented in practice (Iwaniec *et al.*, 2002).

SUMMARY

This chapter has outlined how exposure to family violence, the experience of parental divorce/separation and parental substance misuse can constitute child emotional abuse and place children at increased risk of a number of negative outcomes. Although research in some of these areas has advanced, there is clearly still some way to go: within the field of child maltreatment, and indeed in a UK context, some of these issues remain largely unexplored. While learning from the information in other fields, it is also necessary that researchers in child maltreatment produce clearer, more standardised defi-nitions, and appropriate measures of assessing the impact of these three forms of emotional abuse on child development. In particular, as some of these forms of emotional abuse often overlap (e.g. parental substance misuse and family violence), and may co-occur with other forms of child maltreatment, future research which attempts to disentangle the effects of each upon children is urgently needed. Such research would be of great value in aiding in the design of intervention programmes and strategies. Further to this, greater recognition among those working with children (particularly those involved in child protection) that family violence, divorce/separation, and parental substance misuse can be emotionally abusive to children is necessary in order that interventions are put in place at an early stage.

CHAPTER 4

EMOTIONAL ABUSE AND NEGLECT OUTSIDE THE FAMILY

CONTENTS

INTRODUCTION

A discussion of emotional abuse and neglect in settings other than the family is important, given that Article 19 (1) of the United Nations Convention on the Rights of the Child states:

> Parties shall take all appropriate legislative, administrative, social and educational measures to protect the child from all forms of physical or mental violence, injury or abuse, neglect or negligent treatment, maltreatment or exploitation, including sexual abuse, while in the care of parent(s), legal guardian(s) *or any other person who has the care of the child* (UN Convention on the Rights of the Child, 1989, italics added, http://www.unicef.org).

From the above statement it is clear that safeguarding children from emotional abuse/neglect extends to all individuals and institutions that have some degree of care for children or young persons. Yet the theoretical and research focus within the field of child maltreatment has been primarily upon the family and the family home. However, there has been growing recognition, albeit slow, that emotional abuse can take many forms and occur in a variety of settings.

In the light of the above, this chapter is dedicated to a discussion of emotional abuse/neglect which occurs in three institutional settings outside the family home. It will open with a discussion of emotional abuse/neglect in educational settings, including the issue of peer-to-peer bullying, which has received increasing attention within the field of child maltreatment, and the less well-researched issue of teacher-to-pupil abuse. This will be followed by a discussion of emotional abuse/neglect as experienced in out-of-home care settings and penal establishments, two areas that have received much less focused attention within this field of study. As literature is seriously lacking in a number of these domains, reference has been made to studies beyond the field of child maltreatment with a view to highlighting ways in which some forms of treatment of these young people, or behaviour in these settings, may constitute emotional abuse or neglect of children.

SCHOOL BULLYING: PEER ABUSE

The Extent and Nature of Peer-to-Peer Bullying

It is now widely agreed that peer-to-peer bullying constitutes a form of peer abuse and emotionally abusive behaviour.[1] Since school bullying in particular appeared on the political agenda (in England and Wales) in the late 1980s, it is an area which has received sustained academic interest. Yet there is no one consensual definition of bullying, often leading to problems in measurement, understanding, intervention, and prevention. In spite of this, most agree that bullying can be of three main types: first, intent to cause physical or psychological harm or fear; second, repetition or continuous intent to cause harm or fear over time; and third, the wielding of power over others. Indeed, the UK Department for Education and Employment's (DfEE) definition of bullying is based on these (Percy-Smith & Matthews, 2001).

Bullying can take a number of forms in that it can be physical or verbal, direct or indirect. Direct bullying includes physical attacks (such as hitting or stealing/destroying belongings), and verbal attacks or threats (such as name-calling, ridiculing, and taunting). Indirect bullying, on the other hand, includes behaviours such as spreading malicious rumours and socially excluding or isolating someone from a group (Connell & Farrington, 1996; Espelage & Asidao, 2001; Smith & Sharp, 1994). Studies from many parts of the world have shown that boys tend to bully more than girls and that boy-bullying tends to be physical and direct, while girl-bullying tends to be psychological and indirect (Baldry, 2003; Byrne, 1999; Connell & Farrington, 1996; Espelage & Asidao, 2001; Smith, 1999). Establishing the prevalence of school bullying, however, is far from clear-cut: rates of occurrence vary depending on the

---

[1] This is signalled, in part, by articles on bullying appearing in the *Journal of Emotional Abuse*.

definition employed, the measurement tools used, the period during which they are investigated, and the country/place in which the study takes place. Swearer and Doll (2001) suggest that prevalence rates vary from about 10% when based on definitions of 'extreme bullying', to as high as 75% when based on definitions of ever having been bullied.

Ahmed, Whitney, and Smith (1991) carried out one of the largest surveys of school bullying in England, involving 24 schools and 6 758 pupils, and found that 27% of primary-school children reported being bullied 'sometimes' or more often. Of these, 10% reported being bullied at least once a week. The corresponding figures for secondary-school children were 10% and 4% respectively. Rather than physical attacks, however, this study found that the most frequently reported type of bullying was verbal, taking the form of name-calling (cited in Smith & Sharp, 1994). A similarly large-scale study in Ireland, based on similar definitions and measurements and involving 530 schools, found that 5% of primary-school and 2% of post-primary-school children reported being victims of bullying at least once a week (Byrne, 1999). US studies suggest that between 15% and 20% of children can expect to encounter bullying in their school career, either as victims or perpetrators (Swearer & Doll, 2001). These studies also found that there was little difference in the degree to which boys and girls were victimised. Yet some suggest that certain groups of children are at a greater risk of being victimised, or being victimised in a very particular manner (e.g. racial abuse/ taunts towards children from ethnic minority backgrounds, asylum-seekers, and travellers' children, as well as those with disabilities or body image which is considered unattractive, e.g. obesity).

Characteristics of Victims and Bullies

It has been reported that those who are often the victims of bullying are perceived to be in some way 'different' to other children. At a group rather than individual level, three groups have been identified as being at increased risk of victimization: children with special educational needs (SENs); children with disabilities; and children/young people who are gay, lesbian, or bi-sexual. With regard to his work in Irish schools, Byrne (1999) found slightly higher levels of reported bullying among children in remedial classes. Smith (1999) also reported that those children with SENs and those with disabilities were particularly at risk of bullying. Nabuzoka and Smith (1993), in their research with 179 children (39 of whom had SENs), asked pupils to nominate who they thought were the main victims and perpetrators of bullying. Those children who had SENs were more likely to be nominated as victims (33%) than those without (6%). Further research by Whitney, Smith, and Thompson (1994) matched pupils with SENs and those in main-stream education on a number of background characteristics, and found that those with SENs were 2 to 3 times at more risk of being bullied. Addition-ally, it was found in a study of 140 gay and lesbian young people that overall 80% reported having been teased about their sexuality. Further to this, over half had been physically assaulted or ridiculed by other pupils and/or teachers (cited in Smith, 1999). The following case illustrates the predicament of the bullied child, the range of behaviours resulting from being bullied, and the behaviours of the bullies.

A CASE OF BULLYING

Natasha (15) was referred to the psychologist after prolonged refusal to go to school, exhibiting distressed and anxious behaviour, and showing marked avoidance of peers and teachers. The teachers were aware that Natasha was not very popular at school, because of obesity and her shabby, unkempt appearance, but they were unaware of her being bullied by her classmates. As it was later learned, a group of five very influential and aggressive clique-leaders would put notes on her desk telling her that they did not want her to be in the class because she smelled, looked like an elephant, and her clothes were dirty and shabby. They said that if she wanted to enter the school they would have to examine her first and that she would have to pay a penalty if she did not meet their standards.

Natasha's life became intolerable. She was often called names, laughed at, and humiliated in front of all the class or other children in the playground. After a while the bullies would wait in the school grounds to inspect her. They would pull her hair, kick her shoes, stating that they were unfashionable, and pull her skirt down, leaving her in her underwear. As a rule they demanded money. At first it was £1, then £2 and lastly £5. To avoid torment, Natasha started stealing money from her mother and her mother's partner to pay 'the penalty money': the girls threatened to beat her up and do something nasty that she would never forget, if she told anybody about this.

Natasha's behaviour at home changed dramatically and rapidly deteriorated. She refused to go to school, making all kinds of excuses, and she began to show psycho-somatic symptoms associated with the school phobia. Additionally, she became withdrawn, depressed, irritable, and was unable to sleep. She started to eat for comfort, consuming huge amounts of food, then feeling disgusted and making herself sick: this bulimic behaviour increased in frequency and severity as more pressure was put on her by her mother and the school. Natasha said that she contemplated killing herself as she found it increasingly hard to cope with the situation. She was frightened to tell her mother about her predicament and even more terrified to tell the teachers. At the time of assessment Natasha's self-esteem was at rock-bottom, and she was an extremely anxious and distraught girl.

Natasha's case is also closely associated with physical and emotional neglect at home. Her unkempt, dirty appearance had a long history. In the primary school, children refused to sit next to her, saying that she smelled and that her hair was infested by lice. They seldom played with her or included Natasha in their activities. Unfortunately, the teachers' reaction to the social isolation of Natasha and to the way her peers treated her was not corrected. Thus, Natasha had little support, either at home or at school. The symptoms of Natasha's behaviour were not taken into consideration by the teachers: they observed emotionally disturbed behaviour, but said they did not understand why Natasha's conduct, deterioration in school work, and school attendance became so acute.

There has also been a growing recognition of the possible link between being a victim of child abuse/neglect in the home and being a victim of bullying at school. In a retrospective study of 210 college freshmen, Duncan (1999) found that those who had been bullied as children were more likely to be a victim of some other form of child abuse than those who had not been bullied. In particular, it was found that victims of school bullying reported significantly higher levels of emotional maltreatment by parents. Additionally, the group found to have the highest levels of post-traumatic stress disorder (PTSD) and psychological distress were those who were victims both of child abuse and of school bullying. With reference to this finding Duncan (1999) states that when a child is told by both parents and peers that he or she is not valued, it is not surprising that symptoms of distress surface and even continue into young adulthood.

Where the school often acts as a safe haven for those abused at home, for children also abused in school through peer-bullying this is far from the case. In the light of these findings, Duncan suggests that those working with abused children, or with survivors of child abuse, should also examine the nature of peer relationships as this may be something that should be addressed in therapy.

Olweus (1999) and Baldry (2003) found that some victims of bullying (particularly males) had very strong relationships with their mothers. Olweus found that teachers often reported that mothers of bullied children were overprotective, treating their children like babies, and were overcontrolling in their actions/behaviours (cited in Duncan, 1999; Swearer & Doll, 2001). This type of parent–child relationship would appear emotionally abusive in the sense that it would fall within Hart *et al.*'s (2002) sub-category of 'exploiting/corrupting': i.e. 'encouraging or coercing abandonment of developmentally appropriate autonomy through extreme over involvement, intrusiveness, or dominance'.[2] Smith and Sharp (1994) suggest that the possible effects of such a relationship may be that the child fails to develop the same level of social skills and independence as its peers and that this may make it more vulnerable to potential bullies.

Conversely, there is also a suggested link between being a victim of child abuse/neglect and being a bully. Again, emotional neglect would appear to have some effect, according to Olweus (1993), who found that children who

---

[2] See Chapter 1 for a full overview of these subcategories of psychological maltreatment.

reported bullying others also disproportionately reported that their parents lacked affection or warmth (Smith & Sharp, 1994). Additionally, it has been suggested by many researchers that there is a link between emotionally and/or physically aggressive parents and children who bully. Baldry (2003) also highlights the findings of the Canadian National Longitudinal Survey of Children and Youth when discussing the possible link between interparental violence and school bullying. It would appear that when children witnessed family violence they were almost three times more likely to be physically aggressive and over twice as likely to be indirectly aggressive at school as children who did not witness family violence. In her own study of 1059 Italian school children, Baldry (2003) also found evidence of a relationship between children who were exposed to interparental violence and bullying behaviour. Although it was found that these children were disproportionately more likely to be the victims as well as the perpetrators of bullying, she found a particularly strong relationship between girls who were exposed to family violence and bullying others. It was also revealed that bullies were almost twice as likely as non-bullies to be exposed to interparental violence. The main explanations put forward for the association between experiencing abuse at home and being abusive to peers have been based on 'learnt behaviour' and 'social learning theory'. Bullies at school, therefore, may be victims at home of emotional and physical aggression who modelled their behaviour on parental violence.

The Consequences of Being Bullied

There has been growing recognition of the often severe and long-term consequences of school bullying to the extent that courts in the USA have begun to award damages to some victims (Varnham, 2001). Perhaps the most tragic consequence of severe, prolonged bullying is that it has been identified as a contributing factor in several cases of children who take their own lives in the UK each year (Smith & Sharp, 1994).

The effects of bullying upon children are often immediate, and several short-term consequences have been identified. The most identifiable consequences have been truancy (or school avoidance) and effects upon levels of educational achievement. It has been reported, for example, that children who are being bullied will often avoid going to school out of fear, and, when they do attend, they find it difficult to concentrate (Connell & Farrington, 1996). Smith et al. (1999), in their study of 723 secondary-school pupils, found that 20% of those who had been bullied in the last year avoided school because of bullying and 29% reported difficulties in concentrating while at school. Percy-Smith and Matthews (2001) also point to evidence that victims of bullying are more likely to underachieve in education because of school avoidance or truancy. In fact young people themselves, in offering retrospective accounts of their school careers, often highlight how disengagement from school and underachievement are the result of intense, prolonged victimisation. The following is an interview extract taken from the work of MacDonald and Marsh (2003) on the wider issue of social exclusion. It aptly captures, in the words of a young person (Simon, aged 19), feelings and experiences of isolation and fear caused by bullying and its consequences on his educational career:

> At one point I was beginning to think I was depressed, really depressed about it and . . . basically I was one of them lads who kept meself to meself and didn't talk to very many people or things like that. I just put me head down and got on with it, you know? Just tried to keep myself quiet so no-one'd talk to me or owt like that. Sometimes it just got on top of me and I just didn't wanna go, you know? . . . And basically it ruined my chances up 'cos I, err . . . most of the time was off [absent from school] and, err . . . I could've done better at school.

Absenteeism from school may also be related to physical illness, with a number of studies finding that children who are the victims of bullying also report higher levels of illness than non-victims. Returning to the aforementioned work of Smith and Sharp (1994), their study revealed that 22% of those who reported having been bullied felt physically sick after an incident, and 20% reported having difficulties sleeping. Additionally, Williams, Chambers, Logan, and Robinson (1996), in their research with almost 3 000 7- to 10-year-olds, found that those who had been bullied reported sleep disturbance, bed-wetting, feeling sad, and had more stomach-aches and headaches than those who had not been bullied (cited in Smith, 1999).

Much of the research on the immediate consequences of bullying, however, has pointed to the impact on the psychological well-being of those children who are victims. The most frequently reported outcomes of being bullied are children's lower levels of self-esteem and higher levels of depression, anxiety, and psychological distress (Connell & Farrington, 1996; Kumpulainen, Rasanen, & Henttonen, 1999; Percy-Smith & Matthews, 2001; Smith, 1999; Smith & Sharp, 1994). Kumpulainen et al. (1999), in their longitudinal investigation of bullying behaviour and its consequences, found in the second sweep of data collection (when the children were aged 12), that victims of bullying were the group who scored highest in the Children's Depression Inventory. More than two-thirds of this group, it was reported, scored highly on at least one measure of psychological distress/disturbance. Kumpulainen et al. also go as far as to suggest that bullying may be a contributing factor in the referrals of some children for psychiatric evaluations. Duncan (1999) also points to an investigation of over 2 000 children aged between 10 and 16 years, and argues that there is a link between peer aggression and psychological functioning. These theorists found that victims of serious physical assaults by peers showed similar levels of PTSD to children who had been sexually assaulted. Recently in the UK, the parents of a Pakistani boy sued a school trust for negligence over the physical and psychological racial bullying that their son endured at primary school: three years after he left the school he continued to suffer from post-traumatic stress due to his experiences (*The Guardian*, 12 February 2004).

Taking a more longitudinal or retrospective approach, many have pointed to the long-term consequences of bullying. Smith and Sharp (1994), for example, referred to the many adults they came across in the course of their research who stated that their experiences of being bullied at school had a lasting effect on them. Olweus (1993) examined the long-term effects of bullying on those who had been victims between the ages of 13 and 16 years: following them up when they were 23 years old, he found that they were likely to still suffer from poor self-esteem and to have a high rate of depressive symptoms (Connell & Farrington, 1996; Smith & Sharp, 1994). Taking a retrospective approach, Duncan (1999) sought to examine whether 'traumatic interactions with peers' led to long-term psychological distress which carried through to adulthood. She found that victims of bullying were more likely to have lower levels of self-esteem, confidence, and feelings of self-worth (and higher levels of anxiety and depression) than non-bully victims. In addition, she found that victims of childhood bullying were now more introverted, social avoidant, hypersensitive, and pessimistic about life than non-victims. Conversely, longitudinal research by Dodge *et al.* (2003) found that early rejection by peers, which would be a facet of indirect bullying through exclusion or isolation, was associated with later antisocial and aggressive behaviour.

In sum, it is evident that bullying is endemic in the school environment and that the consequences for victims can be traumatic, devastating, and long-lasting. From the literature reviewed it would appear that there are two particularly important lessons to be learned for those working with children: first, that children who have already been identified as victims of child abuse or neglect are at increased risk of suffering from further abuse by peers, and that the nature of their peer relationships should be explored in detail; and, second, that bullies themselves may also suffer some form of abuse or neglect at home, and this should be borne in mind and not dismissed in any interventions.

EMOTIONAL ABUSE/NEGLECT BY TEACHERS

Most discussions concerning emotional abuse and neglect in schools have tended to focus on pupil-to-pupil bullying (Hepburn, 2000; Hyman & Snook, 1999), the role of the school in helping to identify children who are being maltreated outside schools (Benbenishty, Zeira, & Astor, 2002; Doyle, 2003b; Hart, Brassard, & Germain, 1987), and effects on educational achievement (Doyle, 2003b; Iwaniec, 1995). Much less attention (particularly in Britain), has focused on the school as a potential site of emotional abuse of children by teachers (Tomison & Tucci, 1997). The lack of specific literature on this topic, however, is not to be taken as an indication that these issues are things of the past, but merely that the field of child maltreatment has been slow to move beyond institutional abuse (apart from abuse of a sexual nature). Varnham (2001) noted that while a particularly serious view was taken in respect of sexual misconduct, the same cannot be said about schools when it comes to physical and verbal bullying by staff on pupils. Indeed, Eslea, Stepanova, and Cameron-Young (2002) reported that the issue of, teacher-to-pupil aggression has received minimal attention, illustrating this point by stating that a search on the Web of Science returned no hits. This is despite the fact that Hyman and Snook (1999) argue that 'the incidence of educator-induced [verbal and physical] violence far exceeds that of offenses committed by students. Yet it is little studied, mostly ignored, and in some settings greatly encouraged'.

One must clearly justify the need for examining schooling and schools with regard to emotional abuse and/or neglect of children in order to avoid charges of demonising schools (which are often under-resourced) and teachers (who are often overstretched). Yet, given the fact that schools are perhaps the only social institution through which every child normally passes, they bear a huge responsibility for the welfare of children, and must be held accountable. After all, as Hart *et al.* (1987) state, 'educators are surrogate parents'. Not only do children acquire academic and learning skills in school, but also social and emotional skills, and teachers themselves serve as role models for normative behaviour (Benbenishty *et al.*, 2002). Relationships with teachers are important in that children learn important lessons in empathy, respect for others, and peaceful conflict-resolution: the nature of teacher-child relationships, therefore, may influence the level and quality of learning. As children spend 12 years of their lives in compulsory education (and some will attend pre-school, so the time may be even longer), schools play a significant role in the development of various aspects of personality (Harris, Eden, & Blair, 2000).

THE EXTENT AND NATURE OF CHILD EMOTIONAL ABUSE/ NEGLECT BY TEACHERS

Emotional abuse and neglect, it is argued, can take a number of forms in the school setting (Hart *et al.*, 1987; Hyman & Snook, 1999; Hyman, Zelikoff, & Clarke, 1988; Paulson, 1983). This includes: verbally assaulting, threatening, and bullying children; rejecting, neglecting, or isolating some pupils in favour of others; failing to intervene when pupils are being bullied by peers; having inappropriate academic expectations (either above or well below a child's developmental level); and providing an unstimulating learning environment (either in terms of teaching style, teaching aids, or the curriculum). Hyman and Snook (1999) also point to the practice of having undercover police and random strip-searches on students in American schools as being emotionally, and on occasions, sexually abusive. Although this section will focus primarily on the teacher-to-pupil relationship with regard to emotional abuse and neglect, some of the other ways in which schooling can be institutionally emotionally abusive or neglectful will be touched upon throughout.

Despite gaps in the literature, clear examples of emotional abuse and neglect have been reported, and indeed have been the focus of research in all levels of schooling, from pre-schools (Paulson, 1983) and primary/elementary schools (Hyman et al., 1988; Krugman & Krugman, 1984; Shumba, 2002) to secondary/high schools (Benbenishty et al., 2002; Hepburn, 2000; Janowski, 1999; Olweus et al., 1999). A number of these studies, particularly those whose main focus is child maltreatment, present clear evidence of emotional abuse where intent is often evident. Yet many other studies with a slightly different focus tend to highlight the more subtle forms of emotional abuse experienced by children in school. This most commonly involves behaviour by teachers that they would no doubt perceive as neither abusive nor bullying.[3] Cullingford and Morrison (1996) remind us, however, that 'Children feel hurt and isolated, often as a result of behaviour in which the deliberate intention to cause distress is absent. Such actions can be psychologically devastating, leaving children feeling severely victimised.'

One example they give of this is the subtle ways in which teachers bully children, leaving them feeling embarrassed, alienated, socially isolated, 'picked on', or rejected as 'different'. This behaviour, they argue, may be one reason why pupils physically and/or psychologically exclude themselves from school, and may end up being socially excluded from other aspects of society. These subtle processes are clear examples of emotional abuse by teachers and they come through in much educational and sociological research on the school experience of children and young people but, more often than not, fail to be recognised as emotional abuse.

Emotional abuse by teachers, often in the form of verbal assaults, humiliation in front of the whole class, bullying tactics, and unfair punishments is most often associated with the school ethos of discipline and control. Indeed Hepburn (2000), through a discourse analysis of interviews carried out with teachers regarding the bullying of pupils (among other things), found how

---

[3] See Hepburn (2000) and Hyman et al. (1999) for detailed accounts of teachers' understandings and reasonings of their behaviour.

teachers most often tended to justify or neutralise their behaviour on the grounds that they needed to enforce and maintain control and discipline in the classroom. Byrne (1999) also suggests that teachers may unknowingly be involved in bullying behaviour. Intent, however, is not essential for emotional abuse to occur. While the true extent of emotional abuse of children by teachers is unknown, some, like Hyman and Snook (1999), argue that it is pervasive. Through their research they suggest that between 50% and 60% of any group of citizens will report at least one experience of psychological maltreatment at the hands of teachers. That is, an act which has remained in their memory often many years after the event and which caused some degree of trauma. Of this total, they suggest that the experience is so disturbing in 1% to 2% of cases that it leads to PTSD. There have, however, been few large-scale prevalence studies of emotional abuse or bullying by teachers. One would suggest that this has more to do with the sensitivity of the issue and the litany of methodological aspects surrounding research of this nature than a lack of interest in the issue or a belief that it is something that simply does not exist. Olweus (1999), however, in 1985 studied bullying by teachers in Belzen, Norway. Based on the self-reports of 2 400 pupils he found that 2% had been bullied within the 5 months prior to the study.

A larger-scale and more recent self-report study carried out among 10 410 Israeli students across 161 high schools found much higher reported levels of emotional abuse. Here Benbenishty *et al.* (2002) found that a quarter (24.9%) of all their respondents had been emotionally maltreated by school staff. The main types of maltreatment reported were public humiliation by teachers, and being denounced and ridiculed because of appearance and/or academic ability. For some, a pattern of bullying was identified, in that a particular student would be repeatedly victimised by a particular teacher. Due to the large-scale nature of this study, groups of children who were most vulnerable to maltreatment in schools were also identified: these were males, younger children (i.e. junior high), and those who attended schools which had a high concentration of students coming from low-income families. Although there may be very particular reasons why levels of emotional maltreatment are high in that country, this research revealed a number of interesting issues which could be further explored in other countries, especially that relating to schools located in 'poor communities'.

Although it appears that there have been no large-scale studies of emotional abuse or bullying by teachers in a UK context, smaller-scale research on the issue of bullying (Eslea *et al.*, 2002; Hepburn, 2000) or within the fields of sociology and education (Cullingford & Morrison, 1996; De Pear & Garner, 1996; John, 1996; Kilpatrick, 2003) would suggest that it is a problem which is widespread. While the following subsections outlining a number of forms of emotional abuse/neglect in schools will employ case studies from the literature dealing with child maltreatment, illustrative examples from other fields of research will also be referred to in order to highlight how pervasive and ingrained this form of abuse may be. Interestingly, many of the experiences cited in retrospective accounts of (mainstream) school would fall into the categories of psychological maltreatment outlined by Hart *et al*. (2002).

VERBAL ATTACKS AND HUMILIATING BEHAVIOURS

One of the main forms of emotional abuse perpetrated by teachers comes in the form of verbal attacks on pupils. This includes behaviours such as name-calling, put-downs through insults and sarcastic remarks, verbal threats, and public humiliation of pupils. Paulson (1983), in her observations of 60 to 70 pre-schools for children aged between 2-and-a-half and 5 years found many examples of these types of abuse in her 5 years of study. The following is one incident she witnessed which could fall into a number of categories of emotional abuse:

> A 3-year-old boy comes out of the bathroom struggling to pull his pants up. Teacher shouts, 'Aren't you ashamed to come out like that?' Child does not know what he has done and begins to cry. Teacher shouts 'stop crying'. The child is now sobbing. Teacher 'if you don't stop crying, your mother won't pick you up.'

Within this one incident the child is shamed and humiliated, shouted at to the point where he is made to cry, and then threatened as a means of regaining control over him. Such behaviour would not be appropriate for a child of any age, but Paulson reminds us that the ethos behind early-childhood education is to build self-esteem. Yet many behaviours were observed which could impact upon this, particularly at this key developmental stage as children feel shame very deeply, and as a result doubt their ability to perform various tasks. While the true effects of treatment may not be immediately observable, Paulson suggests that they can diminish a child's confidence and ability to learn. Other behaviours of punishing a child for behaviour which is overlooked in other children can also lead to withdrawal or, conversely, to that child 'acting up'.

Examining the occurrence and effects of sustained emotional (and physical) abuse on a class of first-grade elementary-school children, Hyman *et al*. (1988) came to much more definitive conclusions about effects upon the children involved. Forms of abuse included: tying up pupils who would not sit down to their chairs; taping shut the mouths of those who would not be quiet; humiliating those who needed to use the bathroom during class time by writing their names on the board and punishing them by taking away their play time; verbally assaulting children and threatening them that if they told their parents that they would be made to wear badges saying 'tattle tale'.

Hart *et al.* (1987) noted that these methods of discipline clearly fall under the forms of psychological maltreatment they termed 'terrorising', 'degrading', and 'rejecting' behaviours. With regard to the impact of these experiences, psychological evaluations of 17 of the children from this class found many symptoms being reported, including vomiting, headaches, earaches, stomachaches, insomnia, excessive dependency, anxious behaviour, depression, withdrawal, and avoidance of school. One child pulled out all her eyelashes. Furthermore, the clinical team believed that PTSD was identifiable in about half of these children. Although it is noted that PTSD manifests itself differently depending on a child's developmental level, it is stated that 'the traumatic anxiety may impact on every area of a child's cognitive, emotional, and spiritual growth' (Hyman *et al.*, 1988). Thus, the effect this may have upon a child's development may lead to permanent changes in that child's ability to learn and how it relates to others.

Krugman and Krugman (1984) also reported on the effects of emotionally abusive behaviour of a teacher on a class of 17 children in an elementary school. The teacher in this case was reported to have carried out the following actions: verbal harassment and put-downs; labelling pupils as 'stupid/ dummy'; shouting at children until they cried; allowing pupils to harass and belittle others; inducing fear through various techniques; and imposing unrealistic academic standards. Parents noticed significant changes in their children's behaviour soon after they had started the new school year and entered this teacher's class: they reported symptoms such as excessive worrying about school performance, the emergence of negative self-perception, and a negative attitude to school. Less common (but still significant) were reports of sleep disturbances, withdrawn behaviour, headaches, and stomachaches. Within two weeks of the removal of this teacher from the classroom these symptoms disappeared in all but two of the children. Yet Krugman and Krugman (1984) noted the disastrous effect verbal abuse can have on a child's self-esteem, reporting that in 13 of the 17 children's evaluations the experience had led to a dramatic lowering of self-esteem and other psychological trauma.

These are clear examples of incidents where a specific teacher can emotionally abuse a number of children on one or more occasion. There are, however, examples of teachers behaving in a similar manner towards a particular pupil rather than to the class as a whole,[4] and such behaviour may in turn provoke hostility and bullying by peers. Because these cases were based in the USA in the 1980s does not mean that emotional abuse by teachers is not an international phenomenon or that it is a thing of the past.

---

[4] See Cullingford & Morrison (1996), De Pear & Garner (1996), John (1996), and Kilpatrick (2003) for illustrative examples.

It has recently been reported, for example, that an 11-year-old boy with learning difficulties had his mouth taped shut by a teacher in a school in Cardiff and has been humiliated by the experience (*The Guardian*, 11 February 2004). Recently, a family in the USA took legal proceedings against some staff members of a school: their 14-year-old son was tied to a chair by a teacher who encouraged other students to throw wadded paper towels at him and threaten him with hanging. At the age of 16 the child suffered flashbacks, fear, and anxiety, and feelings of social alienation, anger, and sadness.

Clearly, persistent verbal insults, put-downs, and humiliation by teachers can affect children in a number of ways, from discouraging learning and creating behavioural problems to destroying self-esteem leading to the onset of clinically diagnosed stress disorders (e.g. PTSD). As Brown aptly states: 'kids who are the victims of persistent put-downs don't walk around with bruises on their arms and legs, but often they're damaged just as much as if they'd been physically assaulted' (1979, cited in Hart *et al.*, 1987).

REJECTING AND ISOLATING

Rejecting and isolating children in the classroom setting can be viewed as an act of omission rather than commission. This can include withholding compassion, affection, and physical contact, or rejecting, ignoring, and isolating some students in favour of others. Hyman *et al.* (1999) remind us that teachers, by virtue of their position, are obliged to attend to the needs of pupils and should be 'aware of children's emotional needs as they vary according to age'. Yet Paulson (1983) offered clear examples of teachers withholding compassion and affection to very young children at pre-school. Although referring to these incidents as 'emotional abuse' rather than 'emotional neglect', she described how teachers failed to show compassion to children who fell and cut themselves, and told children who cried to stop without offering them any form of human contact or affection, despite the fact that the very young have strong needs for nurturing (Hyman *et al.*, 1999). Paulson (1983) suggested through her observations that staff simply did not see small children as small children, which might partly account for the problem.

Hart *et al.* (1987) also referred to the research of Good and Brophy (1987) which found that teachers did not ask for, or failed to wait for, the responses of students who were viewed as 'slow or poor': this can effectively lead to those students feeling isolated or ignored. Failing to let pupils communicate effectively in the classroom, it is suggested, can impact upon their understanding of themselves. Also, with regard to pupils being rejected and isolated, Cullingford and Morrison (1996) offered a quotation from one of their interviewees illustrating feelings of loneliness in children:

> I used to think they had favourites . . . and I used to sit there and they sort of blanked me out and talked to the others all the time . . . so I used to sit there most of the time on me own, nobody to talk to. So I used to sit on me own, and then I used to think, oh God, I'm not coming tomorrow. 'Cos I knew if I stayed at home me mum and dad would talk to me, but they [at school] didn't.

It is clear to see that acts of omission such as those mentioned here are examples of emotional neglect within the school setting. Children who are ignored or rejected may respond by 'acting up', withdrawing, and rejecting learning and may, as a consequence, experience low self-esteem.

While these are by no means the only ways in which the school environment may be viewed as emotionally abusive or neglectful (e.g. the pressure to perform), the teacher-to-pupil relationship is perhaps that aspect of schooling over which individual schools have most control. Yet despite large-scale surveys and public-awareness campaigns throughout the 1990s regarding peer-to-peer bullying within schools, no such attention has been paid to the issue of teacher-to-pupil bullying. Nevertheless, examples of emotional abuse by school staff are evidenced in much literature regarding school discipline, and those cases, which are often of the most extreme nature, are periodically exposed in press reports. In Warsaw, for example, it took the suicide of a secondary-school pupil and a resultant demonstration by fellow-students taking to the streets with banners stating 'We want teachers, not bullies', to bring the harsh realities of the effects of emotional maltreatment by education staff to the eyes of the public (Janowski, 1999). Doyle (2003b) pointed out that for those children being emotionally maltreated in the home and then further humiliated in schools the burden can simply be too much to bear. In sum, and as stated by Benbenishty *et al.* (2002):

> Given the importance of educators and schools in the lives of children, and the possible negative effects of maltreatment by school staff on children, it is important to note the paucity of studies that assess the prevalence of the various forms of staff maltreatment.

EMOTIONAL ABUSE AND NEGLECT IN OUT-OF-HOME CARE

Research regarding the incidence and nature of the abuse and neglect of children within the care system is relatively scant. The research base in the UK tends to be made up primarily of official inquiry reports, and the focus has almost exclusively been on physical and sexual abuse. This is despite the fact that a number of authors suggest that children in care are at an increased risk of abuse as opposed to those not in care (Hobbs, Hobbs & Wynne, 1999), and that official reports and figures may hugely under-estimate the scale of the problem (Barter, 2003; Kendrick, 1998a). Of past revelations of the abuse of children in residential care, Colton (2002) aptly states: 'It is a matter of grave concern that many...children who were removed from their families for protective purposes were then placed in residential care and exposed to even greater risks.'

Emotional abuse/neglect can take a number of forms in out-of-home care, including: acts of omission/commission by carers, staff, or peers; regimes and programmes which are inherently emotionally abusive; and poor policies and practices within the care system as a whole. Due to a lack of literature, each of these issues will be discussed briefly, with the focus primarily upon residential as opposed to foster-care, reflecting the imbalance in the literature base.

Abuse by Carers/Staff

Although a number of high-profile cases of physical and sexual abuse perpetrated by staff on children in residential-care homes have been brought to public attention, much less is known with regard to the emotional abuse and/or neglect of children by caregivers or staff. One of the few studies which took account of allegations of emotional abuse by residential-care staff is that of Westcott and Clement (1992, cited in Kendrick, 1998a). In their study of NSPCC teams and projects they uncovered 84 cases of alleged abuse in the year prior to the study: only 4 of these, however, were defined as emotional abuse. In interpreting this finding it is important to note that the authors of this research pointed out that these reported cases probably reflect only the most extreme cases. As highlighted in Chapter 1, emotional abuse, by its very definition, is often viewed as less serious than sexual or physical abuse, and this may in part contribute to the small numbers of reports, particularly within the care system. Kendrick (1998c) also reminded us that it is difficult for children to make complaints against staff members and foster-parents/siblings as they are often fearful of reprisals. Barter (2003) highlighted that most inquiries into institutional abuse in the UK found that children's complaints were often ignored. This was primarily on the basis of stereotypical notions held about the characters and behaviour of children in residential care. Added to this, Colton (2002) argued that a lack of clear mechanisms of accountability in residential care means that there is a lack of safeguards against abuse.

The often difficult task that carers and residential staff face should not be underestimated. Children in care can exhibit appalling emotional and behavioural problems. Lack of appropriate training, supervision, and support often leads to 'burnout' which affects relationships with children. Kendrick (1998c) stated that this often manifests itself in 'increasing negative attitudes towards clients or children including depersonalisation and dehumanisation'. The pressures upon staff and carers, therefore, may be a major contributing factor in emotionally abusive and/or neglectful relationships in out-of-home care situations.

Abuse by Peers

Despite high-profile reports of abuse by staff, it has been suggested that children in residential care in the UK are at more risk of being abused by peers than by staff (Barter, 2003). There is considerable literature on bullying in schools, but much less with regard to peer-to-peer bullying in other institutions, residential care included (Kendrick, 1998b). As such, the problem often remains hidden despite the general belief that it may be part of the institutional culture of this setting. The most recent study of bullying in residential care, for example, found high levels of violent physical and verbal assaults in 11 of the 14 homes investigated (Barter, 2003). A study of 48 children's homes by Sinclair and Gibbs (1998) found that as many as one in four children reported having been bullied while in care (cited in Barter, 2003). Within the residential-care setting, Gibbs and Sinclair (1999) stated that bullying can cause extreme misery in some residents and lead to long-term problems in adjustment. An analysis of calls made to 'ChildLine for Children in Care' in 1994 found that over a quarter of all calls made by boys and 1 in 10 of those made by girls related to bullying by other residents (cited in Kendrick, 1998b). Indeed, in Northern Ireland, the Social Services Inspectorate study found high levels of bullying in all sectors of residential care (cited in Kendrick, 1998b).

It is clear that peer-to-peer bullying is a large problem in residential-care settings. Barter (2003) argued that organisational and cultural factors in residential homes contribute to the level of peer-to-peer bullying (e.g. 'peer pecking order' and 'macho cultures'). Poor supervision and lack of appropriate practices and policies have allowed bullying to flourish and in some instances to become ingrained in the institutional culture of residential-care settings.

Programmes and Systems Abuse

The regimes, programmes, and practices within the care system can also be emotionally abusive/neglectful to children. Tomison and Tucci (1997) referred to emotional abuse inflicted via systems abuse as a consequence of experiences such as of traumatic child-protection investigations, multiple placements, lack of continuity of care, and separation from siblings; added to this list could be experiences of case conferences and lack of continuity in education. More specific programmes within some facilities have also been found to be emotionally abusive. Perhaps the most often cited example of 'harsh, inhumane, or unusual techniques to teach or guide children' was the Pindown technique (Kendrick, 1998c). This was a regime adopted in residential children's homes in Staffordshire between 1983 and 1989. Its aim was to 'pinpoint' and control difficult children through isolating them in special units for weeks and months at a time. They were also denied access to external contacts, punished through losing 'privileges', had their ordinary clothing removed, and were made to wear shorts or nightwear. The resultant Pindown Inquiry (1991) found these practices of isolating and humiliating children to be unethical and unprofessional, and it is clear that such a regime fell into a number of the categories of psychological maltreatment outlined by Hart *et al.* (2002) and Iwaniec (1995).

Although the literature is scarce, that research which does exist highlights the various ways in which residential-care institutions and policies and practices regarding the care of the child outside the family can be emotionally damaging. Given the fact that a sizeable proportion of children in care have already suffered some form of abuse and that they are a particularly vulnerable group, measures to safeguard them from further abuse/neglect should be paramount.

CHILDREN AND YOUNG PEOPLE IN CUSTODY

Inmate-to-Inmate Bullying

The culture of prisons and the various inmate subcultures within them have been issues of continued interest among criminologists for some time, yet it would appear that it was not until the 1990s that the culture of bullying within these establishments (particularly in the form of verbal assaults) received focused attention by academics and policy-makers alike.[5] In fact, it was not until 1993 that HM Prison Service set out a clear national strategy to tackle bullying in all carceral institutions (Dyson, Power, & Wozniak 1997; O'Donnell & Edgar, 1998). Despite new strategies, however, it is suggested that bullying is still rife within prisons (especially those containing children and young people), and that these anti-bullying strategies may have merely led to more covert forms of bullying (Dyson *et al.*, 1997). Recent investigations into bullying in HMYOI Castington, for example, revealed that 55% of inmates reported being involved in a bullying incident in the week prior to the investigation (Howard League for Penal Reform, 2001; *The Guardian*, 10 October 2001).

Connell and Farrington (1996) carried out preliminary research of 20 young offenders in penal institutions in Canada. Employing a more conservative

---

[5] See O'Donnell & Edgar (1998) and Beck (1995) for detailed accounts of the nature of bullying among young offenders in custody.

estimate of bullying than other studies (in that the inmate had to be a victim of certain behaviours about once a week or more), they found that 70% of their sample admitted to being involved in bullying. This comprised 45% who admitted to being bullies and 25% who reported being victims. Interestingly, 4 out of 5 victims reported being bullied on a daily basis. It was also found that a number of inmates believed that some staff ignored bullying, and that bullies were given high status or 'jail respect' by other inmates and staff alike. Even in specialised secure facilities, bullying has been found to be rife. Research at Glenmore Youth Treatment Centre, for example, found that, over a 6-month period, 47% admitted to regular bullying, and 56% admitted to being frequent victims of bullying (Browne & Falshaw, 1996, cited in Kendrick, 1998b).

O'Donnell and Edgar (1998), in their study of two adult prisons and two young offender institutions (YOIs), show how everyday routine victim-isations in such establishments shape their social 'ethos': that 'ethos' is one based on threats, intimidation, verbal and physical assaults (not always of a serious nature), theft, and robbery. They described these 'routine victimisations' as being embedded within prison culture (more so in YOIs than in adult establishments). It is the constant picking on someone (generally those perceived as weak or different), through threats, name-calling, and often mild incidents of violence, they argued, that causes more emotional harm than incidents of serious physical injury. They highlighted that verbal insults aimed at breaking the inmate's spirit can serve to isolate the victim, excluding him from many activities and networks, thus inevitably increasing vulnerability and damaging self-esteem. It is often these subtle and somewhat hidden inmate cultures of consistent verbal abuse and intimidatory behaviour that grind down will and break the spirit.

Beck (1995) found similarly high levels of self-reported victimisation in two YOIs with 1 in 5 (21%) inmates reporting having been bullied while in these institutions. Again, the most commonly reported forms of bullying were of a psychological nature, namely threatening behaviour and name-calling. Within one of these establishments staff reported that physical segregation of inmates did little to prevent bullying as verbal insults and taunts could be heard shouted from windows at night. This is a form of intimidation that has been reported by children in various prison settings (see Howard League for Penal Reform, 2001, 2002 for more details). As Beck (1995) stated, 'this form of public humiliation does not require the bully and victim to be in physical contact but may clearly cause distress to the victim'. Beck's conclusion is similar to that of many others who have examined bullying among young offenders in custody: that it is very much the 'norm' among this particular group and as such is an 'insidious and almost inevitable component of prison life'. This is particularly important and worrying in light of the fact that an enquiry into factors associated with suicide in a YOI in Scotland concluded that inmates who were 'physically assaulted or verbally harassed and teased', from whom 'tobacco was extorted', and about whom there was a campaign of 'whispering, with implied threats', were the most vulnerable to suicide (Scottish Home and Health Department, 1985, cited in Dyson *et al.*, 1997). Bullying among young offenders was also implicated as one of the main causes of inmate deaths in at least one institution in the 1990s (Connell & Farrington, 1996).

Emotional Abuse by Prison Staff

Despite claims by the Prison Service that the ethos and regime within YOIs have changed significantly since the days of Borstals and approved schools, reports of severe physical and emotional abuse by staff upon inmates are still being made. HMYOI Portland, for example, which used to house young men aged between 16 and 21 years of age, has been the focus of a recent legal battle with former inmates. As a result of an out-of-court settlement, 7 former inmates were awarded £120 000 damages for the physical and emotional abuse they had suffered at the hands of guards. Apart from physical beatings, the former chaplain of the institution explained how there was also legitimised bullying, intimidation, and humiliation of inmates (*The Guardian*, 21 January 2004). As recently as 2002 the then governor of the institution also reported that the regime within certain parts of the prison was 'nothing short of institutionalised intimidation' (*The Guardian*, 22 January 2004). This is by no means the only example of the often prolonged emotional and physical abuse some children and young people suffer in such institutions, and several other establishments have been the focus of similar investigations into maltreatment by staff. However, Beck (1995) noted that there has been no systematic research which looks at the sensitive issue of the bullying of inmates by prison staff.

Prison Culture and the Rights of the Child

With regard to the practice of putting some young people in solitary confinement (where the cell is totally bare, there is often no light, ventilation, or sanitary facilities, and the young person is often stripped of all clothing), this can be a humiliating, degrading, and damaging experience. In fact, the use of 'strip cells' for adult prisoners 'at risk' of suicide was found to exacerbate feelings of despair and became regarded as a 'humiliation ritual' (Dexter & Towl, 1995); such experiences would no doubt constitute emotional abuse. Holding an adolescent in solitary confinement for as much as 23 hours a day has been outlawed by human-rights legislation, yet reports continue to suggest that the practice is still very much in use in a number of YOIs (Howard League for Penal Reform, 2004): indeed, recent reports suggest that two young boys were kept in 'strip cells' for more than a year

(*The Guardian*, 11 January 2004). The director of the Howard League for Penal Reform reminds us that if a parent locked a child up in solitary confinement for days on end this would be counted as child abuse. The State must therefore accept its responsibility when it is acting in a parental role (http://web.ukonline.co.uk/howard.league/press/170703.html).

Despite very specific incidents of severe emotional abuse, it is argued by some (the Howard League for Penal Reform, 2002, 2003 in particular) that children under the age of 18 years should simply not be placed in traditional prison establishments. In fact, these and other campaigners go to lengths to highlight how many of the practices within these institutions contravene children's rights. Punishment received through a custodial sentence is loss of liberty, and should not involve further punishment in custody. The statement of purpose of HM Prison Service is, after all: 'Our duty is to look after them [inmates] with humanity and help them lead law-abiding and useful lives in custody and after release' (www.hmprisonservice.gov.uk). The worryingly high levels of suicide, attempted suicide, and self-harm among children in custody would suggest, however, that the prison environment, its routine, and practices are simply not conducive to the emotional well-being of young people (Lyon, 1996). It has been reported that in the case of self-harmers, for example, officers are often dismissive of these children, ignoring their behaviour or labelling it as attention-seeking (*The Guardian*, 10 October 2001). Due to pressures on space young people over the age of 15 who are particularly vulnerable or who have special needs and who, according to the guidelines, should be placed in small units (secure training centres or local authority secure units), almost always end up in prison custody where their needs simply cannot be met (Howard League for Penal Reform, 2002). The Chief Inspector of Prisons reported that some of our most difficult, disturbed, and vulnerable children and young people are being held in conditions were they are at risk of significant harm.

Perhaps one case which illustrates the needs of children in prison, the prison services' lack of ability (for various reasons) to cope with these, and the detrimental effect of incarceration on already vulnerable young people, is the case of a 16-year-old boy who took his own life in 2001:

> Joe was 16 and serving a 4-month sentence for driving offences when he killed himself in prison in 2001. Joe was known to be highly vulnerable. He had a history of self-harm and on his way to prison had tried to hang himself in the van with his shoelaces. He was distressed on arrival and so was put on suicide watch and taken to healthcare. There, he [was] kept in a semi-furnished cell and prescribed anti-depressants but offered precious little in terms of human interaction. After a week, it was considered safe to move him to the main wing, but within a minute of being alone he again tried to hang himself. Joe was taken back to healthcare but still not offered counselling or any other intervention. He continued to be withdrawn and depressed, and told staff he could hear his

dead grandmother talking to him. In spite of these factors and his long history of self-harm, it was decided he should move to the main wing. Left alone in his cell and anxious about the proposed move back, Joe hanged himself by his sweatshirt from his cell window bars (Howard League for Penal Reform, 2002).

Joe was one of 22 children (aged 15 to 17 years) who killed themselves in custody in the UK since 1990. His was a clear case of how emotional needs were neglected though lack of human contact and appropriate intervention, and illustrated how placing vulnerable children in such an environment can damage them emotionally in the most extreme of ways. Despite consistently high levels of reported suicide and self-harm, and continued reports of emotional and physical abuse within these institutions, the UK continues to lock up more children than any other European Union country (Howard League for Penal Reform, 2002).

SUMMARY

Through the use of literature from a variety of sources as well as the author's work with emotionally abused children and young people, the preceding material highlighted some of the ways in which three institutions which have responsibility for the care of the child can be inherently emotionally neglectful or abusive. Yet the almost exclusive focus on the family and parenting in some ways overshadows the fact that, just as sexual and physical abuse and neglect of children can occur in a variety of settings, so too can emotional abuse and neglect. It has been evidenced that within the field of child maltreatment there is a distinct lack of research on emotional abuse and neglect with regard to schools and schooling, out-of-home care and custodial settings.

Although studying emotional abuse in out-of-natural-home settings is difficult, it does not mean that there are not significant problems which require urgent attention and action for change. Children living away from home have an overwhelming set of needs which cannot be met if punitive, humiliating, and degrading methods are used in an aggressive and overpowering way. A warm but constructive approach is needed to help these young people.

CHAPTER 5

ATTACHMENT AND BONDING IN CASES OF EMOTIONAL ABUSE

CONTENTS

INTRODUCTION

A child's love and total dependency on parents or other caregivers is so natural and obvious that we seldom stop and think how the attachment of children to the primary caregivers develops and how it is maintained. Attachment is described as a unique and powerful relationship that develops between an infant and caregiver during the child's first year of life (Bowlby, 1969; Carlson & Sroufe, 1995). The nature and quality of that relationship are essential to establishing a child's interest and sense of safety and security, and influences the infant's fundamental modes of regulating thoughts and feelings internally and in relation to others.

Attachment theorists suggest that children form internal representational models of effect, cognition, and future expectations of themselves and others, based on their relationships with caregivers (Bowlby, 1969; Crittenden &

Ainsworth, 1989). In the context of the parent–child relationship, children develop a concept or expectation of their carer, described in the literature as a 'working model'. This model is based on the experience, memories, and interpretations of the child's relationship with the carer, who then is subsequently judged as a person who can respond to the child's expressions and communication for support and protection. An interdependent model or concept of 'self' develops in parallel, which infers whether the self is lovable, interesting, and a person to whom the attachment figure in the child's environment will respond in a helpful and satisfying way. Experiences of relationships are integrated, and gradually become a feature of the child's identity and personality structure, and facilitate a concept of the kind of person they are through feedback and interaction with others. Once established, internal models of the self and relationships with others are maintained, and tend to function as a self-confirming mechanism. The individual tends to select relationships and social situations which replicate and confirm earlier experiences and expectations established in the working model (Bowlby, 1973).

While attachment is a term usually reserved to describe the child's feelings toward the parent, parents have feelings of connection to the child that – while not technically described as attachment – are as powerful and influential as those of the child toward its parent. These feelings are not always positive. Many mothers report feeling empty, emotionally disconnected, and disengaged from their children, while others project intense aggression and hostility on to their offspring (Lieberman, 1999). These complex and multifaceted feelings and thoughts are thought to be strongly rooted in a mother's own attachment organisation – her own attachment history, which powerfully determines child attachment organisation, parenting behaviour, and the mother's capacity to see herself as providing a secure base for the child. The concept of mother–child bonding – the quality of that bond; and the consequences for the child if the emotional bond is weak or distorted – need to be explored to provide a balanced picture of the parent–child relationship. This exploration is particularly important to the understanding of emotional abuse and neglect and will be discussed briefly in this chapter.

WHAT IS ATTACHMENT?

When talking about children as being attached to the caregiver we mean a child being inclined to have a tendency to seek proximity to and contact with the specific caregiver in times of danger, distress, illness, and tiredness (Bowlby, 1984). Bowlby defined attachment as a 'behavioural control system', and distinguished between attachment as an attribute of the child (in that he/she is strongly genetically predisposed to seek proximity to the caregiver), and attachment behaviour (which describes various forms of behaviour that a child commonly engages in to attain or maintain a desired proximity to the particular caregiver). The infant continually monitors the accessibility of one or a few protective older 'attachment figures' (usually biological relatives such as the mother) and then approaches these individuals for security and protection in times of danger and alarm (Bowlby, 1988). Apart from providing comfort and protection, such individuals also act as a secure base from which the infant can explore the environment. These attachments to only a few people are thought to be formed by the age of seven or eight months. Ainsworth (1982) postulated that there is some basic behavioural system that has evolved in social species that leads individuals to seek and to maintain proximity even when conditions are not satisfactory. Children are thought to become attached whether or not their parents are meeting their physiological needs. Findings that infants become attached even to abusive mothers (Bowlby, 1958) suggest that the system is not driven by simple, pleasurable associations.

THE ORIGINS OF ATTACHMENT THEORY

Attachment theory emerged from two separate roots: the first is Freudian psychoanalysis; and the second root comes from ethology (the science of animal behaviour). Bowlby was particularly interested in how animals form intimate bonds and in their conflict behaviour. Ethological studies with non-human species mirrored his own work with human children. He believed that the parallels between his work and the work of the ethologists verified the validity of the evolutionary perspective on human development.

Attachment theory is built upon the assumption that children come to this world with an inborn inclination to demonstrate behaviours leading to the formation of an attachment relationship, and such inclination would have had survival value in the environment in which human evolution originally took place. Main (1990) postulated that the biologically based human tendency to become attached is paralleled by an ability (also biologically based) to be flexible to a range of caregiving environments. Whereas almost all children become attached, even to maltreating mothers, not all are securely attached, and striking differences are observed. Secure attachment occurs when a child builds a mental representation based on accumulated positive experiences of an attachment figure who is available and responsive to the child's various needs and signals of distress. Insecurely attached children are considered as lacking positive mental representation, because their basic needs are not being attended to (often due to neglect, emotional unavailability, and abuse).

Bowlby (1973) made a point that even ready accessibility to a caregiver is not enough to establish security for the child. Apart from the physical presence of a primary caregiver there must be an emotional presence as well. It is of primary importance that a baby should have emotionally responsive parents when hungry, tired, or cold; when experiencing anxiety-provoking, uneasy events; or when uncertain about the location or behaviour of the parents. Emotional availability and sensitivity of primary caregivers is at the core of development of secure attachment.

PARENTAL SENSITIVITY AND FORMATION OF ATTACHMENT

Early studies on attachment (Ainsworth, Blehar, Waters, & Wall, 1978; Bowlby, 1973) defined parental sensitivity as parental ability to perceive and interpret children's attachment signals correctly and to respond to those signals promptly and appropriately. They proposed that early difficulties, lack of parental responsiveness to many of a baby's needs, and inconsistency and insensitivity in responding to those needs could lead to feelings of insecurity in children, whereas persistent, sensitive responsiveness would build secure bonds between children and parents. Bowlby (1973) also suggested that the parents' childhood attachment experiences would influence the way they respond and relate to their children. For example, parents who were neglected (both physically and emotionally) or ill-treated would be prone to neglect or ill-treat their children.

Infants whose caregivers are sensitive and responsive to signals of distress and cues learn that they can have their needs met and that they can have an effect on the world around them. Such infants grow to believe that they can influence their social environment. Additionally, sensitive caregiving will lead children to believe that they can influence people to achieve their goals. This confidence allows children to function autonomously and with a belief that they will be successful in their efforts. By being successful and appreciated by others, but particularly by the parents, they will build strong self-esteem and a sense of achievement. Thus, continuous influence of attachment is brought forward through effective regulation, behavioural reciprocity, and representation. In contrast, infants whose caregivers are unresponsive or erratically responsive to signals and cues learn that they are not able to influence their social environment to meet their needs. These children do not acquire the confidence to function autonomously; they show constant doubts and lack of self-esteem in social interactions (Sroufe, 1983). Such behaviours and reactions are very characteristic of emotionally abused children and of those whose parents are not emotionally available.

The causal role of parental sensitivity in the formation of the attachment security is now firmly accepted (De Wolff & Van Ijzendoorn, 1997). The validity of this statement is based on a causal analysis of 66 studies consisting of 4000 families as well as on intervention studies directed at parental sensitivity. It was found that the correlational studies on parental sensitivity and infant attachment security showed a consistent association, indicating that more sensitive parents have more secure children. The results of the intervention studies also support correlation evidence in showing that treatment in enhancing parental sensitivity can give greater security to children.

Belsky (1999) argued, from the ecological perspective, that, apart from caregiver sensitivity, the psychological attributes of the mother, her relations with her partner, and the degree to which she has access to support services should also be associated with the security of the infant–mother relationship. Isabella (1994) found that attachment security is affected by social support, even when direct effects of social support do not emerge as expected. He found that high social support significantly predicted high maternal-role satisfaction, and enhanced the quality of maternal care and attachment security.

INDIVIDUAL DIFFERENCES: THE STRANGE SITUATION

The extent and quality of sensitive responsiveness of the parent to the child will determine either secure or insecure attachment (Isabella, Belsky, & Von Eye, 1989). There are individual differences among children and parents in the type and quality of attachment relationship, and these have been the focus of most research describing and characterising them, explaining them, and determining their consequences. Mary Ainsworth and her colleagues operationalised attachment theory, and developed a procedure to observe children and mothers in a standardised stressful separation procedure in order to assess the amount of trust the children had in the accessibility of their attachment figures. Ainsworth *et al.* (1978) delineated three infants' attachment patterns, based on Bowlby's concept of internal working models and on the basis of a laboratory procedure called the 'Strange Situation' (in which the reactions of young infants to separation and reunion with their mothers, in the presence of a stranger, are examined). These internal working models give to children either an accurate or distorted picture of the world. On the basis of painstaking observations three types of attachment styles were identified: secure; anxious/resistant; and anxious/avoidant.

1. *Secure attachment* – The pattern B children are individuals who are confident that the caregiver(s) will be available, responsive, and helpful should they encounter adverse or frightening situations. The caregiver(s) is/are seen as readily available, sensitive to the child's signals, and responsive when the child seeks protection, comfort, or assistance. This security builds

confidence in the child, encourages exploration and competence, and is thought to be consistent with healthy development. Infants use the attachment figure as a secure base from which to explore; their working model of self and other is of someone who is worthy of love and the respect of others, and their caregivers experience little stress when caring for them.

2. *Anxious/resistant attachment or resistant insecure* – The pattern C children are uncertain that their caregiver(s) will be available, responsive, or helpful when needed. The caregiver(s) is/are less predictable with responses, being available and helpful on some occasions but not on others. Parenting is inconsistent. Adults have been either potentially available and responsive or otherwise. The child's working model of self is likely to be of someone who is demanding and needy. The pattern is also promoted by separations from the caregiver and threats of abandonment used as a means of control. The child tends to be clingy and anxious about exploring the world and may suffer from separation-anxiety (Bowlby, 1988). These infants fail to move away from the attachment figure and show little exploration. They are also highly distressed by separations and are difficult to settle after reunion: their physical model is one of cling or attack (Rutter, 1995b). Neglected children tend to be anxiously attached to their caregivers: subsequent caregivers experience great turbulence as the inconsistent, insecure C working model is projected and played out, because on the one hand they appear to be trusted by the child, but when trust begins to be established, the child is likely to either physically or verbally attack the caregiver.

3. *Anxious/avoidant attachment or avoidant insecure* – The pattern A children expect to be rejected by their caregiver(s) when they seek support or care. The caregiver(s) constantly rebuff(s) the child when approached for care or protection, and as a result these children will attempt to live their lives without the love and support of others. Their working model of self is likely to be one in which parenting oneself is seen by the child as the only option for survival. Their physical model is one of withdrawal and inappropriate self-sufficiency. The majority of more severely emotionally abused children are avoidantly attached. If this pattern persists, these children may later be prone to a variety of personality disorders, from compulsively self-sufficient individuals to persistently delinquent ones (Bowlby, 1988). These children explore with little reference to the attachment figure and seem to show ignoring or avoidant behaviour on reunion (Rutter, 1995a). Subsequent caregivers often experience a sense of helplessness from these children who appear to have no faith in parenting itself and who rely on themselves only for self-regulation and comfort.

During the last 20 years a fourth category of disorganised/disorientated pattern has been identified by Main and Solomon (1986). The behaviour of these children did not easily fit into any of the other categories; for example, children with a known history of abuse and neglect may be classified as secure, although their behaviour outside the 'Strange Situation' test may indicate abnormalities (Rutter, 1995a). These children show inconsistent behaviour, confusion, and indecision. They tend to freeze or show stereotyped behaviour such as rocking. This behaviour is thought to result from an extremely unpredictable caregiver's interactive behaviour. Conflict behaviour results because the source of security for the infant is also a source of fear. Many children who are emotionally abused fall into the disoriented/disorganised attachment style.

CHILD-TO-PARENT ATTACHMENT AND EMOTIONAL ABUSE

Development and emotional needs that are fundamental for psychological health – such as security and safety; attention; connection and sense of belonging to others; emotional and psychological development; autonomy and control; purpose and meaning (Griffin & Tyrell, 2002) – are generally thwarted or violated in the context of an emotionally abusive or neglectful relationship. Living in such an adverse environment, where negative effect is incessant and unremitting, excessive parental criticism, denigration, rejection, and the communication that the child is of little value consolidate the child's self-belief that it are 'worthless' and 'bad'. The child's cognitive capacity is insufficiently developed to cope with a carer who is both a source of protection and harm, which often leads to confusion for the child. Contradictory models of the carer develop, which overlap with multiple (and/or incoherent) concepts of the self. Individuals lose their confidence in their carers' availability and responsiveness, subsequently adopting insecure attachment styles as a strategy to cope with their emotional and relationship needs (Bowlby, 1973).

Insecure avoidant styles, where the parent may be authoritarian, yet unavailable, normally result from a parent who has been emotionally abused in childhood, who may be authoritarian and yet is physically and emotionally unavailable. The child in this relationship attempts to cope with this rejection through self-deception, idealisation of the parent, and/or minimising the importance of the attachment relationship (Main & Goldwyn, 1984). This, in turn, is hypothesised to foster a paradoxical experience of dependency, yet inability to trust within relationships, which may explain the high levels of social isolation and interpersonal difficulties in children and young adults with a history of psychological abuse.

Resistant attachment styles in families with a history of emotional abuse may be characterised by 'role reversal'. One or more children within the system behave as parents, as the carer has a sense that the child should meet their own emotional needs. As the needs of resistant child go unmet, he/she may be placed in a vulnerable position, disappointed, and open to revictimisation. As a teenager and young adult he/she is characterised by low self-esteem, an idealisation of partners, and being a compulsive caregiver, which may be connected to the high rate of teenage pregnancies observed in this population.

Families evincing *disorganised attachment* styles are often characterised by fear of abandonment and unresolved personal trauma (Alexander, 1992). As fear and terrorising often characterise the parent–child relationship in emotional abuse the context of the maltreatment may often lead to an overwhelming fear of abandonment. Families where parents present alcohol and substance abuse often result in disorganised attachment styles (Brennan, Shaver, & Tobey, 1991; Cotroneo, 1986). Carers may be repressing their own experiences of childhood adversity through substance abuse, with other members of the family unit, fearful of the consequences of the family break-up, either passively or actively ignoring or perhaps participating in the abuse. Disorganised children as adults would be expected to exhibit the most severe difficulties with affect regulation, including low mood and trauma symptoms, as the individual does not have the coping skills or resources to deal with a carer who is both the source of and the solution to the felt anxiety (Main & Solomon, 1986).

PARENT-TO-INFANT ATTACHMENT (BONDING)

There is little doubt that parental feelings (emotional bonds) towards a child can be as strong, powerful, and enduring as the child's attachment to its parents. These parental feelings can be differentiated in terms of depth, strength, and commitment expressed by action and sacrifice. There is also no doubt that the concept of parent–infant bonding has enjoyed somewhat controversial theoretical evolution (Sluckin, Herbert, & Sluckin, 1983). While certain aspects of bonding theory have fallen in and out of favour (e.g. the existence and nature of a 'sensitive period'), it has, nevertheless, popular appeal among practitioners from different disciplines.

Parent–infant bonding is defined as an emotional tie from parent to infant (Klaus & Kennell, 1982). There are several reasons why the doctrine of parent–child bonding was disregarded. First, an early conceptualisation of bonding failed to recognise the role the father (or the role the infant itself) played in the process; second, it failed to take into consideration those parents who could not have early post-natal contact with the baby; third, the notion of a critical period (skin-to-skin contact) was discredited as it failed to take into account alternative early parenting scenarios (Larkin, 2003). The term 'maternal attachment' was introduced to move away from adherence to a 'sensitive period' hypothesis, and the role of fathers was included in the process through use of the term 'parental attachment' (Mercer, 1990).

Parent–infant attachment is believed to be a bidirectional, reciprocal process involving mothers, fathers, and the infants. It has been defined as a cognitive and social process that tends to develop through positive and enjoyable feedback and satisfying experiences between parent and infant (Mercer, 1990). Parent–child attachment has also been defined in terms of the extent that the interest of a child takes precedence over the interest of the parent, and the perception of a child's occupying a central position in the life of the parent (Iwaniec *et al.*, 2002).

Parental bonding is typically shown by the parents behaving in a certain manner towards their baby, such as fondling, vocalising, smiling, picking up, touching, kissing, gazing, responding to signals, and the like. A mother would be considered to be bonded to her child if she looked after it well, gave it considerable and considered attention, saw willingly to the child's physical and emotional needs, and got considerable pleasure out of these actions.

Parent–child attachment implies a very special emotional relationship between two people which is specific and endures through time. It implies personal sacrifices given freely and willingly; feelings of warmth, affection, and love; a sense of possession and belonging; devotion, protectiveness, and concern for the child's well-being; positive anticipation of prolonged contact, longing to hold, see, and be with the child (if briefly separated); and rewarding experiences with the infant. It also implies unconditional love and caring attitudes which, on the parents' part, are quite likely to last a lifetime (Mercer, 1990; Iwaniec *et al.*, 2002).

Goulet, Bell, St-Cyr Tribble, Paul, & Lang (1998) outlined what they perceived to be three critical attributes of parent–infant attachment in an attempt to identify the essential characteristics of the concept. These include proximity, reciprocity, and commitment. Proximity is seen as the physical and emotional experience of the parent being close to the infant. Reciprocity is described as a process involving sensitivity and responsiveness of the parent towards the infant, whereby the infant plays an active role in eliciting parental responses. Commitment is described as the centrality of the infant in the parents' lives together with incorporation of the parental identity into the child.

SIGNIFICANCE OF THE PARENT–CHILD ATTACHMENT

The parent–infant attachment is central to the parent–child relationship, presumably the most important relationship in life. How this relationship will develop and grow is dependent on many factors, including parental experiences of being parented, wantedness of a child, the child's characteristics, parental mutual support for each other and in relation to childcare, parental health, economic factors, and parental resourcefulness, among other things.

In order for the parents to become attached to the child, and more importantly for the child to become attached to the parents, the parents must create an atmosphere of positive responsiveness to the child and mutual support for each other to meet the child's fundamental needs in a manner which is relaxed and warm.

Failure to establish a responsible and caring relationship between parents and children can result in a number of problems, e.g. development of a poor sense of self with resultant interpersonal difficulties; a tendency towards negative self-evaluation; dysfunctional cognition; and an impaired repertoire of defences and coping strategies (Ingram, Overbey, & Fortier, 2001). The attachment process has also been found to exert a significant impact on parents, as impaired bonding is a potentially distressing and isolating experience. Larkin (2003), on the basis of her study, identified that impaired parental attachment may affect parents in a number of ways, such as: the ability to view the child as their own; perception of the child as rewarding and exchanges with the child as satisfying; motivation to care for the infant; willingness to invest in meeting and prioritising the child's needs; ready acceptance to make sacrifices on the child's behalf; and, importantly, desire to prevent or avoid a relationship breakdown in the face of multiple child or parent problems. These factors may, in turn, influence the parent–child relationship and the quality of caregiving afforded to the child. Available evidence suggests that distorted parent–child attachment is potentially a distressing and isolating experience for both parent and child.

It needs to be recognised that affectionate bonds and relationships between parents and children have their own complex, many-sided developmental histories, stretching over many years. Among the factors which can influence the way parents relate to and behave with their children are their ages, their cultural and social backgrounds, their own experiences of being parented, their personalities, their previous experiences with babies, their desire to have the child and emotional preparation for its arrival, and the mother's experiences during pregnancy and birth. It is also important to take into consideration the support system, which is very useful, especially during the first few months of the child's life. Lack of such help and support can lead to excessive tiredness, depression, and distortion of the parent–child attachment and still, perhaps, fragile relationship. If the baby happens to be difficult to feed, to get to go to sleep, cries a lot, and gives little rewarding feedback, the bond between parents and child will be slow to develop or may have undesirable qualities, and may, in some instances, lead to emotional and physical abuse and neglect. Love, the joy of having a baby, and pleasure in seeing it grow and develop take time. Love and a sense of belonging grow strong as a baby begins to respond to a mother's nurturance and care. It would seem that the attachment bond comes quickly to some, but to others more slowly; the reasons and the range of individual difference is wide. The child's reactions to the parents – the joy shown in seeing them, the baby's responsiveness to their care and attention, and enjoyment of parental nurturance – will powerfully influence the parents in how they feel about their offspring and how they feel about themselves as parents. The magic of the emotional bond, secure and strong, will last a lifetime.

ADULT ATTACHMENT STYLES

It is believed that parents' childhood attachment experiences may influence the attachment relationship with their children. Unresponsive and insensitive parents may have received insensitive parenting themselves and may have been unable to change and provide warmth and supportive care. The idea of inter-generational transmission of good or bad parenting is widely accepted, and so is inter-generational transmission of attachment, but the latter is scientifically difficult to prove. There are very few longitudinal studies available which investigated attachment, and only such studies can link past events and present relationships to have a reasonably valid picture of attachment over time. Life-path experiences, exposure to different people, and opportunities are bound to influence parents' attitudes and lifestyles. The Adult Attachment Interview (AAI) was developed in order to assess the current mental representation of childhood attachment experiences (George, Kaplan, & Main, 1985).

Four types of attachment styles were found corresponding with children's attachment classifications, but using different labels:

- *Secure-autonomous attachment style* has a positive view of self and others. The person feels loved, effective, caring, and competent, and sees other people as available, co-operative, and dependable.
- *Dismissive attachment style* is characterised by a positive view of self and a negative view of others. The person feels self-reliant and finds other people rejective or intrusive.
- *Preoccupied attachment style* is demonstrated by a negative view of self and a positive view of other people. The person feels confused and bad, and considers other people to be unavailable and distant.
- *Unresolved fearful attachment style* is characterised by a negative view of self and a negative view of others. The person feels of low value, ineffective, and dependent, and considers other people to be neglecting, insensitive, unpredictable, and unreliable.

Inter-generational transmission of attachment suggests that adults and children develop similar strategies to cope with negative emotions, e.g. dismissive parents would have children who are *avoidant* of them, *preoccupied* parents would be inclined to have *ambivalent* children, and *autonomous* parents would relate in a secure way to their children. Meta-analysis of 854 parent–child dyads shows that the infant- and parent-attachment classifications are strongly associated (Van Ijzendoorn, Juffer, & Duyvesteyn, 1995). Even at prenatal interview with mothers their attachment security is highly predictive of an infant's security in the first year of life (Fonagy, Steele & Steele, 1991). In about 75% of families the parents determine their infants' attachment security on the basis of their own attachment representation. However, the uncertainty remains regarding the mechanism of transmission of attachment between adult and children. It could be that transmission of genes is involved, similar to the non-human primates (Suomi, 1995).

MOTHERS WHO PROMOTE SECURE ATTACHMENT BEHAVIOUR IN THEIR CHILDREN

Mothers who are sensitive, accepting, and co-operative in interaction with their children show synchrony, responsiveness, involvement, and warmth. There is a sense of harmony and mutual trust between mothers and their children, with well-timed reciprocal interactions and communications of feelings. Mothers show a great deal of interest in and fascination with their children, recognise their needs, and respond appropriately to signals of distress and joy. Mothers who are themselves secure and accessible pick up their babies more quickly and frequently than mothers of insecure children, and, although they have other demands on their time, they remain alert and available to their children. They consider the children's interest first before considering their own. They are ready and willing to make sacrifices in relation to their children and observe parental duties and responsibilities in a positive way.

Mothers who accept their babies as their own show a preference for shared, negotiated strategies to resolve difficulties, and their relationship with their children is that of a flexible, two-way goal-corrected partnership. They recognise and accept both positive and negative aspects of their children's behaviour, accept their individuality, but focus attention on the positive sides of their offspring. In secure homes, parents are able to achieve an age-appropriate balance over issues connected with security and discipline, socialisation and individuality, exploration and safety, and separation and comfort. Parents of secure children use disciplinary methods which are educative and informing, based on reasoning, negotiation, and clear instructions. Such approaches appear to be much more successful in helping children to achieve impulse control, compliance and self-reliance, and confidence.

DISMISSING AND REJECTING MOTHERS

Clinical and research evidence suggests that many emotionally abused and neglected children have experienced dismissing and rejective parenting (Glaser & Prior, 2002; Iwaniec, 2004; Doyle, 1997).

Patrick, Hobson, Cesde, Howard, & Vaughan (1994) found that between 15% and 23% of people show a dismissing pattern of attachment, and that these patterns are distinctive of those who feel anxious in the presence of strong feelings, either in themselves or in other people. Experiences of insensitivity, rejection, interference, and being ignored are associated with insecure attachment. Such mothers lack self-confidence on the one hand, but are driven to exert power and be dominant in relation to the powerless child on the other. When examining interaction of emotionally abused children with the rejecting mothers it is clear that such mothers lack empathy and perceive the child's attention-needing behaviour – a cry for warmth, interest, and gentle physical contact – as deliberate child's action to hurt them, rather than as a call for help. To illustrate such relationship problems let us look at Daniel's case.

Daniel's Case

Daniel, a four-year-old at the time of referral, was born two months prematurely to a family with a one-year-old girl. While in a special baby unit he was seldom visited by his mother as she was not well after his birth, and had to have a gynaecological operation. Having a one-year-old baby, living a distance away and having a husband who was a long-distance lorry-driver and seldom at home, contributed to limited contact with her son. After Daniel was discharged and sent home she found it hard to feed him and generally to look after him, as he was very small and often irritable. Although both parents were pleased to have a son, they were disappointed at his appearance and presentation. The mother also found it difficult to enjoy him as there was little feedback from him, and she firmly believed that he did not like being picked up, loved, and cuddled, so he was left in the pram or cot, quite often away from family interactions. Daniel had a much better relationship with his father, but did not see him on a daily basis because of his work. Daniel was seldom attended to, both physically and emotionally, so his development was seriously delayed. Daniel started to walk at two-and-a half years, hardly used any words, and his social behaviour was causing concern.

Mother–child interaction was limited to care and control, and at such times it tended to be insensitive and cold. The mother found it hard to love him and to respond willingly to his emotional needs. He was, as a rule, left alone in the bedroom with a few toys to entertain himself. As he grew older he began to show very disturbed behaviours, such as a bizarre eating pattern, aggressive defiance, attention-seeking, destructiveness, and toileting problems. He seldom ate at the table with the rest of the family; as a rule he sat on a newspaper-covered floor in order to eat, as his messy eating put his mother off her food. Also, he was seldom played with or interacted with in any way. Quite frequently he was banished to his room as a means of punishment, where he would spend several hours unattended.

Acceleration of emotional and behavioural problems coincided with the birth of his brother, who happened to be a very easy baby to rear and to enjoy. As Daniel's behaviour deteriorated, the mother's feelings and treatment of him deteriorated as well. He stopped talking to his mother and became quite mute, and if he did so he would address her as 'Miss' or 'lady' and would not respond to her requests. At the same time he was extremely attention-seeking, following his mother, but at a distance, and making sure that she was in his vision, which irritated her even more.

The mother–Daniel relationship became hostile and dismissive and, at the end, mutually antagonistic. The mother quite openly stated that she had no feelings for Daniel, that she did not feel that he belonged to her, and that the sheer physical presence of Daniel made her feel anxious, depressed, or hostile. She blamed him for everything that went wrong within the family and within the neighbourhood. She became particularly angry and resentful when people stopped her on the street or the park and made comments about her treatment of Daniel, publicly telling her off. She also stated that she felt very guilty about the way in which she treated Daniel, and wondered what went wrong with her parenting as she had a good relationship with her two other children. She felt that one of them had to go, either him or her, as he did not fit into the family. He was a stranger to her, even though he had lived with her for the last four years.

Dismissing Parents

Dismissing parents seldom acknowledge, in a sympathetic way, the child's expression of fear, anger or sadness, as they find it difficult to connect a child's reaction to their lack of responsiveness to the child's emotional needs or hostility in their interaction with the child. Unfortunately, such a dysfunctional pattern of interaction and communication can become self-sustaining. When negative emotions shown by the child fail to attract the caregiver's interest and positive attention, the child's behaviour can become dysfunctional and contribute to a variety of problems and distorted expressions of pain, hurt, and helplessness, as seen in Daniel's case. Attachment-related feelings of sadness and despair become more pervasive depressive symptoms, because of their long duration, and are expressed by anxiety and extremely aggressive antisocial behaviour.

A carer who feels agitated, distressed, or hostile towards her child causes the child particular difficulties, as such children are unable to channel their behaviour and emotions in a coherent and organised way. The ways in which mothers tended to deal with their children's feelings and their own agitation was to try to control the children's emotional states. Hollburn-Cobb (1996) suggested that a mother might attempt to define how her baby 'ought' to feel or what such feelings mean in a way that suited her needs rather than her child's. A crying baby may be told that he is not really distressed and that there is nothing to be upset about. An inability to reach the child's feelings and tune to them in a sympathetic way is very characteristic of these mothers. In other words they are unable (metaphorically speaking) to put their feet into the child's shoes.

Dismissing mothers have an excessive and unobjective preoccupation with their own attachment relationships or experiences (Crittenden, 1992). This may show as fearful preoccupation and a sense of being overwhelmed by traumatic experiences or may show as a more subtle presentation with the person appearing to be uncritical or unconvincingly analytical. The child's experience of being reared by a dismissing mother is one of being 'punished' and not receiving synchronised, sensitive parenting. Mothers classified as *dismissing* on the AAI were found in Van Ijzendoorn's *et al.* (1995) meta-analysis to be disproportionately likely to have children classified as avoidant or resistant. As the children became adults such individuals experienced an increase in anxiety and nervousness about entering into a close relationship at times when greater intimacy is expected, such as marriage or parenthood.

Dismissing mothers do not recognise or respect their children's independence. They tend to define their children's experience in a manner that is often abrupt, impatient, and aggressive, as seen in Daniel's case. Insensitive mothers fail to read their infants' signals, tending to interact according to their own thoughts, feelings, needs, and wants. Cassidy and Berlin (1994) note that the immediate, proximate function of behaviour associated with resistant attachment is to recruit more care and attention, and this may come out in the form of compulsive caregiving. Parents of resistantly attached children were found to be prone to intrude, control, and overstimulate their children in ways that bore little relation to the child's actual needs.

Preoccupied mothers tend to be less emotionally supportive and helpful, and tend to be cold and controlling. This seems to be consistent with self-description of their own early experience of being pushed to become independent as a child. Such mothers were found by Belsky and Cassidy (1994) as least responsive and affectionate with their children, probably because they had insensitive care in their own infancy. The mother's state of mind seems to indicate an attempt to limit the influence of attachment relationships. There is an over-reliance upon 'felt security', and this is achieved by an overreliance on the self and underreliance on other people. This is the reason why help is often not accepted, as parents feel they can manage themselves. There is evidence of poor insight and poorly developed critical self-evaluation.

Preoccupied mothers were found to be still overwhelmed by their past attachment experiences. They often felt mistreated by their parents: they expressed involved anger when they discussed past and present relationships with their parents (see Jackie's case for demonstration of this problem). The mother's state of mind seemed to indicate an attempt to limit the influence of attachment experience she had as a child and lessen the transmission of those experiences to her own offspring. Preoccupied mothers are responsive towards expression of fear in their babies, but are disinclined to attune to or validate their infants' expressions of initiative and exuberance during play.

CONSEQUENCES OF INSECURE ATTACHMENT

Whether the child is securely or insecurely attached to the primary caregiver can have not only immediate but long-term consequences. Many research findings postulate that insecure attachment in infancy may influence subsequent behaviour, such as impulse control, conflicts and struggles with caregivers, difficulties in adaptations, and seriously problematic peer relationships (Sroufe, 1983; Easterbrooks & Goldberg, 1990). Insecure attachment has also been linked to low self-esteem in six-year-old children in Cassidy's (1988) study. Infants who were insecurely attached at the age of one year were less enthusiastic and compliant, and showed more negative feelings and less positive ones towards their mothers at two years of age in free play and in problem-solving (Matas, Arend, & Sroufe, 1978).

Insecure children were found to be less socially competent with peers, and less flexible, self-reliant, curious, and involved in the nurseries. Equally, children investigated by Sroufe (1983) in the day-nursery between four and five years of age, with a history of insecure attachment, were rated to be less empathetic, had lower self-esteem, and were less socially competent and less ego-resilient than children with a history of secure attachment. The disorganised attachment style was found to dominate in high-risk samples which strongly predicted pre-school behaviour problems (Lyons-Ruth, Alpen, & Repacholi, 1993). It has been found that insecure infants are less competent in their social behaviour when with unfamiliar adults, have more problematic interaction with their parents, and have seriously disturbed interaction with their peers (Main & George, 1985; Troy & Sroufe, 1987).

The 20-year follow-up study of children who failed to thrive (Iwaniec & Sneddon, 2001; Iwaniec, 2004) found that some individuals who were insecurely attached as children made a remarkable recovery if their life trajectory changed for the better, e.g. being satisfactorily adopted, marrying a supportive and caring person, staying in one long-term foster-home, having a good social network at school and in after-school activities, or when parents and children received meaningful and successful interventions.

When attachments as adults were measured, using the Hazan and Shaver (1987) questionnaire, there were differences in comparison with their childhood-attachment assessment as measured by the Strange Situation Classification questionnaire.

Comparison of childhood- and adult-attachment classifications produced some interesting results. There were differences observed in the styles of attachment of the children who failed to thrive. In total, 14 of the 31 children were classified as secure, 9 as anxious/ambivalent, and 8 as avoidant. The picture is slightly different when we look at the attachment classifications of these individuals as adults.

There was an increase in secure attachment from 14 individuals in childhood to 22 in adulthood. There was a marked decrease of anxious/ambivalent style from 9 children to only 1 in adulthood. The number of clients falling into the avoidant category remained the same (8) for both children and adults. Analysis of Chi Square showed there was a significant relationship between the type of attachment observed in the children using the Strange Situation test and the subsequent classification of the adults using the Attachment Style Classification questionnaire (Kendall's Tau b, $p = 0.046$).

- The majority of children who had been classified as secure were also seen as secure in adulthood (13 individuals). Most children classified as secure were younger children at the time of referral. All these children were wanted pregnancies. Eleven were classified as temperamentally easy (Carey Temperamental Test), and only 2 were slow to warm up. Easy babies are thought to be predisposed to be more placid, positive in moods, easy to instruct, not intensive in reactions, and happy.
- Only one person who was secure in childhood was avoidant as an adult. This participant had several traumatic events throughout childhood including her father's suicide. Although she had remained in the home throughout the intervention, there was inconsistent improvement in the emotional environment experienced there. This client was also diagnosed as suffering from mental illness.
- Most of the sample who had been avoidant as children were also avoidant as adults (five out of eight individuals).
- Three previously avoidant individuals were classified as secure adults. In two of these cases the children were removed from the home environment and placed in long-term foster-homes in which they remained all the time. In the third case there was a dramatic change in home circumstances when the mother left the children's father and established a very positive relationship with a new partner. In essence each of these children experienced a new and much emotionally improved environment, either by being physically removed to a foster-home, or by dramatic changes in the home atmosphere.

- There is more variation in the group that had been anxious/ambivalent as children. Only one individual was classified as anxious/ambivalent as both child and adult. Two individuals showed a change from being anxious/ambivalent children to avoidant as adults.
- However, the majority showed a change from being anxious/ambivalent children to secure adults (six individuals). Two of these children were adopted at a very early age, and three children were fostered out long-term. One child remained in the home environment and showed improvement when her mother's new partner moved in (as above). The other two children remained in the home environment throughout intervention.

Intervention with failure-to-thrive children and their families, using various services and therapeutic methods, proved to be beneficial and effective in eliminating or reducing stress levels, which directly or indirectly affected parental reactions towards the failure-to-thrive child and consequently the child's reaction to the caregiver. We could argue that responding to people's immediate needs and dealing with crises (ranging from housing, economics, childcare, etc., through to personal factors) provided necessary help and support for the parents and consequently the child (Belsky, 1999). Equally, relationships between parents and children improved to satisfactory levels. There is ample evidence that intervention and treatment provided for those families and children over a period of time improved the quality and quantity of relationships and interactions between parents and infants. Interventions, such as obtaining care orders where there was no improvement at home and placing children in caring and stable foster-homes, and in two cases having them adopted, proved to be stabilising and wholly helpful strategies. It needs to be noted that these children stayed in one foster-home all the time they were in care and had extensive contacts after leaving care. Those individuals were able to develop secure attachments both with their foster or adoptive parents and later with their romantic partners. It can be argued that early and appropriate intervention can help to provide bases for developing secure and meaningful attachment and trust to parents and other significant people (such as daily minders, nursery nurses, and foster- or adoptive parents).

Clarke and Clarke (2000) argued convincingly that probabilities for developmental changes, both positive and negative, are influenced by biological trajectory, the social environment trajectory, interactions and transactions, and chance events. The life-path of each individual is the result of combined interaction of all four influences emerging during development. There is ample evidence to suggest that early experiences, even if they are of an extremely damaging nature, can be overcome if radical remedial action takes place and emotional stability and security are provided (Clarke & Clarke, 2000; Messer, 1999; Rutter, 1995a). The results of this study support the above-mentioned findings and suggest that attachment style is not static, so changes are probable. These changes appear to be influenced by many factors. (See Chapter 9 for further discussion.)

Individuals who showed attachment disturbances as adults were those who, throughout their lives, experienced insecurity with their parents, then with their peers, and later with their romantic partners. Emotional responsiveness and sensitivity were absent during the period of parental care, and a similar lack occurred later among peers.

Emotionally abused children are without exception insecurely attached to their primary caregivers, either showing anxious/avoidant or disorganised/disoriented attachment patterns. Furthermore, some of them show severe attachment disorders, both at home and at school, and when placed in the foster-home their behaviour and emotional reactions intensify, which often leads to placement breakdown. Early identification of attachment problems, either child-to-parent or parent-to-child, is important to prevent emotional maltreatment of children, as illustrated throughout this book by case studies and outcomes of research findings.

SUMMARY

This chapter discussed the origin and nature of attachment behaviour, and argued that attachment of infants to parents is genetically determined and that it serves as a protection and has survival value. It also examined various factors of attachment classifications, and described components of secure and insecure attachment styles. Additionally, it looked at parent–child attachment and discussed similarities and differences between attachment and bonding theory. Different parenting styles based on Adults Attachment Classification were elaborated upon, linked to the emotional abuse and neglect of children, and illustrated by a case study. The consequences of insecurity in child-to-parent attachment were demonstrated by findings from various research projects, and it was argued that intervention is necessary in more serious cases. Finally, the findings of the author's 20-year follow-up study were discussed: individual attachment styles in childhood were compared with attachment styles in adulthood. Several cases showed changes from insecure to secure attachment styles. Possible reasons for positive and negative changes and no change were discussed.

CHAPTER 6

EMOTIONAL ABUSE AND NEGLECT: EFFECTS ON THE GROWING CHILD

CONTENTS

INTRODUCTION

Human development is viewed in terms of the accomplishment of crucial socialisation tasks. Those tasks will be learned and skills acquired if the socialising agents (such as parents) create an atmosphere and opportunities for the child to learn to the best of its ability. We have seen in Chapters 2, 3 and 4 how neglect and abuse can interfere with a child's healthy growth and development: however, not all children who are emotionally neglected or abused show growth failure, but most of them show developmental delays and various behavioural and emotional problems.

Emotional abuse and neglect affect the speed and quality of development, especially during the early years of a child's life. There is some evidence to suggest that emotional abuse and neglect play roles in inhibiting positive emotional development which can last a lifetime. Adults who experienced such neglect may find it difficult to form warm, intimate relationships, and have problems with the management of hostility and aggression, which, it is claimed, may give rise to depression in later life (Carlson, Cicchetti, Barnett, & Braunwald 1989). There are ample data available to state that maltreatment reflects itself negatively on a child's developmental attainment and that it differs with age (Frodi & Lamb, 1980; Cicchetti & Rizley, 1981; Belsky & Vondra, 1989; Wolfe, 1988; to mention but a few).

Maltreatment demonstrates itself in many different ways and in varying degrees, from lack of care and provision of basic physical needs to lack of attention to stimulation and encouragement of optimal growth and development of children. It also manifests itself by failure to provide love, affection, and emotional availability to the child: at its worst, the child might be rejected and badly affected by parental hostility and dismissiveness. While physical neglect and abuse are more obvious and easier to recognise (because of distinct marks in cases of physical abuse and observable features in cases of physical neglect), emotional abuse and neglect can go unnoticed for a long time. The child might appear well-dressed, clean, and well provided for, but is seldom played with, spoken to, looked at, comforted, attended to when in difficulties, or cuddled. Verbal and physical contact is limited, and emotional input is insignificant in cases of neglect; while harsh, denigrating, threatening, disapproving, and rejecting behaviour is usual in cases of abuse. When children live in such a hostile, anxiety-arousing, or indifferent atmosphere, their physical, cognitive, intellectual, and emotional development is quite likely to be arrested. In infancy curtailed development will tend to show itself in insecure attachment and delayed psychomotor development; in pre-school children it will be manifest in disturbance of social and emotional behaviour; in school-age children it will show itself in serious learning deficits and behavioural problems; and in adolescence it will appear as an inability to become more independent and self-sufficient, and may spark an identity crisis.

Erik Erikson has argued that each developmental stage has to meet certain social demands. At each stage a conflict between opposite poles in a pattern of reciprocity between the self and others has to be resolved. Table 6.1 shows the major hazards of achieving age-appropriate tasks and what facilitates happy and healthy development.

Table 6.1   Developmental tasks

Approximate age period	Characteristic to be achieved	Major hazard to achievement	Facilitators
Birth to 2 years	Sense of trust or security	Neglect, abuse, or deprivation of consistent and appropriate love in infancy; harsh or early weaning	If parents meet the preponderance of the infant's needs, the child develops a stronger sense of trust than of mistrust
2 to 4 years	Sense of autonomy – child viewing self as an individual in his/her own right, apart from parents although dependent on them	Conditions which interfere with the child's achieving a feeling of adequacy or the learning of skills such as talking	If the parents reward the child's successful actions and do not shame his or her failures (say in bowel or bladder control), the child's sense of autonomy will outweigh the sense of shame and doubt

4 to 6 years	Sense of initiative – period of vigorous reality-testing, imagination, and imitation of adult behaviour	Overly strict discipline, internalisation of rigid ethical attitudes which interfere with the child's spontaneity and reality-testing	If parents accept the child's curiosity and do not put down the need to know and to question, the child's sense of initiative will outweigh the sense of guilt
6 to 11 years	Sense of duty and accomplishment – laying aside of fantasy and play; undertaking real tasks, developing academic and social competencies	Excessive competition, personal limitations, or other conditions which lead to experiences of failure, resulting in feeling of inferiority and poor work habits	If the child encounters more success than failure at home and at school, he or she will have a greater sense of industry than of inferiority
12 to 15 years	Sense of identity – clarification in adolescence of who one is, and what one's role is	Failure of society to provide clearly defined roles and standards; formation of cliques which provide clear but not always desirable roles and standards	If the young person can reconcile diverse roles, abilities, and values and see their continuity with past and future, the sense of personal identity will not give way to a sense of role diffusion
15 to adulthood	Sense of intimacy – ability to establish close personal relationships with members of both sexes	Cultural and personal factors which lead to psychological isolation or to formal rather than warm personal relations	If parents allow young people to develop relationships with peers of both sexes, encourage independence, and support youngster to build interest in education and work, then they will be prepared for life

Source: Adapted from Erikson (1965) by Herbert (1989) and Iwaniec (1995).

INFANCY

Parental physical care, attention, and emotional availability are essential for the child to start off optimistically on life's journey. In order to provide those ingredients, parents need to be willing and committed to nurture and to love. They also need to have an environment and means to meet these commitments, as well as guidance and support to exercise their parental obligations and duties.

There are various theories stressing different tasks. Erikson (1963), taking a broad view, stated that the essential task of infancy is the development of basic trust in others. He believed that during the early months and years of life a baby learns whether the world is a good and secure place in which to live, or a source of pain, misery, frustration, and uncertainty. Because a baby is dependent on others for so long, it needs to know that it can depend on the outside world. If its basic needs are met it is thought to develop a 'basic trust' in the world and thus to evolve a nucleus of self-trust, which is more important for later development.

But how does the trust show itself in a child's behaviour early on in life? The first demonstration of social trust in the baby is the ease of feeding, the depth of sleep, and the relaxation of bowels. Later on it is demonstrated when the infant will let its mother out of its sight without undue anxiety or rage. It is thought that if the maternal child-rearing techniques (such as providing comfort, familiarity of images, satiation, and relief of pain) are consistent and predictable then the child slowly develops a sense of ego-identity based on remembered and anticipated sensations of things and people. According to Erikson, a baby who smiles easily demonstrates trust.

What are these early developmental needs? Babies need to be fed regularly and be given appropriate food, to be kept in a warm and clean place, to be changed regularly to avoid nappy rash, to be washed and bathed, and attended to if in distress or discomfort. They also need a place of relative calm and a peaceful nurturing atmosphere. If these basic needs are not given due attention, the child's health, growth, and well-being will suffer. Infants need attention and stimulation to help them to develop basic skills like sitting, crawling, walking, talking, and the social behaviour of participation and sharing. They need sensitive training in bowel- and bladder-control. They need to learn how to eat, to dress, to respond to parental requests, and to acquire self-discipline. They need to develop a sense of belonging and of security, and to build up basic trust for an attachment to their parents and siblings. They need close nurturing physical contact (being picked up when in distress, comforted when they hurt themselves, and soothed when disturbed or frightened). The quality and quantity of basic needs provision will determine a child's development and level of attachment to its carers: it also lays the foundation for future accomplishments and the ways the child will perceive and relate to people around it. Neglected and abused children suffer from the omission of parental care, attention, and affection: as a result their physical and psychological development tends to be impaired. The most common problem resulting from physical and emotional neglect during infancy is failure to thrive (see Chapter 7). Additionally, the development of an affectionate bond between parents and children tends to be weak and insecure: parent–child interaction is often cold, indifferent, and, at times, hostile.

Seriously emotionally neglected and abused infants are observed to be withdrawn, lethargic, apathetic, and, in the most adverse circumstances, depressed. Since they live in an emotional vacuum (unattended and unstimulated) they revert to self-stimulating behaviour like rocking, head-banging, and pulling out hair. They often sit or lie motionless, or are irritable.

ATTACHMENT BEHAVIOUR

Neglected and rejected children do not show distress and do not protest when they are separated from their parents. They tend to go with anybody and do not discriminate between known and unknown persons. While in hospital or in a foster-home, they tend to relate in a similar way to a nurse or a foster-mother: however, because of their insecurity they are unable to move freely to explore the environment in an organised and purposeful way. They either cling to the parents or aimlessly run about in a disruptive fashion. They also appear to be frightened and anxious.

Attachment is assessed in a situation unfamiliar to the child in the presence of the mother, and the child's reactions to separation from, and reunion with, the mother are observed. As outlined in Chapter 5, three patterns of insecure attachment have been identified: anxious-avoidant infants, anxious-resistant infants (Ainsworth, 1980; Aber & Cicchetti, 1984), and disorganised/disoriented infants (Main & Solomon, 1980). Anxious-avoidant infants treat the mother and stranger alike and avoid the mother upon reunion. Anxious-resistant infants show little curiosity about their surroundings, and they often struggle or become rigid when being comforted. Disoriented children behave in a confused way because an abusing parent frequently behaves in two different ways (either being caring or abusive): the source of fear is also a source of comfort, and, therefore, they get very confused. It is suggested that anxiously attached infants are more difficult to care for, and in turn their mothers have been found to be less sensitive and less responsive to their babies. Abused and neglected children will cling to their mothers and/or show negative effects like screaming, fear, apprehension, and rigidity. It has been postulated that maltreatment during infancy produces an insecure attachment over a period of time that adversely affects the child's later intellectual and socio-emotional development (Ainsworth, 1980; Steinhauer, 1983).

Many studies in developmental neurobiology indicate the importance of early stimulation, nurturing, and education which are grounded in three major findings. First, in infancy there are dramatic increases in the number of connections between brain cells. Second, there are critical periods when experience shapes the development of the brain. Third, enriched environments cause more connections to form in the brain than impoverished ones. However, there is evidence that early deprivation can be made good if satisfactory care is provided (Blakemore, 2005).

Brain development begins well before birth. The human baby is born with almost all the brain cells it will ever have. An adult human brain contains about 100 bn brain cells (neurons): at birth the brain has a similar number. However, after birth the brain changes substantially and undergoes several waves of reorganisation. Following birth the increase in weight and volume of the brain is due to the growth of synapses or the connections between the neurons. Babies come to this world with two neural systems which serve different functions. The first system, called experience-expectant, has survival value and is already established at birth, e.g. heart rate, breathing, etc. The second neural system is based on interaction and sensory reaction. The purpose of the neural connections, which are 'experience-dependent', is that they need another person to provide stimulation such as sound, touch, vision, etc. If a child is provided with new experiences (in other words is attended to and stimulated), then new synapses will be created and the existing ones will be strengthened. A fundamental characteristic of brain development is that environmental experiences are as important as genetic programmes. Greenough, Black, & Wallace (1987) examined how the environment affects the brain synapses during development. They found that an child's early enriched environment is very important, but not to be exaggerated. Their experimental work would suggest that extra stimulation leads to an increase in synaptic connections, but it might be more accurate to say that a 'normal' environment, rather than a deprived one, leads to more synaptic connections. It is unlikely that children brought up in any normal child-oriented environment could be deprived of sensory input. The research, however, suggests that there is a threshold of environmental richness below which a baby's brain could be harmed. Children who are seriously neglected, both physically and emotionally, are at risk of being damaged intellectually (Perry, 2004).

EARLY CHILDHOOD

The major developmental task at this stage of life according to Erikson (1963) is the attainment of a sense of autonomy. The child begins to function as an individual, doing its own thing and trying new skills. The child is trying to make sense of the environment and tries to control it; striving for mastery and control often reaches a peak between two and three years of age. Children struggle with the conflicting needs within themselves and against parental control. Toddlers and older toddlers (two to five years of age) are, at the best of times, a handful, and require constant supervision and a lot of patience from their parents. Not for nothing are they referred to as 'terrible twos', and parents often find them demanding and exhausting. Their apparently endless energy, explorations, questions, displays of negativism, temper tantrums, and ambivalence are often perceived by parents as oppositional behaviour and sheer naughtiness, leading to interactional problems and distortion of the parent–child relationship. Pre-school children's cognitive, emotional and intellectual developments require sensitive and supportive conditions to promote their abilities. Parents should allow the child to persist in trying to experiment with autonomy. This helps to build up a strong foundation of self-confidence and delight in independent behaviour. But, as a child is a learner, parents need to be available for them to give instruction, guidance, offer a helping hand (although this is not always accepted), to teach, cajole, and praise. Parents need to allow the child to try tasks that may be beyond it at that stage, for only by encouraging the child to engage in new tasks can the parents hope to promote the youngster's sense of competence.

Continual discouragement and/or criticism of a child by parents inculcate an overwhelming sense of shame and self-doubt in that child. Such children lack confidence in their abilities to perform, and they expect to fail at what they do. In order to avoid criticism they refrain from all kinds of new activities. As a result, the process of learning new skills becomes slow and painful. Feelings of self-confidence, a sense of achievement and self-worth are replaced by constant doubting and consequently developmental delays. Maltreated children tend to develop an unfavourable self-image: they do not like themselves and tend to believe that they are to blame for whatever goes wrong around them. Positive self-attitudes are the basic ingredients of positive mental health, and negative self-concepts are among the critical predispositions of maladjustment. The way parents treat children will determine what those children think about themselves. The expressed attitudes and behaviour of the carers will provide vital information to the children about their achievements, goodness and worth. Living up to parental expectations (or always failing to do so in the case of over critical or hostile parents) will become part of their self-concept (Herbert, 1974).

The major hazards for optimal development during this stage are parental unavailability and hostile restrictions (which interfere with the child's acquisition of personal adequacy and development of skills such as speech, locomotion, toilet-training, competencies in eating and dressing, playing, self-control, and ability to discriminate between emotions in others). Social behaviour with peers and adults tends to be more aggressive on the one hand and withdrawn on the other. Since such children are deficient in social maturity due to persistent abuse, their interaction with other children is fraught and problematic. Their attachment, similar to that of infants, is indiscriminate and unselective. They tend to attach themselves to anybody who shows attention and kindness, and long for physical contact and affection. Neglected toddlers are rather inactive and deficient in social skills.

Severely emotionally abused and neglected children do not communicate with their carers and, at times, are completely mute. They tend to ignore requests and do not respond to parental attempts to engage them in conversation. Language development appears to be most affected in deprived environments: since relationships between the emotionally maltreated child and its siblings are marked by hostility and avoidance, there is little opportunity to practise language skills at home. These children spend a lot of time in social isolation, away from normal family interactions, and this does not promote communication and the development of interpersonal behaviour. Prugh and Harlow (1962) describe this dilemma as 'masked deprivation', where the child is physically at home but emotionally does not belong there. Home observations show that the target child is seldom included (in a positive way) in everyday family interactions. There is a physical distance between parents and the child, and between siblings and the target child. Siblings do not play or communicate with it, and tend to be aggressive and dismissive. The child usually stands 2–3 yards away from them, watching (when the parents are present) or being disruptive (when the parents are not around). Again, the child is seldom seen being close to the others, is never played with, or placed on the mother's lap. Most emotionally abused children are isolated from the rest of the family in order to discipline them; they are often locked up in their bedrooms for many hours as a punishment for any misdemeanour.

Acute emotional abuse and neglect can affect a child's physical growth in terms of poor weight, height, and head circumference. Rapid improvement and acceleration is evident when they are removed to a caring and affectionate environment, such as a foster-home or extended family. A change in social, cognitive, and language development is also observed, although it is not as rapid as physical growth. There is a need to be alert to cruel punishment which is not always visible, but manifests itself as a consequence of maltreatment (for instance, as recurring infections and colds caused by being deprived of bedclothes because of bed-wetting, or by being put into cold water for soiling).

MIDDLE CHILDHOOD

The most commonly identified developmental deficits among 5- to 10-year-old emotionally abused and neglected children are in the areas of academic achievements at school and their ability to relate to the peer group. These researchers found that the maltreated children in comparison with the control sample were two years behind in verbal performance and maths abilities. They also found that maltreated children were seriously failing in one or more subjects and had to have some remedial teaching. Additionally, they discovered that the siblings of maltreated children were also the subject of poor school performance. The latter seems to suggest that academic achievements might be curtailed by a home environment unconducive to learning. It might also be associated with little importance being placed on academic achievements in these families. Belsky (1980) stated that social and family factors (associated with child abuse and neglect) might contribute to the developmental deficits generally. These factors might include: marital strife, lack of social support, inappropriate supervision of children, and irregular school attendance.

In her study of emotionally abused and neglected children, Iwaniec (2004) found that the parents showed a lack of interest in their children's achievements and performance and demonstrated a serious deficit in stimulating and providing opportunities for these children to learn and acquire new knowledge. Out of 31 children, 7 experienced learning difficulties and had poor academic attainments during their primary education. Teachers found that these children were unable to concentrate and to pay attention to the given task. Their problem-solving abilities were poor as were their abilities to read and write. Seven of these children were statemented for special education. Social behaviour in the classroom was marked by aimless overactivity, disrupting their own and their peers' learning, or by an inability to concentrate due to emotional torment experienced at home (e.g. domestic violence) or at school, rejection by peers, and disruptive and antisocial behaviour.

Teachers find children like this attention-seeking on the one hand and detached and uninvolved on the other; such children desperately try to be noticed and accepted by their peers and teachers, but the way they do this is usually aggressive and disruptive, so they are often excluded from peers' play in the playground and outside school activities. They are seldom invited to the birthday parties of other children and are seen as not worthwhile to have around or with whom to make friends. In order to compensate for their rejection by peers some of them will try to become particularly close to the teachers or other adults in the school, like dinner ladies or secretaries: they try to offer assistance (like carrying books or equipment), and tend to follow them around just in case they have the chance to be helpful, appreciated, and wanted. They tend to volunteer to do various tasks at school, or to compete in sport or other competitions, even though they have no abilities to do so. Emotionally abused children, in many cases, show longing and desire to belong and to be wanted, but lack the social skills to get themselves into a circle of peers. Disruptive and aggressive behaviour as well as an inability to observe the 'rules of play' eliminate them from the peer group. Those children who are not performing well academically and who are criticised by the teachers are not easily accepted by their peers.

Additionally, some emotionally abused and neglected children suffer from encopresis and enuresis, and because they smell they are pushed away and rejected by their classmates. Thus the child who has incontinence problems will be isolated and perceived as dirty and revolting. Teachers, too, tend to view them as unpleasant, undesirable, and impossible to manage in the classroom. Sadly, teachers and parents alike tend to believe that soiling and wetting are deliberate and/or the result of sheer laziness to go to the toilet on time, and not because of emotional disturbance brought about by maltreatment. These children might run away from school as a result of ill-treatment there, or might exhibit self-harming behaviour (like scratching to the point of bleeding, wounding with knives or sharp objects, persistent rocking, head-banging, and burning, to mention a few examples) similar to that of psychosocial short-stature children.

All these children, without exception, suffer from very low self-esteem and low self-worth, and their attempts to be accepted, wanted, appreciated, and loved have been unsuccessful at home and often at school. Low self-esteem demonstrates itself in uncertainty, constant doubting, a sense of guilt, a belief that everything which is unfortunate or problematic is their fault, and apologising for everything (whether or not they were responsible for what went wrong) verbally or by writing little notes for parents saying that they love them and they are sorry for being 'bad'. Emotional abuse can also affect a child's physical growth (although not in all cases); it is not unusual to find some children small and thin for their age and showing disturbed eating behaviour (see Chapter 7 on failure to thrive and stunting of growth).

ADOLESCENCE

Adolescence is marked by the biological changes resulting from the onset of puberty and involves navigating and confronting a series of developmental questions as the young person makes the transition from child to adult roles and responsibilities. Challenges relating to independence, social acceptance, levels of sexual activity, and personal identity characterise the pathway from childhood to early adulthood and contribute to long-term psychological health and well-being (Gortmaker, Walker, Weitzman, & Sobol, 1990; Dahl, 2003; Daniel *et al.*, 1999). Psychological maltreatment can compromise young people in their negotiation of these salient developmental tasks. Emotional abuse can significantly interfere with subsequent adaptation, resulting in a host of problems for the individual and for broader society (Cicchetti & Toth, 1995b). A considerable body of evidence suggests that, in addition to the immediate and short-term harm of psychological maltreatment, the consequences of emotional abuse and neglect may not be fully realised until adolescence, and may manifest in a number of behaviours and symptoms.

Mental Health and Interpersonal Problems

Optimal psychological health requires encouragement, love, support, and attention from parents and caregivers. The experience of emotional abuse, for any child, will at least contribute to a setback in the development of psychological adjustment and well-being. Several studies have reported that a history of psychological maltreatment in childhood is strongly predictive of mental-health problems, particularly low moods, hopelessness, and low self-esteem in the teenage years (e.g. Brown *et al.*, 1999; Kaufman, 1991; Kelly *et al.*, 1997; Toth *et al.*, 1992). In comparison with other types of maltreatment (e.g. sexual and/or physical abuse) the experience of emotional abuse appears to have a more deleterious effect on adjustment, and is the stronger predictor of psychological difficulties for adolescents (Crittenden *et al.*, 1994), particularly for females (McGee *et al.*, 1997). Emotional abuse, in the form of parental criticism and verbal hostility, appears to be particularly significant in the development of adjustment difficulties. For example, in a study of 160 young people (aged 11–17), randomly selected from child-protection records, perceptions relating to the levels of parental criticism and verbal hostility were strongly associated with both self-reported levels of internalising and externalising problems (McGee *et al.*, 1997).

In adolescence, the self-concept undergoes its greatest transition and is ultimately consolidated (Oppenheimer, 1990). Excessive parental hostility and the denigration that is implicit in emotional abuse appear to interfere with the development of a healthy self-image. Available retrospective and longitudinal studies have revealed strong associations between levels of parental criticism and excessive self-criticism (Arias, 2004; Koestner, Zuroff, & Powers, 1991). Children and young people appear to internalise the critical voice of the abusive caregiver and come to believe that they are 'bad' and 'worthless'. Continuous disapproval and disparagement are particular problems for the adolescent who remains unreported to child-protection services. As parents/caregivers continue their emotionally abusive behaviour throughout the teenage years, the young person has little relief from parents' opinions and, ultimately, from negative self-perceptions that result. In such an incessant and unremitting adverse environment, young people acquire intensely negative self-images that have evolved over time, and this may limit their abilities to manage their own emotional states, solve problems, and manage new or stressful situations (Kaufman & Cicchetti, 1989; Shields *et al.*, 1994).

Experiences of current or previous psychological maltreatment also appear to place the child at risk of interpersonal difficulties during adolescence. The relationships these teenagers establish outside the abusive care system tend to be characterised by withdrawal, avoidance, instability, and difficulties with trust (Carlson *et al.*, 1989; Varia, Abidin, & Dass, 1996). For such young people, relationships with others are often perceived as a source of disappointment and dissatisfaction, and would appear to limit opportunities for what could otherwise be corrective and supportive experience.

Cognitive Difficulties and Educational Outcomes

Detrimental effects of emotional maltreatment on school performance are among the most thoroughly researched, as is clear from the literature investigating the consequences of psychological abuse and neglect on the child. Difficulties evident in middle-school years appear to continue throughout development, and place young people at the risk of continued academic failure during adolescence (Kelly *et al.*, 1997). Specific deficits are observed in the areas of reading, languages, and maths (Kurtz *et al.*, 1993; Oates, 1996). Teachers report that children with a history of maltreatment struggle in their effort to adapt to the demands and tasks of the school environment. It is possible that these preliminary difficulties interact with the cognitive and emotional consequences of the abuse and intensify the delay and disruption in the acquisition of basic skills. As the learning process is sequential in nature, young people may feel overwhelmed and incompetent as tasks become increasingly complex (particularly in secondary school). As the child progresses through year groups, its academic failure may become more pronounced and can serve as another blow to already fragile self-esteem.

Young people who have been subjected to psychological maltreatment report low educational and vocational aspirations in adolescence (Malinosky-Rummell & Hansen, 1993). Teenagers with a history of emotional abuse and neglect are also more likely to be disruptive, display discipline problems, repeat year groups, be suspended, and finish school without any qualifications (Kendall-Tackett & Eckenrode, 1996). Poor school performance, poor relationships with teachers, little support from parents, and lack of stimulation and/or help with homework provide little incentive to engage in the education process. Prematurely abandoning a school career can independently contribute its own set of problems for the adolescent, as leaving school early is associated with reduced economic opportunities, long-term unemployment, and lower levels of life satisfaction in adulthood.

Social and Behavioural Outcomes

The picture of the young person with social difficulties (having few friends, being isolated, and avoiding peer-interaction) is maintained throughout early adolescence and young adulthood (Hildyard & Wolfe, 2002). There is also an accumulating body of research evidence which would suggest that the experience of psychological maltreatment (whether the behaviour was experienced in childhood, adolescence, or endured throughout development) becomes more pronounced in the teenage years and is manifested in a host of social and behavioural problems, not just interpersonal and relationship difficulties. Self-reported drug and alcohol uses are significantly higher in samples that have been victimised by abuse (Dembo *et al.*, 1990a; Widom & White, 1997).

Many researchers in the field of emotional abuse attribute the high rate of drug use, delinquency, and pregnancy observed among teenagers as coping mechanisms and means of escape from adverse conditions endured in the family home (Latimer, 1998). Young people may use drugs and alcohol in order to manage the trauma of abuse and neglect, as a means of developing relationships with peers, or to cope with a mental-health difficulty with its roots in the experience of childhood or continuous maltreatment (Ireland & Widom, 1994). Teenagers may engage in antisocial behaviour as means of reacting against experiences they currently endure at home or have experienced in the past (Agnew, 1992). Although ultimately self-destructive, the problems are often a direct symptom of the history or current experience of emotional abuse and neglect that teenagers have endured from abusive parents or carers. Unfortunately, the psychological and social consequences of maltreatment set the stage for further difficulties (and contribute to a host of negative outcomes for the person victimised by emotional abuse) which persist into early adulthood (Johnson, Cohen, Brown, Smailes, & Bernstein, 1999; Widom, 1999b).

SUMMARY

It would appear that emotional abuse and neglect may have an overriding role in poor developmental attainment and may contribute significantly to the development of emotional and behavioural problems in children. Neglect and rejection during infancy are associated with insecure and anxious attachment, which (if it persists) may impair a child's intellectual, cognitive, social, and emotional development. At the toddler stage, maltreatment of this kind may delay language development and distort personality formation, peer-relations, and social adjustments. In middle childhood, the maltreatment will contribute to poor performance at school, learning difficulties, lack of motivation, and behaviour problems (Brassard *et al.*, 1987; Garbarino *et al.*, 1986; McGee & Wolfe, 1991), and in adolescence in distortion of identity, development of independence, poor self-esteem, and various behavioural and relationship problems.

CHAPTER 7

FAILURE TO THRIVE AND EMOTIONAL STUNTING IN GROWTH

CONTENTS

INTRODUCTION

During the first year after birth, human growth is quicker than at any other period during childhood, decreasing rapidly until the end of the third year, and then continuing at about one-third of its post-natal rate until puberty. However, there are some children who do not grow at the same rate as others. Instead, they lag behind. These children have been described as failing to thrive, and, compared to their peers, they are significantly smaller and can be expected to have poor outcomes (Iwaniec, 2004). They can be found in all social classes and levels of society. Without help, their physical growth, cognitive progress, and emotional development can be expected to be negatively affected, with a high risk of developmental delays, behavioural problems, abuse, neglect, or even death. If successful intervention does not take place at an early stage, failure to thrive may lead to the distortion of the parent–child relationship, serious attachment disorders, disturbed behaviour, developmental impairments, and emotional stunting of growth (Iwaniec, 1995). This chapter will deal with growth-faltering in babies and more acute failure to thrive, resulting in psychosocial short stature.

WHAT IS FAILURE TO THRIVE?

From the day a baby is born, parents will focus their attention on the child's growth and development; their major preoccupation will be connected with feeding, health, and the baby's contentment, and they will be eager to see how much weight the baby gains, how it responds to their nurturing and what developmental progress it makes. In order for a baby to grow adequately and according to expected norms, it will need to get sufficient nutrition on a regular basis; this should be provided in a manner which will be anxiety-free, enjoyable, and satisfying. So, to give and accept nutrition is at the core of the emerging relationship and interactional synchrony between mother and child. Mutual satisfaction and success of feeding and caring will determine not only the speed of physical growth but also psychomotor development and general responsiveness and alertness. In a secure, caring home, and fuelled by adequate nutrition, children will thrive, giving parents pleasure and confidence in their parenting. In homes riddled with conflict, stress, disharmony, emotional coldness, or indifference, mental illness, substance and alcohol abuse, poverty, or where parents are ill-informed about children's developmental needs, the children's progress may be impaired if nutritional intake and the quality of nurturing are inadequate for their chronological ages.

The term 'failure to thrive' (FTT) is applied to infants whose weight, height, head circumference, and general psychosocial development are significantly below age-related norms and whose well-being causes concern. In the United Kingdom, current practice is to investigate further those children whose weight is below the second centile. Children who drop down two or more percentile curves on the weight chart within a brief period are also likely to be evaluated further to determine what led to rapid loss of weight. In the USA, common practice is to use the fifth centile as a cut-off point for weight.

FTT is generally defined in terms of growth. When children are undernourished they fail to gain weight. After a while their growth in length also falters. Most children are diagnosed as failing to thrive when their weight or height percentiles are low, and others are diagnosed when their growth crosses the percentile line downwards. As undernutrition also impairs brain growth, so the head circumference is measured as well.

Although still identified primarily by physical-growth measures, it is now recognised that FTT goes beyond the physical: the term describes a condition rather than a specific disease, and consequently it has many causes which may be organic or psychosocial, or a mixture of both. It is conceived as a variable syndrome of severe growth retardation, delayed skeletal maturation, and problematic psychosocial development, which are often associated with illness, inadequate nutrition for normal growth, acute feeding difficulties, and motor dysfunction, disturbed mother–child interaction, insecure attachment, family dysfunctioning, and poverty (Iwaniec, 2000).

FTT is normally diagnosed within the first two years of life, although its effects can be observed much later as a rule, resulting in stunting of growth. It can emerge at different times in an infant's life, as a result of illness or trauma, but undernutrition during early infancy can have the most detrimental effects as the nutritional requirements at that time are at their most crucial. Given the rapid period of growth, particularly brain growth, which occurs during the first two years, particular attention should be given to appropriate provision of food and stimulation. Estimates of prevalence have varied from as many as 10% of children seen in outpatients' clinics in both urban and rural areas, to 1% of all paediatric hospitalisation (Bithoney & Newberger, 1987). Skuse, Wolke and Reilly (1992) estimated that FTT probably affects 3.3% of the paediatric population at some time.

The causes of FTT are often divided into three categories: organic, non-organic, and combined. Organic FTT is thought to result from illnesses or genetic conditions, while non-organic FTT may derive from inadequate parenting and from various environmental factors. Combined FTT may have both organic and non-organic origins. In recent years it was recognised that such divisions of FTT are unhelpful and can be misleading as children who are failing to thrive because of illness can also be neglected, abused, and maltreated. Whatever the sources of FTT, it is almost always associated with undernutrition, whether that is caused by a disease that blocks or interferes with the absorption of nutrients or by an inadequate food intake for the child's age and size (Dykman, Ackerman, Loizou, & Casey, 2000).

There is substantial variation in the reasons why some children do not get a sufficient amount of food into their system. Some may have sucking/eating problems and oral motor dysfunction, while others may not be acquiring sufficient nutrition because of parental lack of understanding of what, when, and how to feed. Some may be neglected and others rejected. In addition, some parents may react to presenting problems and to caring tasks in many different ways. Some worry and become anxious about their children's poor intake of food and poor growth; others become angry and frustrated; some may perceive their children's refusal of food as a personal affront, involving rejection by the children themselves; and yet others may assume that their children are simply not hungry. Parental attitudes to food will play a role as well. How food is presented to children, and what is fed to them, will often establish that fears concerning potential obesity of children will be important factors in those parental attitudes. Some will deliberately withhold food, and some will fabricate illnesses; in both instances the children will fail to thrive.

Children will also react differently to parental behaviour: some will be anxious, apprehensive and fearful, while others will withdraw, become lethargic and detached, or be irritable and demanding. Thus, the behaviour of parents and of children may negatively influence each other and lead to aversive and painful interactions, resulting not only in poor growth, but also in distortion of relationships and in neglect and abuse.

All these children and their families need help. Furthermore, help is needed early on to prevent the escalation of problems associated with attachment, interaction, relationships, and inadequate growth and development. Unresolved early difficulties can have a long-term negative affect on both children and parents. These children are not always identified as potentially at risk at the onset of growth-faltering and interactional problems. If a wait-and-see approach is adopted, leaving things to chance, vulnerable children and equally vulnerable parents may suffer. Some children grow out of problems, but some do not; for others, however, as they grow, difficulties grow with them, resulting in emotional stunting of growth due to emotional maltreatment and acute stress they experience.

EMOTIONAL STUNTING IN GROWTH

It is believed that emotional abuse, parental rejection, and associated stress are the major contributory factors bringing about stunting of growth. Children who suffer from such stunting of growth are referred to as having psychosocial short stature: such children are exceptionally short and remain stunted in height for a considerable time, yet there may be no obvious organic reason for this. Weight is below that expected for height, though, exceptionally, weight may be appropriate for height, and the child might appear well-nourished, but such appearances may be misleading at first glance because neither weight nor height is normal for the chronological age.

Medical investigations show that quite often there is microcephaly, and bone-age is, as a rule, delayed. Gohlke, Khadilkar, Skuse, and Stanhope (1998), for example, found that the bone-age in their sample was delayed on average by 1.9 years, and severe delays in bone maturation of more than 3 years was observed in 13% of their patients.

This type of FTT acquired various labels over the years: e.g. it was named 'deprivation-dwarfism' by Silver and Finkelstein (1967), 'linear growth retardation' by Skuse, Gilmour, Tian, and Hindmarsh (1994b), and 'psychosocial short stature' by Spinner and Siegel (1987). These terms describe a syndrome of physical abnormalities characterised by extreme short stature, bizarre eating patterns, disturbed toileting, destructiveness, defiant hostility, acute non-compliance, self-harming behaviour, serious developmental delays, and sleeping problems. Relationships of these children with parents, but in particular with mothers, are marked by hostility, rejection, and mutual antagonism, with pronounced disturbed attachment of children to mothers and lack of a maternal emotional bond with their children. Because such children are unloved and unwanted, and because they are reared in social isolation and an emotional vacuum, their cognitive, emotional, language, and social development is seriously retarded and their behaviour is a cause of concern.

This disorder has been known for many years and extensively studied. Some investigators hypothesise on the existence of a physiological pathway whereby emotional deprivation affects the neuroendocrine system regulating growth. Researchers such as Talbot, Sobel, Burke, Lindeman, and Kaufman (1947), Patton and Gardner (1962), Powell, Brasel, and Blizzard (1967), and Blizzard and Bulatovic (1993) favoured a theory of emotional influence on growth, with secondary-growth hormone insufficiencies as a main cause of psychosocial short stature. Charles Whitten (1976), on the other hand, concluded that such children were simply starved and therefore did not grow.

In recent years there has been a considerable debate about whether psychosocial short stature is the extension of earlier FTT and whether it is in any way qualitatively different as the child gets older and is more mobile and more independent. The point of separation between FTT and psychosocial short stature differs among researchers and clinicians: some have set an arbitrary age-limit, while others have used clinical presentation and findings, including various hormonal studies, to differentiate one from the other. The range for the point of separation has been between 18 months and 4 years. It was argued by MacMillan (1984) that this dichotomy occurred because children under the age of 2 years are difficult to measure in length, but relatively easy to measure in weight. He argued that a child under the age of 2 is more likely to be recognised as being abnormal if it is underweight, as opposed to only being of short stature.

Growth failure, as a rule, begins in infancy during the first few months of a child's life, but stunting of growth can occur much later, even at six or eight years of age if a child is exposed to acute stress, or experiences trauma and all forms of abuse (including sexual abuse). Additionally, attachment discontinuity, caused by being removed from home and placed in care, by witnessing frequent family violence, by acrimonious parental divorce and pressure being put on a child, and by traumatic, unexpected events in family life (like death, threats, and abandonment), can trigger in some children acute emotional distress and helplessness, which in turn can arrest growth-hormone function. Because children so affected are unloved and unwanted and, as a rule, rejected, they do not get support, protection, and help from the parents to buffer them from emotional distress; on the contrary, they are often blamed for traumatic events in the family one way or another.

Most of the short-stature children suffer, or are likely to suffer, significant harm and, therefore, require child-protection attention. How bad the relationship can get between mother and child in cases of psychosocial short stature and what effect it can have on a child can be illustrated by the case of James and Mark.

CASE STUDY

The case is of particular interest as it involved two brothers born five minutes apart, each weighing the same at birth (5 lb 3 oz [2.355 kg]), being of the same length, and both parents delighted to have two healthy babies. At the point of referral (24 months after birth), however, they were almost a lifetime apart.

Let us look at the differences in their appearance, emotional expressions, physical growth, interaction with their mother, demonstration of attachment behaviour to the mother and to each other, their mutual relationships, and expression of self-confidence and self-esteem. We also need to examine differences in maternal attitude towards each child, emotional availability, sensitivity, and level of affection (or lack of it) shown to each of them.

> James was a chubby, rosy-cheeked, boisterous two-year-old, who appeared to be a happy, mischievous boy, who ran, played, talked, and laughed. He went to his mother for help and comfort, and cuddled up spontaneously to her; he responded readily to her attention and affection; she smiled at him, provided comfort, showed concern, picked him up, sat him on her lap, played with him, answered his questions, watched his movements, showed pleasure in his achievements, corrected him in an encouraging way, and warned him when he was in danger. Her voice was soft when she talked to him.

> On the edge of the room, like a stranger, stood his twin brother Mark, his posture rigid, staring fixedly. He was a sad, lethargic-looking child, very small and extremely thin; his pale face threw into relief the dark shadows under his eyes; he remained in one spot, as if at attention; he gazed unswervingly at his mother, who took no notice of him. When asked to call Mark over to her she looked in his direction; as she did so her face hardened and her eyes became angry; she addressed him with a peremptory command; when he hesitated she showed irritation and shouted at him.

> Observations of his interaction with his mother confirmed that she never smiled at him, never picked him up, never sat him on her lap, never played with him, never showed satisfaction when he did something praiseworthy, and never encouraged him in the pursuit of new activities. She told him off for minor misdemeanours, and persistently criticised and shamed him. The only physical contact came about when she fed, bathed, or dressed him, and at such times her handling was rough and she seldom spoken to him. When she approached him he appeared to be frightened, and occasionally burst into tears. He never came to her for comfort or help, and she never approached him, except to carry out the bare essentials of care and control. Living standards

in the household were high, and both children were meticulously clean, well-dressed, and materially well provided-for. However, James and Mark did not play together, but James frequently pushed his brother and smacked him. The ensuing cries of Mark were usually ignored by his mother. Looking at Mark and James it was hard to believe that they were twins who were the same weight at birth. At the point when the case was referred to the social services (some two years after the birth of the twins) it was impossible to see that they were exactly the same age, or indeed were twins at all. Mark was half the size in weight and only reached his brother's shoulders in height. (See Figure 7.1: James' and Mark's growth chart.)

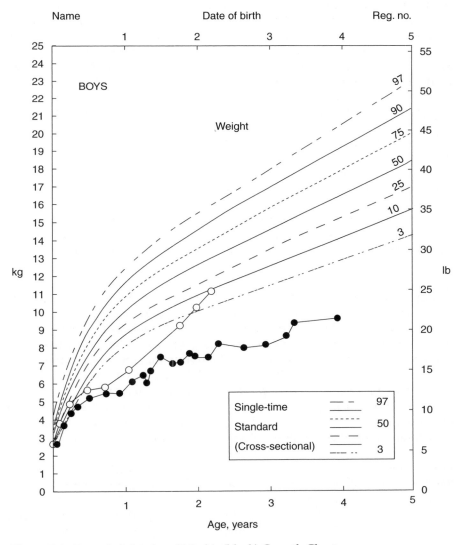

Figure 7.1 James's (white) and Mark's (black) Growth Chart

CAUSAL MECHANISMS

It is believed that prolonged and severe emotional abuse and rejection produces a high and continuous level of stress in children, which affects the rate of linear growth and functioning of the secretion of growth hormones. Even if some of them eat a huge amount of food (if food is available) they remain extremely small for their age. Although the precise mechanism of growth-hormone arrest is not clear, it can be assumed that emotional factors play an important role. Once the child is removed from an abusive environment its growth quickly accelerates, but when returned to it a marked deterioration occurs and behaviour worsens. Observations were made that when such children were hospitalised their endocrine function normalised and growth hormones were secreted again, but the growth hormones ceased to function when these children returned to emotionally insulting homes (Spinner & Siegel, 1987; Skuse et al., 1996; Iwaniec, 2004). Similar observations were made in the foster-homes regarding rapid gain in weight and height and decrease in emotionally disturbing behaviour while being looked after by supportive substitute carers, and equally rapid loss of weight and stunting of growth when returned to an emotionally abusive environment. Interestingly, it is not just a simple matter of merely replacing the growth hormone. Numerous investigative studies have shown that even when, and if, these children are treated with hormone-replacement therapy there is no increase in growth or resolution of other endocrine abnormalities until the child is removed from the continuously stressful and emotionally abusive environment (Goldson, 1987; Iwaniec, 2004). Indeed, many researchers have postulated that diagnoses of psychosocial short stature can be made only on the basis of removal from the stressful environment and subsequent increase in growth velocity.

However, it needs to be noted that while growth in terms of weight and height increases rapidly when these children are cared for by different people and living away from home, behavioural and emotional problems tend to persist for a considerable time. The carers charged with looking after these children require good understanding of why their behaviour is so disturbed, and they need considerable help in managing various emotional and behavioural problems. Frequent breakdowns of foster-placements are associated with unawareness of presenting problems and lack of constructive advice on how to help these very troubled children. Some of them need individual therapeutic work to overcome some deeply seated emotional turmoil and pain. (See Chapters 12 and 14 for therapeutic information.)

Problem profiles of these children are extensive and serious, affecting all areas of their lives, indicating omission of meeting crucial developmental needs in a manner which is supportive, sensitive, and responsive. The parenting style observed in such cases goes far beyond neglect and a deficit in parenting skills, as it is based on rejection and lack of commitment. Scapegoating of these children is a common feature in such families, not only demonstrated by the parents but also by siblings. Behavioural and emotional problems are acute and often of long duration, ranging from defiant aggression, disturbed toileting, destructiveness, and non-compliance, to bizarre eating patterns, self-harming, fire-setting, withdrawal, depressive moods, apprehension, and profound insecurity.

Relationships of such children with parents or carers are marked by hostility and active rejection. At school they are unable to concentrate, follow instructions,

Table 7.1 Profile of psychosocial short stature

Growth retardation	Developmental retardation
Child's height and weight and head circumference below expected norms	Language Social Motor
Physical appearance	Intellectual
Small, thin, enlarged stomach	Cognitive
Disproportionate body fluid	Emotional Toilet-training
Characteristic features	**Behaviour**
(a) Bizarre eating behaviour, excessive eating, an obsessive preoccupation with food, hoarding food, begging food from strangers, eating non-food items, searching for food during night and scavenging food from waste-bins, voracious eating, gorging, and vomiting	Bizarre eating pattern (over-eating), soiling, wetting, smearing, defiance, demanding, destructiveness, whining, fire-setting, attention-seeking, screaming, aggression, short attention-span, poor sleeping, head-banging, rocking, scratching, cutting
(b) Some eat very little – starved appearance, characterised by poor appetite, chronic nutritional deficiencies	**Psychological description**
(c) Attachment disorder Mutually antagonistic relationship Active rejection Hostile or extremely poor mother–child interaction and relationship Addressing mother as 'Miss', 'Lady' (elective mutism) Lack of proper stranger anxiety Insecure and avoidant attachment style	Withdrawal, expressionless face, detachment, depression, sadness, minimal or no smiling, diminished vocalisation, refusal to speak to mother, staring blankly at people or objects, unresponsiveness, lack of cuddliness, lack of confidence, low self-esteem, eager to be helpful and useful, craving for attention and affection, overreaction when given praise or attention, stubbornness
School attainments	
IQ below average, poor learning performance, difficulty in concentrating, poor relationships with peers, disliked by peers and teachers, disruptive, manipulative	

Source: From Iwaniec (2004). *Children who fail to thrive: A practice guide*. Chichester: John Wiley & Sons.

and apply themselves to any work for more than a few minutes. They tend to be disruptive and chronically attention-seeking in the classroom or in the nursery, alienating themselves from the peer group and provoking resentment from teachers. Their school attainments are poor. As a rule they are disliked and avoided by peers, which results in social isolation in the classroom, playground, and in the neighbourhood in which they live. They do not seem to appeal to people with whom they interact because (as is often stated) of their disruptive, attention-seeking, and frequently aggressive and spiteful behaviour. They are seldom invited to other children's birthday parties or to their homes for play. Table 7.1 sets out their characteristics.

HYPERPHAGIC AND ANOREXIC SHORT-STATURE CHILDREN

Children of short stature are divided into two groups. The division is dictated by their eating behaviour: either overeating or undereating. Children who overeat are labelled as hyperphagic, and those who undereat are called anorexic. Their behavioural profile differs somewhat as well.

Hyperphagic children are those who present excessive and bizarre eating behaviour such as: having a high hunger drive; preoccupation with food and eating; drinking excessively, even from toilet bowls or puddles on the street; hoarding food; searching for food during the night; eating non-food items; scavenging food from waste-bins; eating other people's leftovers; and eating voraciously and gorging. Additionally, they are poor sleepers and present disturbed toileting behaviour (smearing faeces over their belongings and urinating in inappropriate places, e.g. over the bed or in the corners of the room). Destructiveness, short attention-spans, and poor social relationships are evident in most cases. They tend to steal things from other children or parents, and lie, either to put the blame on others or to attract others' attention.

Anorexic children are very poor eaters, have little appetite, show faddiness, and refuse to eat. When pressed to eat they heave, store food in their mouths, and chew and swallow with difficulty. They tend to be anxious, apprehensive, withdrawn, passive, and unable to stand up for themselves. Relationships with other family members are poor and marked by fear and apprehension. While at school they tend to be excessively quiet and uninvolved, unable to concentrate, and are often bullied by other children.

GROWTH-HORMONE DEFICIENCIES

Gohlke *et al.* (1998), on the basis of their study, note that some children with psychosocial short stature who have been treated with growth hormone do show an adequate initial response, but this is not maintained, and consequently the child does not grow at the required rate. They recommended that psychosocial short stature should be considered in every patient who presents 'idiopathic' growth-hormone deficiency or ineffectiveness of growth-hormone treatment with isolated or multiple pituitary hormone deficiencies. Symptoms, such as abnormal eating habits, hyperphagia, global and serious developmental delay, emotionally disturbed behaviour, enuresis, and encopresis, should be investigated as well as the possibility of sexual and physical abuse. More often than not these children are physically abused. Iwaniec's (2000) findings, from a longitudinal study of subjects who were classified in their childhood as of short stature, indicated that they were often smacked, pushed, pulled by their hair, or punished in a physically painful way (such as being put into a bath of cold water for soiling or wetting).

It was suggested that the most important indicator is excessive overeating (hyperphagia) and this sign accurately predicts the reversibility of growth-hormone insufficiency. Gohlke *et al.* (1998) state that failure to respond to growth-hormone treatment in a child with growth-hormone deficiency may be another presenting sign of psychosocial short stature. These researchers recommended that all children suspected of having growth-hormone deficiency should have a detailed history taken for hyperphagia, polydipsia, hoarding food, and scavenging for food, as these are characteristic symptoms that predict reversibility of growth-hormone deficiency and subsequent catch-up growth. A long time ago MacCarthy and Booth (1970) suggested that an identifying characteristic of psychosocial short stature was the rapid reversal of all abnormal physical signs, with growth acceleration, when the child was removed from the adverse setting and given no treatment other than normal hospital care.

These children are clearly at risk of gross significant harm on a short- and long-term basis, and require urgent attention to prevent escalation of further harm. The 20-year follow-up study reported by Iwaniec (2000) found that those individuals classified as of psychosocial short stature who remained at home had very poor outcomes on personal, educational, employment, relationship, and self-esteem levels, while those who were removed from an abusive situation did much better or very well in every aspect of life.

MANIFESTATION OF DISTURBED BEHAVIOUR

Short-stature children present very disturbed behaviour in several areas which (when identified) should guide the making of appropriate diagnosis and intervention strategies. Some of the most easily observable behaviours are described below.

Bizarre Eating

Some of the eating behaviours were outlined already in the profile of short-stature children, but it is worthwhile to expand further on some characteristic features and to give a few brief examples from clinical practice and research.

Psychosocial short-stature children, primarily those falling into the overeating group (hyperphagic), show an obsessive preoccupation with food. This tends to emerge at an older toddler stage (although an early feeding history is that of undereating, typically characteristic of many failure-to-thrive children). As a rule most parents, when asked at what point overeating and an excessive interest in food started, would say when a child became more mobile, could feed itself, and was more independent. Preoccupation with food is manifested not only by eating more than expected, but by constantly talking about food, asking for food, and making inquiries as to what and when they are going to eat. The first thing a little boy of four would ask (as soon as he came to the nursery) was, 'What is for lunch?' He would follow the nursery nurse, repeating the question until she told him, and then he would engage in some activities. The same pattern of behaviour is often observed and described by nurses in hospitals, especially during the first few days. The impression is that these children fear that food may be withdrawn from them or they may be denied food, so they seek reassurance that they will be fed.

Distorted behaviour around food is expressed by hoarding it in most peculiar places. A girl of seven years used to make little parcels with pretty ribbon bows and neatly store them on the shelves where her toys and books were kept: these parcels contained bread, sausages, chips, and even mashed potatoes. Food is often hidden under beds and pillows, in cupboards, under furniture, and in various drawers.

Begging food from strangers is quite common in severe cases: some children may stop a complete stranger on the street, in the park, or by the house gate, and ask for biscuits, fruit or drinks, saying that they are hungry. This is particularly difficult for the parents to cope with, as they feel they may be judged as neglectful or starving the child. Such parents tend to get very angry, which often leads to punishing the child by withdrawing the next meal to teach a lesson.

Bizarre eating is demonstrated by eating non-food items, such as cotton wool, soil, pieces of paper, cat- or dog-food from bowls on the floor (one boy ate all the fabric from the inside of his continental quilt), and/or drinking from toilet-bowls, from puddles on the street, or the water coming out from drainpipes. Getting up at night in search of food is very common, and such children tend to go through cupboards, fridges, and pantries, and will eat whatever they can find, in enormous quantities.

Nigel, who was eight years old, used to get up at three or four o'clock in the morning, and often ate five to six cans of baked beans, with a whole loaf of sliced bread and a packed of margarine or pot of jam, and drank two litres of milk. Once the parents became aware of his nocturnal eating habits they closed the doors or cupboards or put the food away out of the child's reach. Seldom do those strategies work, as the child will hoard food during the day and eat it at night. Many of these children tend to scavenge food from rubbish-bins both at home and in public places. Nursery, hospital, and school staff have reported that they take food from other children's plates or eat leftovers. Teachers reported that these children steal food from other children's lunch boxes, and parents often complain that they steal food, leaving other members of the family with nothing to eat for breakfast. These children tend to eat quickly and voraciously, hardly chewing the food (to the point of gorging and vomiting). It is not uncommon to find that these children do not eat with the rest of the family; instead they might be given food sitting on the floor away from the table, excluded from normal family interaction at meal-times. This in itself is rejective and dismissive parental behaviour which is questionable and requires attention. The most frequent method of punishment is withdrawal of food. These children are often sent to bed without dinner, even for minor misbehaviour, or are asked to leave the table when they eat messily, to keep their hands up, and to watch others eat. Such food deprivation has been reported to happen even three or four times a week in some cases (Iwaniec, 2004).

Disturbed Toileting

The majority of psychosocial short-stature children show very disturbed toileting behaviour which manifests itself in urinating all over the bed, furniture, or personal belongings, or defaecating into pants, corners of the room, or under the table, as well as smearing faeces on walls, toys, and other people's belongings. Tipping the contents from the potty all over the room is not unusual, and hiding dirty pants in the most unlikely places are common features among these children. This type of behaviour indicates a high level of emotional turmoil and distress, and appears to be aggressive retaliation directed at the primary caregivers to start with, and then extending itself to other people, such as teachers. This kind of behaviour is very offensive to everybody, and it can lead to peer-rejection if it occurs at school. Such children are perceived by schoolmates as disgusting and dirty. Because of the smell they usually become isolated in the classroom (as nobody wants to sit next to them), and in the playground as they are not considered rewarding to play with; thus opportunities to make friends and to engage in social activities, such as swimming and school trips, are eliminated. They react to peer-rejection either by being aggressive and disruptive or by being withdrawn, detached, and avoidant of children's company. They tend to play on their own away from other children or remain in the classroom looking very distressed and sad. There are times when teachers have to send them away from the classroom or send them home because of severe soiling and other children's refusal to be near them.

At home these children are often punished for soiling and wetting in a cruel way, e.g. forcing a child into a bath of cold water to teach it a lesson, making a child wear badly soiled clothes the next day, or not changing wet or soiled bedding. They are called nasty names, are deprived of treats, and more often than not are hit, slapped, and pushed away. At school they are bullied both physically and verbally.

Destructiveness

Most of these children suffer from extremely low self-esteem and lack of confidence. They feel that they are unworthy to have anything, that they are bad and therefore do not deserve to have anything belonging to them. Some of them stated as adults that tearing their clothing and breaking toys was done as self-punishment. Others remember tearing bedclothes to pieces, pulling down wallpaper, splashing paint on the walls, setting fire to curtains or starting fires in the rooms as outbursts of anger and helpless despair were experienced at home and at school. Some also said that they were made to believe that they were the major reasons for the family quarrels, disputes, and unhappiness. Feelings of self-blame predominated in everything they did, resulting in confused destructive behaviour.

Behavioural Problems Including Self-Harming Behaviour

There are several ways that these children want to attract other people's attention to their unhappiness, hurt, confusion, and unmet needs. This usually manifests itself in severe head-banging against the furniture, walls, floor, and other objects when the child is distressed and hurt. These reactions tend to be triggered when food is withdrawn as a punishment; when the child is locked up and isolated from the rest of the family; when it is denied a treat while siblings get it; or when it is unfairly punished; e.g. banished to the bedroom for many hours. Some of these children bite, cut or scratch themselves to the point of bleeding, and this tends to occur when they are confused, frustrated, or cruelly criticised, blamed for everything and degraded, and also when they are unable to do or get what they want. Because they suffer from extremely low self-esteem they may punish themselves for their misdemeanours or express hurt and pain to get some care and attention. Some children will injure themselves by putting a hand or a foot into a fire or burn personal belongings.

These children are characterised by either high levels of overactivity or passivity. Many of them, due to a lack of energy and depression, are withdrawn and lethargic, while others run from one activity to another due to emotional insecurity, unable to concentrate and maintain on-task behaviour. These children are described by parents as moody and unpredictable in their reactions. Once in a bad mood it can go on for many hours. They tend to present as either temperamentally difficult or slow to warm up, which can make their daily care demanding or unrewarding. Additionally, they are poor sleepers, with frequent waking and wandering around the house. Some of them lie motionless in bed with opened eyes, staring at the ceiling looking extremely unhappy and depressed.

Developmental Retardation

Psychosocial short-stature children show significant developmental delays in language, and in social and cognitive development. Their motor skills can be impaired as well, frequently losing balance and bumping into furniture or falling down, and they may have poor verbal skills and poor practical reasoning abilities and skills in problem-solving. All of them have short attention-spans: they also find difficulty in concentrating, and in storing and processing information. Their receptive and expressive skills are, as a rule, impaired. The most worrying impairment is in intellectual development: their IQ is well below average and educational attainments are extremely poor. Once placed in a nurturing and stimulating environment IQ scores increase and intellectual performance improves. Early intervention, therefore, is essential to reverse impaired potential.

Lying and Stealing

Psychosocial short-stature children are characterised by mindless stealing and lying when they get older. This type of behaviour is also seen in other types of emotional abuse, not only in short-stature children. They take things which are of no use to them, and when confronted they say that they did not do it, implying that someone else put it there. They take other children's food or belongings at school, and although they are found to have done so, they will vigorously deny their wrongdoing.

Lying tends to take place when they want to put blame on another child or fabricate a false story to get another child into trouble. It would appear that such children want to see others suffering in the same way as they are suffering, being blamed as they are being blamed. As their sense of justice and fairness is grossly distorted, due to their emotional maltreatment, they are unable to empathise with their victims. Foster-parents and teachers find these behaviours very difficult to cope with and understand. Foster-parents, in particular, have problems in tolerating lying, especially when a child refuses to admit that he/she has lied, and shows no remorse. These behaviours tend to drop in frequency once the child feels more secure, wanted, and appreciated. Moral reasoning, e.g. teaching the child what is right and wrong and why, helps alter behaviour for the better, and gives a child some degree of insight as to what is appropriate and what is not.

Psychological Description and Mother–Child Relationship

The most characteristic feature in social behaviour of short-stature children is antagonistic and disturbed interaction between the parents (usually mother and the child), and, to a lesser degree, other members of the family. The child seems to be an outsider in family activities, never fully involved in family life, and excluded from any participation in decision-making and being taken into consideration by other members of the family. It is quite common to see such a child standing or sitting a few meters away from the rest of the family and nobody taking any notice of him or her. It seems that life goes by without being a part of family interactions. Interaction is marked by dismissal or indifference: parents avoid the child, and at times its mere presence creates a heavy atmosphere of tension and anxiety.

Quite recently the author was told by a mother that her best time was when her son went to the nursery; when he came back, her stomach churned and her heart sank. The tension and anxiety did not leave her until he went to bed. She stated that it was extremely difficult to have any physical contact with her son and to tolerate his presence without getting upset. She also found it difficult to find anything positive about her child. There was nothing she liked about him.

Extreme defiance and stubbornness are prevalent, and these children seem to be oblivious to requests and commands which, in turn, bring about hostile parental reactions. Parents tend to revert to quite cruel and harsh discipline to exert control and authority which they do not use with their other children when they misbehave. Disciplining may involve getting rid of a child's favourite toy or pet; locking the child up in a bedroom, dark cupboard, or shed for many hours; tying a child to a bed; making a child stand for a prolonged period in one spot; forcing a child to keep hands on its head to stop it taking or touching things, usually food; smacking; and shouting. However, the most common way of punishing a child, as was said earlier, is withdrawal of food and drink. It is not unusual to see how the child is left out when treats are given to other children. There is always some justification given as to why this child is not given treats while others are. These may include observations of disobedience, cheek, or destructiveness, but often turn out to be of small importance.

Sibling–child relationships in many instances are hostile or indifferent; siblings usually ignore the child, do not include it in their activities, blame the child if something goes wrong, and behave towards it in the same way as the parents. Because parents seldom take the side of the target-child, it is smacked or pushed, and toys are frequently snatched from it. It is not unusual to see that the child is being bruised or hurt otherwise, by its siblings (even the younger ones).

It is not an uncommon feature in severe short-stature cases that a child will not speak to the mother, will not answer her questions, and seems to dismiss any attempts of contact she tries to make with him or her. Some children do not address their mothers as 'Mum' or 'Mummy' but refer to them as they would to a teacher at school or nurse in the nursery. They sometimes call them 'Miss', 'Mrs', or 'that Lady'. Mutual dislike becomes more acute as the child gets older and the battle of wills intensifies. As an already fragile relationship and a sense of belonging deteriorate, the child becomes an intruder in the family. Attachment disorders are evident and they tend to attach themselves indiscriminately to strange people who give them some attention and show interest in their needs. It has been observed that some of them call strange women 'Mummy' and go willingly, without any protests, with strangers and never show separation-anxiety. Due to maternal hostility and rejection, their attachment style is anxious-avoidant and these children feel unworthy of love.

The following passage demonstrates vividly the distortion of the mother-child relationship (Iwaniec, 1995, p. 45).

An example of psychosocial short stature: 'John'

> John will not speak to me (I know he can – he speaks to other people). I heard him swearing at me when I put him into his room. When I asked him to repeat what he said, he would not – even a swear word from him is better than nothing. He would not answer my questions – he would just stare at me. He refers to me as 'Miss' or 'this Lady' – he never calls me 'Mum'. He would position himself in a provoking way, for me to see him. He makes this awful noise, in a high-pitched, squeaking voice, which drives me mad. I just cannot stand him, I cannot bear having him near me – he deliberately behaves like that to hurt me – so for his own good I put him into his room, for his safety and my sanity, so that I do not have to look at him. I cannot allow him to annoy me so much. And yet, I worry so much about him – even though I do not like him. I keep wondering where I went wrong, what has happened. I get on so well with my two other children. I feel so guilty and ashamed and desperately unhappy. People like my family do not believe me that he is, and has always been, so difficult to care for and to enjoy. I went through hell trying to feed him when he was a baby. My whole life revolved around feeding John and coping with his crying and screaming. I tried to defeat him but he has defeated me instead. He does not want me and I do not want him. One of us has to go. He does not fit into this family: I feel that someone has dumped him on me and forgotten to take him away again.

Figure 7.2 shows the characteristics of psychosocial short-stature children.

Check list for psychosocial short stature	Yes	No	Do not know

• Child is very small for the age
• Child stunted in growth for several months
• Child's weight and height below second percentile for considerable time (minimum six months)
• Bizarre eating behaviour
• Excessive hunger drive
• Voracious eating habits – eating quickly and gorging to the point of vomiting
• Eating huge amounts of food
• Wandering around the house at night in search of food
• Hoarding food
• Eating non-food items, e.g. cotton wool, pieces of paper
• Drinking from drainpipes, toilet-bowls, puddles on the street
• Eating from dog or cat dishes
• Begging food from strangers
• Eating leftovers when in public places
• Scavenging food from waste-bins
• Constantly asking for food
• Stealing food from other children at school
• Having a poor appetite
• No interest in food
• Exceptionally long time eating
• Heaving and vomiting when pressed to eat
• Consuming small amounts
• Soiling
• Smearing
• Wetting bed
• Wetting pants during daytime
• Urinating over personal belongings
• Defaecating in inappropriate places
• Lying awake and motionless in bed for long periods
• Self-harming behaviour:
   ○ head-banging
   ○ cutting, scratching, and self-biting
   ○ rocking
   ○ burning
• Severe non-compliance and stubborn defiance
• Reluctance to communicate with the mother
• Destructiveness (tearing clothes, breaking toys, pulling off wallpaper, destroying things)
• Fire-setting and burning things
• Short attention span
• Poor ability to concentrate and to complete tasks
• Disruptive behaviour when in the company of other children (including classroom)
• Attention-seeking and attention-needing
• Withdrawn, lethargic, passive behaviour
• Depression
• Irritability
• Hyperactivity
• Poor relationships with siblings and peers			

Figure 7.2   Characteristics of psychosocial short-stature children
Source: Iwaniec (2004). *Children who fail to thrive: A practice guide*. Chichester: John Wiley & Sons.

Check list for psychosocial short stature	Yes	No	Do not know
• Attachment disorders • Rejection by the primary caregiver • Negative parental attitudes (dislike, rebukes, belittling, screaming, and shouting, dismissiveness of child's attempts to please a caregiver) • Physical abuse • Possibilities of sexual abuse • Emotional abuse • Emotional neglect • Developmental delays:			
○ motor ○ language ○ cognitive ○ social ○ emotional			
• Acceleration of growth in terms of weight and height when removed from home, e.g. hospital, short-term care • Deterioration of growth and behaviour when returned home • Age of identification:			
○ toddler ○ early childhood ○ middle childhood			
• Being unappealing to other people • Eagerness to be helpful and useful (teachers, nurses) • Shortness • Thinness • Playing alone • Weight for height normal or greater			

Figure 7.2   (Continued)

TWENTY-YEAR FOLLOW-UP STUDY

The author recently completed a 20-year follow-up study of 31 subjects who failed to thrive as children. Fifteen out of 31 were classified as of psychosocial short stature, 8 falling into the hyperphagic group, and 7 into the anorexic group.

The long-term outcomes varied among them and appeared to be determined by 2 factors: the onset and length of psychosocial short stature, and type of intervention. Children with a long history of failure to grow and who remained at home had disappointing outcomes. Six subjects out of these 15 were removed from neglectful and abusive homes. They achieved better outcomes than the 9 remaining in unsatisfactory homes. Two subjects who were adopted at 3 and 5 years respectively, and who experienced severe adversity when living with parents, have done extremely well, both personally and professionally. Their new life provided warm nurturing, feelings of being wanted and loved, sustained security, much-needed social stimulation, and encouragement to learn and to enjoy various activities. They both managed to make good their impaired intellectual potential, as demonstrated by being able to finish higher education, obtaining good employment, and leading stable emotional lives. Children who were fostered out (3 subjects) at the ages of 4, 5, and 7, had lower educational attainments: they were not so successful in securing satisfactory and permanent employment. One subject who was accommodated with his father at the age of 11 years manifested similar problems.

Nine out of the 15 who remained at home (3 on the At-Risk Register on and off for a long time) developed serious antisocial habits, such as delinquent behaviour, running away from home, glue-sniffing, drug abuse, and destructive behaviour. Seven of them were 'statemented' for special education. While at school they had severe difficulties with concentration and learning and were reported to be disruptive and attention-seeking. They had no playmates at school or in the community, and generally were not popular or liked by their peers and their teachers.

Six subjects had, on average, three to four episodes of short-term foster-care lasting between four and eight months. During their stays with foster-parents their weight and height, as a rule, accelerated, bizarre eating or poor appetite normalised, and disturbed toileting and destructive behaviour improved. On returning home the growth in terms of height slowed down, they lost weight, and behaviour became even more problematic. Three subjects did not want to return home but were made to do so.

All the subjects reported being badly treated as children by parents, in particular mothers, and sometimes by siblings. They reported being deprived of food, often isolated from the rest of the family, locked up in bedrooms for a long time, and persistently criticised and rebuked. Furthermore, there was little affection and attention shown to them by the members of the family. Withdrawal of food as punishment for any misbehaviour was common and frequent, which begs the question as to whether these children were offered adequate food. What parents say and what actually happens might not be true, and caution is needed when carrying out assessment. Taking into consideration the very poor relationship of the child within the family – often open rejection and insecure attachment – and remarkable recovery when care is provided by other people but deterioration on returning home, should keep us alerted to possibilities of severe maltreatment and abuse. The following statements would indicate how cruel parental behaviours were and their effect on the children, but specifically on a child's actual nutritional intake:

- I was sent to bed without having tea at least three or four times a week if I was lucky.
- I was so hungry I could not sleep.
- No amount of crying and screaming and saying that I was hungry would do any good; the door was locked and that was that.
- If I did eat quickly and made a mess, she would take my plate away from me, and ask me to get up from the table. I had to sit still and watch the others eat.
- Of course I have hidden food, even under the carpet – wouldn't you if you were hungry all the time?
- I felt so miserable that I often cried myself to sleep.
- I did break things and smashed my toys and scratched myself until blood started to run. I don't know why, I guess I was hurting inside – I guess I wanted to let my mum know I wanted someone to see how unhappy I was. No one took any notice of me anyway.
- Often I had to sit on the floor to eat while all of them sat at the table.
- I was so hungry at times that I could not sleep. I would go downstairs when everyone was asleep to find something to eat.
- Treats were not for me – I was told I did not deserve them. Others were given crisps or sweets; I was seldom given any.
- Well, I was a burden to them all – I was told often enough that I was stupid, sick, and good for nothing.
- Whenever I brought home something I made at school she would not even look at it. I was so hurt.
- I got so angry at times that I would break everything I could put my hands on.

The above statements made by the ex-short-stature subjects are based on their memories and interpretations of experiences from their childhood. A comparison with statements made to the author by the parents of those children during the assessment stage 20 years earlier shows very different views of the problems.

However, there were some unexpected and positive outcomes in four cases. Two subjects who were adopted at the ages of four and five years respectively received higher education and were in successful jobs and had stable marital relationships. One of them had a two-year-old son, thriving and well-cared-for. The other two, in spite of extremely poor relationships with their mothers as children and the consequent reception into care of one of them (the other went to live with his father), gradually rebuilt their contacts with their natural families. It needs to be said that they received considerable therapeutic help. Once they established their own families and had children themselves the relationships with their mothers warmed up somewhat, and they reappraised their own attitudes.

OTHER FINDINGS

The most worrying and long-lasting defect appears to be in the cognitive area in 40% of the cases. School attainments in those cases were poor or very poor. Six subjects had not passed any exams such as GCSE, and seven were moved to special education due to their slowness in learning and maladjusted behaviour. It is important to point out that six of these children remained at home with the parents, where difficulties were noticeable all the time, such as lack of stimulation, lack of interest in the child, and prevailing insecure attachment to family members. Five subjects are semiliterate and four have considerable difficulties with reading and numeracy in spite of finishing secondary education.

Difficulties with maintaining employment are apparent where the ability to read and act upon written information and instructions is necessary. Six subjects had had between seven to ten different jobs since they left school. These findings are in line with other shorter-term follow-up studies indicating that children who fail to thrive exhibit significant deficit in cognitive development, and that the problems can prevail if active intervention does not take place to remedy early deficit (Oates & Yu, 1971; Drotar & Sturm, 1988; Achenbach, Howell, Aoki, & Rauh, 1993).

SUMMARY

Psychosocial short-stature children present serious and urgent problems to be dealt with as soon as they are identified. They are in danger of being physically and sexually abused, and they are, as a rule, emotionally abused and rejected. These children are exceptionally small for their age as a result of persistent stress which affects growth-hormone function. In spite of excessive appetite they remain stunted in growth and their general development is retarded (in particular in cognitive and emotional areas). The long-term outcomes are very poor if constructive and decisive intervention does not take place early in the child's life. Children presenting a bizarre eating pattern, disturbed toileting, attachment disorders, and self-harming and destructive behaviour. When removed from their stressful homes they rapidly put on weight, begin to grow in length, and their behaviour calms down, but when returned to their homes they lose weight, become stunted in growth, and their behaviour worsens. The environment in which they live and the care they receive are very stressful; it is clear they are suffering significant harm.

CHAPTER 8

CHILDREN WITH DISABILITY AT RISK OF EMOTIONAL ABUSE AND NEGLECT

CONTENTS

INTRODUCTION

Children with disabilities represent approximately 3% of the total child population (Department of Health, 2000). It has been defined by the Disability Discrimination Act (1995) as: 'a physical or mental impairment which has substantial and long-term adverse effect on a person's ability to carry out normal day-to-day activities'. There are many conditions that are categorised as disabilities. A child can present one or more of the following: specific learning disability (e.g. auditory or visual perceptual and processing problems); significant developmental delay; sensory impairment; autism and pervasive developmental disorders; emotional and behavioural difficulties; physical impairment; medical or health-related disabilities; traumatic brain injury; and communication difficulties.

Problems in categorising and labelling emotional abuse contributed to a reluctance to name and make child-protection decisions (Glaser, Prior, & Lynch, 2001). For no group of children has this been more evident than for children with disabilities (Goddard, 1996). Historically, there was little evidence to support the existence of emotional abuse and neglect in this population. Cultural beliefs and attitudes towards disability contributed to the erroneous belief that such children did not experience abuse (Sobsey, 1994). Early research in the field often excluded children with impairments from their samples, or adopted rather arbitrary definitions of disability, yielding low and grossly inaccurate prevalence rates of maltreatment. Changes in social and political attitudes to disability led to a growing awareness and emphasis on the rights of protection for these children. An emerging research field ensued, contributing to an acceptance that children with disability are vulnerable to emotional maltreatment at what seems a very high rate. It is now clear that emotional abuse and neglect towards children with disabilities are endemic in today's society and findings are presented as critical issues that need to be addressed.

In this chapter, prevalence rates of maltreatment of children with disabilities, the links between typologies of caregiving behaviour and specific conditions, and presentations of disabilities are discussed. Relationships between disability and ways in which children with impairments experience emotional abuse and neglect are considered. Vulnerability and risk-factors are examined within an ecological framework. Clinical issues of assessment, intervention, and preventative measures (based on current research and relevant to a wide variety of professionals) are highlighted, in order to offer guidance on optimising developmental outcomes.

INCIDENCE AND PREVALENCE RATES

Children with disabilities are no different from their non-disabled peers in their need for nurturance, social relationships, and stimulation. Yet they are disproportionately vulnerable to experience a type of caregiving which disregards their emotional and social developmental needs. Reports exploring prevalence rates in child-protection services indicate that children with registered impairments are significantly over-represented (Cross, Kaye, & Ratnofsky, 1993). Evidence from early studies in the area examining child-protection registers concluded that children with disabilities were 1.7 times more likely to experience abuse and neglect than their non-disabled peers (Cohen & Warren, 1987; Cross, Kaye, & Ratnofsky, 1993). Smaller UK-based studies have reported comparative levels of abuse (Kennedy, 1989; Westcott, 1993).

More recent epidemiological evidence suggests that the prevalence rate may indeed be considerably higher. Sullivan and Knutson (2000) integrated reports from social services, child-protection agencies, and educational records of more than 50 000 children. The authors identified that 31% of children with a diagnosed case of disability had experienced some form of maltreatment, compared with 9% of children without any such conditions. Sullivan and Knutson (2000) noted that children with disabilities were 3.14 times more likely to be emotionally abused, 3.76 times more likely to be neglected, and 3.8 times more likely to be physically abused than children without any registered impairments. The most common form of maltreatment appeared to be neglect, yet for these children abusive caregiving was not limited to one type of cruelty. Based on their findings the authors concluded that children with disabilities were much more likely to experience maltreatment 'multiple times and in multiple ways'.

Perpetrators of abuse are known to victims in almost all cases, as with children without disability (Westcott, 1993). Conversely, males are most likely to be victims of the abuse (Sobsey, Randall, & Parrila, 1997). Children with disabilities are much more likely to experience maltreatment at a younger age than their non-disabled peers, with a vulnerability to abuse which extends throughout adolescence and adulthood (Verdugo, Bermejo, & Fuertes, 1995).

These children are exposed to the same forms of psychological maltreatment as their non-disabled peers (see Chapter 2). However, because of disability they are vulnerable to emotional abuse and neglect in a way that children without such impairments do not experience. Lack of understanding of disability and unrealistic expectations of abilities and skills; intrusive and/or disrespectful application of medical photography and medical rehabilitative programmes; lack of stimulation; overprotection; isolation and confinement; lack of appropriate supervision according to the impairment and developmental need; and overmedication are just some of the common means by which the self-esteem, self-worth, and development of these children may be compromised (Newport, 1991). The *nature* of the impairment can be particularly important, as acts not normally considered as maltreatment may indeed be viewed as abusive, with similar long-lasting and negative effects on psychological health and well-being. For example, refusal to speak to a child with an audio impairment within its known range of hearing or withdrawal of a communication device from a child with speech and language difficulties are just two ways in which a child with an impairment can be mistreated. It is also worth considering that current definitions and conventional methods of ascertaining abusive practices may be insufficient for children with disabilities, and that the true extent of emotional abuse and neglect may far exceed known prevalence rates.

There is some evidence to suggest a relationship between specific conditions and the type of emotional abuse and maltreatment experienced by the child. The three most common forms of disabilities (namely developmental delay, specific learning difficulties, and emotional and behavioural disorders) are also the most prevalent impairments among children who are victims of maltreatment. Children with behavioural and emotional difficulties are at most risk of neglect and physical abuse; children with speech and language impairments are five times more likely to experience neglect and physical abuse than children without any recorded difficulties; and children with developmental delay are four times at risk for all types of maltreatment compared with their non-disabled peers (Sullivan & Knutson, 2000).

The presence of *multiple* impairments can further augment risk (Department of Health, 1999). Children with more than one condition are much more likely to experience *frequent* and *severe* episodes of maltreatment. The 'degree' of disability also appears to have a strong influence in how carers respond to the child and ultimately the severity and type of maltreatment the child experiences (Benedict, White, Wulff, & Hall, 1990). Ammerman and Patz (1996) reported high levels of vulnerability for verbal abuse for those with *mild* impairments in a study of 132 mothers of 2- to 8-year-old children with and without disabilities. Parental difficulty adjusting to appropriate developmental expectations was suggested as a possible explanation for the increase in verbal attacks towards these children. Alternatively, there is also evidence to suggest that the risk of neglect and emotional abuse is highest for children whose impairments are most *severe*. The child's emotional and social needs are most likely to be ignored in this group when parents feel unable to provide a level of care necessitated by the child's impairment (Jones, Peterson, Goldberg, Goldberg, & Smith, 1995; Rycus & Hughes, 1998). Some parents feel ashamed of having a child with a disability, and in such cases they are isolated from normal family interaction and activities and, more often than not, hidden from visitors. Rejection and resentment are often present, and contact with such children is limited to control and care. Social isolation and understimulation are common as is lack of attention to basic physical and emotional needs.

The extent by which the disability is caused or compounded by maltreatment is unknown. Thus far there are no prospective studies charting developmental pathways of maltreatment for specific conditions. Disregarding the child's emotional and social development is likely to have a significant effect on the child's overall capability (and therefore degree of impairment). Additional research is needed to unravel this conundrum.

RISK-FACTORS

Early conceptual models proposed a 'dependency-stress' framework to explain the disproportionate amount of maltreatment experienced by children with disabilities. Many researchers proposed that risk of maltreatment was dependent on the severity of the child's condition and the care demands required to effectively manage and support the child. Advocates of these theories (Friedrich & Boriskin, 1978) hypothesised that families and caregivers respond to this inordinate amount of *stress* by abusing the child. Certainly, caring for a child with a registered condition (where the 'duty of care' is higher than for children without any impairments) can impact parental well-being and family functioning (Sobsey, 1994). A considerable body of evidence would suggest that the unidirectional relationship between care demands, stress, and abuse is oversimplified and that a number of parents and families cope well with the level of care and responsibility required (Byrne, Cunningham, & Sloper, 1988; Sobsey, 1994).

Drawing on ecological perspectives of maltreatment, where individual, family and social factors are given equal emphasis (Belsky, 1993; Bronfenbrenner, 1979), has been particularly informative in attempting to unravel risk-factors for emotional abuse in this population (Sobsey, 1994). Several key elements relating to parents, children, families, and systems of service delivery may increase the likelihood of emotional abuse for children with disabilities. It would seem the *interaction* of these significant factors makes children with disabilities more vulnerable to emotional abuse and neglect.

Child-Related Risk-Factors

Factors intrinsic to the child are at the centre of ecological models explaining behaviour. Several specific child-based characteristics have been reported by researchers exploring aetiological links associated with child abuse. These include: difficult temperament; poor ability to form relationships; behavioural and emotional problems; lack of physical attractiveness; and premature birth (Christian, 1999). Having a disability, however mild, either directly or indirectly also appears to make a child vulnerable to emotional abuse and neglect (Jonson-Reid, Drake, Kim, Porterfield, & Han, 2004; Sobsey, 2002). In some cases, depending on the amount of care which the child requires or the level of physical disability, the impairment can compromise the child's ability to defend itself by escaping or reporting the behaviour. As a result, perpetrators may see children with disabilities as 'safe victims' and presume that the abuse will go undetected (Wolcott, 1997). Many children may find the power imbalance too overwhelming to escape from and/or avoid maltreatment and, having an impairment, are even more at risk.

Children with disabilities have a tendency to please and acquiesce (Marchant, 1991). There may be an increased vulnerability to comply with authority, which could result in the failure to recognise inappropriate behaviours as abusive (Sullivan, Knutson, Scanlan, & Cork, 1997): for children with cognitive deficits this is an additional difficulty. They may lack the full knowledge or ability to understand maltreatment, believe that the caregiver knows best, and may be unable to differentiate inappropriate from appropriate caregiver behaviour (Ammerman, 1992; Steinberg *et al.*, 1998). When children do recognise improper behaviour from carers, they may feel immobilised to initiate a complaint, possibly out of fear of losing the relationship with the caregiver on whom they are emotionally and practically dependent (National Clearing House on Child Abuse and Neglect Information, 2001). The extent to which each of these characteristics elicits abusive caregiving is unknown: however, it is likely that they in some way *interact* with parental, environmental, and system factors to prompt maltreatment.

Parental and Family-Related Risk-Factors

As previously discussed in Chapter 2, certain parental and family factors are associated with an increased risk of caregiving that is both emotionally abusive and neglectful. The same topics that were highlighted as potential risk-factors for children without impairments are relevant to children with disabilities. Parental substance abuse, previous childhood experience of emotional abuse, poor coping skills, poor impulse-control and a history of domestic violence, and low self-esteem and mental-health difficulties have been associated with increased risks of psychological maltreatment. Additional environmental factors such as low income, poor employment prospects, and low levels of educational attainment have also been linked with increased vulnerability to abuse (Jaudes & Diamond, 1985; Knutson, 1995; Morrison, Frank, & Holland, 1999; Vig & Kaminer, 2002). Parental disabilities (such as physical impairments and/or health complications) are over-represented in prevalence rates of perpetrators of maltreatment, in particular physical abuse (Milner & Chilamkurti, 1991). Parents with cognitive impairments are also highly represented among families investigated by child-protection services for maltreatment due to neglect. Estimates of 45% of families having one or more children diagnosed with 'failure to thrive' have been recorded when one or both parents were recorded with a learning disability (Seagull & Scheurer, 1986). This is due to poor understanding of children's very basic developmental needs, and poor retention of information given by the helping agencies on how to provide adequate food, when and how to feed, and properly to interpret signals of distress. Furthermore, it is essential to differentiate between what these signals indicate, i.e. hunger, tiredness, a need to change a nappy, illness, and so on.

Although not the primary cause of emotional abuse and neglect in this population, certainly the caring role for a child with disabilities often places tremendous emotional, physical, economic, and social demands on families (Benedict *et al.*, 1990). There may be extra demands on time due to medical or service-related appointments that caregivers are invited to attend. Adapting the family home to accommodate the child's impairment and securing services for the child may present an additional financial burden. Fears about the abusive nature of hired caregivers, and/or difficulties in securing respite services, may prevent parents leaving the home, which further inhibits opportunities to develop social networks or allow for breaks from care demands. Parents of children with a wide range of disabilities often report feelings of social isolation and that nobody understand, difficulties coping with their child, helplessness, and depression (Kaufman, Johnson, Cohn, & McCleery, 1992; Sloper & Turner, 1993). It is possible that, at times when parents feel overwhelmed by the competing care difficulties for the child alongside their own needs and those of other children within the family, a less than optimal caregiving may occur.

The risk of maltreatment may be mediated by a number of factors. Feelings of *grief* and *anger* may continue to emerge as the family 'mourn' the loss and disappointment of giving birth to a child with a disability (Cunningham & Sloper, 1977; Rycus & Hughes, 1998). Parents may re-experience loss at different times throughout the family life cycle (Vetere, 1993); for example, after the birth of subsequent children; when a younger sibling reaches developmental goals the child with disabilities is yet to attain; or when decisions which further segregate the child from mainstream society need to be made.

Parental/family perceptions around *stigma* and/or causes of impairments may further increase the likelihood of emotional abuse and neglect. Some parents may view their child's disability as a punishment for their behaviour in the past; for some mothers this may be health-related behaviour during pregnancy (Burrell, Thompson, & Sexton, 1994). These factors may, in turn, promote a cycle of self-blame and pessimism about the future which could independently contribute to mental-health problems for parents, and increase vulnerability to abusive interactions with the child. In certain cultures (e.g. Asian) children with a disability are still seen as punishment on the parents, particularly the mother. Giving birth to a disabled child is seen as shameful and vindictive. Mothers of such children have no support or sympathy, as it is seen as a punishment that they have to bear.

Early and frequent disruptions in caregiving are common for families with a child diagnosed with a disability, which can lead to complicated *attachment relationships*. Repeated separations due to hospitalisations or unresponsive or unexpected interactions with the child may lead to difficulties establishing a close emotional bond (Ammerman & Patz, 1996; Sobsey, 1994). Depending on the nature of the child's impairment, its severity, and whether it co-occurs with additional developmental difficulties, each child will also react differently to both the challenges of the disability and the environment attempting to address its need. Children will develop their own styles and methods of communication as well as behaviours, which may indicate that fundamental needs are not being met (Murphy, 1994). Parents may view behaviour problems as aspects of disability and become exasperated when traditional methods of addressing childhood difficulties fail. Relationship difficulties may be further compromised when parents have insufficient information about the impairment, appropriate developmental expectations for their child, and how the child should be supported. Inadequate knowledge of positive behaviour-management and of how to appropriately stimulate and educate the child may lead to a lack of warmth and negative attitudes towards the child which can incite incidences of emotional abuse and neglect. Parents may engage in more neglectful or abusive practices and come to believe that they are the only effective means of managing their child's behaviour (Sullivan *et al.*, 1997).

How families and parents cope with these challenges will differ. Concerns and worries about care needs and quality of life for the family and the child will vary. For the person with the disability, additional difficulties may arise if their wishes are in conflict with those of parents and other family members. Parents may underestimate the child's skills as they develop throughout childhood, adolescence, and early adulthood. Families may overprotect their child and consider daily-living skills to be an issue only when they consider the care burden as elderly parents. Alternatively, parents and families may not fully accept the consequences of the impairment, and may overestimate their child's skills, contributing to poor feelings of self-worth for the child who cannot meet parental demands. To illustrate this point Sarah's case is presented, indicating the emotional abuse and exploitation of Sarah over many years.

CASE STUDY

Sarah, aged 14 years, the eldest of the family of 4, was a girl with a learning disability attending a special school. She had learning problems and wore a single hearing aid.

Sarah presented herself as a passive, withdrawn child, eager to help and oblige, who looked extremely tired and undernourished, and was shabbily dressed. Both parents spoke of Sarah as a difficult child – very stubborn, disobedient, and hard to enjoy. They felt that she was lazy, and would not wash and clean herself: but she looked different and would do all these things if she stayed with her uncle and aunt.

Sarah was responsible for looking after her three-and-a-half-year-old sister during the day, before and after school, and always since her birth during the night. She had to feed, bathe, change, and attend to her during the night. Additionally, she was often asked to do things for her younger brother, e.g. getting him ready for school in the morning and looking after him after school. If things were not done according to parental, but in particular maternal, expectations, she was smacked, screamed at, called names, and deprived of food. Quite often she was kept at home to look after her siblings, and on such occasions she had to dress, feed, wash, and change them while both parents were still in bed. Responsibilities given to her and the demands put upon her were much above her chronological and, above all, mental age.

Sarah's relationship with her parents (in particular her mother) was very poor. Sarah's mother was ashamed of her and never took her anywhere to avoid (as she said) people making remarks about her (e.g. that she was thin, frightened, and anxious). The mother used to criticise, rebuke, and belittle Sarah on a continual basis, and had totally unrealistic expectations of her disabled daughter. Sarah presented as an insecure girl because of the parental emotional unavailability, lack of sensitivity, and unpredictability in parental behaviour (characterised by overestimation of her learning ability). Sarah was trapped in helpless despair as she did not comprehend what was expected of her, and cognitively was not able to store and use information properly in order to perform various tasks correctly and speedily.

Sarah was emotionally abused and neglected all her life and was given responsibility which can only be described as exploitation. Her shy, withdrawn, passive, automatic or frightened and anxiety-driven behaviour was the result of parental emotional and physical maltreatment. Lack of stimulation of and attention to her basic needs exacerbated her learning disability.

Realisation of the consequences of impairment at each stage of the family's life will be interpreted differently and will have different meanings for each family. Implications of additional provision needed may contribute to increased stress for parents and/or within the family and result in conflict and cruel behaviour towards the child with disabilities (Vetere, 1993).

Care Systems and Policies Relating to Disability

Because of the nature of their impairments, children with disabilities are involved in a range of systems. Although organisations, institutions, respite services and schools provide a much-needed and valued service they also increase access to possibly inappropriate caregivers.

Rogow (2002) suggests that 'abuse in human services is a quiet epidemic' (p. 11). Overmedication, use of physical restraints, isolation, and segregation are often used as means to manage children with disabilities, and as observers we are right to be concerned. Lack of co-ordination and communication among carers and organisations also exists, and has led to critical gaps in care systems, further neglecting developmental, social, and emotional needs (Marchant & Page, 1993; Rogow, 2002; Westcott & Jones, 1999). Care providers may be prone to some of the similar dynamics which characterise parent–child relationships. Poor understanding of a child's condition, overwhelming feelings regarding the management of care needs of the child, difficulties in forming attachments and bonds to children with impairments, and limited social and community support may initiate a pattern of interaction that is both emotionally abusive and neglectful. Since some children are physically unappealing, physical and emotional contact tend to be limited, and interaction for pleasure is almost non-existent.

Systems and policies towards people with disabilities need to be considered when considering factors which contribute to the aetiology of emotional abuse and neglect. Children with impairments may be at increased risk of abuse due to society's response to their disabilities rather than because of their impairments themselves. Policies that 'devalue' children with disabilities and imply that they are less entitled to educational, social, and vocational experiences than children without such impairments may reinforce feelings of low worth and separateness. Assumptions that caregivers working in services with vulnerable children are 'good' and 'special' people (who would never perpetrate such abuse), and that children with impairments do not experience abuse, may result in failure to scrutinise services for abusive practices. Erroneous beliefs (e.g. children with disabilities do not completely understand abusive or neglectful behaviour, and as a consequence do not suffer or feel physical or emotional pain) are additional myths contributing to the vulnerability of these children (Grossman, 1995; Sobsey, 2002). By devaluing and reducing social worth of children with disabilities, violence and abusive behaviour are often excused and justified.

PRACTICE ISSUES

Identification and Reporting

Children with disabilities (like other children) need caregiving which facilitates healthy and vigorous development and promotes self-esteem. When emotional abuse occurs, it needs to be identified and reported. Clinicians, paediatricians, educators, care providers, and other professionals involved in the lives of children with disabilities are well-placed to identify and detect emotional abuse and neglect. Due to the high rates of maltreatment that children with impairments experience, vigilance is crucial. Professionals should be mindful of and alert to the signs and symptoms that are suggestive of abuse (e.g. events which occur due to a lack of supervision; lack of interest in the child; or a refusal to adapt the environment to the child's impairments). Although caregiving practices to manage children with impairments will, of course, not always be abusive, professionals have a duty to question the quality of care when suspicions are aroused. The responsibility to alert professionals to the experience of abuse should not remain that of the child, but of the many professionals and caregivers with whom he/she has contact (Sullivan et al., 1997).

Assessment

Once identified and reported to the relevant child-protection service, assessments of emotional abuse and neglect require well-integrated, multidisciplinary procedures, with dual expertise in both child protection and disability issues

(Marchant & Page, 1993). On a more individual level, developmentally appropriate interview and assessment procedures are necessary. As no two children are alike, and children with disabilities will vary in the severity and complexity of their condition, each assessment/interview schedule may require considerable adaptation to accommodate developmental needs. It will be important to be mindful of the limitations of some approaches (e.g. facilitated communication), and of the possibilities of erroneous charges against caregivers that may result. Some preliminary work utilising cognitive techniques have shown some promise for adults with learning disabilities (Milne & Bull, 1996), yet further work in developing structured assessment tools for this population may be important to yield accurate and convicting information.

Abuse may indeed be masked by and attributed to the child's condition. Practitioners need to be aware that symptoms which might be indicative of possible abuse (e.g. self-harm) could also be a means of dealing with and communicating emotional distress by a child with disabilities (Murphy, 1994). Assessment is further complicated when there is a query about the child's cognitive understanding and its ability to discern if caregiving behaviour is inappropriate. Another important consideration for professionals is to question whether symptoms of maltreatment which warrant investigation (e.g. low mood, withdrawal, unresponsiveness) are a result of discrimination and isolation from family and mainstream society or whether the behaviour of children is a direct consequence of abusive practices (Kennedy, 1990).

Clearly, for any assessment of maltreatment, an extensive evaluation of the child's environment is needed. The child's surroundings, family, parent–child relationships, and contact with services (including school, respite care, or institutional support) should be evaluated by thorough 'functional analysis', in order to establish both risk and resiliency factors in the child's environment (Clees & Gast, 1994).

Helping Strategies

Not only is it important to strengthen systems of reporting and to investigate symptoms and signs of emotional abuse, but it is also imperative to develop appropriate and relevant systems of treatment. Historically, adults and children with disabilities have had little or no access to therapeutic services; however, following recent publications emphasising the compatibility of therapeutic approaches for this group (Waitman & Conboy-Hill, 1992; Willner, 2005), the situation is gradually changing and therapeutic services are increasingly on offer, particularly for adults. In children's services, therapeutic services normally cater for staff (Nagel & Leiper, 1999) or are provided to parents/caregivers (Froelich, Doepfner, & Lehmkuhl, 2002; Saunders, Mazzucchelli, & Studman, 2004). Parent management-training (see Chapter 12) can be extremely helpful in facilitating positive parental interactions with children: there is ample evidence to suggest that these techniques are equally beneficial for children with disabilities. In a study of 36 families of children with developmental disabilities, Feldman and Werner (2002) reported that equipping parents with positive teaching techniques and how to use functional assessment methods for behavioural problems yielded significant results for families (which were maintained 5 years after the intervention). The 18 families that experienced the intervention reported an overall reduction in behavioural problems, enhanced parental self-efficacy, and quality-of-life perceptions, as well as reduced perceptions of parental stress compared to controls (18 families). The extent to which these types of treatment programme prevent additional maltreatment is unknown; however, they do show some promise for children who may be at risk from abusive caregiving within the family.

Direct face-to-face therapeutic services are often unattainable; in addition, mental-health services specialising in child protection may not cater for children with disabilities (Little, 2004). In some care systems, a child's case may be seen as the sole responsibility of a particular service (e.g. paediatrics); professionals, however, while mindful of the child's experience, may continue to focus on the more obvious developmental needs normally catered for within the organisation, while overlooking the possibilities of the child's being abused. In other services, referrals may be made to address the emotional consequences of the abuse. Cases are often bounced back and forth from disability to mental-health services, while professionals decide on care and treatment responsibilities (Marchant & Page, 1993; Rogow, 2002; Westcott & Jones, 1999). Whatever the situation, the child's emotional needs may be subject to neglect, and the child may continue to suffer and to feel unsafe and insecure. Communication and collaboration between services is essential to appropriately address these issues. Clear policies and procedures regarding protection concerns, care and treatment responsibilities need to be developed and integrated into services to ensure responsive and appropriate treatment (NSPCC, 2003).

Prevention

The contributions to the aetiology of emotional abuse are multifactorial and interrelated. Effective prevention needs to be multifaceted and target many levels of a child's social ecology. Although services and government agencies may view the recommendations suggested within this discussion as too expensive, the price cannot be so great that it overrides the physical, emotional, and financial cost of emotional abuse to the child and society at large.

Society System/Service-Based

One of the major ways to prevent abuse is for society to accept and believe that children with disabilities experience emotional abuse and neglect. Government bodies and educational and health-care professionals have an important role in educating the general public and those who work in social services about issues of disability. In addition, promoting inclusive practices, encouraging the value of children with disabilities, as well as challenging negative attitudes and behaviours towards this vulnerable group, will hopefully initiate a change in the broader views towards children with disabilities (Sobsey, 1994, 2002).

Schools, institutions, and disability services can play major roles. Services can develop and promote definitions of good practice; make a clear commitment to child protection; develop clear policies and procedures on how to manage suspicions of emotional abuse and neglect; and encourage a working environment that is open to scrutiny and subject to review (Marchant & Cross, 1993; NSPCC, 2003). Organisations can schedule time for staff support and supervision. Employers and service providers can make available funds which enable effective staff/client ratios. Staff attitudes towards children with disability, as well as references, should be thoroughly checked as part of the recruitment process (Kragthorpe *et al.*, 1997; Sobsey, 1994; Steinberg *et al.*, 1998).

Providing regular and extensive in-service training may further complement these aims (Marchant & Cross, 1993). Increasing staff awareness of the nature of emotional abuse and neglect and understanding how abusive relationships can develop may serve to encourage more positive relationships between caregivers and children. Promoting sensitivity to issues of disability; positive behaviour-management strategies; child development; appropriate expectations for the client group and individual child; and children's rights to protection are important topics to consider for all staff who work in the area. To prevent cases 'falling through the net', service providers, institutional and residential care facilities, and schools need to develop protocols by which cases of suspected abuse are evaluated.

Family-Based Services

Children with disabilities are very dependent on their parents and families. Recognising that the duty of care is higher for parents of children with disabilities is important when developing support services for these families (Westcott & Jones, 1993). Home-based assistance, in addition to pastoral and emotional support, may be helpful in encouraging coping with problems and developing positive relationships with such children (Hollingworth,

1987). Regular information sessions on children's condition, general issues of child development, and how developmental progress may be compromised by any impairment will be important topics to address. Parenting programmes, as well as being a vehicle to promote positive behaviour-management strategies, can give the parents of children with disabilities opportunities to meet other parents, instil in them a sense that they are not alone and encourage them in the belief that they can cope and manage their family situation (Santelli, Turnbull, Marquis, & Lerner, 1997). Establishing good links with service providers who are sensitive to their difficulties may further reduce risk.

Child-Based Prevention

Delivering structured prevention programmes to children with disabilities, with the goal of encouraging and facilitating mechanisms of self-protection and assertiveness, may in some way contribute to reducing vulnerability to emotional abuse and neglect (Mitchell & Buchele-Ash, 2000). Ammerman and Baladerian (1993) highlight the following issues and topics that should be considered when designing and delivering child-focused prevention programmes to children with disabilities:

- to define what is emotional abuse and neglect;
- to show how to report abusive caregiving;
- to demonstrate how to communicate to others that abuse is happening; and
- to teach the children with disabilities how to express emotions related to their experience of emotional abuse and neglect.

Child-focused programmes need to be responsive to issues of disability and to accommodate developmental needs which the child presents. Programmes need to be accessible (at a practical and developmentally appropriate level) and sensitive to differences, e.g. ability, skills, culture, and gender. Sessions should also be inclusive and cater for children with a variety of disabilities, not just those who may seem more developmentally aware or responsive (Ammerman & Baladerian, 1993; Kragthorpe *et al.*, 1997; Steinberg *et al.*, 1998).

Abuse-prevention programmes could be integrated into assertiveness workshops and presented in conjunction with safety and self-defence skills. Sessions may need to be repeated, and booster sessions may be required to inform, empower, and support children. The processes of absorbing information and increasing confidence in using newly learned skills are likely to be long, but perseverance and patience are needed to give children the means and coping skills to understand what emotionally abusive behaviour is, how to protect themselves, and to be aware of how to deal with it.

SUMMARY

Children with disabilities are at higher risk of emotional abuse and maltreatment than children without such impairments. A number of factors interact together to increase the vulnerability of these children to maltreatment. These include: attitudes and beliefs toward disability; policies and systems designed to meet the care and practical needs of children with disability; and family factors, such as increased care demands and factors specific to the impairment and/or factors intrinsic to the child. The key components of preventative services are child-focused programmes; family-support interventions; professional training and policy development; and co-operation and collaboration between families and services supporting the children. In summary, the degree of awareness of families and professionals needs to be raised regarding emotional abuse and neglect. Additional research (possibly prospective studies) needs to be undertaken to explore developmental pathways leading to emotional abuse and neglect for children with disabilities. Practitioners need to adopt a community approach to working with, managing, and preventing emotional abuse and neglect of children who are vulnerable to maltreatment, particularly children with disabilities.

CHAPTER 9

RISKS AND RESILIENCE IN CASES OF EMOTIONAL ABUSE

CONTENTS

INTRODUCTION

It has long been recognised that stressful life experiences may have an adverse effect on children's and young people's well-being, and predispose them to physical and mental disorder. Some children and young people live in families and communities where there is a high level of environmental stressors of long duration; the last are often referred to as chronic adversities, which also include acute negative life events (e.g. parental psychopathology, poverty, community and domestic violence, parental death, child abuse, interparental discord, removal of children into care, and child ill-health and disability [Friedman & Chase-Lansdale, 2002]).

It is believed that severe and long-in-duration chronic adversities are hazardous to a child's growth, development, and emotional adjustment. Many studies in the last two decades or so drew our attention to the individual differences of how chronic adversities affect some children (but not others) in spite of the same stressors being present. The question is why some individuals come out of it unscathed and unharmed, as though immune to stress, and why some are crushed and damaged by the experiences. It is important to know what are the risks and vulnerabilities which can lead to child emotional abuse and neglect and what are the protective factors which can shelter the child from adversities and build protective resilience.

Some years ago most of the literature on assessment concentrated on stressors in the family and a child's vulnerability when exposed to many risks within the family and community. In recent years the question 'what makes for a vulnerable child?' has been replaced by 'what makes for a resilient child?' In the past attention was focused almost exclusively on victims, e.g. on children who experienced deprivation, abuse, and neglect. However, it became apparent that not all materially deprived children developed into damaged and ineffective people. Many of them, in fact, were remarkably successful in overcoming acute early difficulties. As clinical impressions and anecdotal evidence gave way to empirical studies we have learned that stressors and their impact are moderated by many social, genetic, and personal factors (Clarke & Clarke, 2000; Herbert, 1998a; Rutter, 1990a). It is the search for these other factors that dominates current research and literature. There are, on the one hand, biological and psychosocial factors that make some individuals particularly susceptible while, on the other hand, there are protective influences that serve a differing function. These may include factors associated with the biological predisposition of a child (easy or difficult temperament, intellectual potential, disability, good or bad health, etc.) or with parenting factors (such as cohesive or dysfunctional family, secure or insecure upbringing, cold or warm emotional nurturing, and so on). In fact, it is a combination of biological and social factors that is most successful in differentiating children according to vulnerability.

How do we then define risk and protective factors? Risk-factors are characteristics of an individual or the environment that are associated with increased probability of that individual experiencing negative outcomes (Compass, Hinden, & Gerhardt, 1995). Protective factors buffer the effects of a risk-factor and may reduce the likelihood of maladaptive outcomes (Rutter, 1987). Resilience refers to the ability to demonstrate adequate development and adaptation within the context of adversity, despite the presence of risk-factors (Fonagy et al., 1994; Garmezy & Rutter, 1983). Rather than constituting a fixed characteristic of an individual as either vulnerable or invulnerable to risk, resilience is viewed as a relative resistance to risk (Rutter, 1999).

According to the cumulative risk model, the presence of a greater number of risk-factors is linked to increased risk of vulnerability to psychological, social, and developmental difficulties. Conversely, an increase in protective factors shelters the effects of risk-factors, thus reducing the likelihood of maladaptive outcomes (Rutter, 1987). The presence of protective factors and buffers, at any level of the ecology, may help to explain why some children display successful adaptation in the face of adversity (Cicchetti, Rogosch, Lynch, & Holt 1993; Cicchetti & Toth, 1995b). It is in situations where the cumulative effects of multiple risk-factors outweigh protective resources that children are susceptible to the social, cognitive, and psychological problems that can lead to significant difficulties throughout the life course (Mullen *et al.*, 1996; Rutter, 1985, 1986, 1999; Widom, 1999a).

This chapter examines risk and resilience in relation to emotional abuse. It explores numerous child and family factors that may increase the risk of emotional abuse occurring, and numerous ways in which experience of such abuse can enhance vulnerability to negative outcomes. Case studies are presented to illustrate some risk and resilience, and positive or negative outcomes. The case studies are not representative of all risks or possible protective factors; they merely illustrate some of the points in these peoples' lives.

RISK AND RESILIENCE FACTORS FOR EMOTIONAL MALTREATMENT

Risk and resilience for emotional abuse involve a complex interplay between processes at work at the level of the individual, the family unit, and the wider community, and are well framed within an ecological framework (e.g. Bronfenbrenner, 1979). Research and practice have identified numerous pathways to child abuse and neglect. However, the causal routes between factors operating at various levels of the family ecology and risk for psycho-logical maltreatment remain unclear (Belsky & Stratton, 2002).

It is clear, however, that emotional abuse may increase a child's vulnerability. The extent to which emotional abuse exerts an impact upon a child's life appears to be determined by a number of factors. For example, Emery and Laumann-Billings (2002) have identified at least five broad classes of variables that determine the consequences of abuse for children. These include: the nature of the abuse, including factors such as frequency, intensity, and duration of the abuse; individual characteristics of the victim; the nature of the relationship between the child and the abuser; the response of others to the abuse; and factors associated with the abuse that might exacerbate its effects or account for some of the consequences of the abuse. Cicchetti and Rizley (1981) devised a transactional model of factors relating to the child, the parent, and the environment that act to determine risk or resilience for maltreatment: first, enduring vulnerability factors include long-lasting parenting and environmental factors that potentiate maltreatment (such as a parent's history of being maltreated); second, challengers include short-term conditions and stresses such as the experience of loss; third, enduring protective factors including permanent conditions that decrease the likelihood of maltreatment (such as positive parental relationships); and finally, factors that protect a family from stress (such as improvement in family finances).

Mitchell (2005) refers to triggering factors of emotional abuse in terms of vulnerability as 'the soil in which such abuse thrives'. This very appropriate metaphor points to the following risks: poverty and social exclusion; early parenthood and large families; family violence; substance misuse; family breakdown; physical illness and disability; mental disorder; learning difficulties; and parental preoccupation. These risks are most often identified in daily practice of childcare workers and guardians, in assessment, and intervention.

Family Factors

Research to date has not established a very clear picture about the types of families that experience increased risk for psychological maltreatment. In addition to the multitude of potential risk-factors for emotional abuse, this lack of clarity is linked to the fact that available data often fail to consider psychological maltreatment as a separate entity of child abuse. However, it is clear that while psychological maltreatment appears to be found in a broad range of families, it is more prominent in families where stressors exceed supports and where risks are greater than protective factors (Belsky, 1980, 1993). Doyle (1997, 2003b) found that a combination of multiple family variables was a better predictor of emotional abuse than any single family variable, pointing out that emotional abuse can also occur in families who are free of obvious stressors and interpersonal problems, such as rejection.

Although some researchers claim that it is difficult to determine the extent to which socio-demographic variables increase risk for emotional abuse and neglect in families (Cawson, Wattam, Brooker, & Kelly, 2000; Black et al., 2001) it is widely known that being poor increases vulnerability for child-rearing and, therefore, can contribute to child maltreatment. It was identified by Sedlak (1997) and Iwaniec (2004) that children from lower-income families, children whose race was described as 'different', children with disabilities, and older children were at increased risk of psychological abuse.

Certain parental personality factors are also believed to increase the risk of emotional abuse. These include: anxiety symptoms, aggression, hostility, lower self-esteem, less engagement in social activities, dysthymic symptoms, lower verbal reasoning, and frequent illness (Lesnik-Oberstein *et al.*, 1995).

Emotional abuse has also been associated with parents' own histories of maltreatment and less than optimal relationships with carers (Glaser & Prior, 2002; Hart *et al.*, 2002; Iwaniec *et al.*, 2002). The experience of such abuse has been noted to affect parents' ability to cope with and manage stressful situations in the family home, and they may later develop insecure attachment and relationship styles with partners and their own children (Iwaniec, 1995). Mothers classed as psychologically abusive are found to have less affectionate relationships with their husbands, and to report greater levels of verbal and physical aggression (Crittenden & Ainsworth, 1989). Further, parental factors such as parental depression, substance abuse, and family violence have also been found to increase the potential for emotionally abusive behaviour (Chaffin, Kelleher, & Hollenberg, 1996; Glaser, 2002; Thoburn *et al.*, 2000).

Child Factors

Just as there appears to be no one type of family that is more vulnerable to emotional abuse, there appears to be no one type of child who is more likely to experience psychological maltreatment in terms of age, gender, ordinal position in family, or health status. Unlike sexual abuse, where females are more likely to present as victims to child services, both males and females are equally vulnerable to experience emotional maltreatment. However, children with birth defects – premature babies, temperamentally difficult children, and those with a physical or intellectual disability – are dispropor-tionately vulnerable to experience a type of caregiving which disregards their emotional and social development. Reports exploring prevalence rates in child-protection services indicate that children with registered disabilities are up to 3.14 times more likely to experience psychological abuse and neglect than children without any registered disabilities (e.g. Sullivan & Knutson, 2000). It is possible that these particular groups are more vulnerable to emotional abuse because of the greater potential for disruptions in the parent–infant bonding process and for greater parenting stress (Crittenden & Ainsworth, 1989, Doyle, 1997; Tomison, 1996a).

CASE STUDIES

There is no better way to illustrate vulnerability and resilience than by exploring the life histories of adults who, as children, were subjected to emotional abuse, whose life trajectories either led to recovery from early and severe adversity, or continued throughout life.

Len and Tom

Len and Tom were born (one year apart) as illegitimate children in the late 1940s. Their mother was a housekeeper in a well-to-do farming family. Len was a product of his mother's relationship with the farmer, the identity of whom was never disclosed.

The shame and stigma of bearing children outside marriage during the 1940s and the demands of the farmer's family forced the mother to leave the village when Len was seven and Tom was six years old. The farmer, who was fond of the boys' mother, persuaded her to leave the boys behind and promised to provide a better quality of life for them. The farmer's family did not share his wish to take care of the boys, yet agreed to maintain them to work as farmhands when they were older. The boys' lives were marked by shame, isolation, and loneliness: they were called derogatory names, publicly referred to as 'bastards', and routinely told they were different and unwanted. They were excluded from family activities and special occasions, and banished from the house when visitors arrived: apart from using them for work purposes, the family seldom interacted with, spoke to, or paid attention to the boys.

Both boys very much missed their mother, yet they were forbidden to talk about her and were never told what happened to her or why she left. Len became very detached, seldom spoke, appeared depressed, and often burst into tears when criticised or reminded that he was the illegitimate and unwanted son of the farmer: he became obedient and did not complain about the maltreatment he experienced. Len was particularly fearful of the farmer's wife and remained in permanent fear when near her. He was a constant reminder of her husband's infidelity, and she hated him for it.

Tom screamed or shouted when derogatory remarks were made or when subjected to extensive and or unreasonable demands; when possible, he spent his free time away from home in the fields, watching birds and animals. Both boys excelled academically but Tom, in particular, demonstrated considerable ability, and eagerness and enthusiasm to learn. He was vivacious, sought the company of children who were kind to him, was imaginative, organised plays or other group activities, and became popular.

The boys' shabby, dishevelled appearance and poor growth alerted the attention and concern of teachers. Their maltreatment was so intense that Tom began to present significant erratic mood swings and bizarre behaviours. It became clear that Len was somewhat protected by the farmer from abusive caregiving and that the maltreatment Tom experienced was more severe and came from everybody. This prompted the intervention of the headmaster who requested Tom's reception into care. Tom left the farm to live in a well-run and supportive children's home for boys at the age of 12, where he spent 6 years. He established a very warm relationship with a care worker who helped him to come to terms with his past. Tom finished school with good marks and developed some friendships. He went on to university and studied law. During his postgraduate studies, he developed a relationship with a fellow student whom he subsequently married. His wife's parents and brother welcomed him into the family and provided him with a supportive family base. Tom became a very successful barrister, and a good husband and father.

Len remained 'second best' in the farmer's household and was unable to escape from the hurtful and disrespectful treatment he received from the farmer's family, especially the wife. He gradually came to believe their assertions that he was 'different' and 'unworthy'. Frequent negative remarks about his appearance and awkward social behaviour made him shy away from relationships and contact with others. In spite of an attractive appearance and gentle manner, he felt that he could not possibly attract any girl's attention and that he would only experience hurt and rejection. However, at the age of 26 the farmer (his natural father) became terminally ill and decided that Len should be married. An arranged marriage took place, but Len's wife was an extremely dominant, rigid, and demanding woman with whom he felt unable to assert his opinion. After his wife humiliated him at a social gathering, Len left home and never returned. His whereabouts or whether he is alive or dead is unknown.

Looking at the distribution of vulnerabilities and protective factors between Tom and Len summarised in Tables 9.1 and 9.2, it is clear that Tom's protective factors exceeded vulnerabilities by about 40%, while Len's vulnerabilities stood at 60%, and protective factors at only 40%. Tom's life chances were so much better once he was removed from the abusive environment and provided with support and therapeutic input by the residential key-worker. Len, on the other hand, had no such opportunities for change and the healing of his pain.

Table 9.1   Tom

Vulnerability	Protective factors – resilience
Loss of mother	Good intellectual potentials
Disruption of attachment	Placid temperament
Rejected by carers	Appealing personality
Denigrated/humiliated	Good school attainments
Socially isolated	Support from teachers
Physically and emotionally neglected	Support from his brother
Emotionally abused	Popular among peers
Exploited	Rescued from abusive environment
Separated from his brother	Constructive and sustained help from the residential worker
Some difficulties in early adjustment to a new life	Continued support from teachers and peer group
Low self-esteem and self-doubts	Successful in sport and making positive relationships
	Reading for comfort
	Good romantic relationship
	Right educational and professional achievements

Table 9.2   Len

Vulnerability	Protective factors – resilience
Sudden loss of mother	Good intellectual ability
Disruption of attachment	Placid temperament
Sullenness, depressive moods	Support from his brother
Denigration and humiliation	Some support from his father
Failure to thrive (physical and emotional neglect)	Good school performance and support from teachers
Low self-esteem – feeling unworthy of affection	
Profound social isolation, inside and outside	
Lack of support from peers	
Inability to communicate	
Loss of his brother	
Avoidance of people and contact with them	
Poor problem-solving ability	

Isabella

Isabella's parents and her younger sister were killed in a car accident when she was almost 4 years old. Isabella survived the accident, and was not badly hurt. She was asleep when the accident happened, yet could recall seeing her parents and sister covered in blood when taken to hospital. Isabella subsequently lived with her much-loved grandmother, who unfortunately developed liver cancer when Isabella was 5 years 10 months old and died 3 months later. Isabella subsequently developed a fear that everybody she loved would be killed one way or another leaving her alone.

After the loss of her grandmother, Isabella went to live with a maternal aunt, her husband, two daughters, and one son. Isabella described her aunt as sympathetic and caring. Her uncle did not like her and frequently demonstrated his resentment at being forced to bring up somebody else's child. Isabella was singled out for criticism, derogatory remarks, and punishment. He was a violent man and there were frequent episodes of domestic violence. Isabella was very fearful for her aunt's safety and often had panic attacks as a result. The uncle often made unrealistic demands of her while in the family home. The cousins were also cold, distant, and unsupportive and frequently played on their father's dislike of Isabella, which often got her into trouble. Her aunt tried to shelter her as much as possible, yet Isabella felt unwanted by other members of the family and was petrified of her uncle.

School, supportive teachers, and friendly peers provided Isabella with some respite and escape from an adverse home environment. She was fortunate that the headmistress of the primary school had been her mother's best friend; this person provided her with extensive emotional support and often invited her away to

Table 9.3 Isabella

Risks and vulnerabilities	Resilience and protective factors
Sudden loss of parents and sister	Pleasant personality
Loss of grandmother	Attractiveness
Changes in caregiving from supportive and loving to cold and detached	Bright and resourceful
Feeling unwanted by her uncle and cousins	Support from teachers and an aunt
Domestic violence	Good school performance and good relationship with peers
	Membership of Girl Guides (which she enjoyed) and support from leaders and the other girls

spend weekends with her. The headteacher told Isabella many things about her mother and provided her with an opportunity to talk. Isabella drew a great sense of comfort and support from the contact with her mother's friend and learned to treasure the memory of her mother. Isabella's school achievements were good, given her experience, and she finished school with positive results. After leaving school she went to study nursing. In agreement with her aunt, both decided that it would be better for her to live away from the difficulties she was subjected to at home. Isabella completed her training and developed a successful career.

Being a very attractive girl with a pleasant, generous, helpful, and friendly personality, she gained popularity and respect among peers and colleagues. In addition, she stated how she had learned how to avoid confrontations with her uncle and where to seek support when feeling sad and despondent. Isabella felt that the reasons she had survived major tragic events and emerged from them relatively well were due to several factors: her aunt's persistent, quiet support and protection; the interest and support of schoolteachers; good relationships with peers; and membership of the Girl Guides. She felt wanted, appreciated and valued by the Girl Guides' leaders and enjoyed the activities and the company of the other girls enormously.

CASE DISCUSSION

It is clear that emotional abuse may increase a child's vulnerability. It would appear from examining the cases of Len, Tom, and Isabella that all three children were exposed to significant emotional maltreatment. Current understanding of possible mechanisms or processes underlying risk mediation (and how and why certain risks operate and lead to psychopathology in some children but not in others) is somewhat limited (Rutter, 1999). Several key factors do appear influential in determining the consequences and impact of abuse for children exposed to emotional maltreatment (see Emery & Laumann-Billings, 2002). Predisposing factors such as early caregiving experiences; precipitating factors such as the frequency, intensity, and duration of the abuse; factors intrinsic to the child such as working models of the self and others; internal or external attributions; and behavioural and coping strategies, self-esteem, and disposition are important to examine in abusive cases. Additionally, external factors (such as school influences and availability of supportive relationships) need to be taken into consideration in terms of their survival value and support. Reference will be made to the cases presented here as illustrations, but not as generalisations, or claiming universal evidence based on three cases.

PREDISPOSING FACTORS

Early Caregiving Experiences

Tom, Len, and Isabella all enjoyed early experiences of loving, caring, and supportive relationships. Unfortunately, all three children experienced the loss of their primary caregivers. For Isabella this was compounded by the subsequent and untimely loss of her grandmother. Healthy experiences in early childhood and attachment security are believed to protect children against the later effects of psychological maltreatment and predict later adaptive psychosocial functioning (Shonkoff & Phillips, 2000). However, the likelihood of positive trajectories appears primarily related to a *continuation* of sensitive, supportive care than simply to good relationships with significant others which may come to a premature end (Egeland, Kalkoske, Gottesman, & Erickson, 1990). When parent–child relationships are discontinued, a secure attachment in infancy may not necessarily predict later adaptive psychosocial functioning (Thompson, 1999). Thus, while early experiences of loving, caring, and supportive attachment relationships may have initially boosted resilience, the subsequent loss of these supportive relationships and substitution of psychologically abusive patterns of caregiving may have counteracted the advantages associated with early positive care experiences. The reverse may be the case as well, e.g. early negative experiences may be compensated by proper intervention and life chances (Clarke & Clarke, 2000; Iwaniec, 2004).

PRECIPITATING FACTORS

Context of the Abuse – Frequency, Intensity, and Duration

The nature of the abuse (together with its frequency, intensity, and duration) plays a part in determining the extent to which emotional abuse exerts an impact upon a child's life (Emery & Laumann-Billings, 2002). Friedman and Chase-Lansdale (2002) highlighted the importance of focusing on the comprehensiveness of environmental characteristics and of looking at whether adversities are widespread and of long duration. Both Tom and Isabella experienced similar risks to Len, but were exposed to these risks for a shorter amount of time. Their experiences were less widespread and pervasive due to the fact that they had fewer risk-factors and access to a greater range of protective factors such as outside supports and personal attributes, in addition to more positive life chances.

Although many of a child's difficulties remit when removed from an abusive system (Clarke & Clarke, 2000; Iwaniec, 2004; Skuse *et al.*, 1996), a considerable number of children still show signs of dysfunction many years after the abuse has terminated, particularly if they remain exposed to a number of risk-factors and if emotional support and help is unavailable (Iwaniec, 2004). Both Tom's and Isabella's difficulties seemed to resolve when they were removed from the source of their abuse. Len was not so fortunate. His marriage, although providing an opportunity to escape from the unsatisfactory home, perpetuated the cycle of maltreatment through constant criticism, fear of the farmer's wife, and unreasonable demands. For Len, the cycle of abuse had become so ingrained that it was extremely difficult for him to become a different person. His life chances did not give him the opportunity to re-emerge from adversities and to start again. In spite of intellectual abilities he did not succeed. A number of adversities exceeded a number of protective factors, and continuity of emotional ill-treatment, compounded with sensitive personality make-up, seriously damaged him.

FACTORS INTRINSIC TO THE CHILD

Working Models of Self and Others

Emotionally abused children are likely to be insecurely attached to their abusive caregivers and to develop 'internal working models' of distrust and rejection which they expect from all their key relationships (Doyle, 2001; Iwaniec, 2004). The rejection that Tom and Len experienced due to their mother's departure without explanation may have led them both to assume that they were unworthy or unlovable. The subsequent maltreatment they experienced would have consolidated this belief. For Isabella, the experiences of multiple and traumatic losses appeared to foster a world view that people that she loved died, leaving her alone and unsupported. Her uncle's violent behaviour and cruelty possibly facilitated a belief that carers were uncaring and unsupportive. Being able to get respite from school and peers helped her to survive and manage her unsatisfactory existence at home.

Behavioural/Coping Strategies

The development of behavioural strategies in order to function in the face of adversities, such as emotional abuse, may either facilitate or disrupt resilience. Crittenden and Ainsworth (1989) describe two behavioural strategies that abused children may develop with implications for both short- and long-term outcomes. First, a *compulsive compliant* strategy may consist of excessive social vigilance, superficial compliance, and inhibited anger in situations in which others seem threatening or powerful. Although adaptive in the short term, as it reduces the risk of parental violence, by adopting this strategy the child is learning to suppress his or her own feelings, and may risk enduring long-term maladaptive outcomes associated with a diminished sense of satisfaction and achievement.

Conversely, an *overtly resistant* strategy may consist of confrontations with others who seem threatening or powerful. This strategy is described as being more risky in the short term because children who employ this strategy may be more likely to experience parental anger and active abuse; as they are less likely to deny their own feelings, or to defensively exclude or misinterpret information, this approach may thus be more protective in the long term (Crittenden & Ainsworth, 1989). A constellation of externalised behaviours, demonstrably poor health, and deterioration in well-being can attract the concern and attention of teachers or people in the community. Adopting a more resistant style to manage emotional problems may lead to more damaging consequences in the short term, but in the long run may lead to positive change (e.g. in Tom's case it led to his subsequent removal from the abusive context and functioned as a means of rescue).

Disposition

Dispositional attributes, such as an easy temperament, distinguish stress-resistant children from stress-vulnerable children and may enhance resilience in the face of adversity (Friedman & Chase-Lansdale, 2002). Tom was outgoing and bright, and was able to mobilise support and intervention, which ultimately helped him somewhat to withdraw from the abusive home. Isabella was attractive, bright and resourceful, which in some way may have helped her establish and secure positive relationships outside the family home. Len was more withdrawn and subdued, presented poor social and interpersonal skills, and found it difficult to build relationships, thus increasing his vulnerability and limiting his opportunities and stamina to pursue change.

ENVIRONMENTAL FACTORS

School and Neighbourhood

Abused children often present in the school environment with an overarching concern with security issues and an underlying expectation of unresponsiveness and rejection from adults. Nevertheless, school can provide an opportunity for maltreated children to gain the social, emotional, and practical support they need. However, difficulties (such as failing schoolwork or difficult peer relationships) may perpetuate any negative self-perceptions and render some children particularly vulnerable (Cicchetti & Toth, 1995b). Tom, Len, and Isabella all demonstrated good intellectual ability and academic performance: for all three, school functioned as a respite and as a distraction from the abuse they experienced within the family home, as well as providing an opportunity to develop positive relationships. Skills and interests were established, particularly for Tom and Isabella, in specific subject areas and extra-curricular activities (such as sport and Girl Guides) that enhanced self-efficacy and self-esteem.

Peer Relationships and Organisational Groups

Relationships with same-age peers, siblings, adults outside the abusive system, organisational and religious groups, pets, and toys can function as lifelines for children who have a history, or who are currently victims of, maltreatment (Doyle, 1997). Tom and Isabella established good relationships with peers, were well-liked, achieved, and maintained relationships that were pleasurable and rewarding. In their relationships with peers they learned how to relate to others in an appropriate manner and learned that others could be caring and trustworthy. Both Tom and Isabella also had access to community resources (the children's home and Girl Guides respectively) which provided them both with a sense of stability and predictability. In addition to the care and support given by these organisations, Tom and Isabella experienced consistency, from which they gained a sense of security which was lacking in their family homes. Len was not able to engage in, or have access to, community supports, or have the ability to form peer relationships (because of the emotional harm he experienced), which may have contributed to his increased vulnerability and poor outcomes.

Support

It has been documented that the presence of a supportive relationship can buffer the impact of emotional abuse and promote resilience. For example, Clarke and Clarke (2000), Doyle (1997), and Rutter (1990b) found that, of a number of internal and external factors that acted to protect children from the damaging effects of emotional abuse, the most important single survival factor was the presence of at least one person who gave unconditional, positive regard, who thought well of them, and made them feel important. There are multiple ways in which supportive relationships can exert a protective function for children who experience emotional abuse.

For example, according to Crittenden and Ainsworth (1989), supportive relationships can help children through difficult experiences; can modify working models to include more positive images of the self and others; can help feelings of satisfaction; and can increase the likelihood of forming subsequent close or supportive relationships with others. The availability of a supportive person can also promote resilience to the damaging effects of abuse by assisting a child in developing capacity to make decisions, in developing a sense of right and wrong, in detaching emotionally from the abusive carer, and in engaging in other relationships (Briggs & Hawkins, 1996). A supportive individual may also enhance resilience by helping a child to make sense of how and why the abuse occurred, thereby enhancing a sense of control (Madge, 1997). Indeed Tomison and Tucci (1997) point out that adaptive functioning of children who have been emotionally maltreated may be enhanced by a constant supportive person, and by teaching abused children to structure experiences, enhance social competence, and strengthen socio-emotional bases for relationship-formation (Gilligan, 2001; Wolfe, 1991).

COMMENTS ON RISK AND RESILIENCE

According to the cumulative risk model, the greatest psychopathological risk comes from the cumulative effects of multiple environmental and genetic risk-factors whereby accumulation of risk-factors renders children vulnerable to negative outcomes (Rutter, 1985, 1986, 1999). In addition, because some risk and protective factors operate across a wide range while others are quite specific in their effects, it is necessary to focus on risk and resilience with respect to particular risk experiences and particular psychopathological outcomes (Rutter, 2002). There has also been a recent drive within risk and resilience literature to explore the 'how' and 'why' questions of why some children achieve adaptive outcomes in the face of multiple and chronic adversities. Currently we have no empirically based theory of how, or to what extent, early experiences shape long-term development (O'Connor, 2003). However, evidence points to the significance of the timing and ordering of events. It would appear that resilience changes over time and according to circumstances. For example, the ordering of major life events (e.g. finishing at school/university, marriage, and child-rearing) has been found to be significant for long-term development.

When investigating resilience, it is necessary to consider present, past, and continuing experiences because outcomes are influenced by a complex pattern of interconnected risks throughout the course of development (O'Connor, 2003). The effects of adversity are influenced by a reduction of negative and an increase of positive chain reactions (Rutter, 1999). It has also been found that new experiences can open up 'turning-point' effects and that positive experiences can neutralise some risk-factors (Rutter, 1999). The case studies convincingly illustrate these points.

Clearly, Len's life history shows that the prolonged systematic emotional harm inflicted on him damaged his personality in terms of low self-esteem, self-doubt, inability to make his own decisions, passivity, loneliness, depressive moods, apathy, lack of confidence, inability to stand up for himself, social isolation, difficulties in building social and romantic relationships, and poor communication skills. Len had nobody to help him to come to terms with his sad past, and no means of escape from a rather humiliating and unsupportive environment – he was stuck, perceived as an awkward intruder who had to be tolerated but not accepted. Losing his brother, the only remaining support and attachment, was devastating and further compounded the earlier loss of his mother.

In contrast, the cases of Tom and Isabella convincingly illustrate how, despite an experience of severe adversity, traumatic loss, emotional pain, and rejection, an individual can achieve a satisfying and successful life path with extensive and appropriate practical and emotional support, intervention, and life chances. Although Tom and Isabella's emotional maltreatment was pervasive and relentless, opportunities for alternative experiences functioned as protective factors which facilitated resilience and ultimately healthier outcomes. Both persons had pleasant and engaging personalities: they could engage in good peer relationships, developed interpersonal skills, and attracted and maintained the interest of adults who intervened and supported them. Within the context of positive relationships they learned to attribute the abuse to external factors, were able to advance a positive identity, and learned to trust and develop confidence in others (and, ultimately, in themselves). Hobbies and contacts with community supports and academic interests provided respite from the maltreatment, and fostered healthy self-concepts and self-esteem, as well as the professional skills which eventually provided avenues for independence and financial security. With appropriate support, behavioural strategies, and life chances, Tom and Isabella achieved adaptive outcomes in spite of the chronic adversity and emotional abuse they experienced in childhood.

In addition to the timing and ordering of events, the level and severity of adversity experienced has also been shown to influence resilience. It was found that individuals who experience a greater number of adversities tend to be at greater risk for adverse outcomes. For example, children exposed to multiple risks are much more likely to show psychopathology than children who are not. Jenkins and Keating (1999) found that while children without exposure to risks had a 10% rate of psychiatric disorder, children exposed to four or more risks experienced a 50% increase in rate of psychiatric disorder. Similarly, Rutter (1979) found that while children with a single risk-factor were at no greater risk for disorder than children without, children with two risk-factors experienced a 5% increase in risk for disorder and children with four or more risk-factors experienced a 20% increase in risk for disorder. Overall, individuals showing resilience tend to be those who have been exposed to fewer risks for a shorter time (Rutter, 2002).

Much variation in vulnerability to psychosocial stress and adversity is due to a complex interplay between genetic and environmental factors (Rutter, 1999). Genetic factors are implicated both in individual differences in exposure to environmental risk and in the mediation of risks associated with factors defined in environmental terms (Rutter, 2002). Both genetic and environmental factors have been found to interact in a complex manner to influence resilience, with each perceived to exert a roughly equal impact (Rutter, 2000). For example, while genetic factors have been found to increase vulnerability to high-risk environments, the effects of genetic risk-factors have been found to be less damaging in the absence of environmental risk.

Protective factors are variables that are found to modify a person's response to a risk-factor (Rutter, 1987). Rather than being opposite to risk-factors, protective factors exert some kind of indirect, interactive, or catalytic effect. It is important to consider the particular mechanisms involved that interact to provide protection in the face of adversity.

Protective factors for children in high-risk environments include caring and supportive relationships; secure attachment; availability of supportive extended family members; affectionate ties with parent-substitute (such as grandparents or older siblings); family cohesion; emotional warmth; and absence of discord (Daniel & Wassell, 2002; Doyle, 1997; Iwaniec, 2000; Mitchell, 2005; Thoburn et al., 2000).

The protective impact of supportive relationship was found to be of notable importance, especially for older children. The presence of a greater number of good relationships was needed to provide protection. Sources of support have also been found to be significant. For example, children with multiple risks and absence of a good relationship with people other than parents tended to display high levels of difficult behaviour (Herbert, 1998a). The mechanisms through which relationships protect and promote resilience are unclear: however, it is thought that such relationships promote well-being through a sense of belonging, coherence, and co-operation, and of integration within a community.

Protective mechanisms operating at the 'person' level have been found to include features such as autonomy, self-esteem, and a socially positive orientation (Garmezy & Rutter, 1983); positive and high expectations; strong belief in personal control; internal locus of control; a sense of coherence, a feeling of confidence that one's internal and external environment was predictable and that things would probably work out well; and experience of pleasurable success in one arena or another (Daniel & Wassell, 2002; Rutter, 2002).

The ways in which individuals process experiences may also influence the development of resilience. Cognitive coping strategies have been found to play an important role in adjustment. In their study of the cognitive coping strategies of resilient child sexual-abuse survivors, Himelein and McElrath (1996) found four protective factors to be associated with high adjustment. These included: disclosing and discussing; minimisation; positive reframing; and refusing to dwell on the negative experience. Self-enhancing distortions of reality such as exaggerated perceptions of personal control and unrealistic optimism were also found to assist adjustment.

At least average intelligence has been found to affect resilience, with this effect partially mediated through educational failure and associated social consequences. However, the mechanisms through which levels of cognitive functioning impact upon resilience remain unclear (Rutter, 2002; Widom, 1999a).

EARLY ADVERSITIES AND RECOVERY

As can be seen from Tom's and Isabella's life histories, people can recover from serious adversities and build a normal, satisfactory life, providing they receive adequate help (of good quality) and the necessary support. Much will depend upon the type and duration of problems, their history in the individual, genetic factors, and certain life chances that may or may not occur. There are ample examples in the literature based on empirical evidence, indicating positive outcomes in spite of severe early difficulties (see Clarke & Clarke, 1999, 2000 for a full discussion). The outcomes of the Romanian orphans' study (Rutter *et al.*, 1998) illustrate considerable recovery from extreme deprivation.

After the collapse of Ceausescu's regime in Romania the horror of abandoned babies living under appalling conditions in the large orphanages was discovered. Many of these children were adopted by people from western countries. In the United Kingdom these children have been followed up and compared with the progress of other adopted children by Professor Rutter and his colleagues. Rutter *et al.* (1998) reported some very interesting findings. The babies who had been reared in severely deprived conditions, with poor nutrition, ill-health, or little sensory or social stimulation, were seriously retarded in all areas of development. Rutter and his colleagues found a close association between the duration of deprivation and the severity of the child's intellectual retardation. A significant proportion of the Romanian adoptees studied also showed autistic-like patterns of behaviour, such as indiscriminate approaches to strangers, clinging, and narrow, obsessive interests. However, the indication of the recovery of intellectual capacities and improvement of autistic-like behaviours of the severely neglected children in these studies was remarkable, but not complete, for those who at the time of rescue were over six months old. Most babies made a good recovery – certainly in their sensory capacities (walking and talking), and their social and emotional skills improved. This research does suggest that even very deprived children can recover to a large extent if given extensive and dedicated remedial stimulation and care.

Equally, Iwaniec's (2004) longitudinal study showed that children classified as psychosocial short stature with serious global developmental retardation, when removed from the emotionally abusive environment and placed in a nurturing home, recovered remarkably well and began to function satisfactorily socially, cognitively, and emotionally. Those who were removed into a caring home showed an increase in their IQ by the end of the first year, and a marked improvement in social and emotional development. Additionally, those who were adopted made a particularly good recovery.

Let us look now at the widely publicised case of the Czech twins who recovered from unbelievable cruelty and acute adversity which lasted for a few years. Jarmile Koluchowa (a personal friend of the author and Czech professor of psychology) published a fascinating story (1991) of identical twins, both boys, born in 1960. Their mother died shortly after giving birth to them. They were received into care where they spent a year, and then were looked after by the maternal aunt for 6 months. At the age of 18 months their development was described as normal. The twins' father remarried and they were returned to his and his new wife's care. The stepmother disliked the children and treated them in an extremely cruel way. She beat and starved them, and eventually banished them to the cellar where they spent 5.5 years. The children were discovered at the age of 7 when they did not register for school, but there was no record that they had died. At 7 the boys were seriously stunted in stature, lacked speech, suffered from rickets, failed to understand the meaning of pictures, and were totally unsocialised. Medical examination predicted permanent damage to physical and mental health. After being removed from parental care they received massive medical treatment and physiotherapy and then went to a school for children with severe learning disabilities. They were then adopted by a very warm and kindly woman and her sister and went to a normal school. What is remarkable here is that due to exceptionally good care and attention they caught up with age-peers on intellectual, emotional, and social levels. After finishing secondary education they went to technical school, training as typewriter mechanics, and then went to study electronics. They went to do National Service, married, and had children.

The follow-ups confirmed that they became fully adjusted, stable, and normally functioning people.

Children exposed to acute adversity can not only survive, but can also recover and can catch up developmentally if strong and appropriate remedial intervention is provided. The cases illustrated here showed remarkable recovery due to life-chances and dedicated care provision. Such examples tell us that early experiences, regardless of how bad they are, can be reversed if there are no genetic or congenital abnormalities. Skuse (1984) and Skuse *et al.* (1996) found that children of psychosocial short stature put on weight and grew rapidly in height if removed from an emotionally and physically insulting environment, but when returned to it they lost weight and behaviour worsened. Decisive action and good substitute care helped them to catch up in growth, intellectual functioning, and emotional stability.

SUMMARY

Emotional abuse is a contributing factor to all types of child maltreatment. It is characterised by a chronic pattern of carer behaviours which involve active rejection or persecution of the child and/or an unwillingness, indifference, or inability to meet their needs. This type of maltreatment compromises a child's social, emotional, and cognitive development and increases vulnerability for long-term psychological damage. As there are often no immediate physical consequences (except in cases of failure to thrive), cases often go undetected by professionals, parents, and victims.

Table 9.4   Checklist of factors associated with increased vulnerability or resilience in cases of emotional abuse

Factors associated with increased vulnerability	Protective factors associated with increased resilience
Balance of risk and protective factors	*Balance of risk and protective factors*
• Presence of more risk than protective factors	• Presence of more protective than risk-factors
Nature of the abuse	*Nature of the abuse*
• Timing of the risk	• Timing of the risk
• Longer duration of exposure	• Shorter duration of exposure
• Frequent, intense, widespread, and pervasive	• Intermittent and restricted
Caregiver factors	*Caregiver factors*
• Insecure attachment relationship(s)	• Continuity of attachment
• Family violence	• Positive early caregiving experiences
• Mental-health problems	• Good health
• Social isolation	• Supportive relationship between parents

- Learning disabilities
- Substance misuse
- Family breakdown
- Poverty and social exclusion
- Single-parent families

Child factors
- Loss of primary caregivers
- Lack of support at home or outside
- Low self-esteem and self-efficacy
- Disability or illness
- Low IQ
- Inability to come to terms with the abuse
- Difficulties interacting with peers
- Poor problem-solving abilities
- Difficult temperament

External factors
- Limited opportunities for respite from the abusive environment
- Limited opportunities to develop skills, hobbies or interests outside home
- Few friendships
- Poor school performance and lack of support from teachers
- Social isolation

- Good problem-solving abilities
- Reasonable economic standards

Child factors
- More than average intelligence
- Higher levels of self-esteem and self-efficacy
- Level temperament
- Positive school attainment
- Ability to mobilise support
- Social competence
- Problem-solving ability
- Physical attractiveness
- Peer group which is pro-social
- Availability of at least one supportive caregiver
- Availability of outside interest and support

External factors
- Opportunities for respite from the abusive environment
- Availability and use of external support systems
- Skills, interests or membership of organisations
- Friendships
- Good school performance and support from teachers
- Additional lifelines such as pets or toys

It is helpful for professionals to be aware of issues that could be considered in an analysis of risk and resilience factors in cases of psychological maltreatment. Assessments and decision-making processes in child-protection services need to consider strengths and weaknesses of the child, family, and community system. Risk and protective factors for vulnerability and resilience exist at many levels within the child's social ecology. A comprehensive analysis of risk and protective factors for emotional abuse is illustrated in Table 9.4.

SECTION 2

ASSESSMENT OF EMOTIONAL ABUSE AND NEGLECT

CHAPTER 10

ASSESSMENT OF EMOTIONAL ABUSE AND NEGLECT

CONTENTS

INTRODUCTION

Assessment, decision-making, and intervention are major activities of any practitioner working with children and families. These tasks are never easy, but they are particularly difficult when dealing with issues of abuse and neglect and, specifically, with the emotional maltreatment of children and adolescents.

Although knowledge about emotional abuse and neglect has increased considerably over the last decade or so, making decisions based on well-informed assessment (that the child has suffered or is likely to suffer significant harm because of emotional abuse) is still difficult. We have developed a reasonable understanding (thanks to many research projects) of what emotional abuse and neglect are, and how we can identify such abuse, but knowing where and when to draw a line between harsh and unsympa-thetic treatment of a child by carers and significant harm still presents a real challenge. The assessor also has to take into consideration the probability of harm occurring in the future if abusive behaviour continues. These predictions are hard to make as things can change and a child may show exceptional resilience and ability to buffer itself from the effects of emotional abuse as it grows older and becomes more independent. Again, it would be unwise to assume that all children are so resilient that they will bounce back into emotional stability and social adjustment regardless of their experiences. If risk-factors in a child's life are far greater than protective factors, then serious consideration has to be given as to what to do to protect the child from likely harm.

There are a few requirements for conducting assessment on emotional abuse and neglect, regardless of what assessment framework we adopt as a guideline. As long as we adopt the position that it is a child's welfare we are assessing, we will do a reasonable job, as wisdom gained in practice and through experience will help. However, there are a few principles to be observed during the assessment process. First, in order to do the child and the carers justice, sound knowledge of what constitutes emotional abuse (and how it comes about) is needed. Second, in order to be able to differentiate between what is emotionally harmful and what is just less affectionate emotional nurturing, the severity, duration, frequency, and intensity have to be carefully examined, and the child's age needs to be taken into account. Third, the effects of emotional abuse and neglect on a child have to be scrutinised and evaluated. Fourth, exploration of parental attitudes, mental health, childhood experiences, parenting capacities, and personal and environmental factors (or stressors) have to be explored. In order to accomplish this, sound knowledge of child development and developmental needs and hazards is necessary. Equally, we need to learn what makes parents or other caregivers react and rear a child in an anxiety-provoking, painful, and often cruel way, and why the parent–child relationship and interaction should be explored in great detail during any assessment.

This chapter provides a schedule of assessing children (who are emotion-ally abused and/or neglected) and parents or carers (who are abusive and neglectful). The schedule is partly based on the *Framework of Assessment* issued by the Department of Health (2000) for assessing children in need, but also on risk-factors. As emotional abuse deals with children in need of support, help, and allocation of services (as well as in need of protection in serious cases), both family support and protection aspects of assessment are addressed. Many check-lists and tables have been developed over the years by the author and tested for their usefulness and applicability for emotional-abuse assessment. An ecological approach is used, looking at family, child, and environment factors.

DEPARTMENT OF HEALTH *FRAMEWORK OF ASSESSMENT*

A new framework for assessing children in need was issued in the United Kingdom by the Department of Health (DoH) in 2000, with the stated intention of providing holistic, child-centered, and much more targeted help for all children who are in need of help or protection. The assessment framework is multidimensional, addressing parental capacity, children's developmental needs, and family and environmental factors. The assessment is based on ecological theory, postulating that children's development is influenced by the quality of parenting which, in turn, is influenced by the characteristics of their families, social network, neighbourhoods, communities, and the interrelations among them (Belsky, 1984; Bronfenbrenner, 1993). Risk and resilience (as seen in Chapter 9) have also been considered within the same ecological theory.

The philosophy of the new framework aims to redirect assessment focus from the risk and blame culture to the developmental needs of children (and ways of meeting these needs in the families and communities in which they live) by providing services for those who require help and avoiding State intervention (in terms of court proceedings and removal of children from parental care) unless it is absolutely necessary. Additionally, it is argued that the 'wait-and-see' approach needs to be avoided when dealing with cases where evidence suggests a poor prognosis for change in parenting. Quick decision-making is often essential in order to avoid further deterioration and increase of difficulties (leading to significant harm and consequent care proceedings). There is emphasis on providing better distribution of resources for all children in need of help, and to narrow the gap between protection and family support. Because emotionally abused and neglected children were formerly at the end of the queue for resource distribution, and because such abuse was not considered dangerous (as far as child protection is concerned) this is a change for the better, providing that philosophy is matched to resources, that there is an awareness that emotional abuse is at the core of all types of abuse and neglect, and that its effects can be deeper than the effects of physical or sexual abuse.

Assessment of needs is a useful tool, but presents problems when it comes to child-protection cases, as it is very general, avoiding focusing on the very problem presented in the referral (which clearly may indicate concerns about the child's safety and risk to his/her welfare).

PARENTING DUTIES AND PROBLEMS

As we have seen in the previous chapters, many research projects have identified a number of aspects of parent–child interactions and relationships which
differentiate emotionally abusing and non-abusing parenting. A comparison
of emotional expression by these two groups in interaction with children
shows many and varied differences. However, on closer examination, differences are mostly notable in the frequency and intensity of emotionally
abusive parental behaviour, experiences of being parented as children,
and availability of advice and support regarding the developmental needs
of children and an understanding of children's behaviour. Research results
may, at times, be interpreted that abusive families are qualitatively different
from non-abusive families in their everyday behaviour and relationships. In
the majority of cases such families appear to consist of very ordinary people
in need of help and correction in parenting their children. Only a small
proportion of parents are wilfully harmful to their children, and their children
need prompt action to protect them. Additionally, characteristics of children
and their circumstances have to be taken into consideration in order to make
sense of what is going on and to devise appropriate helping strategies or to
take protective action.

We know that parents or carers bring to relationships and interactions with
children their personal histories of being parented, different personalities, sets
of attitudes to child-rearing, expectations, and current lifestyles and functioning.
Children, also, have individual characteristics (such as temperamental
attributes, good or ill-health, disability, or particular vulnerability [e.g.
premature birth, low birth weight, etc.]). The quality of the relationship
between a child and its parents will be determined by mutual responsiveness
to each other's needs. It is argued that parenting behaviour is influenced by a
child's behaviour, and the child's reaction to its parents is determined by the
parenting that he or she has experienced (Frude, 2003). So the parent–child
interaction is a two-way process, one influencing the other either positively or
negatively. The assessment, therefore, has to address these issues. The way
parents rear their children is also influenced by the culture to which they
belong and by the beliefs and standards of communities in which they live.

Belsky (1984) argued convincingly that competent parenting is multiply
determined, and proposed that influences fall into three categories:

1. the parents' characteristics;
2. the contextual sources of support (e.g. marital/partner relationship, family
   unity and support, help and support from extended family, friends,
   neighbours, and wider community); and
3. the child's characteristics (e.g. temperament, physical appearance, health,
   child's behavioural responses to the parents).

These dimensions will be explored in this chapter from the point of view of needs and risks.

Assessment of parenting has to take into consideration the nature of the relationship between parent and child. The 'goodness of fit' between the characteristics of the child and parents needs to be assessed within the context of their relationship. What is important when assessing the parenting of emotionally abused and neglected children is not so much how well-informed, skilful, and competent the parents are but, more importantly, how their skills and any information they acquire are translated and expressed when dealing with children within the context of the parent–child relationship and the strength of the emotional bonds within the family. The interviewing schedule in Table 10.1 is a useful tool focusing on child-rearing attitudes and

Table 10.1   Interview schedule with parents

1. It looks to me that you are experiencing some problems in parenting your child. What kind of problems are they? Can you describe each of them?
2. How do you handle these behaviours? Can you give me an example of how, for instance, you deal with defiance or attention-seeking?
3. How do you discipline your child? What do you do to help the child to behave in a pro-social way?
4. What is your reaction and behaviour when the child (according to your thoughts) misbehaves?
5. Do you often criticise, tell off, and show anger and resentment when dealing with the child's behaviour?
6. Can you describe rules and routines in your family? Are children aware and informed of what is acceptable and what is not?
7. Do you threaten your child in an anxiety-provoking way (e.g. of being abandoned, killed, thrown out from the home, etc.)? How often would you do that?
8. How do you correct, instruct, and teach the child to behave, or do things well and according to the child's age? Can you give me a few examples?
9. Do you punish your child by sending him/her to their room for a long time, or locking him/her away from everybody in odd places (e.g. cellar, cupboard, etc.)?
10. Do you, at times, humiliate, and embarrass your child by saying critical and unkind things in front of peers or other family members?
11. Do you regret hurting your child by being overcritical? Do you ever apologise for being unkind, but explain that you did not mean what you said?
12. How do you help the child to learn different skills (eating, dressing, toilet-training) when small, and later to interact with peers, doing homework, helping in the house?
13. Do you ask your child to do things which may be too difficult for his or her age?
14. Do you praise the child and show pleasure in his/her achievements?
15. How much time do you spend with the child and what do you do together?
16. Do you show your child feelings of love and devotion by touching, kissing, smiling, and hugging? Do you encourage your child to come to you for comfort, reassurance, and support?

Table 10.1   (Continued)

---

17. Do you do things with the child? Describe these mutual activities.
18. Do you enjoy your child's company, and do you know why?
19. Does your child bring you pleasure and satisfaction? Can you talk about it?
20. What do you like about your child? Describe these likeable qualities to me.
21. What are your expectations for the child?
22. What do other members of the family think about him/her?
23. Can you describe how you get on together?
24. Does your child bring you a lot of worry and aggravation?
25. How does he/she get on with brothers or sisters?
26. Are you proud of your child and why?
27. How often do you tell your child that you love him/her?
28. How does your child get on with other people when in their company?
29. Do you blame the child if things go wrong in the family, or for you?
30. Do you take an interest in your child's schoolwork and other activities?
31. Do you remember your child's birthday and celebrate it?
32. Do you acknowledge your child's distress, sadness, and anxiety, and try to help your child?
33. Do you think that your child feels loved, wanted, and appreciated?
34. Do you consider that your child's needs come before your needs?

Let us look now at the early history of your child.

35. Did you want to have your child? Was he/she planned?
36. What kind of pregnancy, labour, and birth did you have with him/her?
37. What was she/he like as a baby in terms of feeding, sleeping, contentment, responsiveness, and health?
38. What were the major difficulties (if any) when he/she was a baby?
39. Did you feel close to your baby early on and how do you feel now?
40. Could you tell me what his/her development was like in terms of achieving various milestones (when he/she sat, crawled, walked, first words, sentences, toilet-training, etc.)?
41. How would you like to change the present situation so both of you are happier together?
42. What help and assistance do you need to make things work for the child and family?
43. Would you be willing to work with us so that we could improve the present situation?
44. Would you agree to devise an action plan together, based on mutual agreement as to who is going to do what, when, and how?

---

practices, emphasising possible emotional abuse. It needs to be stressed that some information may not be disclosed by the parents during the interview. If there is suspicion of particularly serious abusive behaviour, it needs to be investigated with the help of other people (e.g. health visitor, extended family, neighbours, older children), who need to be interviewed as well.

ASSESSMENT OF BASIC CARE

Emotionally abused and neglected children require basic provision of physical care (such as food, shelter, clothing, appropriate hygiene, bedding, and medical and social care), as do any other children, and an environment which is peaceful and not overwhelming. As emotional abuse occurs in all types of families, rich and poor, the physical care of the child might be adequate or even very good at first glance. Closer examination might show, in some cases, obsessive preoccupation with tidiness and cleanliness (where there is no freedom of play and a child is not allowed to get dirty), or with allowing play with only a few toys at the same time. Equally, provision of basic care might be 'clinical and mechanical', and devoid of warmth and pleasure in caring for the child. In cases of neglect (both physical and emotional) resulting in failure to thrive, provision of food and the manner of feeding need to be carefully examined by direct observation (e.g. what amount and when the child is fed, noting the intake of food and measuring the rate of weight-gain). Basic care of children who fail to thrive also requires careful observation and identification of subtle clues which are demonstrated by parental attitudes towards food and weight, or the parental emotional relationship with the child (see Iwaniec, 2004, for full discussion). The questions in Table 10.2 need to be addressed when assessing

Table 10.2   The quality of nutritional and physical care of a child
Rate the quality of nutritional and physical care provided for the child, based on observation and interview data. The higher the score, the greater the cause for concern over the child's welfare.

Name: _____   Date: _____

Overall Rating: _____

Section A	Most of the time	Sometimes	Not very often
	1	2	3

Nutrition

Is the child regularly fed?
Is the child given enough food for his/her age?
Is the child being picked up when fed?
Is the child encouraged to eat by being prompted
   and praised?
Is food presented in an appetising way?
Is the food suitable for the child's age?
Are the signals of hunger or satiation properly
   interpreted?
Is the manner of feeding comfortable and anxiety-free?

Table 10.2   (Continued)

Section A	Most of the time 1	Sometimes 2	Not very often 3
Is there availability of food?			
Is the child handled patiently during feeding/eating?			
Is the child encouraged to eat?			
Is there reasonable flexibility in feeding/eating routine?			
Physical care			
Is there awareness of child being too thin, small, or unwell?			
Is the child's medical care being seen to, such as: medical examinations, vaccination, eye and hearing tests, etc.?			
Is medical advice sought when the child is unwell?			
Is there recognition and concern about the child's well-being?			
Is the child appropriately dressed for the weather?			
Is the child changed and clean?			
Are medical or other health or welfare agency appointments being kept?			
Do the parents administer required medication for the child?			
Is the safety for the child observed?			
Is the child supervised and guided?			
Is the child protected from a smoking environment and other unhealthy substances?			
Total for Section A			

Section B rates parental attitudes and behaviour regarding feeding and food.

Section B	Most of the time 3	Sometimes 2	Not very often 1
Does the caregiver appear angry during the feeding/eating period?			
Is there evidence of frustration during the feeding/eating period?			
Is the child punished for not eating?			
Is food withheld as a means of punishment?			
Does the caregiver restrict the child's intake of food (or dilute the formulae) to prevent possible obesity?			

Table 10.2   (Continued)

Section B	Most of the time	Sometimes	Not very often
	3	2	1
Does the caregiver restrict the child's intake of food and variety of food due to fabricated illnesses, e.g. allergies, etc.?			
Are the caregiver's attitudes to food and eating negative (e.g. dislike of food, preoccupied with healthy food, strictly vegetarian, or vegan)?			
Has the caregiver a history of being anorexic, bulimic, or experienced other eating problems?			
Total for Section B			

Source: From Iwaniec (2004). *Children who fail to thrive: A practice guide*. Chichester: John Wiley & Sons.

nutritional and physical care of the children, specifically those who fail to thrive.

PARENTAL CHARACTERISTICS

Emotionally nurturing parenting may depend on many factors, e.g. cognitive abilities of parents, the socio-economic situation within the family, experiences of being parented as children, emotional ties with the child, and the relationship between parents. Major characteristics found in emotionally abusive and neglectful parents are:

- unresponsiveness to the children's emotional needs;
- absence of warmth and attention;
- hostile attitudes towards children;
- lack of empathy;
- unrealistic expectations of children's behaviour and achievements;
- poor relationships with children; and
- generally aversive interaction.

Emotionally abusive parents give little attention to their children and do not seem to be interested in what they do and how they feel. The little attention that is paid to them is negative and often anxiety-provoking. Observation of parent–child interaction persistently shows that they seldom look at the child but, if they do, the look is hard and forbidding (Burgess & Richardson, 1984; Diaz, Neal, & Vachio, 1991). Lack of warmth is also demonstrated in the parent–child relationship. Research on interaction between such parents and children consistently indicates significant lack of enjoyment of having and being with their children, and being less satisfied with them. Additionally, abusive parents perceive child-rearing as difficult and a burden (Iwaniec, 1995, 2004; Reid, 1986; Tricket & Susman, 1988). Parents also show little positive behaviour such as physical affection (touching, smiling, cuddling, close physical contact), seldom, if ever, praise good behaviour and, strikingly, seldom speak to children unless giving orders or to tell them off (Doyle, 1997; Glaser & Prior, 2000; Iwaniec, 1997, 2004). It seems that emotionally abusive parents tend to exhibit low levels of positive child-directed or child-responsive behaviour, and when they do it is often inappropriate and negative in nature. Dilalla and Crittenden (1990) found that these parents were, more often than not, hostile in the way they perceived a child, talked about it and expressed their attitudes regarding a child. There is also evidence that emotionally abusive parents or carers generally show low levels of empathy towards the abused child (Doyle, 1997; Iwaniec, 1995; Herbert, 1998b).

Unrealistic expectations of what a child should or should not do are quite common among emotionally abusive parents. Research indicates that some of these parents have extremely high expectations of their children in terms of their compliance and achievements, and are angered by what they take to be the child's defective or deliberately defiant or lazy behaviour (Frude, 2003; Herbert, 1998b). Lack of knowledge about normal child development may be the reason for unrealistic expectations of how clean, compliant, or self-sufficient the child should be at a certain age, and how advanced it should be in relation to speech, toilet-training, self-feeding, motor skills, and mobility. This is the reason why developmental counselling is so important for these parents, for their own and their children's sake (Frude, 2003; Iwaniec, 1997; Stern & Azar, 1998; Sutton, 2000).

The following caregiver characteristics require attention when assessing cases of emotional abuse and neglect:

1. unresponsiveness to the children's needs;
2. lack of sensitivity when dealing with the child;
3. absence of warmth in interaction;
4. absence of physical affection;
5. lack of praise and encouragement;
6. hostility or indifferent interaction;
7. lack of satisfaction and enjoyment of the child;
8. hostile in attitudes and behaviour towards a child (e.g. negative actions, threats, complaints, humiliation, anger);
9. lack of empathy;
10. unrealistic expectations of a child's behaviour and achievements;
11. parental attributions – inaccurate interpretations of a child's behaviour;
12. depressive moods;
13. experiencing feelings of loss, bereavement, or abandonment;
14. low self-esteem and self-efficacy;

15. poor marital/supportive relationship;
16. being socially isolated and unsupported;
17. family violence;
18. feelings of guilt and failure as a parent;
19. rigidity or chaotic disorder in child-rearing;
20. alcohol and drug abuse; and
21. presence of mental-health problems.

Table 10.3 offers a check-list of parental emotionally abusive behaviour.

Table 10.3   Check-list: parental emotionally abusive behaviour
Often is a negative measure, almost never is a positive measure

Parental abusive behaviour	Often	Occasionally	Almost never
1. Child not included in the family circle			
2. Ignored, not taken notice of			
3. Not allowed to play an active part in family activities			
4. Seldom spoken to in an easy way			
5. Persistently deprived of privileges and treats as a means of discipline			
6. Frequently punished for minor misbehaviour			
7. Persistently ridiculed and criticised			
8. Never praised			
9. Not acknowledged or reinforced in any good behaviour or positive action			
10. Shamed, denigrated and put down in front of peers, siblings, and other people			
11. Disregarded in any attempts to please caregivers			
12. Ignored and discouraged when attempting to attract attention or affection			
13. Not allowed to mix with peers			
14. Socially isolated			
15. Told he/she is disliked or unloved			
16. Blamed when things go wrong in the family			
17. Not properly supervised or guided			
18. Mis-socialised in various ways			
19. Encouraged in prejudices such as religious, racial, cultural, or other hatreds			
20. Not allowed to get physically close to caregiver			
21. Not permitted to show emotions			
22. Unrealistic developmental expectations			

Table 10.3   (Continued)

Parental abusive behaviour	Often	Occasionally	Almost never
23. Negative attitudes towards the child (can't find anything good and pleasing about the child; always finding faults)			
24. Lack of interest in the child (seldom interacts, shows concern, not interested in child's activities, schoolwork, or feelings)			
25. Does not remember child's birthday			
26. Does not attend events at school which child is taking part (Christmas play, sports day, parents' evenings)			
27. Not showing empathy and concern when child is upset, distressed, or worried			
28. Lack of sensitivity and warmth in responding to signals of distress			
29. Emotional unavailability to the child			
30. Terrorising the child (threatening to abandon, kill, or kill pet or destroy loved object, etc.)			
31. Cruel teasing and tormenting on a regular basis			
32. Locking child in dark cupboards, cellar, or shed as a means of punishment			

Source: From Iwaniec (1995). *The emotionally abused and neglected child: Identification, assessment and intervention*. Chichester: John Wiley & Sons.

ENSURING SAFETY

Ensuring that a child is adequately protected from harm and danger is a very important factor to consider. This can be an issue with children exposed to fabricated illnesses, or active inducement of illness (so-called Münchausen's syndrome by proxy). Such parents (usually mothers seeking attention by presenting fabricated symptoms or self-induced symptoms) seek medical treatment for a child or for themselves. Such children, at best, are exposed to unnecessary physical pain because of various examinations and operations and, at worst, permanent damage to health or even death.

Practitioners should be alerted to possible mistreatment or müismanagement if a child improves rapidly when living away from home (e.g. with an extended family, in short-term foster-care, or when hospitalised). This is particularly important with psychosocial short-stature children. In cases of this kind the assessor should examine what is done differently to produce desired outcomes or improvement in a child's behaviour, health, or development. The overprotected child, on the other hand, is developmentally 'paralysed' by parental exaggeration of keeping the child safe. Such a child is prohibited to go anywhere or do anything, being told that the outside world is a dangerous place to be. Parental behaviour of this kind is emotionally abusive as it prevents development of independence, identity, and self-confidence.

EMOTIONAL WARMTH

One of the major characteristics of emotionally abusive parenting is lack of emotional warmth shown to the child. Parent–child interaction is riddled with indifference or hostility and tension. The emotional bond between child and parent tends to be weak (as indicated by low frequency of affectionate interaction), and a poor relationship is manifested by the lack of pleasure in being in each other's company. In the majority of cases the child-to-parent attachment is insecure and troubled by unpredictable or hostile parental behaviour towards the child.

Direct observation and interviews with the parents, and with older children, will provide information on the way a child is nurtured and treated by the family members, and to what degree he or she is supported and encouraged in mastering developmental tasks and being socialised. Table 10.4 describes emotionally caring parenting and emotionally uncaring (inadequate) parenting. Many children who are emotionally abused and neglected experience inadequate emotional caregiving.

Table 10.4 Emotional care of the child

Adequate (good)	Inadequate (poor)
Affection Frequent physical contact, admiration, touching, holding, comforting, making allowances, being tender and loving, saying nice things about the child, showing concern, talking softly and warmly to the child	**Affection** Limited physical contact, child seldom picked up and given attention, signals of distress ignored or dealt with harshly, seldom talked to in a warm, reassuring way, child talked about in a negative, critical way, lack of satisfaction and emotional commitment persistently shown to the child
Security Continuity of care, predictable environment, consistent control, settled patterns of care and daily routines, fair and understandable rules, harmonious family relationships, stability and security of home and family	**Security** Tense and changeable environment, child cared for by different and unsuitable people, confusing and inappropriate rules and routines, hostile relationships between family members, frequent threats of being abandoned, set away, disruptions in family functioning and unity

Table 10.4   (Continued)

Adequate (good)	Inadequate (poor)
Guidance/control Discipline appropriate to the child's stage of development, provision of models to emulate, indication of boundaries, insistence on concern for others	**Guidance/control** Unrealistic expectations of child's ability to behave and react in a manner parents want, physical and emotional punishment applied in an inappropriate way, parental behaviour not a good model from which to learn, poor teaching of what is right and wrong, failure to establish fair and clear rules of behaviour, disregard for the feelings and needs of others
Independence Creation of opportunities for him/ her to do more for self, make decisions, first about small things but gradually about larger matters; all requiring a balance between being lax (laissez-faire) and overprotective	**Independence** Negligence in teaching a child to acquire skills to function independently but appropriately, prevention of a child from being able to make his/her decisions, being either dictatorial or overprotective on the other hand, or neglectful and not paying attention to these development needs on the other
Stimulation – new experiences Encouragement of curiosity and exploratory behaviour, responses to questions, engagement in play, promotion of training/educational opportunities	**Stimulation – new experiences** Restriction of a child in exploration of environment, failure to engage a child in new activities and seeing new things, lack of response to a child's questions, lack of provision of materials for play, low interest in child's school performance, poor help with the encouragement of homework, no help or development of interests, hobbies, or talents

Source: Adapted from Iwaniec, Herbert & Sluckin (2002). Helping emotionally abused and neglected children and abusive casers. In K. Browne, H. Hanks, P. Stratton, & C. Hamilton (Eds.), *Early prediction and prevention of child abuse: A hand book*. Chichester: John Wiley & Sons.

PARENT–CHILD INTERACTION

Parent–child interaction in emotionally abusive cases tends to be chronically problematic. The quality and nature of interaction determines the quality of relationship and the feeling of being loved and wanted, or of being disliked or rejected. The responsibility to create a non-abusive relationship and avoid hostile interaction, lies with the parents as they have the cognitive maturity to do so and power over the child.

It needs to be remembered, however, for care-planning purposes, that parent– child interaction is a two-way process, which powerfully affects the way parents and children relate to each other, perceive each other, and influence each other's behaviour. The parent and the child each play a major part in determining (and in disrupting) the other's behaviour. It would appear that a lack of sensitive and contingent reciprocity between parent and child is present in emotionally abusive families. The notion that a child is a passive, ineffective participant in parent–child interaction has long been dismissed (Schaffer, 1977; Thomas, Chess, & Birch, 1970). Children come to this world with unique and specific characteristics which will have profound effects on how parents feel about them and behave towards them. Thus an infant's behaviour and reactions will either encourage or discourage parental caregiving activities. If parents receive positive feedback from the child, like smiling, reaching out to parents, taking food, responding to attention, then they will try to engage with the child more often. On the other hand, if the child gives little back in terms of showing pleasure in seeing the parent, responding to the parent's emotional overtures, crying and being difficult to pacify, then the parent will interact less. Observation of parent–child interaction and exploration of parental thoughts and feelings often reveal (in cases of emotional abuse) disappointment, or unfulfilled dreams of a perfect child. A downwards spiral of destructive and painful (to the child) interactions rolls on, distorting development of the emotional bond between parent and child, and standing in the way of any evolution of secure attachment of the child to its parents.

Parent–child interaction is at the core of indicating the quality of the relationship and the child's well-being. Table 10.5 is a useful tool to measure

Table 10.5   Interaction between caregiver and child
The following questions need to be considered when assessing the quality of interaction between the child and the caregiver.

Rate the quality of interaction, based on observation and interview data. The higher the score, the greater the cause for concern over the child's welfare.

Name: _____   Date: _____

Overall Rating: _____

Section A

Does the child:	All of the time 1	Most of the time 2	Sometimes 3	Seldom 4	Never 5
Play freely?					
Laugh and appear happy?					
Spend time running?					
Talk freely?					
Come for help?					
Come for comfort?					

Table 10.5   (Continued)

Does the child:	All of the time	Most of the time	Sometimes	Seldom	Never
	1	2	3	4	5
Cuddle up to the caregiver?					
Respond to affection?					
Respond to attention?					
Appear at ease when the caregiver is near him or her?					
Join in activities with other children?					
Appear not too frightened when approached or corrected by the caregiver?					
Eat as quickly as other children of the same age?					
Eat a wide variety of food?					
Ask for food or indicate hunger in some other way?					
Appear relaxed during mealtime?					
Show steady weight-gain?					
Show absence of vomiting?					
Show absence of diarrhoea?					

Total for Section A

Section B

Does the caregiver:	All of the time	Most of the time	Sometimes	Seldom	Never
	1	2	3	4	5
Talk to the child?					
Look at the child?					
Smile at the child?					
Mark eye contact with the child in a loving or gentle way?					
Gently touch the child?					
Play with the child?					
Cuddle the child?					
Kiss the child?					
Sit with the child on his or her lap?					
Handle the child in a gentle way?					
Give the child requests (as opposed to commands)?					

Table 10.5   (Continued)

Does the caregiver:	All of the time 1	Most of the time 2	Sometimes 3	Seldom 4	Never 5
Help the child if it is in difficulties?					
Encourage the child to participate in play and other activities?					
Appear to be concerned about the child?					
Pick the child up when it cries or when it is hurt?					
Answer the child's questions?					
Not ignore the child's presence?					
Emotionally treat the child the same as other children?					
Total for Section B					

Section C

Do the siblings:	All of the time 1	Most of the time 2	Sometimes 3	Seldom 4	Never 5
Play with the child?					
Talk to the child?					
Participate in activities with the child?					
Accept the child?					
Treat the child well?					
Push the child away and reject it?					
Blame the child for everything that happens?					
Protect the child?					
Help the child when in difficulties or in trouble?					
Scapegoat the child?					
Total for Section C					

Table 10.5   (Continued)

Section D

Adolescent's reactive and
proactive behaviour

Does the teenager:	All of the time	Most of the time	Sometimes	Seldom	Never
	1	2	3	4	5

Get on well with parents?
Get support from one parent?
Get on well with at least one sibling?
Get support from extended family?
Get support from at least one adult
(teacher, family friend,
youth-club leader)?
Use friends, peers for support?
Use activities outside the home?
Use sport or leisure activities?
Use school as escape from home?
Feel loved and wanted at home?
Feel secure within the family?
Communicate with parents?
Be listened to and taken
   notice off?
Be shown understanding and
   affection?
Get help and protection?
Get encouragement and
   reassurance?
Achieve at school?
Feel good about him/herself?
Feel confident?

Total for Section D

Section E

Does the caregiver:	All of the time	Most of the time	Sometimes	Seldom	Never
	1	2	3	4	5

Listen to the teenager?
Like his/her company?
Provide advice and guidance?

Table 10.5   (Continued)

Does the caregiver:	All of the time 1	Most of the time 2	Sometimes 3	Seldom 4	Never 5
Show interest in activities and schoolwork?					
Show affection and love?					
Give reassurance and encouragement?					
Praise achievements and good behaviour?					
Demonstrate satisfaction with teenager's contribution to family life?					
Protect from harm, inside and outside the home?					
Encourage independence?					
Think and feel positive about the teenager?					
Show concern and worry when teenager is distressed or worried?					
Help when in difficulties?					
Protect from negative influence corruption?					
Resolve conflict by discussion and negotiation?					
Use age-appropriate discipline?					
Treat teenager with respect?					
Total for Section E					
Total Score (Sections A + B + C + D + E)					

Source: Iwaniec (2004). *Children who fail to thrive: A practice guide*. Chichester: John Wiley & Sons.

frequency and intensity of interaction (both positive and negative) between parents and children, and the child's responsiveness and reactions when in the parents' company. As siblings' reactions to an emotionally-abused (rejected) child are often negative (based on observation of parental behaviour towards that child), a checklist of sibling-child interaction is also provided.

RATING CRITERIA

This is a five-point scale. Rating of quality and nature of interaction is based on observation and interview data: the higher the score, the greater the cause for concern over the child's welfare.

1. All of the time – Indicates a very good interaction and relationship between parents and children, and positive, free, happy reactions of children to parents. Very good interaction with siblings.
2. Most of the time – Good enough parenting. Positive child's reaction to parents, and siblings' positive interaction.
3. Sometimes – Indicates problems in interaction and possibility of neglect and abuse. Family support is required to improve relationship and quality of emotional parenting.
4. Seldom – Indicates severe risk of emotional abuse and hostile or non-existent interaction between parents and siblings. Child's reactions are fearful, avoidant, and anxious, indicating very poor relationship with members of the family.
5. Never – Child is suffering significant harm and action needs to be taken to protect the child from further harm.

STIMULATION

Emotionally abused and neglected children receive less stimulation from their parents as they spend little meaningful time in their company but, even if they do, they are seldom spoken to, played with, and given attention or affection. Neglected, rejected, and ignored children are often reared in social isolation, spending a lot of time in their bedrooms or in the pram in the garden, away from everybody and from family activities. When older they are seldom allowed to interact with peers or take part in after-school activities.

Different cultures, however, perceive giving stimulation to children in different ways. These differences are often misunderstood. The African saying that 'it takes a village to bring up a child' means that from very early on members of the extended family and neighbours will be involved in caring for a child. Traditionally, women are charged with looking after small children and men are seldom involved in childcare when they are young. Western cultures have seen a huge expansion in men's involvement in basic childcare in recent years. It needs to be stressed that cultural differences have to be taken into consideration when assessing emotional abuse and neglect, but not at the expense of the child's welfare. The duty of the social services is to identify problems and promote welfare for all children regardless of race, religion, or nationality.

When assessing these children and families, the level of parental involvement (both physical and verbal) and its quality need to be taken into consideration.

It is necessary to find out how much time is spent with the child on an average day and what is the content of mutual involvement. Direction observation, or keeping a diary of daily activities by the parents, is a good method of assessing parental involvement and availability.

GUIDANCE AND BOUNDARIES

Children are learners, so from a very early age they need to receive instruction as to what they can and cannot do, and why. They also have to learn what is appropriate and inappropriate and to become aware of the limits and boundaries of their behaviour. Guidance enables the child to regulate its own emotional state, and to develop an internal model of conscience and appropriate behaviour, while also promoting pro-social interpersonal behaviour and social relationships. A child's socialisation process will depend upon parental ability, awareness, willingness, and motivation to guide the child in establishing a moral code by giving instruction and providing an appropriate model of behaviour from which he/she can learn. This involves reasoning, giving instructions, correcting, supervising, explaining, guiding (by providing appropriate parental models from which the child may gain knowledge), and discriminating between what is right or wrong, what is painful to others and should not be done, and helping a child to develop a good sense of empathy and fairness.

Unfortunately, in cases of emotional abuse and neglect, parents may apply either iron rules (which are hostile and uncompromising) or no rules or boundaries at all. Emotionally abused children are expected to behave well but are not provided with examples and instructions, and are given no guidance about how to behave; as they experience hostility, criticism, denigration, being ignored, and lack of sympathy from carers, their behaviour to others (e.g. their peer group) tends to lack empathy as well. Abused children, when observing the distress of peers in George and Main's (1979) study, responded by showing disturbed behaviour such as fear, anger, or physical attack, while non-abused children showed sadness, concern, and empathy. Sroufe (1983) found that many abused children were hostile and isolated at school, lacked empathy, and tended to respond maliciously to peer distress. This can partly be explained with reference to behavioural reciprocity as Frude (2003) puts it – 'Just as a kind act tends to elicit kindness from the recipient, so hostility tends to elicit hostility.'

Assessment needs to cover awareness of the existence of fair rules, routines, and boundaries, and how these are explained to children and implemented. Emotionally abused children who have a difficult relationship with caregivers will find it difficult, if not impossible, to develop an internal moral code which derives from positive experiences and examples. Children who are rejected and unloved have no such experiences on which to build their own codes of behaviour. They, and their carers, need help in establishing fair rules and routines, and in learning what is right and wrong.

STABILITY

Stability in a child's life will create a strong sense of belonging and permanence. A sense of permanency in a child's life and familiarity with the environment in which it lives are the bases on which to build confidence that people who matter will always be there for him/her. Stability means continuity of care, predictable environment, a settled pattern of care and daily routines, harmonious family relationships, the feelings that one's home and family are constantly present, always there to which to return and to which to be welcomed. Frequent changes of home, place, and caregivers destabilise a child's life and create a sense of insecurity and emotional upset. Emotionally abused and neglected children's lives are stable only in the misery they experience, threats they receive, torment to which they are exposed, and denigration they feel. Their emotional life, therefore, is very unstable and requires attention.

Table 10.6 offers questions to be asked when assessing parenting.

Table 10.6 Assessment of parenting

The following questions need to be asked when assessing parenting.

Is there evidence which would indicate:

- acceptable/unacceptable physical care, e.g. feeding, dressing, changing nappies, bathing, keeping clean and warm, acceptable sleeping arrangements, safety, as evidenced by
- positive/negative attitudes towards parental duties and responsibilities as evidenced by
- positive/negative attitudes towards the child as evidenced by
- parental lifestyle which might be contributing to the child's poor care and attention as evidenced by
- harmful habits (alcohol, drug-abuse, criminal behaviour, prostitution) as evidenced by
- personal circumstances affecting positive parenting (single parents, poor housing, poverty, social isolation, poor health, unemployment, mental illness, immature personality) as evidenced by
- level of partner and family support as evidenced by
- parents' intellectual capabilities – level of education, cognitive abilities as evidenced by
- passivity, withdrawal, inertia – learned helplessness as evidenced by
- parental childhood experiences of parenting as evidenced by

- awareness of children's developmental needs
  as evidenced by
- concern about the child's physical and psychosocial well-being
  as evidenced by
- ability to interpret child's behaviour and respond to it in a sensitive and helpful way
  as evidenced by
- availability of clear and fair rules and routines and boundaries
  as evidenced by
- they show affection and demonstrate a positive bond with the child
  as evidenced by
- the level and quality of parent–child interaction
  as evidenced by
- the level and depths of parent–child relationship
  as evidenced by
- was help and assistance provided for parents to overcome parenting difficulties
  as evidenced by
- what use they made of the help available to them
  (a) level of co-operation with workers
  (b) working constructively towards set goals
  as evidenced by
- they are able to understand what is going wrong in their parenting and they are able and willing to work at it
  as evidenced by

CHILDREN'S DEVELOPMENTAL NEEDS

Health

Emotionally abused and neglected children do not present major health problems apart from, in some cases, failure to thrive. However, emotional abuse might trigger off behaviours which can be harmful to a child's health. Enuresis and encopresis (which are common in emotionally abused children) can lead to various complications such as urinary-tract infections, sores, and physical discomfort. Soiling, induced by emotional stress, can lead to chronic constipation as a result of withholding faeces, and the necessity to take medication to evacuate waste, etc.

Self-harming behaviour resulting from acute emotional stress can endanger such children's health. For example, scratching, cutting, burning, severe head-banging, and running away quite often bring consequences related to ill health. Above all, attempted suicide or successful suicide occasionally takes place (as discussed in Chapter 4). Doyle (1998) reported that 14% of the registered children attempted suicide or made serious attempts to harm themselves. Chris's case in Chapter 1 is a good example of how rejection can drive some children or young people to destruction. Unsuccessful attempts at committing suicide can have serious health consequences (e.g. drug overdose can affect liver function, and jumping from a window can lead to permanent disabilities). Emotional abuse is one of the reasons leading to eating disorders; in childhood it is seen in psychosocial short-stature children (Iwaniec, 2004), and in adolescence in anorexia nervosa and bulimia (Rorty *et al.*, 1994).

Drug abuse, glue-sniffing, and excessive drinking are often a means of escape from miserable and abusive lives for some of these children, or may be the results of mis-socialising or the corrupting influence of caregivers. The author dealt with 5 cases where children as young as 6 years were encouraged to drink alcohol during the parents' (and their companions') drinking orgies. Two of them, at the age of 16 and 17 respectively, were addicted to alcohol and had to undertake detoxification treatment in hospital. Glaser *et al.* (2001) reported that a child aged 7 was given alcohol and exposed to drugs, including cocaine. Münchausen's syndrome by proxy is undoubtedly emotionally abusive and harmful to children's health. Being treated or operated on repeatedly for fabricated illnesses is not only health- but soul-destroying as well.

Education

Children who are emotionally abused or neglected present themselves as underachievers for various reasons: an inability to concentrate because of more or less permanent distress prevents completion of tasks and recollection of what was read or thought; poor peer relationships and being perceived as rather stupid and odd inhibits school attendance; unsatisfactory progress and avoidance of criticism is a common feature in older children and teenagers who commit frequent truancy. Children whose parents chronically abuse alcohol are frequently absent from school, or regularly arrive at school late. Additionally, they present themselves as tired, hungry, dirty, withdrawn, and apathetic. Their parents never attend special events at school (such as the Christmas play, sports days, or parents' evenings) and do not show interest in their children's schoolwork. Non-school attendance in Glaser *et al.*'s (2001) study of registered children was 25%, and Doyle (1998) reported 21%. In addition, children who are overprotected are often kept at home because of assumed bullying or for the caregiver's own emotional needs, as illustrated by Sonia's case in Chapter 1.

Again, children living in homes where there is family violence miss a lot of schooling, and their school attainments are poor; they worry excessively about the victim-parent being left at home alone, or with the abusive and often drunk partner. Even if such children attend school they are unable to concentrate or to work at the speed of other children. Additionally, some have panic attacks, and occasionally develop school phobia, as a result of worry that when they are at school their mothers might be killed (McSherry, Iwaniec, & Larkin, 2004).

Emotional abuse and school underachievement are not only restricted to emotionally abusive parental behaviour, but are also linked to emotional abuse by teachers and peers. This issue has been fully discussed in Chapter 4. Schools for disabled children are of particular concern (as reported by Sobsey [2002]) because the children cannot protect themselves in, or escape from, at times, an oppressively abusive environment. Bullying is a widespread problem, and vulnerable children are targeted as victims. Many children emotionally abused at home become emotionally abused at school, which is particularly devastating for a victim-child as it has no place to which it can escape. However, for many children who suffer emotional abuse at home, school may be a haven of safety, peace, and support, and can provide a means by which morale is boosted and confidence enhanced. School may serve as an escape from adversity, and can have immense value as an environment in which to survive and perhaps flourish. Certain personalities may blossom and, given reasonable intellectual potential, some children may succeed in schoolwork.

Emotional and Behavioural Development

Emotional development of children is facilitated by the quality of emotional care they receive from their parents or caregivers. If parents respond to their children's emotional and other needs regularly, and in a sensitive way, the children will build trust in their parents' availability to attend to them when they are distressed or in need of assistance. Good emotional development (establishing in a child a sense of security and safety) is determined, there-fore, by parental responsiveness. Parents who are sensitive and attentive tend to have children who are securely attached to them, as they feel they can always rely on their parents when they need them. Parents who are consistently responsive to children's efforts to seek closeness or comforting engender secure attachment, while parents who are inconsistent, rejective, neglectful, and insensitive produce an insecure attachment style in children. In a well-functioning attachment system, the caregiver is sensitive and psychologically available to give comfort, support, warmth, and positive contact, as well as to provide opportunities to build new relationships and to make new contacts as they get older (see Chapter 7 for full discussion on attachment).

Secure attachment (infant-to-parent) may be indexed by the baby's:

1. interest and attentiveness when with the parent (looking, gazing, listening);
2. relaxation and/or calmness in the company of parents;
3. dependence behaviours, e.g. holding, proximity-seeking (later when more mobile going for comfort and help), directed at the parents;
4. evident preference for the parent to others;
5. curiosity and exploration, using the parent as a base;

6. pleasure, enthusiasm, joy (e.g. smiling, vocalising) in the presence of the parent; and
7. protest, displeasure, concern when separated from the parent: comforted when she/he returns.

Emotionally abused children, as a rule, are insecurely attached to their parents because the parenting they have received has been devoid of affection, sensitivity, and gentle physical contact; their parents have not provided a secure base from which trust and a sense of security is developed. Research on attachment of emotionally abused children to their mothers shows that the majority of children are insecurely attached (Crittenden *et al.*, 1994; Iwaniec & Sneddon, 2002; Main & Goldwyn, 1984; Sroufe, 1979). A growing body of evidence strongly suggests that the quality of attachment has profound implications for emotional health and interpersonal functioning. Research has repeatedly demonstrated that insecure-attachment history is a risk-factor for maladaptation in a few areas of development. One of the mechanisms through which insecure attachment affects maladaptation is an internal working model which portrays early parent–child interaction, and shapes future behaviour and ability to form positive relationships with peers and adults. Without help, or better experiences, children's abilities to form meaningful and warm relationships may be affected; emotionally abused children (if help is not provided early on) carry such negative representations into adulthood and parenthood (Doyle, 1998; Egeland & Erickson, 1987; Iwaniec, 2000, 2004). It is important and necessary, therefore, to assess the quality of attachment and to apply corrective measures to prevent long-term negative consequences.

Table 10.7 gives a description of each type of attachment, parental behaviour, children's reaction, and how emotionally-abusive or neglectful behaviour influences each attachment pattern.

Table 10.8 shows insecure attachment styles and types of emotional abuse or neglect. Each category of emotionally abusive behaviour can be fitted into each insecure attachment style.

Behavioural Development

Children's development is viewed in terms of the accomplishment of crucial socialisation tasks; these will be learned and skills acquired if parents or other carers provide models of behaviour which the child can copy (given instruction, correction, encouragement, praise, and supervision). Children need to be educated and helped to achieve social competence and to behave in a pro-social manner appropriate for age and gender. Emotionally abused children show a number of behavioural symptoms which are of some concern if these behaviours occur frequently and intensively, and are considered developmentally inappropriate (e.g. temper tantrums at two to

Table 10.7   Types of attachments, parental behaviour and child's reactions (outcomes)

Types of attachments	Carer's behaviour	Effect on child's developmental outcomes
Securely attached children	Sensitive; responsive to signals of distress; warm, reassuring; supportive; encouraging; patient; comforting; available; concerned; engaging; protective	Self-confident; high self-esteem; social leaders; empathic; popular; show good developmental attainments; open; trustful; sociable; skilful in interacting with others; adaptable; mature emotionally; stable; friendly
Avoidant/anxious	Hostile; rejective; critical; persistent rebuffing; unsupportive; unresponsive to signals of distress; uncommunicative; avoiding physical contact with a child	Unselective attachment; treats parents and strangers alike; over-friendly with strangers; poor self-confidence; poor concentration span; disruptive; destructive; developmentally delayed; difficulty in building relationships with peers; attention-seeking
Anxious/ambivalent	Neglectful; unsupportive; disorganised; insensitive; dismissing; chaotic	Apprehensive; confused; passive; detached; withdrawn; developmentally retarded; poor self-confidence; chronic doubts; poor socialisations
Disorganised/disoriented	Unpredictable; frightening; frightened; changeable; secretive	Confusion; anxiety; undirected expression of fear and distress; dazed or disoriented facial expression; emotional and thought conflicts; disorganised behaviour; apprehension

Source: Iwaniec (2004). *Children who fail to thrive: A practice guide*. Chichester: John Wiley & Sons.

three years of age are not a cause for concern as they are normal and appropriate behaviour for this age-group, but acute temper tantrums occurring at five or six years of age are cause for concern). Kinard (1995) found that both mothers and teachers rated abused children as manifesting more behaviour problems than non-abused children, and concluded that intervention strategies must take into consideration children's behavioural problems as well as those of the parents. Perry and Doran (1983) found that abused children were more cautious, shy, and antisocial, and Iwaniec (1997, 2004) found that deficit behaviours such as withdrawal, depression, apprehension, apathy, sadness, enuresis and encopresis, and conduct problems (including defiance, aggression, demanding, stealing, and eating difficulties) were

Table 10.8   Insecure attachment styles and types of emotional abuse or neglect
Each category of emotionally abusive behaviour can be fitted into each insecure-attachment style.

Insecure-attachment styles	Type of emotional abuse/neglect
Avoidant/anxious Triggered by insensitive care-giving, rejecting, neglecting, and interfering	Spurning, rejecting, denying emotional responsiveness, exploiting, and corrupting
Ambivalent/anxious Triggered by inconsistent and insensitive care	Denying emotional responsiveness, neglectful caregiving
Disorganised/disoriented Triggered by early consistent care, and later inconsistent care	Spurning, rejecting, terrorising, isolating, and denying emotional responsiveness

present. Although we cannot always blame parents for their children's behavioural problems (as there are some children who are very difficult to rear), in the majority of cases children's disturbed behaviour comes about as a result of parental mishandling and abuse. Abusive parents seldom recognise and accept that a child's problematic behaviour is a reaction to parental hostility or confusing and aggressive treatment of a child. Assessment of parental perceptions of a child's behavioural problems, and ways of dealing with them, is essential to stop abuse and to improve the relationship between parents and child. Table 10.9 gives a check-list of problem behaviours, and Table 10.10 is a record chart of problematic behaviours and parental feelings.

Children's Temperamental Attributes

Parents need to recognise that each child comes to this world, not as a *tabula rasa* (a blank, empty being), but with certain genetic characteristics, which are unique to that particular child. One of these characteristics is a temperamental attribute – an individual behavioural style which might pose different child-rearing problems or challenges. Thomas and Chess (1977) view temperament as neither purely genetically circumscribed nor environmentally determined, but as an interaction between predispositions and external influences. The infant is considered in a much more positive way as a proactive and competent being, and its own contribution to shaping its environment from earliest infancy is taken into account.

Three clusters of temperamental characteristics were recognised, and were grouped under the terms of 'difficult', easy', and 'slow-to-warm-up' infants. Characteristics of each temperament are described in Table 10.11.

Table 10.9 Check-list of problem behaviours

Behaviour	Often	Occasionally	Almost never	Is it seen as a problem?	
				Yes	No
Attention-demanding					
Destructiveness					
Disobedience					
Disturbing dreams					
Depressive moods					
Inhibition					
Apprehension					
Withdrawal					
Mutism					
Slyness					
Inability to concentrate					
Lying					
Stealing					
Bed-wetting					
Soiling					
Smearing faeces					
Self-harming					
Rocking					
Unselective attachment					
Aggression					
Overactivity					
Running away					
Negativism					
Regression to baby-like talking and behaviour					
Fire-setting					
Sombreness					
Jealousy					
Overdependence					
Irritability					
School refusal					
Wandering					
Eating problems					

Source: Herbert (1998b). *Conduct disorders of childhood and adolescence* (2nd ed.). Chichester: John Wiley & Sons.

Some children are very easy to bring up: they are regular, predictable, happy, easy to satisfy and distract, and they sleep and eat well. Others are far more challenging to rear and will require more time, patience, and energy to look after. They may be very sensitive, changeable in moods, irregular, and unadaptable. Some will learn new skills and ways of behaving quickly and

Table 10.10   Record chart

Child's name: _____
Behaviour being recorded:

Date and time	What happened beforehand?	(i) What did your child do? (ii) What did you do? (e.g. ignore, scold, smack, argue, etc.)	What was the end result?	Describe your feelings

Table 10.11   Individual behavioural characteristics (temperamental attributes)

Easy child

Rhythmicity:	Rhythmic in biological functioning, e.g. eating, sleeping, naps. The carer can organise daily activities as the child is predictable.
Adaptability:	Adapts relatively easily to new circumstances and changes: e.g. from liquids to solids; from baby-bath to big bath; from cot to big bed; from home to school, etc.
Approach/withdrawal:	Gets used to people easily and interacts with them without too much apprehension or distress.
Intensity:	Reactions, e.g. crying or laughing are moderate. Can be distracted or pacified easily.
Mood:	Positive in mood, happy, jolly, and easy to satisfy.

Difficult child

Rhythmicity:	Unpredictable in biological functioning. Difficult to establish routine in sleeping, feeding, toileting, etc., if changes from day to day.
Adaptability:	Takes a long time to adapt to new food, textures, smell, and different types of food. Adaptation to new things (such as big bath, bed, different room, nursery, school, people) is long.

Approach/withdrawal:	Gets withdrawn, upset, uncooperative, and stubborn when exposed to less well-known people. Difficult to engage.
Intensity:	Very high in intensity, loud crying, loud laughing and talking, very involved whatever it is doing.
Mood:	Frequent negative moods lasting a long time, difficult to jolly out of a bad mood. Often looks miserable and unsatisfied.

Slow-to-warm-up child	
Activity:	Unlike easy and difficult children, slow-to-warm-up children are very low in activity. They sit a lot, move slowly, and walk rather than run. They do everything slowly.
Approach/withdrawal:	Withdrawn when approached by people, does not get involved, avoids new people, uncooperative, stubborn.
Adaptability:	Takes a long time to adapt to new foods, new textures, smells, etc. Adaptation to new things is long, e.g. from liquids to solids; from baby-bath to big bath; from cot to bed; from home to school, nursery, etc.
Intensity:	Low in intensity, quiet. Does everything and reacts to things in a calm, low-key way.
Mood:	Frequent, negative moods lasting a long time but expressed in a quiet manner. Tends to be miserable for prolonged periods of time.

Source: Iwaniec (2004). *Children who fail to thrive: A practice guide*. Chichester: John Wiley & Sons.

enthusiastically, while others will find mastering developmental tasks frustrating and difficult.

If practitioners are familiar with the child's individual temperamental characteristics and rearing difficulties, which may stem from it, they can advise parents on how to manage certain types of behaviour and reactions. For example, a child of difficult temperament requires persistency and predictable rules and routines, which are fair but firm. Slow-to-warm-up children, on the other hand, require parental patience and perseverance in teaching different skills. These children are more timid and more cautious when trying new things. Once they learn the skill they do it well. Parents are advised to wait and encourage instead of worrying and criticising.

INTERVIEW WITH THE CHILD

The interview is an important method for discovering children's problems. This is particularly difficult to do if a child is guarded as to what to say, is suspicious of professional involvement, and may be frightened to disclose what is happening with the family, and how he or she is being treated. Frequent threats experienced by an emotionally abused child may create a barrier to free and open communication. Young children tend to be talkative once rapport is established, but are limited in their ability to reflect insightfully about their experiences. Adolescents are usually reflective, but tend to be monosyllabic when asked personal and maybe threatening questions.

Children are not very good at expressing fears, confusion, and uncertainties, and find it difficult to describe feelings, but they can communicate with us through play, story-telling, and so-called projective techniques. Projective techniques include: sentence or story compilation, puppets and dramatic creations (which are invaluable if used cautiously as a means of communicating with children). Herbert (1988) stated that

> caution refers to interpreting the protocols – the made-up stories about pictured events, or the posted messages (containing statements of feelings) to members of the family. It is believed that children identify with the main characters in the stories, project their own feelings (especially difficult-to-acknowledge impulses or attitudes) onto the fantasy figures, and attribute various motives and ideas into the play or other situations and plot.

The sentence completion may shed some light on a child's experiences and events of significance. The 'memories' exercise is designed to help a child recall what has happened and may still be happening in its life.

Complete the following sentences:

I can't understand why _____

I wish _____

I used to be _____ but now I'm _____

If I were older _____

Other kids ————————————————————————————————

My favourite place is _____

If I was a different person, I'd like to be _____

I would be happy to be _____

Sometimes I feel _____

Sometimes I dream _____

If my family needed my help I would _____

Sometimes I have to do what I don't want to. I mind if _____

Memories

I remember _____

A great birthday for me was when _____

A disappointing birthday was when _____

A day in my life I'd like to live again _____

I felt lonely when _____

When I've been shouted at I've felt _____

Mealtimes at my mum's house _____

Being scared when _____

When I was ill _____

A happy Christmas memory _____

A sad Christmas memory _____

When I was ignored by _____

Not telling the truth when _____

When friends were teasing _____

Being ashamed when _____

The funniest thing that ever happened to me _____

OBSERVATION OF CHILDREN

Assessment of children regardless of age, but in particular younger ones, goes beyond questions and answers; it has also to include interpretation of affect, behaviour, and body language. Observation can be recorded by taking notes, or making a video and examining a video-tape. Observation is an extremely important tool when assessing children who are emotionally abused. Small children in particular are not cognitively mature enough to know what is normal and what is abusive. They have no life experience to recognise abusive behaviour and communication skills to tell us about it. However, they can disclose many problems through play, reaction to questions, drawings, and body language.

Observation should focus on the following aspects of child's behaviour: verbal and non-verbal communication.

Direct Observation of Children's Behaviour and Emotional Reactions

1. What does the child's showing of emotion tell you?
2. What does non-verbal communication tell you?

3. What does the child's behaviour tell you?
4. How is the child coping with the anxiety of the interview?
5. How able is the child to answer the questions?
6. What questions distract/alert the child?
7. Have you noticed the change of mood?
8. What questions/topics caused the mood to change?
9. What questions/topics led to the change of behaviour?
10. What questions made the child to interrupt or distract the interviewer?
11. What topics does the child avoid completely (by not answering, talking about something else, getting agitated)?
12. What play material does the child choose?
13. What toys or play material does the child avoid?
14. How does the child respond to the interview (i.e. too distant, too friendly, engaged, not participating)?

Identity

Part of human development is establishment of self-identity as a separate individual with specific personality characteristics, likes and dislikes, talents, interests, race and culture, which are accepted and valued. As children grow they begin to identify themselves, first as part of the family, then as part of the neighbourhood and community. But in order to build a strong and positive image of oneself one has to be valued by others. Children who are emotionally abused suffer from very low self-esteem and self-efficacy because of persistent denigration, criticism, and belittling; they are seldom praised, their achievements are not acknowledged or appreciated, and they are often made to feel unwanted, stupid, and incompetent. Living in rejective homes and being subjected to constant dissatisfaction by parents with their behaviour and performance does not promote the establishment of positive self-identify; on the contrary, they feel worthless and different (Iwaniec, 1995; Rohner & Brothers, 1999).

Social Presentation

The majority of emotionally abused children are generally well provided for: they are meticulously dressed, clean, and have expensive toys. However, behind that good presentation of care may be a very restricted child who is not allowed to get dirty or play freely using these expensive toys. Behind the availability of smart clothes or toys may be a source of harsh discipline and unreasonable restrictions.

Children who are both physically and emotionally neglected are almost always dirty, smelly, shabbily dressed, infested by lice, and generally look unkempt. Exposing children to humiliation of this kind and, because of their dirty appearance, rejection by peers, is emotionally abusive in itself and highly damaging to children's social behaviour and to the development of positive relationships with peers. Some children feel very conscious and embarrassed about their appearance, so they shy away from other children's company, avoid school, and start truanting. Shabby presentation, also, can lead to bullying.

Family and Social Relationship

Families of an emotionally abused child, or children, are not a homogeneous group, and they do not differ much from any other families who experience some child-rearing problems. As a rule there is only one child in the family who is rejected or scapegoated, while other children are treated well emotionally and have a good relationship with the parents; they seem to be contented and develop according to expected norms. In acute situations (as presented in the twin study, Chapter 5) the signs of rejection were clear and not hidden. The mother openly stated that she disliked the child and interacted with him in a dismissive and hostile way. In the majority of 'singled-out' children the signs of abuse are not so obvious at the first glance. Careful assessment, however, can provide many clues, e.g. there is no physical contact (sitting on the lap, smiling at, cuddling), the child does not come for comfort and cuddle its mother, does not feel at ease when in parental company, and appears to be isolated and uninvolved in family activities (see Table 10.5 for further factors). Other clues involve differential treatment (e.g. no birthday party, modest presents, worst room, fewer privileges, harsh discipline, and negative attitudes towards the child). This is shown by constantly talking in a negative way about the child, finding faults or ignoring the child, and not showing empathy when child is hurt or distressed.

Attention should be given during an assessment to siblings and target-child interaction and relationship. Quite often siblings pick up parental hostile behaviour and treat their brother or sister in a similar way. They smack, push away, snatch toys from, ignore, or blame that sibling for any incident or mishap to avoid parental disapproval. The causal factors for rejecting a child in the family are varied: premature birth; lack of bonding; the child arriving at a difficult time for the family (e.g. bereavement [loss of previous child], or some form of tragedy at the time of the child's birth [loss of a partner, severe marital problems, divorce]); or the child representing a shameful part of the family history (e.g. child as a result of a rape, illegitimacy, or unwanted pregnancy; difficult labour and birth). Relationships between parents and extended family are fraught as various family members blame one of the parents (usually the mother) for the state of a child. There are also noticeably poor relationships between the parents, and many were found in Iwaniec's (2000) study to separate or divorce some years later. Equally, social contacts and relationships with neighbours and friends tend to be sporadic and of poor quality.

Some emotionally abusive families are dysfunctional, and child-rearing fluctuates between good and attentive to neglectful or indifferent. Children are looked after by different people, and occasionally a complete stranger is asked to take care of them while parents go for a holiday or engage in other activities. A considerable number of children are taken to social services' offices and left there, or are threatened to be put into care because of financial difficulties or behaviour problems. Abandoned children are extremely distressed and show a range of emotional problems, confusion, and insecurity regarding their future and parental availability.

A mentally ill parent, substance-misusing ones, and those involved in domestic violence, are unable to provide nurturing care for their children. In many instances children living in such families become carers for their troubled parents, or are mis-socialised and corrupted by being given alcohol or drugs. Social relationships in such families are deviant, having an aversive effect on children's socialisation and emotional adjustment.

Family and Environmental Factors

For parents to provide 'good enough' childcare they need personal commit- ment and certain resources to fulfil that role. But, in order to fulfil these obligations, their needs as parents and individuals have to be met too. Parents, as people, have certain requirements such as basic material needs for shelter and subsistence, and psychological requirements for support, recognition, and approval from the family and community in which they live. It is not enough to assume that intellectual understanding and competence in parenting are sufficient to make for a satisfactory family environment. Emotional responses also require understanding – their proper interpretation, sensitivity, and willingness to accommodate other people's feelings within the family – especially those of children. There is no doubt that parenting entails sacrifices of time, money, interest, and energy, and that parenting creates, as well as interferes with, life opportunities.

Family History and Functioning

Knowing how to parent children comes from experiences of being parented as a child. These experiences may be unpleasant and difficult, such as being neglected, abused, ignored, and unsupported. The background history of emotionally abusive parents indicates lack of emotional nurturing and security as they grew up. Forty-seven per cent of Iwaniec's 1983 sample cited lack of warmth, empathy, consideration, and physical closeness when they were children. They were seldom helped and assisted when they became parents, and the relationship remained distant and unengaging. Some of these parents tried very hard to become better parents themselves, but received little help from their partners, extended family, and neighbours. In addition, the marital relationship was problematic in 50% of the cases and, at the 20-year follow-up, 55% of parents were not living together (Iwaniec, 2000). The major reasons for the family breakdown were family violence, alcohol abuse, and mental-health problems. In cases of the couple's mutual support and family harmony, early problems in building a warm relationship with the child and managing behavioural difficulties were resolved relatively quickly as both parents recognised the problem and asked for help and support. Van Bakel and Riksen-Walraven (2002) found that high levels of marital support and satisfaction were associated with skilful parenting. The quality of marital support also served as a buffer for a child emotionally neglected by one of the parents. In cases where both parents were emotionally abusive, children found it harder to survive and to cope with harsh and insensitive parental behaviour. Those who were befriended by a member of the extended family, or someone from the community (e.g. schoolteacher, youth leader, librarian, member of the church community, or a close friend) described these supportive contacts as a lifeline, and escape from tension, sadness, and distraction. In dysfunctional families, emotional abuse is compounded with physical, medical, and educational neglect. Children living in such families are left to their own devices, witnessing violence, alcohol abuse, and unruly parental behaviour. Family cohesion and functioning require careful assessment. The following questions need to be explored:

1. Do members of the family spend a fair amount of time in shared activity?
2. Are segregated activities, withdrawal, or avoidance rare?
3. Are warm interactions common, and hostile ones infrequent among family members?
4. Is there full and accurate communication between members of the family?
5. Are valuations of family members generally favourable and critical judgements rare?
6. Do individuals tend to perceive other members as having favourable views of them?
7. Are members visibly affectionate? and
8. Do members show satisfaction and good morale, and are they optimistic about the future stability?

See also Table 10.12 on family functioning.

Family Violence

Family violence, as we have seen in Chapter 3, is very emotionally disturbing to children, generating fear, anxiety, and feelings of insecurity. It is also mis-socialising and corrupting as it teaches children to be aggressive if things do not go their way or when they are angry. At times a violent parent tells untrue stories about the victim in order to justify the violence and to

Table 10.12 Family functioning

Is the family able to:	Most of the time	Occasionally	Almost never
1. resolve conflicts?			
2. make decisions?			
3. solve problems?			
4. encourage development of a sense of individuality in each member of the family?			
5. respond effectively to change/stress?			
6. respond appropriately to feelings?			
7. promote open communication; so members are heard, not interrupted, not spoken for, not shut up?			
8. avoid collusion across the generations leading to conflict?			
9. produce closeness between family members to promote meeting their physical and emotional needs?			
10. work together as parents to promote children's welfare and good development?			
11. support each other when faced with problems?			
12. have good organisation in running daily life?			
13. put children's needs before their own?			
14. avoid open conflict between parents affecting other members of the family?			

Source: Iwaniec, D. (2004). *Children who fail to thrive: A practice guide.* Chichester: John Wiley & Sons Ltd.

make a child turn against the abused parent. Table 10.13 offers a profile of children's problems while living in violent homes. Table 10.14 provides a check-list of family violence. It is a useful way to find out how children are involved and how frequently violent episodes occur.

Income, Housing, and Employment

Emotional abuse occurs in all social classes and it cannot be claimed that low income, poor housing, and unemployment are the major triggering factors for emotional abuse. However, poor living conditions and stress can contribute to parental abusive behaviour which, as a rule, is not intentional. To have a more realistic judgement as to what brings about emotional abuse we need to look at what is common to all those who abuse and neglect regardless of status or wealth. The author dealt with very sophisticated and

Table 10.13   Profile of children's problems while living in violent homes, shown at different developmental stages

Effects of domestic violence	Yes	No

On Infants and toddlers
- Poor health
- Poor sleep
- Screaming
- Irritability
- Fear of being alone
- Immature behaviour
- Severe shyness
- Low self-esteem
- Toileting problems
- Regression in language
- Behavioural problems
- Attachment problems

On pre-school children
- Socially isolated
- Diminished age-appropriate activities
- Depression
- Impoverished and confused social and cognitive development
- Aggressiveness in play
- Outbursts of anger
- Poor impulse control
- Chronic fear
- Hypersensitivity to threat
- Loss of appetite or overeating

On school-age children
- Withdrawal
- Anxiety
- Low self-esteem
- Aggressiveness
- Delinquency
- Conduct problems
- Overeating for comfort
- Difficulties in making and maintaining friendships
- Poor academic performance
- Poor problem-solving abilities
- Poor concentration span
- School avoidance behaviour
- Feeling unwanted and unloved
- Sadness
- Tendency to bully other children
- Lack of empathy

Table 10.13   (Continued)

Effects of domestic violence	Yes	No

On adolescents
- Hopelessness
- Emotional adjustment problem
- Low self-esteem
- Poorer parent–child relationship
- Poor relationship with siblings
- Suicidal thoughts
- Mental-health problems
- Offending behaviour
- Substance misuse
- Post-traumatic stress disorders

Table 10.14   Family violence check-list

	Often	Occasionally	Almost never
1. Child exposed to parental fights/quarrels			
2. Child sees mother/father being physically attacked (i.e. beaten, kicked, pulled by hair, pushed)			
3. Child hears the physical and verbal abuse but is not present in the room of assault			
4. Child witnessing emotional abuse of the mother/father (i.e. name-calling, threatening, degrading)			
5. Child tries to protect the victim-parent			
6. Child is beaten, pushed away, etc., during family violence			
7. Child is drawn into the dispute and violence by one or both parents			
8. Child worried/anxious that a victim-parent be killed			
9. Child wants to be at home to protect the victim-parent			
10. Child shows school-avoidance (phobia) behaviour			
11. Child is forbidden to report or tell anybody about the family violence			
12. Child is threatened with punishment if he/she protects or takes the side of the victim-parent			
13. Child is told untrue stories about the victim to justify the violence			
14. Child shows emotionally disturbed behaviour			

Table 10.14   (Continued)

	Often	Occasionally	Almost never
15. Child calls police to protect the victim-parent			
16. Child used as interpreter if mother does not speak English			
17. Child seeks refuge with neighbours or extended family			
18. Child assumes a role of protector, advisor, counsellor			
19. Both parents drunk when domestic violence occurs			
20. One parent drunk (father) when domestic violence occurs			
21. Child used as a hostage to make mother/father stay			
22. Making child spy on a parent			
23. Violent partner threatens a child while in the mother's arms			
24. Making a child watch or even participate in violence			

affluent parents who, nevertheless, treated their children (or a particular child) in an abusive way. The major reasons were found to be: mental illness, alcoholism, unwanted pregnancies, general dissatisfaction with life, poor marital relationships, family violence, disruption in mother's career, social isolation, and disappointment with the child. It was found that if the child did not live up to parental dreams and expectations then rejection, denigration, tormenting, and ignoring were present.

Family's Social Integration

Social isolation in emotionally abusive and neglectful homes has been reported by most studies. Social isolation tends to be caused by several factors such as: depression; difficulties in building and maintaining relationships and social contacts; perceptions that neighbours and people in the community do not want to be friendly; low self-esteem; and acute shyness. Some of those parents are openly rebuked by neighbours for threatening children in a hostile way and depriving them of love and attention. To avoid criticism they distance themselves from the people in the community, and, by doing so, they become lonely and angry and feel incompetent. In addition, they do not allow their children to mix with other children in the neighbourhood, so their children become isolated as well. The lifestyle of some abusive parents alienates them from the community, integration, and support. This is often due to alcohol abuse, drug use, the children's unkempt appearance, family violence or poor social behaviour.

Support for these parents is seldom available and they are not invited to participate in various community activities. As a result they become even more isolated and depressed. This, in turn, has serious effects on children as their carers become physically and emotionally unavailable and unable to meet their basic needs. When such problems are identified and assessed, every effort should be made to help them to break the social interaction barrier and connect with local groups and organisations.

Community Resources

For the reasons stated above, availability of necessary facilities and suitable services in the community where the parents live serves as a buffer and protection from abuse and neglect. Good services and appropriate facilities help parents, not only in parenting tasks and meeting children's developmental needs, but also give often overwhelmed mothers social contact and mutual support. Easy access to health services, schools, and day services (such as family centres, nurseries and play-groups) enables parents to use these services independently. For children who are isolated at home, who do not experience warm and friendly interaction, attendance at playgroup or family centre may be a helpful place to which to go to build resilience and obtain support.

SUMMARY

Assessment of emotional abuse was discussed, exploring caregivers' behaviour, attitudes, and range of feelings shown to the child. Parent–child relationships and mutual interaction were elaborated upon and check-lists provided to help with assessment and content.

Attention has been paid to the effects of emotional abuse on children over long and short periods. Children's emotionally disturbed behaviour and various adjustment difficulties have been discussed. Check-lists (including behavioural, attachment, and temperamental factors) are provided, as well as some suggestions as to how to interview children and young people (and how to observe and interpret their behaviour and enhance communication).

Environmental and economic factors and family functioning have been included in the assessment schedule (e.g. family violence, alcohol and drug abuse, mental-health problems, and social isolation). Availability and uses of community resources and facilities were discussed and the importance of community help was emphasised.

Throughout this chapter, links have been made to relevant research literature and to previous chapters in this text.

SECTION 3

TREATMENT AND INTERVENTION OF EMOTIONAL ABUSE AND NEGLECT

CHAPTER 11

LEVELS OF INTERVENTION AND SERVICE PROVISION IN CASES OF EMOTIONAL ABUSE AND NEGLECT

CONTENTS

INTRODUCTION

A package of intervention defined and tested for its efficiency addressing emotional abuse and neglect is as yet poorly developed and evaluated. With a few exceptions such as Garbarino *et al.* (1986); Iwaniec (1995, 1997); Iwaniec and Herbert (1999); Iwaniec *et al.* (2002); Iwaniec, Donaldson, and Allweis (2004); Doyle (1998, 2001); Glaser and Prior (1997); Glaser *et al.* (2001); Hart *et al.* (2002); Thoburn *et al.* (2000), little has been written about availability and suitability of services in terms of prevention and the therapeutic methods used when emotional abuse has been identified. However, services and therapeutic techniques and intervention methods that have been designed to address other forms of child maltreatment can be adopted and integrated into a treatment package to ensure the welfare of the child and to facilitate functional relationships between the family members. The nature of the mother–child relationship should inform intervention, which should be introduced as soon as emerging problems are spotted.

Intervention will normally involve a multi-systemic or multi-model treatment programme to address problems and issues associated which contribute to the onset, maintenance, and consequences of the abuse. Service provision may include a day-nursery or family centre so that the child may improve its developmental attainments; such facilities should provide nurturing environments to build trust in people, and to provide appropriate models of social interaction. Service provision may need to address parental problems such as mental health, (e.g. depression or substance addiction), family violence, economic difficulties, housing, and employment. Since emotional abuse appears to be multidimensional in nature, it is important to address each of these dimensions in order to work out appropriate intervention strategies. Dealing with only a fragment of a problem is not going to resolve emotional abuse or neglect.

Equally, provision of therapeutic services has to match the needs, abilities, and differences of individual families. There is a necessity to avoid uniform packages and 'one-size-fits-all' tendencies. It is essential to have a tailor-made programme of intervention to suit a particular family in its special circumstances. Intervention programmes can take many forms, follow different routes, and may require the use of various services and therapeutic methods and approaches to deal effectively and suitably with the problems presented by the child and the carers. Working with parents and carers typically involves behavioural-cognitive work, family therapy, marital counselling, psychoeducation, parent-training, play therapy, attachment-work, social skills and assertiveness training, and intervention strategies aiming to improve relationships with the child and other members of the family. It is important not to overwhelm people with a variety of interventions. Doing more is not necessarily better – quality matters, as does the focus on problems identified by carers and worker together.

As with other types of child maltreatment, service provision should be based on comprehensive assessment. Intervention priorities would need to be highlighted and promptly addressed. Allocation of services and types of therapeutic methods chosen would depend on individual and family needs, with emphasis on the nature, severity, and impact of the abuse on the child, and a review of the family's strengths and weaknesses. It is now generally accepted that a combination of interventions and use of different services and working methods produces better results in the long term than a single approach (Wolfe & Wekerle, 1993; Iwaniec, 1995, 1999b, 2004). Equally, full participation of caregivers in assessment of difficulties, planning intervention, and decision-making regarding choices of helping methods have proved to enhance more positive outcomes (Iwaniec, 1997, 2004).

The primary aim in intervention of emotional abuse and neglect is to ensure emotional well-being, psychological safety, protection from harm, and opportunities for healthy and rigorous all-round development of a child. Additionally, ensuring adequate and mutually rewarding parenting to help in building a child's trust and sense of security, enhancing parenting skills, promoting parental sensitivity and responsiveness to the child's emotional needs, and assisting in the development of positive interaction and relationships are all important. Addressing parents' personal difficulties (such as history of abuse in childhood, substance misuse, mental-health problems, marital difficulties, family violence, etc.) would be additional requirements of immense importance. No amount of service provision is going to help the child and secure a sense of belonging if the parents do not receive sufficient assistance to resolve their own difficulties and change their functioning and relationships within the family. Equipping parents and family members with strategies to manage difficulties that normally lead to the abuse, neglect, or exploitation of the child is a necessary target to be integrated into the intervention package. This chapter will discuss levels of intervention and prevention and will explore difficulties in service provision for emotionally abused children and their carers. Some practical suggestions are provided, especially those that have been evaluated by the carers as helpful.

LEVELS OF PREVENTION AND INTERVENTION

Before discussing various types and levels of intervention in cases of emotional abuse and neglect it would be worthwhile to look at the policy, legal framework, and service availability to all children and their families. Most countries (especially developed ones and welfare states) have legislation and social policies to promote children's health, psychosocial development, education, leisure activities, and protection from harm and abuse. This simply means that there are services available to safeguard child welfare set up and financed by either central or local governments, and delivered by statutory or voluntary agencies. The governments also sometimes employ the private sector to provide required services for families and children in need on their behalf. In cases of emotional abuse and neglect, it may involve carrying out assessment, home visitation, and other forms of family support in terms of service provision (e.g. nursery) in order to obtain improvements in parent–child relationships and the emotional well-being of the children. In child-welfare work (such as assessment of needs, allocation of basic services, and monitoring), positive conclusions may be reached concerning the termination of outside involvement, but also State intervention if required changes are not achieved and the child's welfare is cause of serious concern. In the UK, accommodation of children with an extended family or foster-home is used on a voluntary basis when families experience childcare difficulties, or are faced with temporary problems which may jeopardise safety and the well-being of a child. If there is any evidence that a child is in danger of harm (e.g. being frequently abandoned by parents, exposed to drugs or serious antisocial behaviour, or rejected), and the chance of producing sustainable change is remote, then long-term substitute care may be considered as necessary to protect the child from harm. The major consideration in child-welfare and protection work is to ensure good developmental outcomes for all children (remembering, however, that some may need more help because of adverse social circumstances, functional difficulties, cognitive limitations, or mental-health problems).

Little and Mount (1999) argued that good outcomes across children's services result from a combination of prevention (universal level – with the entire population involved to stop identified problems from escalating), early intervention (to stop an existing problem getting worse), treatment (to help those who are victims of the acute problems), social prevention (to minimise the social sequelae for those who have succumbed to the problem), and better diagnosis. The model proposed by Little and Mount stressed that practitioners should use developmental perspective to take into consideration developmental needs of children, parental capacity, and ability to make appropriate judgements regarding what services are needed in order to help. In child welfare and protection, most countries have three levels of intervention: universal services, selective services, and court-sanctioned intervention. In the United Kingdom there is an additional level which comes before court intervention. It is often called targeted registration level.

UNIVERSAL PREVENTION/INTERVENTION

It has been indicated throughout this book that emotional maltreatment, if severe and persistent, can have more negative effects on children's growth, development, and well-being than other forms of abuse and neglect. Furthermore, such children (if help is not provided at early stages) often grow to become parents who are insensitive, cold, and unresponsive to their children's needs (Egeland & Erickson, 1987; Hart *et al.*, 2002; Glaser, 2002; Iwaniec, 1999b, 2004). Faced with worrying empirical evidence it is necessary to review what preventive and protective measures are available to deal with this growing problem.

As has been noted earlier, the prevalence of emotional abuse in the UK and in America is widespread. The degree and severity of such abuse differs, and only the most serious cases are registered, so we have only approximate and far from accurate figures of how many children are exposed to emotional maltreatment in the general population. Much emotional abuse could be prevented if effective universal services were provided. Teaching expectant parents about the importance of emotional care of babies and children and what constitutes emotional nurturing would prevent much pain for both parties. Early guidance and advice for those who run into relationship difficulties would be of significant prevention value, in many cases eliminating the necessity of service providers to get involved in a more intensive way when problems escalate.

Universal services are available for all citizens in the United Kingdom. These include: community and hospital medical services, education, social services, social security benefits, and other local services which are free and can be used by everyone. In the British system all children up to three years of age are visited by health visitors as a matter of routine statutory work. Major concentration is on the child's physical growth and development. All children are assessed in terms of weight, height, and developmental milestones to ensure that they are thriving and developing according to expected norms. During home visits, health visitors provide advice on how to feed, what to feed, how to attend to children's physical needs, how to stimulate and engage in mutual activities, and how to manage behavioural problems. They also advise on how to meet emotional needs of children, and how to protect children from potential dangers and hazards. The primary role is to monitor babies' and toddlers' growth and development and to refer those who are causing concern (due to neglect, poor parenting, abuse, disabilities, or other family difficulties) to the social services for comprehensive assessment of need or protection.

However, because of large numbers of cases on health visitors' caseloads, their input to prevent emotional neglect and abuse is limited. As emotional ill-treatment is difficult to recognise and its effects on a child's development and well-being are not understood very well, prevention in this area of children's lives is not well established. Additional training on manifestation and identification of emotional abuse and neglect is needed for all primary-care workers, so they can spot emerging difficulties in emotional care of children early, and give advice on what to do, or refer the child for further and more specialised help if the parent–child relationship and interaction are particularly negative. It cannot be stressed strongly enough how important early advice is to a young inexperienced mother or father (who often struggle to establish routines or deal with sleeping, feeding, and crying problems). Some parents become disillusioned about parenthood, get frustrated with inability to satisfy the child, and in the end get angry with and resentful of the child – which can lead to disturbed development of attachment behaviour. 'Prevention is better than cure' may be a cliché, but is very true and accurate in cases of emotional abuse, as to change established parental hostility and insensitive responsiveness to a child is extremely difficult. Children too, as a result of parental anger and lack of warmth, can become apprehensive or anxious and distressed so mutual interaction becomes unrewarding and potentially dangerous to the child. Once the damage is done it is difficult to do repair work or to engage parents willingly and openly in the treatment programme. Olds *et al.* (1999) suggested that families reject programmes that are deemed to be stigmatising by singling them out for child-abuse prevention; therefore targeting whole communities and a universal approach are what is required. There is some evidence that these families fare better with a traditional model based on the provision of information and linkage with community resources. Developing an early intervention programme to stop further and more serious difficulties is advocated and should be considered as good and wise practice.

One informal but very useful way to help parents understand their children's emotional needs and emotional developmental processes is mothers' drop-in centres, or mothers' groups attached to churches or voluntary organisations, where well-informed advice is given in a matter-of-fact and non-threatening way. The author was involved in setting up such a service, and working out with parents what topics would be of interest to them. A list of topics and dates was put on the board so that mothers could decide whether they would want to pop in to listen and to participate in the discussion of a topic of interest. An informed short introduction and discussions over coffee took place and lasted as long as it seemed necessary according to an expressed interest. Some mothers wanted to share worries and concerns regarding children or the relationship problems with a particular child privately so opportunities for an individual chat were facilitated as well. Topics for discussion included:

1. why babies cry and what to do at such times;
2. how children could be encouraged to eat a variety of foods and adequate amounts for their age;
3. why playing and talking to children is important;
4. how children could be helped to feel secure;
5. how children's difficult behaviour might be managed and dealt with;
6. why toddlers are frustrated and throw temper tantrums;
7. toilet-training;
8. how trust and a warm/positive relationship are developed between parents and children;
9. how to set up fair and clear rules and routines;
10. dealing with sleeping problems.

Drop-in sessions were quite well attended and there were lively discussions in which the mothers asked many questions (not necessarily because they were experiencing problems but rather to gain knowledge in order to prevent problem development). They genuinely wanted to be better informed and confident in child-rearing. They evaluated this service and average scoring was 9 out of 10. However, there will always be some parents and children who will require more intensive work to solve relationship problems. For them the next level of intervention will be necessary.

SELECTIVE PREVENTION/INTERVENTION

Selective intervention refers to specific, more intensive family support when problems cannot be resolved at a universal level. Selective intervention is voluntary, and aims to prevent further escalation of difficulties and to provide suitable services to deal with presenting problems.

The concept of family support (as a preventive measure) was introduced in the United Kingdom following the implementation of the Children Act 1989 in England and Wales (c. 41) and the equivalent in Scotland (c. 36) and Northern Ireland in 1995. It replaced and widened the Children and Young Persons Act 1969 (c. 54), which was passed in order to provide services and financial help to prevent children coming into care. The aim of the Children Act 1989 was to rebalance provision of services from almost exclusive child-abuse and protection work to all children in need who required provision of help and services generally. Thus family support means stepping in to help parents who are experiencing a range of difficulties which are affecting, or may affect, child welfare.

FAMILY SUPPORT

Family support emphasises interventions with agreement from and in partnership with parents. The concept of 'need' was left deliberately wide by the legislators and not precisely specified in order to reinforce the emphasis on preventive help and support to families having other needs and not necessarily child-protection problems. The lack of precision in interpretation of the 'children-in-need' concept and lack of sufficient resources to facilitate this worthwhile philosophy have created a lot of confusion and tension as to how to prioritise allocation of scarce resources. In reality, resources have been provided mostly for cases of physical and sexual abuse, and very little for cases of emotional abuse and neglect and other child-welfare needs (Thoburn *et al.*, 2000).

Several factors prevent effective management of cases of emotional abuse (Iwaniec & Hill, 2000), not only in the United Kingdom but elsewhere as well. Insufficient resources have been made available for full engagement in effective preventive and intervention work. As Hart *et al.* (2002) point out, intervention programmes for emotional abuse in the USA require substantial resources that are often over and above the budget available to child and family services. Apart from financial shortcomings, cases of emotional abuse tend to be overshadowed and treated as less of a priority than other types of abuse that present more obvious and explicit evidence and require a more urgent response. Cases of emotional abuse are often not seen as urgent or serious enough to warrant immediate action and service allocation. In assessing individual needs, attention has be given to the existing strengths and skills of the families referred for family support, in order to enhance awareness, skills, capacity, and motivation to overcome difficulties. The emphasis is on keeping children with their families and on avoiding State interference. It is also stressed that families who experience difficulties have the right to receive sympathetic support and help in their lives, regardless of whether the 'need' results from family difficulties or the child's circumstances. Having this spirit in mind the assessment of 'need' and subsequent service provision have to be undertaken in an open way, and should involve those caring for the child, the child him/herself and other significant persons. In cases of emotional abuse and neglect, attention has to be paid to the parent–child relationship, quality of interaction, and level of attachment security of children to parents. It is essential to assess a child's developmental attainments and the level of emotional and behavioural disturbances manifested by the child as a result of parental emotional hostility in cases of abuse, and indifference (often described as emotional unavailability) in cases of emotional neglect.

It is often useful to provide placement for a child in a day-nursery or a family centre to facilitate opportunity for experiencing positive interaction with caregivers, get appropriate stimulation, and to learn how to play, share, communicate, and interact with peers. It is equally important to give such children a chance to be in a less stressful environment, feel free to explore interests, get engaged in activities, and build trust in carers' willingness to help and support. Provision of day-care services should not only mean escape for a few hours to a happier place, but also an opportunity to address the child's developmental deficit and emotional problems. Family-centre or day-nursery staff should be made fully aware of each child's problems and of developmental deficits in order to adopt an appropriate approach and plan specific helping activities.

Parents can be encouraged to attend family centres to get involved, and to learn parenting skills: e.g. how to play, discipline, communicate, show affection and attention, encourage and engage the child in worthwhile activities, and acknowledge a child's achievements by praise (showing appreciation, pleasure and affection). Parents are encouraged to observe how difficult behaviour is managed and how conflicts between children are resolved without becoming angry and verbally abusive. Many family centres run parenting training programmes on an individual or group work basis (including mothers' groups) in order to provide a forum for social support and exchange of tips and ideas.

However, selective intervention (in the majority of cases) is provided by social workers using social casework, counselling, support-giving, parent education, and monitoring. Quite often complicated cases are referred for

more specialised help to other agencies or professional groups for therapeutic or support purposes, in order to prevent a deterioration of already
existing concerns to assist parents in resolving their own and their children's
problems.

The majority of children who are emotionally maltreated, and who come to
the attention of social services, will come into a category of selective
intervention using various family services as well as drawing on a range of
therapeutic methods.

Issues and Dilemmas with the Use of Accommodation

Voluntary reception into care, so-called accommodation, was perceived by
the legislators of the Children Act (1989) as a family support service giving
parents a break and a breathing space when in difficulties in caring for their
children. Accommodation was meant to be short-term, mutually agreed,
with parents having the power to discharge their child from care at their
will. However, Hunt, Macleod, and Thomas (1999), in their examination of
the legal process, noted that accommodation had become a significant entry
point to the legal process and that 25% of the cohort of 63 children studied
became the subject of a care order application after admission to accommodation. Equally, Donaldson and Iwaniec (*in press*) found that 33% of the
sample they investigated became looked-after through the provision of
accommodation and then subject to care order application. Donaldson
(2003) found that there was no systematic approach to the task of sifting out
what outcomes were most likely in what cases. There was confusion among
social workers about the policy underpinning the purpose of accommodation.
Some workers felt that accommodation should be offered to children in the
first instance no matter what the circumstances of the child. The most
obvious evidence of accommodation provided as a safeguard to the child, as
opposed to being a support to the parents, was where the child's name was
put on the Child Protection Register. In such cases court proceedings were
almost bound to follow. In Donaldson's study (2003) at the time of the
second case-file examination 18 months later, over 90% of accommodated
children whose names were on the Child Protection Register had become
subject to a care order application. The interviews with parents and social
workers indicated that parents were not always made aware that the case
was still likely to go to court. There was ample evidence that parents were
given an ultimatum to agree to accommodation, otherwise the case would
go to court. There was also evidence that when parents requested discharge
of a child from accommodation they were told that an application to the
court would be made if they persisted.

There are many disadvantages for the child and the parent caught in this
kind of situation where accommodation is 'enforced', as opposed to being

truly voluntary. Such children's future is unresolved; new attachments are made and broken; children and parents become alienated; sense of identity and belonging get confused; and sense of security is upset. The length of accommodation, parental involvement in the process, parental commitment and ability to change, and provision of therapeutic help while the child is accommodated need to be taken into consideration early on, to make appropriate decisions regarding the child's future.

The Use of Coercion in the Provision of Accommodation

The use of coercion in the provision of accommodation was noted in several studies (Hunt *et al.*, 1999; Packman & Hall, 1999; Brandon, Thoborn, Lewis, & Way, 1999). The practice of 'forced' accommodation and the acceptability of such practice gradually developed after implementation of the Children Act (1989). The temptation of social services to avoid testing rather poorly evidenced cases (such as emotional abuse or neglect) in the court became widespread. The need for fairness, due process, and respecting the rights of parents diminished over time, with courts being reluctant to disturb such practice, and are cited as reasons for discontinuing the way cases were dealt with. The damaging effects for the child of emergency proceedings and the importance of providing a 'cooling-off period' in order to avoid court have been put forward as supporting the use of 'forced' accommodation in some circumstances. Although the use of coercion was often criticised by researchers, it was conceded that, at times, it provided a valuable breathing space for parent and child. There seems to be a qualitative difference between accommodation as a service and its use as a 'breathing space' when at the brink of legal action, and safeguards needed to be worked out to prevent children drifting into long-term insecure care.

Packman and Hall (1999) argued that there was a dilemma in having 'true voluntariness' and to protect children at risk, but they also questioned the legality of situations where parents were threatened with court action if they opposed accommodation of the child. The use of coercion was also examined by Brandon *et al.* (1999) who drew a distinction between 'forced' accommodation, where parents were inadequately informed, and where there was no other way to deal with crises and cases where 'some coercion' was used. In such cases the alternative of an application for an emergency protection order or care order was explained and limited choices were given to parents. Some parents were very reluctant to part with their children and wanted them to return from accommodation; most, however, agreed and considered accommodation to be 'the lesser of two evils'. It needs to be remembered that many children who are accommodated because of emotional abuse are returned home before therapeutic intervention takes place, to improve parent–child relationship and before the sense of belonging and security is established. Many of them are rejected again and are again accommodated but often with different people. Accommodation might give parents a break but will not resolve relationship difficulties. Discharging children to unchanged situations, attitudes, and feelings is unwise and counterproductive. Caution needs to be taken in deciding what kind of family support is needed and whether family support is a suitable intervention for more acute and chronic cases.

The Review of Children Act (DoH, 2001) suggested that the use of accommodation needed to be refined and scrutinised, and more attention should be given to the individual circumstances of the children 'in need'. While provision of accommodation as a family support service was considered as a worthwhile resource, it was also argued that its use in 'safeguarding' cases required a review of policy and practice.

TARGETED PREVENTION/INTERVENTION
MULTIDISCIPLINARY APPROACH

The third level of intervention applies to cases where intensive selective intervention does not produce the desired outcome and when parental participation and commitment to resolve the problem are poor. It usually applies when attempts to assist parents working in partnership with them to protect a child's welfare and to improve the quality of care fail to materialise and there are serious concerns about neglect or abuse. In the United Kingdom the child-protection level is delivered on a multidisciplinary basis, so different agencies have responsibilities to work together to protect children, including assessment, attendance, and participation at case conferences, as well as taking into account the existence of the Child Protection Register (Department for Education and Employment, 2000). Obligation of professionals to protect children means that important decisions have to be made on an interdisciplinary basis. For example, children can be placed on or removed from the Child Protection Register only by a formal case conference attended by various professionals involved in some way with the child or the family (who may have relevant information which can help in decision-making). Registration of children is not a legal procedure but a matter of good practice involving the child-protection guidelines of co-operation, communication, co-ordination, exchanging information, concerns, planning action, and service provision, and making decisions as to whether the child is at risk of abuse thus requiring further action or not (Gough, 2002).

General statistics in relation to emotional abuse and neglect indicate that the number of child-protection registrations has increased substantially in the recent years on both sides of the Atlantic, but very few have found their way to the courts, especially those registered solely for emotional abuse. Statistics have to be viewed with caution, as they differ considerably not only across the country, but also the way they are collated and what criteria are used for registration. The figures for emotional abuse alone in England and Wales rose by 18% in 2000–2001, and in Australia the Institute of Health and Welfare in 1995–96 reported 31% of substantial emotional-abuse notifications and such notifications of emotional abuse to the child-protection services in Victoria in 2000–2001 had increased by 15%. In the USA some form of emotional abuse is officially reported in approximately 18% of all cases of child abuse, and government statistics show that between 3% and 4% of referrals to the Children Protection Services (CPS) are concerned with emotional maltreatment. Apart from registration of emotional abuse alone, this abuse accompanies other forms of child maltreatment, and is considered more damaging than acts of physical or sexual abuse. It is also estimated that its prevalence is much higher than reported by the government (Higgins & McCabe, 2001).

Recent statistics in the UK provided by the Department for Education and Skills (DFES) show a drop in emotional-abuse registration of approximately 40% between 2000 to 2003 (cited in Mitchell, 2005). There are fewer registrations within the category of emotional abuse than in any other category. It is not surprising that emotional abuse in its own right is infrequently registered in spite of high prevalence as reported in community studies (Doyle, 2001; Hart et al., 2002; Glaser et al., 2001). For example, Glaser et al. (2001) reported that of 94 children registered under this category the length of time between first referral of expressed concern and eventual registration ranged from 8 months to 14 years and 8 months – the mean for the sample being 4.06 years.

The reasons why policy-makers, resource-allocators, the courts, and child-protection workers give inadequate attention to (and do not take sufficiently seriously) emotional maltreatment are perceptions that emotional abuse is the least serious form of child ill-treatment. As a result only a relatively small number of cases is referred to social services or other childcare and child-protection agencies (e.g. NSPCC). Limited numbers (after repeated referrals) are assessed and put on the Child Protection Register with only some services allocated for family-support purposes; only a fraction finds its way to the courts, and in even fewer cases are care orders granted. This state of affairs does not mean that there is not a significant problem and that emotional abuse is somehow less hurtful or harmful to a child; it may be less dangerous in the short term, but far more damaging psychologically in the long run.

CASE CONFERENCES

The case conference is reserved for situations where there is evidence to substantiate a suspicion or allegations of serious abuse or neglect. Sole emotional abuse (until recently) was seldom considered serious enough to warrant calling a case conference; however, it has always been seen as serious when identified as a part of physical or sexual abuse. Different countries and societies will have varying views of the borderline between 'serious' and 'not-so-serious' abuse: what is considered abusive in one country might not be in another, for the threshold criteria and level of tolerance may substantially differ. The case conference in the United Kingdom is the key forum for deciding the way forward in more serious cases. A central consideration should be the degree of risk of further harm to the child's development and safety in the current situation, what should be done, and what specialised help should be provided to stop abuse and to repair damage. However, in the mix of professionals and parents present at the conference and the varying levels of knowledge of the family, this central issue can often be overlooked. For example Farmer and Owen (1995) found that case conferences focused their attention on establishing that alleged abuse occurred and on the possibility of it being repeated again. They were surprised to find that only a few minutes were spent discussing and deciding how to help these families or what action needed to be taken in respect of the child. Failure to plan appropriate service provision and to establish who is going to do what, as well as making sure that agreed action is implemented, is unlikely to stop maltreatment.

An effective child-protection process also depends upon sufficient knowledge of child development (Bullock & Little, 2002). Unfortunately, such knowledge is scarce among childcare and child-protection workers. Yet, being well informed about developmental tasks, risk, and hazards of different developmental stages and recognition of what is going wrong and why is essential for decision-making as to how to help the child and its family. Furthermore, it is imperative to have such knowledge when assessing significant harm, and working out a care plan for an abused child. Theoretical knowledge and empirical evidence are of the essence here.

Allocating services for children who are developmentally impaired (and therefore requiring help) has been found to be problematic and in some instances puzzling in terms of what criteria have been used to make a decision on service provision for such children. For example, Axford, Little, Madge, and Morpeth (2001) made individual assessments on the seriousness of need for 668 children in a deprived inner-city area in England. They found that the development of 38% of children was impaired and that in 11% of cases that impairment was significant. Contrary to expectations that services would be allocated first to those who showed significant impairment, it was found that intervention was offered to those who showed only marginal or no impairment at all at the time of assessment in 39% of cases, and 15% of children with serious developmental deficit were not in touch with children's services. While it is important to spot difficulties early on and provide help to stop the escalation of problems, as a preventive measure it is difficult to justify omission on such a scale for those who need it most.

MULTIDISCIPLINARY INTER-AGENCY CO-OPERATION AND SERVICE DELIVERY

A targeted level of intervention requires a multidisciplinary approach apart from case-conference activities. Sadly, inter-agency co-operation is far less evident at the point of service delivery, despite ample evidence that emotionally abused children have a variety of needs which cannot be met by one profession alone. It is often assumed by other professionals that social services will implement case-conference recommendations and will become the sole provider for children presenting various needs. In order to distribute roles and responsibilities and allocate special tasks to suitably qualified professionals, a service agreement can be negotiated at the end of the case conference. Service contracts are ordinarily used as a reminder for all parties of what is involved, who is going to do what (and how), the time-span, and statements of expectations and directions. They also provide useful bases for evaluation and monitoring of work and progress. These agreements or contracts cover a variety of goals, from resource provision to therapeutic tasks. A copy of the service contract should be given to everyone involved, including parents, and should be signed by all concerned (Sheldon, 1995).

Service agreements have several uses and advantages:

- they spell out what is expected from caregivers and professionals involved;
- they clearly state the problems, concerns, and goals of the required intervention;
- they clearly define who is going to do what, as well as the time, place, and assumed duration of an involvement;
- they provide a structure for the work to be done between caregivers, the child, and the professionals involved;
- they enhance communication on a multidisciplinary basis;
- they discipline and motivate all parties involved in problem-solving;
- they are good reminders of what is intended and hoped for;
- they obligate all parties to focus on the child's needs and remediation of those needs;
- they provide dates for regular evaluation and monitoring of the case (case reviews);
- they provide a set of expectations and priorities to work on mutually agreed tasks;
- they protect all parties in the event of dispute;
- they involve all concerned in decision-making.

To illustrate service agreements in action, the case of a two-and-a-half-year-old boy is presented.

CASE STUDY

Referral

A child, aged two-and-a-half years, was referred to the social services by the health visitor, who was seriously concerned about the child's physical and psychosocial development and general well-being. John looked extremely thin, withdrawn, unresponsive, and physically ill. The parents appeared to be neglectful and dismissive (or unaware) of the child's nourishment and nurturing needs. The social worker visited the family and was alarmed by the child's physical appearance and by the indifferent mother–child interactions and relationship. The mother expressed feelings of hostility, resentment, and dislike of the child as he was causing anxiety and was difficult to feed and satisfy. The father, on the other hand, did not see anything wrong, and was angry that people were bothering them 'about nothing'. A case conference was called, and the child placed on the Child Protection Register. Both parents attended a case conference. A protection and care plan was drawn up and a service contract written and signed by all concerned.

Problems Identified at the Case Conference and as Shared by the Social Worker and the Health Visitor

1. The child's weight was significantly below second percentile.
2. The child's development was retarded in all respects.
3. The mother–child relationship was at best neglectful and indifferent.
4. The mother–child bonding appeared to be weak.
5. There was little stimulation and attention given to the child.
6. Physical care was found to be poor.
7. Both parents had insufficient parenting skills.
8. Marital frictions and family dysfunctioning was present.
9. The mother appeared to be depressed and without hope.

Problems Presented by the Parents

1. John was difficult to rear from early on, and was difficult to feed.
2. He slept badly and cried a lot.
3. He was defiant and stubborn.
4. He always preferred to be left alone – when he was picked up he cried and was miserable.
5. The mother felt that he was deliberately annoying her because he disliked her.
6. His behaviour irritated her, so she shouted at him a lot and kept him away from her so as not to hit him.
7. The mother felt defeated and helpless.
8. The mother did not know how to cope with the child.
9. The father did not help, as he did not see it as his duty to do so.

Significant Difficulties Identified

1. Development of child delayed due to the lack of parental nurturing.
2. Non-organic failure to thrive predicted due to parental physical and emotional neglect (failure to thrive needs to be medically investigated).
3. Development of child's positive self-esteem, sense of achievement, sense of belonging, and other aspects of socialisation affected by distorted parent–child relationship and hostile interaction.

Action Plan

Case conference recommendations

Step 1   G.P. to refer John to the paediatrician to investigate any possible organic reason for the child's poor growth and development (for immediate action).

Step 2   Comprehensive psychosocial assessment to be undertaken by the social worker.

Step 3   Child's weight to be monitored by the health visitor on a fortnightly basis (after medical investigation).

Step 4   Help, advice, and supervision regarding eating (nutritional provision and appropriate management during this process) to be provided by the health visitor.

Step 5   Developmental counselling to be provided by the health visitor.

Step 6   Attendance of the child at the family centre or day-nursery to be organised on a part-time basis (two days a week) to help the child with its developmental deficit.

Step 7   Social worker to help to improve distorted and harmful interaction and relationship between mother and child, and to work towards better family functioning and fair role distribution between parents.

Step 8   To review this case in three months' time (or earlier if the key worker or any other person involved requests to do so if there is serious concern).

Step 9   To allocate a key worker responsible for co-ordination for this case.

Step 10 If progress is slow and there is still serious cause for concern, expert assessment and help will be arranged.

Care Plan – Service Agreement

This agreement is drawn up between *North and West Unit of Management and Mr and Mrs Blank regarding John Blank*, age 2½ years, D.O.B. 18.11.99, who is a subject of the protection plan.

In keeping with the requirements of the case-conference decision of deregistration of *John*, we agree to work towards the goals set out below.

To improve the quality of care and *John's* well-being as evidenced by:

1. steady weight-gain;
2. improvement in his general development;
3. improvement in parent–child interaction and relationship; and
4. improvement in family functioning.

All people concerned agree to keep the following arrangements:

Mr and Mrs Blank (parents) agree to:

1. *take John every other Monday morning to the health centre to be weighed;*
2. *take John every Tuesday and Thursday to the family centre;*
3. *work with the health visitor (Mrs King) and the social worker (Mrs Smith) to help them to resolve concerns regarding John's well-being, physical growth, and retarded development; and*
4. *keep the appointments and communicate any difficulties that might occur during that time.*

Mrs King (health visitor) agrees to:

1. *be at the clinic every other Monday morning at an agreed time to weigh John;*
2. *help Mrs Blank with John's eating difficulties, and will advise the parents how to help John to catch up in his development;*
3. *visit the family every day at lunchtime for the first weeks (apart from Tuesday and Thursday when John is in the family centre), and then twice a week for the next two weeks; and*
4. *keep a weight record, and evaluate the work done jointly with the parents.*

Mrs Smith (social worker) agrees to:

1. *make arrangements for John to attend the family centre on Tuesdays and Thursdays.*
2. *provide counselling for both parents to better understand John's physical and emotional needs, and to help them improve John's care. She will also help them to resolve their marital frictions.*
3. *help the parents to learn how to play with John, how to deal with his irritating behaviour, and how to deal with the mother's negative feelings towards John. She will also help to deal with John's anxiety, fear and apprehension towards his mother.*
4. *provide six sessions over a six-week period.*
5. *keep a record of work done, and evaluate progress. These tasks will be jointly conducted with the parents.*

Dr Green (the GP) agrees to:

1. *make arrangements with the paediatrician at the hospital to conduct medical investigations.*
2. *see John at the surgery once a month to monitor his physical health and development (more frequently if there is a need or request by parents or professionals involved).*

All parties agree to fulfil their obligations and to observe times of appointments. If for any reason any parties are prevented from keeping an appointment, they must communicate this to the person concerned and make an alternative arrangement.

This care plan will be reviewed in three months' time. All involved should communicate their concerns and progress to the key worker, *Mrs Smith*.

1. Case review *10 June 2001*

Signed: _____ Mr *Blank*

Signed: _____ Mrs *Blank*

Signed: _____ Mrs *Smith* (social worker)

Signed: _____ Mrs *King* (health-visitor)

Signed: _____ Dr *Green* (GP)

Date: _____

Signed: _____ Case conference chair

CIVIL COURT INTERVENTION

The fourth level of intervention applies to children who are at serious risk of suffering or who have suffered significant harm, and where action urgently needs to be taken. Such children require removal from an abusive or dangerous environment as a matter of safety, through the court system. The criteria for significant harm vary between countries and over time. In countries where child welfare and protection are legislated for and regulated by policy and procedures, substantial services at all levels are available, while in less-developed countries there are very few and they are difficult to access. The non-court level of child protection in such countries may be much more limited. It may be little more than an investigation resulting in referral into the court system, or referral to get some local support services but without monitoring and management of child-protection issues. Quite often a case is closed after initial brief investigation (Gough, 2002).

There is little doubt that more persistent and serious emotional abuse requires investigation and comprehensive assessment, and suitable service provision for both the caregiver and the child. It has been estimated (Iwaniec, 1997; Doyle, 1998) that about 10% of emotionally abused children reach the criteria of significant harm requiring serious attention. Although emotional abuse is seldom seen as life-threatening, it indicates in some cases a risk to life. This can be seen in some cases of rejection which lead to depression, attempted and successful suicides, running away from home and living on the streets, drug and substance abuse, and acute eating disorders.

Most children, when removed from home, are placed in foster-homes on a short- or long-term basis, and some will be considered for freeing for adoption if the possibility of rehabilitation back home is remote or impossible. Sometimes the child is placed with its extended family if this is considered safe and the family is willing. Such kinship care can be arranged voluntarily without taking a case to court. Not all such placements are satisfactory and some are highly inappropriate (Lernihan, 2003). In the majority of cases parents of children in care have a right to reasonable access to their children. They can see them quite frequently, and access is either supervised or unsupervised. If the child were removed from home because of Münchausen's syndrome by proxy, or because of sexual abuse, the access visits would be supervised, as they would also be in cases where the parents are addicted to alcohol and/or drugs. The frequency and nature of access visits in the United Kingdom is advocated by social services and determined by the court.

Recent years have seen some changes and less rigid arrangements for adopted children. So-called 'open adoption' is considered for each child, which gives a range of possibilities for contact with birth-parents such as: two or more face-to-face contacts a year and contact in exceptional life events, as well as exchange of photographs, birthday cards, or letters. The nature of contact is determined by the best interests of the child in terms of security, stability, and social adjustment. It is well known that children who have occasional contact with their biological parents have a better-developed sense of identity and less unrealistic and disturbing fantasies about their parents. The 20-year follow-up study of children who failed to thrive as children (Iwaniec, 2000; Iwaniec & Sneddon, 2001, 2002) found that children who were adopted satisfactorily overcame acute adversity of childhood experiences and became well-adjusted individuals and parents in later life. Children in long-term, undisrupted, and well-selected foster-homes have done equally well. Those, however, who had frequent admissions into care on a voluntary basis, but remained at home, have done less well in terms of stability, attachment to peers and romantic partners, educational attainments, employment, and self-esteem.

It is very important to emphasise that children in this category require intensive intervention when placed in substitute care in their own right to eliminate or minimise emotional disturbances and to make good developmental deficit. Provision of day-care services, play therapy, and systematic, positive monitoring of behaviour by various forms of reinforcement is essential to avoid break-up of the placements. Substitute carers require support and active help to guide them to understand and deal with children's difficult behaviour and disturbed emotions. Some of the intervention methods which are suitable will be discussed in the following chapters.

In spite of recognition that emotional abuse alone is most damaging psychologically, and of long-term and serious consequences, proving significant harm exclusively emerging as a result of such abuse is still very difficult. The issues of significant harm, decision-making, and court proceedings in relation to emotional abuse and neglect will be discussed fully in Chapter 16.

SUMMARY

This chapter discussed the concepts of multifactorial prevention and intervention in emotional-abuse cases. Both provision of appropriate services (and therapeutic input) at different levels of prevention and intervention were outlined and analysed for the usefulness of helping emotionally abused children. The importance of early prevention and the necessity to have in place suitable services at a universal level were emphasised, and examples were given of who can help and how parents can be helped to provide good emotional care for their children. Selective intervention as a family support for parents and carers who are experiencing childcare difficulties was discussed, exploring a variety of services which could be used to resolve emerging relationship problems between the child and parents. Targeted registration levels for more serious cases warranting case-conferencing and child-protection registration were brought to attention, emphasising the difficulties of proving that emotional abuse can have very serious negative effects on a child's growth, development, and well-being (in particular on self-esteem, confidence, and attachment security). Finally, civil court intervention was briefly discussed.

CHAPTER 12

BEHAVIOURAL-COGNITIVE APPROACHES IN HELPING EMOTIONALLY ABUSED AND NEGLECTED CHILDREN AND THEIR FAMILIES: THEORY, PRACTICE, AND RESEARCH

CONTENTS

INTRODUCTION

Emotional abuse and neglect have been grounded in a number of theoretical perspectives, with behavioural and cognitive ones among them. Numerous methods and techniques, which will be described in this chapter, derive from social learning theories, and will be outlined as some of the helping strategies to deal with this type of child maltreatment. Behavioural methods are used to help both parents and child to improve aversive interaction often leading to emotional abuse or neglect, and to change parenting style in managing children's behaviour and parental emotional responses to the child. Cognitive theory and methods will be presented to illustrate ways of changing parental attitudes, beliefs, and attributions towards the emotionally ill-treated child, learning how to control anger, manage stress, and solve problems.

Some evaluative research findings will be presented to point out 'what works' when trying to help these children and their parents. A case study will be presented to illustrate use of some methods described in this chapter.

BEHAVIOURAL WORK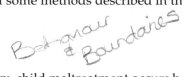

According to behavioural theory, child maltreatment occurs because parents have not learned, or become aware of, more effective ways, strategies, or relationship skills when bringing up a child. Behavioural theorists assume that parents draw on their own experiences of childhood, where they too were possibly a victim of abusive parenting (Hyman & Zelikoff, 1987). In the absence of significant, positive, corrective, or compensating experiences, this dysfunctional pattern of behaviour is maintained, resulting in a parenting style which has a detrimental effect on the child's development. Behavioural theory postulates that maladaptive behaviour is *learned* and *reinforced*, i.e. the individual learns how certain behaviours correspond to specific outcomes. Over time, patterns of interaction evolve, whereby the behaviour is repeated, and an expected and specific outcome occurs. At some level, an association is made between the behaviour and its consequences through positive and negative reinforcement.

Positive reinforcement occurs when a parent attends to or reacts to a child's behaviour. For example, the parent may respond to the child with attention, hostility, criticism, nagging, smacking, or aggression. The child who is starved of affection or attention may engage in behaviour which he/she has learned as yet may elicit an abusive reaction from the parent. Although the abuse is far from pleasant, it may be preferable for the child to engage in this type of relationship to elicit some kind of contact or communication with the parent. *Negative reinforcement* occurs when the experience of an aversive event or situation ceases following a specific behaviour or response. *Negative reinforcement* involves increase in frequency of behaviour which avoids unpleasant events; unlike punishment it activates a response rather than deactivates it. Abusive parenting can be negatively reinforced when a child complies with parental demands to bring to an end a particularly intolerable, hurtful, or distressing situation or interaction. Similarly, a child's eating-problem behaviour is negatively reinforced when a parent discontinues a feeding programme because the child persists in crying, screaming, and refusing to eat, so the parent negatively reinforces the child's behaviour by discontinuing feeding as a way to lessen the child's obvious emotional distress but, at the same time, not solving the problem.

Both parent and child learn to meet their needs by engaging in specific behaviours. The association of maladaptive interactions with personal gain is established through a process termed *conditioning* (where the person strives to engage in reinforced behaviour) and *extinction* (where the person actively avoids reinforced behaviour). The cycle or pattern of dysfunctional interactions is a result of both proximal and distal factors, which interact to *shape* and *maintain* hurtful relationships. In cases of emotional maltreatment, dysfunctional patterns of parent–child interaction become painfully routine for carer and child, increasing in frequency and intensity, and automatically employed in distressing or displeasing situations.

Children may also develop a repertoire of maladaptive behaviours and relationship skills as observers to a dysfunctional marital relationship. As witnesses to domestic violence, for example, the child learns the action, impact, and consequences of maladaptive behaviour. Attempts to engage (appease the more volatile partner, or diffuse an emotionally intense situation) are learned and can become established strategies for the child to approach a maladaptive interaction with the parents and other people in the future. The parental/marital relationship, albeit dysfunctional, becomes a blueprint for the child, who may learn to adopt similar behaviours in subsequent interactions with others, thus maintaining and reinforcing a cycle of abusive and coercive relationships.

Patterson (1982) has provided convincing evidence that parenting style characterised by aggression, threats, hostility, and anger tends to train children in the use of aggressive behaviour by modelling such action. Such children learn to be aggressive by being exposed to an aggressive model of parenting. The child's environment in these families is characterised by aggression and hostility, manifesting itself in physical and emotional abuse between members of the family.

BEHAVIOURAL METHODS AND TECHNIQUES

Interventions rooted in social-learning theory suggest that just as behaviour is learned, it can also be 'unlearned' or modified when more adaptive or appropriate information on how to behave is presented (Herbert, 1974, 1987; Sutton, 1999). With particular reference to the child's emotional, social, cognitive, and physical needs, social-learning theory suggests that parents can be taught to encourage optimal development and functional relationships. Several strategies or 'parent-training' programmes have been developed based on these principles; generally they involve teaching parents about child development, behaviour-management, suitable reinforcement contingencies, and more appropriate strategies to discipline or interact with their child.

Mapping the Cycle of Behaviour

Using diaries or incident records, parents are encouraged to document situations and events that lead to abusive incidents. Alternatively, the therapist may observe the family at home and note times when the parent threatens, criticises, nags, or demeans the child, as well as the child's reaction or response to parental behaviour. When sufficient information is collected, the therapist presents the findings to parents, illustrating the pattern of events, behaviours, or situations which lead to a cycle of relationship difficulties between parent and child. Precipitating events are discussed with the parent to highlight where appropriate changes can be made (Herbert, 1987; Iwaniec, 1999a; Sutton, 2000).

Positive Reinforcement Strategies – Increasing Desirable Behaviour

This stage of intervention is followed by teaching parents how to shape more appropriate interactions with their child, as well as attending to, responding to, and reinforcing desired or wanted responses and reactions from the child. Parents are encouraged to 'catch the child being good' and follow through with rewards to reinforce adaptive patterns of interaction. Parents too have to change their behaviour and reactions to the child, and, in cases of emotional abuse, the primary focus in therapeutic intervention is to increase parental understanding of antecedents of problem behaviour and help parents to interact with the child in a positive way. Using social, symbolic, or activity rewards is particularly important in building self-esteem and self-confidence in children (see Figure 12.1).

- *Social rewards* (such as praise, smiles, hugs, and kisses) should be lavished on the child in an effort to promote pro-social behaviour and to boost positive morale. These techniques, although they sound simple, may be particularly difficult for a parent who has failed to establish any positive connection and feelings with the child. The therapist may have to start, and model phrases for the parent such as: 'You are such a good boy', 'You are such a clever girl', 'I really like the way you tidied your toys away today'. Appropriate phrases have to be used with older children and adolescents: 'I am proud of you'; 'I like being with you'; 'You make me feel good'. These statements can be practised in session as a way of fostering successful parent–child interactions and increasing the child's self-esteem.
- Parents may also choose to give *symbolic rewards* matched to the interests of the child, such as football stickers or other tokens such as pictures of flowers, animals, cartoons, cars, etc., which are often quite cheap to purchase or make by cutting out pictures from books or magazines. These stickers can be presented on a chart and displayed in a place that the child may view it regularly and others may have the opportunity to comment on and praise him/her. For older children 'token economy' may be used (see Herbert [1987] for description of the method).
- Parents could also choose to give the child a *tangible reward*, when they have earned a sufficient number of stickers or tokens on their chart. These could be a special treat such as a magazine, small toy, or favourite meal.

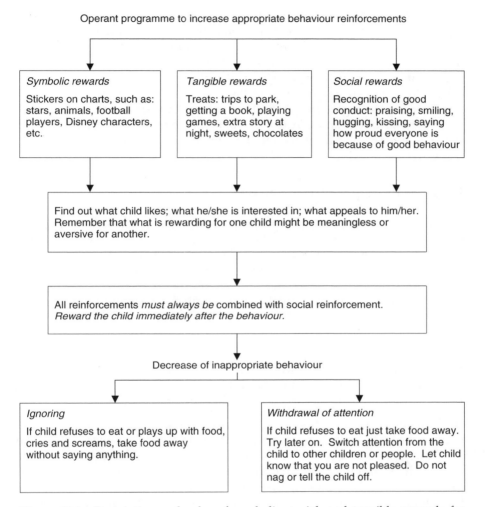

Operant programme to increase appropriate behaviour reinforcements

Symbolic rewards

Stickers on charts, such as: stars, animals, football players, Disney characters, etc.

Tangible rewards

Treats: trips to park, getting a book, playing games, extra story at night, sweets, chocolates

Social rewards

Recognition of good conduct: praising, smiling, hugging, kissing, saying how proud everyone is because of good behaviour

Find out what child likes; what he/she is interested in; what appeals to him/her. Remember that what is rewarding for one child might be meaningless or aversive for another.

All reinforcements *must always be* combined with social reinforcement. *Reward the child immediately after the behaviour.*

Decrease of inappropriate behaviour

Ignoring

If child refuses to eat or plays up with food, cries and screams, take food away without saying anything.

Withdrawal of attention

If child refuses to eat just take food away. Try later on. Switch attention from the child to other children or people. Let child know that you are not pleased. Do not nag or tell the child off.

Figure 12.1   Description and rules of symbolic, social, and tangible rewards for good pro-social behaviour
Source: Iwaniec, D. (2004). *Children who fail to thrive: A practice guide*. Chichester: John Wiley & Sons.

Again, something that the child likes will always promote more interest and motivation. Tangible rewards could also include *activity rewards*, such as a trip to the park or cinema, or an extra story at night. The therapist should stress to the parent that both *tangible* and *activity* rewards should be relatively inexpensive and within the means of the family.

As relationship difficulties will be the reason for the referral, *activity rewards*, which involve the parent and child, directly target treatment aims and may prove more beneficial for parent–child relationships. Arranging and encouraging time together that is pleasant, non-stressful, and fun hopefully will alter negative perceptions parent or child may hold about one another. Taking the opportunity to spend time together should serve to reduce anxiety, fear, and apprehension that may exist about the mutual relationship. When activity rewards are successful, and the time spent together is pleasant and non-aversive, both parent and child can learn that their actions and interactions are welcomed and can be enjoyable. Over time both should draw a sense of appreciation from the relationship and an indication that they are respected and liked.

Decrease of Inappropriate Behaviour

A similar level of importance is given to teaching parents how to 'extinguish' unwanted, inappropriate, or undesired behaviours. The therapist models how parents can selectively ignore difficult behaviour. The parents are also coached on how to let the child know that they are displeased with the behaviour and how to 'discourage' the child by withdrawing any attention for a behaviour which has prompted a coercive interaction in the past.

This may include, although not limited to:

- walking away from the child;
- refusing to give eye contact to the child;
- distracting and being occupied in another activity.

Additional features of this component of the programme may include identifying a 'time-out' area for the child. This could be a place where the child can go that is safe, free from distraction or reward. Identifying a specific area, such as 'sitting on the step' on the bottom of the stairs, not only will provide the child with a negative consequence for engaging in undesirable behaviour, but also will provide the child with an opportunity to calm down and relax, and for the parent to cool off and avoid emotionally and often physically abusive interaction.

Prevention Strategies

Behavioural casework goes beyond concentrating on changing parental and child behaviour and their mutual interaction. It also includes teaching the parent additional skills to promote a more functional atmosphere in the family home. This may include reorganisation of routines and activities or teaching the parent relaxation skills such as visualisation and breathing exercises. These strategies or techniques could prevent an escalation of negative or overwhelming feelings in the parent which would otherwise be directed at the child. Coaching the parent in relaxation and visualisation techniques can also help parents to remain calm, and aid coping ability to help them to follow through the programme during times when the relationship is particularly strained.

Scheduling pleasant activities, or at least developing a plan for the day, may also prevent coercive interactions occurring between the parent and child. Devising a structured routine which includes the parent's household tasks and chores, yet takes full account of the child's needs, will also be of some assistance. The situations or events which were identified at assessment as leading to difficulties should be considered and relied upon when devising daily plans. Allowing the child time to play after school (rather than engaging in homework directly after a demanding day); occupying the child with activities (such as toys or books when parents are out of the home environment); organising interesting and engaging activities for the child (such as painting or cooking); or encouraging them to join groups or clubs (such as the Guides, Scouts, or a sports club) will not only keep them occupied but will also boost self-competence and self-esteem as well as providing opportunities for friendships and building resilience (Scott, 2002). However, children have to learn that they must do homework, and help at home, once they have relaxed for a while after school. For a more in-depth discussion on behavioural techniques and parent training intervention methods, see Webster-Stratton (1991); and Webster-Stratton and Herbert (1994).

Essential Components

Behavioural interventions can often be brief and time-limited, ranging from 8 to 12 sessions. Behavioural methods are easy to communicate and can be delivered in group or individual sessions in a clinic, community, or home-based environment. Throughout the intervention (but especially in the early stages) the therapist is actively involved, taking the lead, modelling the style and tone of requests, praise, and instructions, as well as establishing a more general and appropriate way of interacting with the child. Role plays, video-recording, and immediate feedback can reinforce the skills and strategies taught in the programme. Booster sessions to reorientate the parent to strategies covered in the treatment or phone calls may be helpful to remind the parent how to approach a particular task or situation with the child. Over time, as the family adapts to the different ways of behaving, the child's and parents' interactions will be less aversive. This, in turn, should boost the parents' confidence in parenting skills and promote interest as well as affection for the child as the relationship becomes more positive and rewarding for both parties (Patterson, 1982; Sutton, 2000; Webster-Stratton, 1991; Webster-Stratton & Herbert, 1994).

Empirical Support

Studies highlighting the benefits of behavioural interventions are well supported, particularly for children presenting with conduct disorder, delinquency, learning disabilities, and/or physical and sexual abuse. Parent-training has also been observed to reduce behavioural problems and promote positive family relationships with considerable competence (Serketich & Dumas, 1996); with gains maintained at least one to three years after treatment (Forehand & Long, 1996). In research specifically examining the effects of behavioural interventions, with families where maltreatment has occurred, Brunk, Henggeler, and Whelan (1987) and Wolfe, Edwards, Manion, and Koverola (1988) reported improvements in parental mental health and reduced feelings of stress. Although the programme delivered by Brunk *et al.* (1987) was less effective in promoting parent–child relationships than in the comparison group who received multi-systemic family therapy, the authors reported that social difficulties lessened as a result of the programme. The intervention was delivered in a group format, which enabled the parents to establish social support networks and decrease their feelings of isolation. Based on parental observation, Wolfe *et al.* (1988) reported a significant reduction in their child's behaviour problems and less aversive interactions with their child. These improvements were supported by child-protection workers, who concluded that the risk for maltreatment reduced post-intervention, in comparison to parents who received psychoeducation on topics of child development and behaviour management alone.

In a more recent study involving families where child maltreatment had occurred, Hughes and Gottlieb (2004) reported a significant improvement in parental involvement with their child. Parents received 16 weekly 1-hour sessions based on a parent-training programme developed by Webster-Stratton (1998). After the intervention the authors observed how parents praised, comforted, and attended to their child's needs at a much higher level. Less impact was made on the parents' ability to foster autonomy and support their child. Interestingly, no advantages or differences were directly observed for the children in the group ranging from 3 to 8 years old. The authors state that while behavioural interventions appear extremely beneficial for families involved in the child-protection system, they suggest that additional sessions should be offered, exceeding what is typically delivered to parents with conduct problems. Scheduling additional sessions may be necessary to have a significant impact on a relationship where a pattern of dysfunction is particularly entrenched and established.

Iwaniec's (1997) study compared the effectiveness of individual parent-training with one group, with individual plus group parent-training with another group of emotionally abusive and neglectful families. Individual parent-training was provided weekly in the family home, addressing:

1. exploring and teaching age-appropriate expectations of what children can and cannot do, emphasising individual differences in speed and nature of development by providing psychoeducation;
2. improving parent–child interaction and relationship by exploring parental child-rearing attitudes and feelings about their child and to put them into an interactional context. Appropriate play and skills were modelled and rehearsed using video-feedback and planned activity;
3. managing children's and parents' problematic behaviour using behavioural approaches.

In addition to individual parent-training, the second group of 10 families (both parents involved) received group training to address the personal needs of the parents who presented low self-esteem, social isolation, high anxiety and stress levels, poor anger control, and poor problem-solving skills. The group work aimed to develop stress management, self-control, and problem-solving.

The results indicated (as examined by independent assessors) that both groups improved in the way they interacted and related to their children, but group two (who received additional parent-training) scored lower on the anxiety and depression scale, suggesting that the social contact and hearing others' problems, facilitated by the group, had a beneficial effect. The lesson learned from the study strongly indicates that, in order to help children, parents have to be helped too, and that parent-training is an effective way to deal with emotional abuse of children and changing parental perceptions about themselves and their children.

'Parent-training', using behavioural methods, has been found effective for children and families across the age range, with positive results reported for parents and children during the pre-school, middle childhood, and adolescent years (Corcoran, 2000). Based on the research examining the efficacy of behavioural interventions in cases of child maltreatment, it would appear that a particular subset of parents may be well-suited to this type of intervention. For example, parents whose thinking is more concrete and less reflective may gain more from an intervention which is problem-focused and goal-oriented. Behavioural methods may also be of benefit for parents who are obliged to attend treatment or for those currently unable to address interpersonal difficulties. As parent-training does not seek to assign blame or examine the histories or experiences of the parent (although information may be volunteered through the course of regular contact), a training of skills or educational approach to family difficulties may be more accessible, less threatening, and more acceptable to some parents (Azar & Wolfe, 1998; Kaufman, 1991). Behavioural approaches are easy to understand and follow, which demystifies therapeutic processes and aims, not only for adults but also for children.

USE OF COGNITIVE METHODS OF INTERVENTION

One of the common characteristics of parents who maltreat their children is their self-defeating thoughts and beliefs about their abilities to cope effectively with different life tasks. These dysfunctional thoughts lead to dysfunctional feelings and, consequently, to negative outcomes for the parents and the child. Parents who engage in abusive patterns of caregiving also have a tendency to hold unrealistic expectations of their children's developmental abilities, have poor problem-solving skills, attribute negative intentions to the child's behaviour, and assume that the child's difficulty or inability to meet parental demands (thus creating emotional distress) is intentional. In cases of emotional abuse of children, parents often think that the child deliberately wants to annoy or provoke them. As a consequence the parents may become angry, frustrated, or uninterested in the child, withdraw their affection and interaction, limit support, respond less often to the child's signals of distress, and their general caregiving may become more hostile or indifferent. Such parental behaviour may increase the child's vulnerability for emotional abuse and neglect (Azar, Robinson, Hekimian, & Twentyman, 1984; Azar & Siegel, 1990).

The way in which we interpret things happening around us, and what we tell ourselves, can have a profound effect on our feelings and, subsequently, on our behaviour. Many parents who experience some difficulties in bringing up children tend to run themselves down, saying 'I am useless', 'I can't cope', 'I can't even make my child do simple things', or 'Whatever I touch goes wrong'. Reassuring people that this is not the case may not be sufficient, as they may believe that what they say is the absolute truth. Equally, because of the repetition of such thoughts and statements, they may not realise how pervasive and influential such thinking is for them. Everyone has some 'dysfunctional automatic thoughts' which are activated in response to particular situations or events. Beck (1976) suggested that there are certain automatic thoughts which guide our daily lives and 'colour' much of our emotions and feelings. For individuals who have experienced a series of misfortunes, erroneous self-perceptions, assumptions and interpretations may result, leading to a view of self, the world, and the future as negative and hopeless; in some instances, perceptions may become destructive and resistant to change, and dysfunctional thoughts can generate depressive feelings and a sense of helplessness. Being in such a state of mind generates apathy and may lead to serious neglect of a child's physical and emotional needs. Dysfunctional and distorted perceptions of the child and its behaviour can trap parents in a self-defeating cycle, whereby they cannot generate adaptive solutions to manage the child or interact with it in a positive way. This, in turn, appears to strengthen distorted and unrealistic beliefs and dysfunctional interpretations, and confirms negative self-perceptions about general ineffectiveness as parents. Alternatively, parents may feel that their child dislikes them and is purposely causing distress. Such maladaptive attitudes and beliefs about child-rearing are assumed to be linked to parents' feelings and emotions, such as chronic frustration and anger, which consequently lead to coercive physical and emotional responses fundamentally damaging to the child (Hansen, Pallotta, Tishelman, Conaway, & MacMillan, 1989).

Advocates of cognitive theory propose that distorted perceptions, although far from the truth, are linked with an intense emotional response, consolidated in deep-rooted assumptions or 'core beliefs' characterising most of our responses, communication, and behaviour in everyday life (Ellis, 1973). In the absence of positive information and experiences, dysfunctional thoughts and beliefs can become part of a person's outlook on life; in other words, they become well-established and automatic, confirmed by everyday experiences and events.

Beck (1976) identified a number of cognitive distortions that characterise thought processes, which may also be important in early child-rearing. Let us consider an example of a mother trying to improve her child's weight-gain and increase the child's food intake in order to illustrate how distorted beliefs can be linked to parent–child difficulties and vulnerability for emotional abuse.

When the carer is obviously successful and can report substantial increases in the child's weight and food intake, she can draw a lot of pleasure from the achievement, and may begin to feel and think differently about the child. However, if the mother is involved in a feeding programme which fails to improve the child's weight or feeding status, the mother may resort to traditional thought patterns which perpetuate the cycle of emotional difficulty and maladaptive interactions with the child. The carer's thinking may be *black* or *white*: assuming that success on the feeding programme is achieved only when large gains in weight are made. In circumstances where no large gain occurs, the carer assumes that her efforts resulted in failure. Some carers may *selectively focus* on one aspect of the feeding programme and judge their success as a parent based on this issue. Alternatively, parents may *overgeneralise* – they believe that one difficulty or misfortune will characterise subsequent attempts to deal with the issue, or *magnify* the significance of setbacks and difficulties. Carers may personalise or blame themselves for situations that are beyond their control or assume that just because they feel a certain way about an issue that it is a fact, e.g. 'I feel that I cannot improve my child's weight, so therefore my child's weight will not increase and I am useless as a parent.'

The aim of cognitive work with parents, and indeed with older children, is to help them to begin viewing things in a way which generates positive thoughts, beliefs, and feelings about their capabilities of learning new ways of coping with life stresses and caring for their children in an emotionally nurturing manner. It also aims to generate emotional energy and the will to take action, based on the conviction that they are able to produce change. It is a collaborative process between the client and the therapist which supports 'reality-testing' in a safe environment. The therapist helps to identify the problems and then works with the patient in suggesting ways to test out the parent's ideas and in teaching various coping strategies. As Beck and Weishaar (1989) note, 'Cognitive therapy initially focuses on symptom relief, including distortions in logic and problem behaviours. Ultimately it aims at modifying underlying assumptions and correcting systematic bias in thinking.'

This therapy also points to the successful aspects of parents' lives, so that they can take comfort from them and redirect their thinking to constructive strategies of problem-solving and feel good about it. The success of cognitive work lies in the promotion of self-efficacy (Bandura, 1977). This literally means that a change in cognition occurs when a person says 'I can do it', 'I will find a way to stand up for myself and my children', 'I will make an effort to show warmth and sensitivity to my child.'

Cognitive work with emotionally abusive parents should also address attitudes and perceptions of parental duties and responsibilities in order to raise awareness of children's developmental needs, identify problems in child-rearing, and work out alternative caring strategies which would facilitate positive change. For example, if parents believe that playing with children or talking to them is childish and stupid or that, in order to help children to behave in a pro-social manner, it is helpful to tell them off, scream and shout, or to degrade, persistently criticise, and belittle them, then those beliefs have to be challenged, explored, and changed. Little can be achieved in any intervention if cognitive change does not take place. Change can occur only if the parent is engaged in the problematic situation and experiences effective arousal. This tapping into 'hot cognitions' can occur by use of *in vivo* exposure, imagery, or reality-testing. Thus, a mother who finds physical contact with her child difficult (as is the case in child rejection) may begin by imagining what it is like to sit a child on her lap (and the accompanying emotions), and gradually progress during the course of therapeutic work to making physical contact. Reasons why particular emotions are aroused at each stage will be examined and tested.

Cognitive-behavioural interventions suggest that maladaptive behaviour and distressing emotions can be modified by challenging 'dysfunctional thoughts' and inaccurate beliefs that are linked with vulnerability for maltreatment. Building on behavioural techniques and processes to remedy difficulties in the parent–child relationship, such as development of skills and distraction techniques, cognitive-behavioural therapy (CBT) approaches emphasise challenging maladaptive thoughts and attitudes which appear to have negative outcomes, while simultaneously encouraging adaptive coping methods, self-talk, and problem-solving strategies as a means to promote pro-social behaviour, affection, warmth, and positive relationships with the child (Kolko & Swenson, 2002).

ESSENTIAL COMPONENTS OF COGNITIVE TREATMENT

Mapping Thoughts

In CBT approaches the initial emphasis is identifying and mapping out 'cognitive distortions' or dysfunctional 'automatic thoughts' held by the parent that are linked to feelings, expectations, or behaviour that in some way contribute to difficulties in the parent–child relationship. This may take a number of sessions and will involve 'thought records' or diaries to monitor incidents, emotive reactions, and responses of the child and its parents' inter- pretation of the event. Parents are encouraged to record unhelpful thoughts and link them to the accompanying feelings experienced at the time of distress. Coercive incidents are documented, as well as events or times with the child that are pleasant, enjoyable, and rewarding, as a way of promoting a positive connection with the child. The diary/thought record is reviewed in each session and links are made to promote an understanding of how thoughts are related to events and how they can influence behaviour and well-being.

Cognitive Restructuring

In successive sessions, the therapist and the parent focus on the cognitive distortions and underlying schemas which are linked to maladaptive outcomes for the child. The parent is encouraged to be aware how 'automatic' but falsely held beliefs can trigger maladaptive interactions and to consider alternative explanations for their ideas. The validity and evidence for dysfunctional thoughts are considered and questioned. For example, parents can be asked to rate how much they believe a certain statement, on a scale of 0 to 100 for example. Together, both therapist and parent generate alternative explanations for the parents' interpretations, which act as models for the parent to be adopted with the child. Additional cognitive restructuring or self-statements are discussed and practised by the parent in neutral and stressful or emotive situations with the child. Parents are encouraged to reward themselves in some way when they come to the conclusion that their distortion was invalid, in a process termed *challenge–test–reward*.

A practitioner may find it more beneficial for the parent to adopt more concrete or visual methods to challenge dysfunctional attributions, which can be particularly helpful for parents who feel that they have failed the child, and cannot cope, change, or even interact with them. The parent could be asked to rate a dysfunctional thought on a scale of 0 to 10, using categories that it was 'due to me', 'happens in all situations', and 'will not change'. In situations where parents consistently show maladaptive assumptions, the practitioner may need to be the source of alternative perceptions and explanations, and assert different possibilities, such as: 'The parent was having a bad day', or 'The parent was trying to cope with several pressures and stresses in addition to managing the child.' Encouraging an attributional style which is external, specific, and temporary, should hopefully promote a positive way of thinking about and relating to the child.

Self-Talk Statements

As well as examining what leads to an aversive incident with the child, suggesting alternative ways of behaving and thinking to avert dysfunctional exchanges can be helpful to reduce arousal and prevent child maltreatment. The parent can be taught to engage in helpful 'self-talk' or statements spoken aloud or quietly to themselves, for example:

- I am going to talk quietly;
- I am not going to lose my temper;
- I will not swear, scream, or shout.

It may be helpful for the parent to role-play these situations and practise implementing these strategies with the therapist. Generating a list of helpful statements that the parent could use may help the parent feel in control, reduce stress, and disrupt the cycle of frustration, anger, arousal, and abuse. (This technique will be discussed fully later in this chapter.)

Behavioural Techniques

Through psychoeducation, diary-keeping and a focus on cognitions, the parent learns that activities/events, thoughts, feelings, and behaviour are interrelated. Integrating behavioural techniques, scheduling pleasant activities with the child, and teaching relaxation training and stress management will all hopefully increase positive perceptions of the child. It may be that, for some carers, specific parenting activities are particularly daunting and overwhelming. In these situations the parent may need additional assistance to approach these tasks and break them down into small, manageable, and achievable goals and activities.

Once the parent can readily establish links and associations with negative thoughts and aversive childcare, it will be important for the therapist to simultaneously attend to and highlight positive thoughts, feelings, and successes, or at least situations where an aversive interaction was avoided or failed to materialise. Generating emotional energy, fostering hope, and facilitating a conviction that parents are capable and can produce change are equally important in the development of positive parent–child relationships.

Problem-Solving

Limited problem-solving ability often accompanies rigid and dysfunctional thoughts and traps parents in a self-defeating cycle whereby they cannot generate adaptive solutions to manage the child's behaviour, or set developmentally appropriate tasks for the child. Specific problem-solving strategies, although a fundamental part of a CBT intervention, can also be implemented as an independent and separate technique, depending on the level of risk and difficulties the family presents. These will be discussed in detail at a later point in the chapter.

CBT approaches are goal-oriented and time-limited. The therapist works in an atmosphere of active 'collaboration' with the parent. The therapist is also directive, sets tasks for the client to address in between sessions, and explains to the parent exactly what is expected and what is the rationale behind treatment strategies. CBT is relatively brief in nature and generally ranges from 6 to 19 sessions, depending on the level, intensity, and focus on either psychoeducation, cognitive restructuring, or problem-solving. Interventions can be applied in a variety of settings, and can include individual work with parents in a clinic, family home, and/or community group. Although CBT approaches have primarily been used with families who have been referred for physical abuse, findings are positive, with specific improvements observed in carers' attitudes to parenting, a reduction in child-abuse potential, and reported levels of parenting stress which precipitated most abusive incidents prior to the intervention (Acton & During, 1992). Additional improvements have also been observed in more positive perceptions of the child, coping ability, discipline strategies, and anger-management (Iwaniec, 1995; Schinke et al., 1986). In comparison with a family therapy intervention, families with histories of physical abuse reported lower levels of aggression; those who had received cognitive-behavioural treatment packages (consisting of psychoeducation, coping, and self-control strategies) experienced episodes of useful physical discipline. Moreover, parents refrained from abusive discipline strategies far longer with training in CBT techniques (Kolko, 1998).

Self-Control and Self-Instruction Training

Experiencing occasional anger towards one's children is a natural part of being a parent. Most parents who maltreat their children have difficulties in controlling frustration and anger, so they lash out physically and verbally.

This kind of behaviour seems to be self-reinforcing because it brings immediate (although not long-lasting) relief. Screaming and shouting at the child
can become a chronic problem indicating poor parenting skills and inability
to interact with the child in a peaceful, problem-solving way. As time goes
on parents hit harder and more frequently, scream, and use degrading and
anxiety-provoking abusive language with greater passion, believing this is
the only way to make children behave. But, even if they know that anger
always brings bad results they find it difficult to control frustration and
'short-fused' emotional responses. Self-control training is designed to give
such parents a more effective means of manipulating the eliciting, reinforcing, and discriminative stimuli which affect their behaviour. The first
task in this training is to examine what leads to this type of behaviour and
what are the consequences of that behaviour. The second task is to explore
the ways in which, and then to make suggestions as to how, these events can
be altered. They may be changed either in a physical or cognitive way in
order to achieve a greater degree of behaviour control (for example, learning
to control verbal aggression, drinking, physical violence). The parents are
asked to make a list of behaviours over which they would like to have more
control. If self-control training is carried out in a group of parents then each
group member has to produce a list and to describe an episode using ABC
analysis, in order to practise understanding of the behavioural sequence:

A	Antecedent events	– What triggered off angry behaviour, what started it?
B	Behaviour	– What did you do, what was the behaviour-action?
C	Consequences	– What was the result of that behaviour, what feelings did it inspire?

An example of ABC behaviour analysis:

Antecedent event	– Six-year-old Tony soiled his pants.
Behaviour	– Mother screamed at him, called him a stinker, a lazy bastard, and locked him in the bathroom for two hours as a punishment. When he called for help she screamed more and called him degrading names.
Consequences	– The child was hurt emotionally and physically. Such parental behaviour is destructive as it damages a child's self-esteem and distorts child–parent interactions and relationships.

ABC analysis with the parent, or group of parents, helps one to see clearly
and explicitly what happens when one gets angry, and when such anger is
not controlled. This type of analysis is particularly useful to do with
emotionally abusive parents, as it shows them the sequence of events – what

leads to what, and negative consequences to the child and deterioration of the relationship between parent and child.

Parents, with the help of a therapist, devise various ways of controlling anger, resentment, violence, hostility, and frustration. A list of mutually identified self-control techniques is produced and their application discussed and linked with experienced incidents. It is useful to role-play such incidents so parents can see and hear what they may sound like in real life, and then discuss and suggest alternative ways of coping with anger-provoking situations.

Modelling and rehearsing alternative ways of coping with anger give parents extra confidence when dealing with children. A list of useful techniques in self-control is given below as a series of self-instructions:

1. Go to another room to get away from the child.
2. Close your mouth very tight, grind your teeth.
3. Go to the kitchen to make a cup of tea or drink a glass of water.
4. Pinch yourself to stop screaming and shouting.
5. Take a deep breathe three times.
6. Go to the garden or outside the house and walk around to distract yourself.
7. Go to the bathroom and put your hands under the cold water.
8. Put the radio or music on to take your mind away from the anger-provoking situation.
9. Do some heavy physical work, e.g. vacuum cleaning, washing the kitchen floor, or digging the garden, to get rid of negative emotional energy.
10. Try to recall positive and pleasing aspects of the child's behaviour.
11. Sit down away from the child and read a newspaper or a page or two of a book.
12. Look at the list of coping strategies and remind yourself of the ABC analysis.
13. Try to remember that a child is a learner who is bound to misbehave.
14. Once you have calmed down sufficiently, talk to the child in a quiet and corrective way.

Stress Management and Anger Control

An extension of self-control procedures lies in the development of techniques specifically designed for the control of anger and stress. Novaco (1975, 1979, 1985) developed a stress-management training programme to help people in managing provocation and in regulating their anger arousal. Anger-management does not seek to remove anger but rather seeks to encourage self-regulation of cognition, emotion, and behaviour through the application of methods of self-control. There are three components of this programme: first, 'cognitive preparation' to educate individuals (e.g. parents) about their anger and its causes and effects; then 'skill acquisition' in which coping strategies, including self-statement modification, relaxation, and assertion skills are trained; finally, 'application training' in which the newly acquired skills are put to the test in a range of supervised *in vivo* and role-play settings.

Parents are encouraged to conceptualise anger as a state which is aggravated by self-presented thoughts, and to view arousal as a series of stages, rather than as an all-or-nothing state. Attention should be paid to identifying and altering irrational beliefs (for example, 'She is doing it on purpose to hurt me', or 'He knows how to do it, but he is just lazy'). Coping strategies include the use of self-instruction to reduce arousal when this is identified. Types of self-instruction that may be used include those that encourage a focus on the task to be accomplished (for example, 'I must keep calm', or 'What is it I have to do here?'), and those that encourage other incompatible behaviour such as getting a cup of tea or relaxing (for example, doing relax-ation exercises for a few minutes, or simply telling oneself just to relax or take a deep breath). Parents are advised to use coping skills early in a chain of behaviour and to offer self-reinforcement for success. In other words, parents are advised to interfere with anger-provoking thoughts as soon as they begin to occur, and to instruct themselves in how they are going to deal with the problem. In emotionally abusive situations, especially those where the child may be unliked, unwanted, or rejected, the sheer presence of the child, or minor misbehaviour, often brings about hostile feelings and angry reactions to the child, so early interference with anger-building thoughts is essential to stop the escalation of abuse. For example, if a mother manages to stop herself getting angry and hostile (because her child wet itself) she can tell herself, 'Well, I managed that quite well. It is only a child, these accidents happen to most children that age. I must be more tolerant; I shall just change the clothes and ask the child to remember to go to the toilet on time, for this is not a major disaster. I had better make myself a cup of tea and relax a bit, to stop myself screaming at the child.' Such self-talk helps the parent to feel better, and stops an abusive episode.

Stress- and anger-management can be taught individually as well as in a group of parents. Group members, or individuals at home, are given stressful scenarios and are asked to devise various stress-management strategies. Those scenarios are role-played and discussed, accommodating individual needs for understanding and ability to apply them in real-life situations. A video-tape may be used to show how one can use self-talk to prepare for:

1. provocation;
2. reacting during the confrontation; and
3. coping with arousal.

Self-talk is a useful technique to use with emotionally abusive parents as it helps parents to be in control, and it helps to reduce stress. Since the accumulation of stresses contributes to child maltreatment, knowledge of how this affects the child, and knowing techniques that could help to prevent an outburst of anger directed at the child, are of great benefit to both parents and child. When people are under stress and are besieged by problems with which they feel they cannot cope, they will privately tell themselves all sorts of defeating statements such as: 'I can't cope any longer with this child..., there is no point trying..., I have done all these before..., whatever I do is wrong..., I can't help feeling bad about my child..., there is no hope..., one of us has to go..., I feel very guilty not being able to love my child..., nothing is ever going to change..., I am a failure.' Such self-talk is extremely common among emotionally abusive carers, and it goes together with observable behaviours such as social withdrawal, weepiness, insomnia, detachment, lack of energy and enthusiasm, depression, and so on. Stress is evident, and needs to be dealt with for the parent's and child's sake. Several sets of procedures are taught in order to control impulsive reactions and hostile feelings. Preparing for provocation is important in order to face difficulties, as the illustration below demonstrates:

John is a three-year-old toddler who has had a long history of failure to thrive; he has been seen by the paediatrician (who was alarmed by the poor mother–child interaction, by her indifference to the child and by the continuous poor weight-gain and stunting in growth). John lost weight since the last outpatient visit, and his behaviour worsened. The mother was told that John's growth and development was worrying and that she must make an effort to ensure that he ate more, and that her management of him was kinder and more caring. Her efforts to feed him had been difficult and unsatisfactory for a long time. There were arguments regarding her parenting with her husband, his family, and even neighbours, and she felt very anxious and under a lot of pressure when it came to feeding him. She always anticipated problems, so the problems occurred. As time went on and difficulties escalated, she began to feel very resentful towards John, feeling that he had made her life miserable on every front. Each meal-time became a battlefield: screaming, shouting, force-feeding, smacking, and making him sit at the table for two to three hours. Anger, frustration, and stress became regular features of the eating interaction. It was necessary for the mother to prepare herself for the difficulties and not to feel defeated before she even started. The mother was asked to tell herself:

1. This is not going to upset me.
2. I know what to do.
3. I am going to stay calm.
4. I am going to take John to the kitchen and tell him what I am going to prepare to eat.
5. If I realise that I am getting upset or anxious, I will take a deep breath and tell myself that I will do my best.
6. I will smile and talk to John in a calm way.
7. I will encourage him to eat.
8. I will not get angry.

If John refuses to eat, however, reactions during the confrontation are important, and certain self-instructions should be used:

1. If he does not eat now I will try to feed him later.
2. I am not going to put pressure on him.
3. There is no point in getting angry, because being angry makes things worse.
4. If I get upset I will lose control, so I must not get upset, and therefore remain in control.
5. I must stay calm, and continue to relax.
6. I must remember to talk warmly and in kind tones.

However, it may be difficult to control anger arousal and it is necessary to learn techniques of coping with it. The following self-instruction can be of help:

1. I am getting tensed up, so it is time to relax and slow down.
2. Getting upset will not solve the problem.
3. It is just not worth it to get so angry.
4. I have every reason to be annoyed and anxious, but there is no need to 'blow up'.
5. I had better relax by taking a few deep breaths.
6. I know what to do, and am going to rehearse that again.
7. I need to tell myself what to do again.
8. I am not going to take all the blame.
9. I am going to say what I think.
10. I am going to be rational.
11. Negatives lead to more negatives.
12. It is important to think first before I act.

Accumulation of stresses in the lives of parents contributes to emotional neglect and abuse of children. It is therefore necessary to teach parents how to manage stress by providing some general rules and specific techniques to cope with everyday difficulties. Some life stresses are not in our power to change, but we can control a lot of them if we put our minds to it. At the end of stress-management training a list of suggestions as to how to monitor stress in everyday life may be helpful:

1. Keep a list of stresses in your life – the accumulation of them can make life unbearable and unrewarding.
2. Positive self-talk helps one to remain in control and to feel positive about oneself.
3. Do not think that you have to do everything at once, and that every problem has to be eliminated 100%. Be satisfied with small changes. Even a small reduction in each stress can lead to a big difference in your ability to cope.
4. Do not try to assist everybody all the time. Take a rational view of your commitments in your daily life pattern. Try to leave a little time for yourself and for some privacy.
5. Think positively and believe that you can change things if you put your mind to it; think with determination.
6. Learn to say 'no' if you feel that demands which are being made on you are unreasonable.

7. Be free to put your point of view. Communicate your thoughts and feelings, and do not store them, because they will only accumulate and explode, hurting people who least deserve it, like children.
8. If you cannot cope, ask for help, and keep asking until you get it.
9. Ask your friends, family, or neighbours to give you a hand if you feel overwhelmed with problems.
10. Ask your GP or a health visitor for help, advice, and assistance. Do not feel that you are a burden or nuisance, because it is their job and they are being paid to help you. They can also refer you to appropriate people for help.
11. Do not wait until things are totally out of control.
12. There is nothing unusual in having difficulties relating to your child – or to have difficulties in teaching children how to behave.
13. Try to share your worries with your partner; ask him to help you, to give you a hand and to support you. It is also his duty to care for the child.
14. Social workers do not only protect children – they also protect families. Turn to them for help if you feel you cannot cope any longer.

RELAXATION TRAINING

Relaxation training has become a valuable part of stress management. Clients are taught how to relax when they are overwhelmed with tension and anxiety. They are taught how to identify tension in different parts of the body and how to deal with it. Anxiety shows itself and affects people in different physiological responses (increased heart rate, sweating, muscle tension): behavioural responses (shown by avoidance behaviour); and cognitive responses (negative self-defeating thoughts). In order to break this negative cycle, it is necessary to learn to control anxiety and to be able to recognise the onset of anxious feelings and situations that trigger off anxiety. Relaxation is an ideal way to cope with these crippling and self-defeating feelings.

Relaxation techniques should be practised several times to encourage the acquisition of necessary skills in relaxation, as described hereafter. Each person was given a 30-minute tape to practice relaxation at home at least twice a day. One session should be allocated to teach, demonstrate, and discuss individual applications of different relaxation techniques, including:

1. Listening to the relaxation tape and practising deep-muscle relaxation (demonstration).
2. Meditating (remembering or imagining something pleasant and enjoyable). This has proved to be a particularly helpful exercise in cases where feelings of defeat, lowness or distress are experienced.
3. Listening to music of individual preference which may have a soothing effect.

4. Employing personal techniques suitable for relaxing individuals, such as reading, walking, watching television, cooking, sporting activities, and so on, and discussing and encouraging those aspects. Useful tips are given as to how to build them into everyday life for self-satisfaction and reduction of anxiety.

The author used relaxation exercises with mothers of failure-to-thrive children, and with emotionally abusive parents. The results (as evaluated by the parents) were very positive and most parents found them useful. Relaxation training was done individually in parents' homes and in parent groups. A relaxation tape was used to start with, simply to help individuals to locate anxiety in different parts of the body and to teach the techniques. Once learning had taken place there was no further need to use the tape, and relaxations were done only on those parts of the body affected by anxiety. There are many relaxation tapes currently available, and these should be heard so that the most suitable can be selected (for further reading see Ollendick & Cerny, 1981). An example of a training script is given below.

Hands and arms: Make a fist with your left hand. Squeeze it hard. Feel the tightness in your hand and arm as you squeeze. Now let your hand go and relax. See how much better your hand and arm feel when they are relaxed. Once again, make a fist with your left hand and squeeze hard. Now relax and let your hand go. (Repeat the process for the right hand and arm.)

Arms and shoulders: Stretch your arms out in front of you. Raise them high up over your head and way back. Feel the pull in your shoulders. Stretch higher. Now just let your arms drop back to your side. Stretch again. Stretch your arms out in front of you. Raise them over your head. Pull them back, way back. Pull hard. Now let them drop quickly. Notice how your shoulders feel more relaxed. This time have a great big stretch. Try to touch the ceiling. Stretch your arms way out in front of you. Raise them way up high over your head. Push them way, way back. Notice the tension and pull in arms and shoulders. Hold tight. Now let them drop very quickly and feel how good it is to be relaxed. It feels good and warm and lazy.

Shoulder and neck: Try to pull your shoulders up to your ears and push your head down into your shoulders. Hold in tight. Now relax and feel the warmth. Again, pull your shoulders up to your ears and push your head down into your shoulders. Do it tightly. You can relax now. Bring your head out and let your shoulders relax. Notice how much better it feels to be relaxed than to be all tight. One more time now. Push your head down and your shoulders way up to your ears. Hold it. Feel the tenseness in your neck and shoulders. You can relax now and feel comfortable. You feel good.

Jaw: Put your teeth hard together. Let your neck muscles help you. Now relax. Just let your jaw hang loose. Notice how good it feels just to let you jaw drop. Bite down hard again. Now relax again. Just let your jaw drop. It feels so good just to let go. One more time. Bite down. Hard as you can. Harder...Oh, you're really working hard. Now relax. Try to relax your whole body. Let yourself go as loose as you can.

Face and Nose: Wrinkle up your nose. Make as many wrinkles in your nose as you can. Now you can relax your nose. Now wrinkle up your nose again. Wrinkle it up hard. Hold it just as tight as you can. You can relax your face. Notice that when you scrunch up your nose your cheeks and your mouth and your forehead all help you and they get tight, too. So when you relax your nose, your whole face relaxes too, and that feels good...Now make lots of wrinkles on your forehead. Hold it tight, now, then, let go. Now you can just relax. Let your face go smooth. No wrinkles anywhere. Your face feels smooth and relaxed.

Stomach: Now tighten up your stomach muscles. Make your stomach hard. Do not move. Hold it. You can relax now. Let your stomach go soft. Let it be as relaxed as you can. That feels so much better. Tighten your stomach hard. You can relax now. Settle down, get comfortable, and relax. Notice the difference between a tight stomach and a relaxed one. That is how it should feel: loose and relaxed. Once more. Tighten up. Tighten hard. Now you can relax completely. Now this time, try to pull your stomach in. Try to squeeze it against your back-bone. Try to be as skinny as you can. Now relax, because you do not have to be skinny now. Just relax and feel your stomach being warm and loose. Squeeze in your stomach again. Make it touch your backbone. Get it small and tight. Get as thin as you can. Hold tight now. You can relax now. Settle back and let your stomach come back out where it belongs. You can really feel good now. You have done well.

Legs and feet: Push your toes hard down on the floor. You will probably need your legs to help you push. Push down, spread your toes apart. Now relax your feet. Let your toes go loose and feel how good that is. It feels good to be relaxed. Now push your toes down. Let your leg muscles help you push your feet down. Push your feet. It feels so good to be relaxed. No tenseness anywhere. You feel warm and tingly.

Conclusion: Stay as relaxed as you can. Let your whole body go limp and feel all your muscles relax. In a few minutes you will be asked to open your eyes and that will be the end of the session. Today is a good day, and you are ready to go back to class feeling very relaxed. You have worked hard in here and it feels good to work hard. Shake your arms. Now shake your legs. Move your head around. Slowly open your eyes, and enjoy well-being in your body and your mind.

PROBLEM-SOLVING

Through the course of the assessment it may become obvious that either the parent and/or the child has marked deficits in their approach to addressing practical and/or emotional issues and problems that often present in family life. Parents may have a tried and tested approach to child-rearing, possibly based on their own experience of childhood, which they subsequently adopt with their own child. Parents may not have had access to alternative approaches and may continue to use these methods with their own children, based on the belief that 'it didn't do me any harm'.

Parents with limited problem-solving ability can often present with rigid and dysfunctional thought patterns about their child and their own ability to parent. When difficulties arise, and strategies fail, parents can feel overwhelmed, unable to cope, and disempowered to try new approaches with their child. They can become trapped in a self-defeating cycle, which reinforces their negative assumptions about their child and their own inability to cope or adequately parent. These parents demonstrate particular difficulties in their ability to generate adaptive solutions to manage the child's behaviour, or set developmentally appropriate tasks for the child. They may give up, refuse to interact, or lose interest in a child who does not respond to their style of parenting and may even grow to dislike it. As we know, children who have experienced maltreatment often tend to have difficulty concentrating and can be aggressive or impulsive; these difficulties can augment parenting problems, resulting in a downward spiral which the parents feel they are incapable of addressing and which can lead to abuse.

Equipping parents with problem-solving skills to tackle practical and emotional tasks can be a helpful process in managing and mastering challenges the carer encounters in everyday parenting. Adopting a problem-solving approach to practical problems can also reduce the parents' perception of stress, of feeling overwhelmed, and of experiencing pressure. This should reduce the child's vulnerability to maltreatment as the parents will be less inclined to engage in negative interchanges with the child.

Cognitive problem-solving training can be used as an independent therapeutic technique or helpful adjunct to a cognitive-behavioural-oriented treatment package. In this type of intervention, parents can be taught how to:

1. identify and define problems;
2. generate alternatives;
3. consider the pros and cons of possible solutions, select appropriate decisions;
4. implement a plan;
5. review their progress and the success of their decision. (D'Zurilla & Goldfried, 1971; D'Zurilla & Nezu, 1990)

The practitioner co-ordinates the session, models the techniques, and provides feedback until the skills are well-developed and can be generalised from the sessions to the family home. Parents are taught and encouraged to follow a 'decision tree', similar to the one described in Table 12.1 to help define possible options to address difficulties and arrive at an appropriate solution.

Table 12.1 Problem-solving decision tree

When you have examined a situation and decided that a particular issue is a problem:

- Ask yourself: what's happening here?
- Talk over the situation with yourself.
- What does the problem mean?
- What are the possible consequences of this issue?

Examine the situation from different perspectives

- Consider your feelings, and the feelings of your child and other people involved in the situation. Are your feelings intense? If so, you need to relax first before continuing with the issue.

Describe possible solutions

- Try and list as many possible ways of dealing with the problem.
- Talk the problem over with your partner, friend, or social worker to get their ideas.
- If you cannot manage to speak to someone, think about someone supportive whose advice has been helpful in the past.
- If you were in your child's position, what do you think that *they* would like to happen?
- If your friend Jenny were in this situation, what would she do?
- If your therapist were in this situation, what would she do?
- Do you need to involve specialist or have other professional support to get advice on possible choices and solutions to deal with the problem?

Decide if the change is manageable and controllable

- If you decide the problem is out of control (although this is rare, it could apply to some temporary difficulties) – call friends, family, or professional help for emotional and practical support, such as childcare arrangements, or someone who will listen to your difficulties.
- If you feel change is possible, and/or wish to pursue the issue further, continue with the decision tree.

Evaluate the consequences of each option and possible solution

- Consider the positive and negative aspects of each option.
- Select the option that appears to have most positive consequences and fits in with what you think is most important.

Choose a solution and try it

- Follow through on your decision and put every effort into carrying out what is involved.

Learn from your decision

- Did it work?
- Why? Why not?
- If it didn't work, return to the list of possible solutions and select the next 'best' option.
- If it did work, praise your decision-making!
- Ask yourself why it worked.
- What other options could you try in these situations?
- What did you learn about yourself?

Remember

- Avoiding difficulties does not make them disappear.
- Decisions may not work every time, but they may help you find the best solution!

The practitioner can initially focus on non-emotive topics for the parents, to introduce the decision-making process. Role play may be introduced to provide a safe and supportive environment where the parent tackles difficult and stressful situations, or more emotive topics. The practitioner is available to model or generate alternative options, when the parent is having particular difficulties. Parents may want to list the situations that cause most difficulty for them, or the family, and make a list of accessible resources for how they plan to approach their difficulties in the future.

Encouraging the parent to consider the short- and long-term outcome or impact of a decision, as well as supporting and encouraging the parent to break down tasks into a sequence of goal-directed activities, can supplement this approach, and enhance the carer's ability to manage stressful and aversive situations and incidents with the child (Shure & Spivack, 1971).

The whole family can also be invited to participate. Although the process may seem quite complex, studies have shown that even young children can learn how to break a problem into manageable tasks. Planned activities and encouraging role play for the family allow both children and adults to identify the issues that frequently cause difficulty, yet permit them to rely on the practitioner to shape alternative and possibly more adaptive methods or approaches to their difficulties. The intervention can also be useful for couples where parents have difficulty in agreeing on child-rearing methods.

Promising findings have also been reported for families with adolescents, where relationship difficulties can centre on the young person's requests for autonomy and independence (Robin, Kent, O'Leary, Foster, & Prinz, 1977). Initial sessions may focus on teaching family members to define problems on neutral topics in an atmosphere that is non-blaming and non-coercive. The family is invited to brainstorm options, explore advantages and disadvantages, agree on a plan, and implement and evaluate their decision. For families with adolescents, problem-solving training can also include an element of communication skills, such as active listening, attention to verbal and non-verbal expressions, praise, and questioning family members (Patterson & Forgarchm, 1987; Foster & Robin, 1989).

How the family can be helped in identifying and trying to solve some problems is illustrated below.

CASE STUDY

A family of 7 children (2 boys and 5 girls aged between 5 and 17 years) were referred as *at risk* for emotional abuse of all of them and failure to thrive in 4 (2 very serious ones). Interim care orders were issued pending further investigation and expert assessments.

It was found that the parents' relationship was fraught; fights and quarrels were regular features in their lives, and the three older girls (aged 17, 15, and 14) presented as very troubled, disturbed, and insecure teenagers, whose relationship with their parents had broken down. They would not take any notice of parental rules, reprimands, and requests. They stayed out late at night, did not ask for permission to go out, would not say where they had been, and said that the parents had no right to tell them what to do and that it was not their business to ask such questions. They did not participate in everyday chores, did not come for meals, and simply did not take any notice of their parents and their siblings. The younger siblings became scared of the three older sisters as they were tormented and bullied by them. The relationship between the girls and parents had been extremely bad for a considerable time. They screamed and shouted at each other, using degrading, abusive, and threatening language. The older girls felt unloved, insecure, and unwanted, and all 7 children worried and felt permanently anxious about the constant abusive fights between the parents and parents and children. The teenage girls felt that they were not doing anything wrong, but could not cope with the persistently emotionally explosive atmosphere at home and mutual verbal abuse. The situation worsened when the eldest girl (who had a lifelong history of severe failure to thrive) was diagnosed as anorexic and required hospitalisation. The parents and children were made aware that unless family functioning and relationships improved to an acceptable level, the local authority would have no choice but to seek care orders to stop the escalation of the already evident significant harm.

The comprehensive assessment revealed:

1. Hostile relationships between parents and children, especially with the older ones.
2. Acute insecurity experienced by all children due to parental insensitivity in responding to their needs and threats of abandonment.
3. Relationship difficulties between parents and emotionally hostile and abusive behaviour between them, always witnessed by the children.
4. Father's abuse of alcohol.
5. Lack of rules, routines, and boundaries within the family. They functioned as individuals, doing what each of them wanted, and not as a family group.
6. Unruly behaviour by the three older girls which was beyond parent control.
7. Four children failing to thrive (one became anorexic).
8. Severe encopresis suffered by one child.
9. Four children suffering from primary nocturnal enuresis.

A problem-solving approach was used initially to deal with four areas of difficulties identified by the family as most important to them. The parents and children were involved in exploration and identification (brainstorming) of areas of mutual concern and discussing the effects these had on the parents and children; they then were encouraged to look for a solution and alternative ways of behaving in order to make life more pleasant for everybody in the family. The practitioner helped the family to work out what would be required from each person to improve communication, functioning, and relationships; what each person should and should not do; how to make mutual decisions, taking into consideration the welfare of all; and how to negotiate, compromise, and agree on how to behave and implement changes. They all agreed to monitor progress and to make necessary adjustments on a weekly, or even twice-weekly, basis. A list of rules, consisting of two columns ('what I should do' and 'what I should not do') was worked out together and given to each member of the family. The family as a whole identified the following problems of major importance to them:

1. For parents and children to restrain from screaming and shouting at each other, calling each other degrading names, and to stop being verbally abusive.
2. To work out what family members are allowed and not allowed to do. To set up clear, but fair, rules and routines such as for bedtime, and for the older children not to disrupt the younger ones' sleep when they came home late at night; to make beds, and get ready for breakfast and school in the morning; to help with homework; to have the evening meal at a set time (5.30–6.00 p.m.), and Sunday lunch at 1.30 p.m.; and every member of the family to be at home for meals;
3. For the older girls to be able to go out to meet their friends three to four times a week, and for the parents to trust them and not always look for the worst. To ask for permission to go out, tell their parents where they are going to be, and to return home at the agreed time (10 p.m.).
4. For the father to reduce his beer consumption from six cans a day to three cans a day.

All the family felt that they needed quality time as a family to reduce anger, frustration, and constantly getting at each other, so a Sunday afternoon outing, to mutually chosen places, was put in place.

Table 12.2 shows a problem-solving schedule for one of the older girls.

ABC Analysis

ABC analysis was used with both parents to illustrate how the triggers or 'setting events' tend to lead to particular difficulties, and what are the consequent 'pay-offs' for the children to behave in the way which is problematic for everybody. Being shown graphically (several examples) the sequences of behaviours – what effect, what and why – helped children and parents to better understand what is involved and how it is learned. Table 12.3 shows functional analysis conducted with the family regarding Jane's behaviour as an example.

Parents become aware that specific situations will give rise to negative emotional states, such as their own fear, anger, or low mood, which, in turn, tend to precipitate an abusive incident. Adopting other cognitive-based

Table 12.2   Problem-solving schedule (for Liza)

I should	I should not
Come for the evening meal and Sunday lunch at the agreed times of 5.30–6.00 p.m. on weekdays, and 1.30 p.m. on Sunday.	Scream and shout at parents and siblings.
Get up in the morning when woken up, dress, make bed (if the bed is wet, take sheets downstairs to put in the washing machine). Always have some breakfast.	Go out without permission and come back late at night.
Always ask for permission to go out.	Use nasty language and swear-words.
Help with the housework twice a week. Do homework daily.	Disrupt my younger sisters' sleep when coming back at night.
Speak nicely and quietly to parents and siblings.	Be aggressive and bullying younger sisters and brothers.
Apologise for misbehaviour.	Miss any of my meals because of low weight.

Table 12.3   ABC analysis of Jane's behaviour

Antecedents *What happened before the situation became a problem?*	Behaviour *What is the problem?*	Consequences *What do I do to manage the problem? What happens to my child?*	Prevention *How can I prevent this problem?*	Solutions *What can I do when I encounter this problem?*
Mother asked where Jane was going at night.	Jane said that it is not her business to know, called her mother nasty names, pushed her away from the door. Mother called her nasty names too.	Jane is getting involved with bad people. She is smoking and drinking. She may get pregnant. Mother feels powerless, unable to communicate, exaggerates problems.	Set up clear rules, negotiate with Jane what is reasonable, reason with her. Set out consequences.	Be calm, less abusive. Trust her, do not look for bad all the time. Make firm agreement as to what is acceptable, and what is not.

techniques by paying particular attention to what parents tell themselves in these situations and challenging these ideas may intervene and prevent the cycle of maltreatment. Increasing parental awareness of this link will help parents identify how circumstances can often lead to problems for the family or their relationship with their child. Not only will this alert the parent to particular situations which could be avoided, but, possibly with

Table 12.4   Dysfunctional thoughts, beliefs, and feelings, and alternative ways of thinking and feeling

Self-defeating thoughts and feelings				
Event	Parental Belief	Parental Feelings	Parental Behaviour	Outcome
Child destroyed his toys and a new jumper	He is naughty, wicked, mad, there is something wrong mentally with him	Acute anger Frustration Hostility	Child is called hurtful names; locked up in the room for many hours; not given any food	Child's emotionally disturbed behaviour intensified. Parent–child relationship and interaction became even more hostile and painful
Cognitive change – alternative ways of thinking				
Event	Parental belief	Parental feelings	Parental behaviour	Outcome
Child destroyed his toys and a new jumper	He feels unworthy of having nice toys and clothes, because we criticise him and tell him that he is naughty and wicked	We will change. We will tell him that we love him and that he is a nice and good boy. We will praise him	Parents stopped screaming at the child, showed warmth and praised him whenever he did something good	Child became happier, more responsive to parental requests, interaction more positive. Improved relationship

Source: Iwaniec (2004). *Children who fail to thrive: A practice guide*. Chichester: John Wiley & Sons.

the help of the practitioner (if necessary) the parent can develop a plan on how to manage those problems when they present. Being forewarned is being forearmed! The items in Table 12.4 may be helpful.

Evaluation

The problem-solving (after initial squabbles) went relatively well and some good solutions were worked out. They worked out rules, routines and expectations; meal-times; the number of times they could go out per week; the time to come home at night; the manner of speaking to each other; help with doing homework; the amount of drink the father was allowed to take and going out as a family at least once a week.

There were eight intensive sessions to work out the problems and solutions and six follow-up monitoring sessions. The evaluation at six months and one year showed considerable improvement in some areas and moderate in others (see Figure 12.2).

Problem-solving approaches are future-oriented, with the aim of promoting hope that problems are manageable, and that either the parent or outside resources can tackle and successfully address a difficulty. The parent learns not to dwell on past mistakes, but learns to view prior efforts as a learning experience which supplements their information and knowledge of how to handle stressful situations. Adopting cognitive problem-solving techniques can be encouraged as a viable option and tool to orient the parent to face

Evaluation Sheet

Name: *Smith Family*   Date: *20 April 2005*

Level of improvement and outcomes

-2	-1	0	+1	+2
Very poor	Poor	No change	Good	Very good

	Baseline	1 month	2 months	6 months	1 year	Comments
For parents and children to stop screaming and verbally abusing each other	-2	+1	+1	+1	+1	Remained at +1 – no change from 2 months evaluation, 6 months and 1 year
To set up clear rules and routines for meal-times, bed-times, homework, getting ready for school, coming home at night	-2	-1	+1	+1	+2	Improved somewhat. The same at 2 and 6 months evaluation. Very good at 1 year
For older girls to be allowed to see their friends three times a week, tell parents where they are going, and return home at agreed time	-2	+1	+1	+2	+2	Improved considerably
For the father to reduce consumption of beer by half	-2	-2	+1	+1	+1	Remained at +1 somewhat improved

Figure 12.2   Evaluation of problem-solving

problems rather than turning away from them. Although the strategy of a problem-solving technique may not reach an effective resolution each time, it may be helpful, and can generate possibilities that should eventually provide some assistance for the family.

MOTIVATIONAL INTERVIEWING

Motivational interviewing (MI) is a straightforward, transparent set of therapeutic techniques, based on the principles of cognitive-behavioural therapy. MI adopts the assumption that challenging maladaptive thought patterns can affect behavioural change and diffuse emotional responses which perpetuate a maladaptive cycle. It is also assumed that motivation to adopt new, more adaptive parenting behaviour is related to a personal read-iness to change that behaviour, rather than a fixed, unchanging character-istic of the carer's personality. According to practitioners who advocate MI, an individual will repeatedly rotate through a cycle of different stages, proposed by Prochaska & DiClemente's (1982) transtheoretical model, commonly known as the Stages of Change, before permanent effective change in unhealthy behaviour occurs. As child maltreatment incurs immense psychological and physical costs to the child, it is important to consider cycles of change in parenting attitudes as the way to promote optimal well-being for the child. These stages include:

- *Pre-contemplation* – where an individual does not consider the possibility of change and is unlikely to participate in treatment options, although referred for specialist intervention. Increasing the parents' awareness of the problem and difficulties for the child will be an important challenge for practitioners working with parents at this level.
- *Contemplation* – a carer may be considering that his or her parenting style may have an adverse influence on the child, yet is ambivalent to make changes to the child's care. Clinicians can facilitate discussions relating to risk and the consequences of maintaining current behaviours. For some parents this may include removing the child from the family home and will need to be explored.
- *Planning* – a parent may be keen to take action, and may have decided on a number of changes he or she may wish to make to improve the child's situation, although has yet to implement these strategies. In some cases this may involve leaving a partner who is physically abusive or obtaining additional support to address a substance-abuse issue.
- *Action* – when active attempts have been made to change aversive behav-iour this may involve participating in a parenting or drug and alcohol programme, or leaving the family home in cases of domestic violence. Parents will need extensive practical and emotional support as they initiate this difficult step in the pathway to better psychological functioning for

both themselves and their child. Cognitive techniques can be particularly helpful during this stage if a parent doubts the benefits of their decision. Coping strategies such as problem-solving, previously discussed, can be used as a tool to prevent problem behaviour and avoid triggering situations for problem behaviour.

- *Maintence* When parents have made a deliberate and concerted attempt to address their difficulties, they are in the maintenance phase of change. Although relapse may occur and the parent may return to a state of ambivalence, practitioners should focus on the benefits of the parents' experience of the change process, their strengths and vulnerabilities, and skills to avert difficulties.

Motivational interviewing acknowledges that many people are ambivalent about changing patterns of behaviour, and accepts that there are barriers, difficulties, advantages, and disadvantages to initiating change. MI could be applied to cases of child maltreatment to explore the importance of current parenting styles; to build confidence in the possibility of change in the parent–child relationship; to generate goals, targets, and behaviours for change; to provide accurate information about treatment strategies and the process of therapy and to remove barriers and increase access to treatment options.

Miller and Rollnick (1991) highlight five basic principles that need to be considered when encouraging motivation and facilitating change in maladaptive behaviour which can be easily integrated into interventions with parents in cases of child maltreatment:

1. *Be empathic* – facilitate an atmosphere of respect, acceptance, and interest in the client, to enhance self-esteem and self-efficacy, which is essential for change to occur.
2. Look for *inconsistencies* and *discrepancies* between the parents' view of their current relationship with their child and how they would like it to be. Encourage the belief that these goals can be reached with support.
3. *Avoid arguments* – arguments, labelling, and blaming the parent are counterproductive and may lead the parent to withdraw from services.
4. *Roll with resistance* – question and clarify parents' difficulties with an intervention or treatment process. Highlight their current situation, progress, and hopes for the future.
5. *Support parents' self*-esteem and *sense of responsibility to change* – when difficulties in a treatment programme occur, parents can often assume a sense of failure. It is important to reframe negative perceptions so that difficulties are part of the process and accepted. Encourage parents to focus on their strengths for highlighting the issue and asking for help.

Practical suggestions to facilitate change include:

- reflecting on parents' circumstances and difficulties as ways to manage resistance;
- rephrasing negative self-statements in a positive manner;
- breaking down patterns of problematic behaviour so the parent can address the issue in stages;
- revisiting treatment goals throughout the intervention to reinforce progress and to determine whether priorities have changed;
- utilising 'scaling questions' (such as on a scale of 0 to 10, how keen are you to feed you child at a set time each evening?). Answers can be challenged by probing the parent and increasing their discrepancy, 'You said 6. What makes you a 6? Are you sure you are not a 7? What would it take to make you a 7? (Miller & Rollnick, 2002; Rollnick & Miller, 1995).

Motivational interviewing can be used as an independent therapeutic technique or helpful adjunct to a cognitive-behavioural-oriented treatment package. It can be used early in the treatment process to promote child protection and safety, to encourage parents to adopt adaptive parenting patterns, and/or facilitate participation in additional treatment options if necessary. Although research studies based on MI with cases of child maltreatment are rare, some promising findings and suggestions for practice have been reported to engage and facilitate maternal supportiveness in cases of sexual abuse. Adopting MI techniques may be particularly helpful for families where previous attempts at addressing parenting issues have failed, and concern and interest in the child's well-being has reached a significant low. The author used this technique when doing independent assessments and planning intervention with parents.

SUMMARY

Behavioural and cognitive approaches in helping emotionally abused and neglected children and their parents have been discussed and illustrated by some specific methods and techniques. As behavioural/cognitive approaches are reached in techniques and methods, only some of them were described in greater detail, specifically those which the author used when dealing with emotional-abuse cases, and which have been evaluated for their effectiveness (e.g. positive reinforcements to help the child to build self-esteem and self-confidence; parent-training in cognitive restructuring, anger control, and relaxation; behaviour management; problem-solving; and motivational interviewing). Problem-solving has been illustrated by a case study and some tips and ideas have been provide for practical purposes.

Behavioural and cognitive theories have been discussed briefly and linked to emotional abuse and neglect, demonstrating theoretical application and explanation of the problems. Some research findings, illustrating 'what works' in helping emotionally abused and neglect children and their parents, have been presented.

CHAPTER 13

IMPROVING PARENT–CHILD RELATIONSHIP AND CHILDREN'S ATTACHMENT TO PARENTS: PSYCHODYNAMIC APPROACH – THEORY AND PRACTICE

CONTENTS

INTRODUCTION

According to attachment theorists, a baby is born with an innate set of behaviours that are thought to elicit caregiving. Parenting that responds to these behaviours, is sensitive, and anticipates a child's needs is thought to be fundamental in the development and acquisition of physical, social, and psychological wellbeing, as well as and basic skills. In the context of these early interactions with caregivers, a child is thought to acquire a sense of security and trust on which it can depend, and from which it can develop a sense of autonomy and confidence in itself and its environment appropriate to its age. Experiences of early relationships also provide a framework whereby children develop 'internal working models', concepts or expectations of themselves, and their roles in relationships. Depending on the quality of the relationship, a child concludes whether it is, for example, lovable, interesting and/or a person to whom the attachment, figure or others in the child's environment will respond in a helpful or satisfying way. Expectations of the carer develop in parallel. Based on the experience, the child will decide if the parent is attentive, accepting, responsive, and a source of safety and protection. (Ainsworth, 1989; Bowlby, 1973; Sroufe, 1979).

Emotional abuse, like all forms of child maltreatment, can be thought of as 'relational failure' between the parent and child (Cicchetti, Toth, & Bush, 1988). Parent–child relationships, characterised by a chronic pattern of negative interaction, where negative effects are incessant and unremitting, communicate that the child is of little value. Parental indifference, lack of affection or attention, or failure to respond to signals of distress (such as pain, hunger, or discomfort) supplement the child's self-belief that it is 'unworthy' and 'bad'. Children lose confidence in their carers' availability and responsiveness and may subsequently adopt insecure attachment styles as a strategy to cope with their emotional and relationship needs (Bowlby, 1973). The child's cognitive and emotional capacities are often insufficiently developed to cope with contradictory models generated by a parent who is a source of both protection and harm (Crittenden, 1988; Tomison & Tucci, 1997; Crittenden & Ainsworth, 1989). The child comes to believe that the carer (and by extension other adults) is lovable, but also rejecting and untrustworthy. Relationships with others are subsequently considered as both a source of pleasure and of emotional pain (Bowlby, 1973; Doyle, 2001). Experiencing such paradoxical and unpredictable parenting renders the child less confident, inhibits a capacity for emotional expression, and undermines its capacity to manage its emotions, address stressful situations, and understand its environment (O'Hagan, 1995; Iwaniec, 1997).

Negative experiences, particularly a history of abuse in his or her own childhood (and any unresolved loss), may severely affect a parent's ability to bond with, attend to, or like his or her own baby. Additional difficulties (such as conflicting family relationships, parental mental-health problems, and interruptions in care arrangements) may augment attachment problems and interact with a parenting style which is unresponsive, insensitive, and rejecting, thus increasing the child's vulnerability to emotional abuse and neglect. Given that many parents with attachment problems have themselves experienced histories involving negative caregiving and loss (Bifulco, Brown, & Harris, 1987), preventing an inter-generational cycle of abuse is an additional aim at the forefront of attachment-based interventions (Youngblade & Belsky, 1990). Interventions addressing attachment difficulties for the child and an improvement of parent–child relationships have the broad aim of providing trusting compensatory relationships characterised by mutual respect and acquisition of behavioural skills necessary to relate to others (Hart *et al.*, 2002; Iwaniec, 1995, 1999a).

This chapter will discuss and demonstrate how children can be helped to develop secure attachments to parents or carers, and how parents can facilitate the strengthening of attachment behaviour. Various techniques based on psychodynamic therapy which have been used with good effect will be briefly outlined. Since foster-parents often have to grapple with attachment disorders and emotional disturbances in children placed in their care, examples are given of how they can be informed about basic principles of attachment problems; suggestions are made as to how they can help a child who is confused, hurt, and angry.

BUILDING SECURE ATTACHMENT

There are numerous ways in which children with attachment disorders can be helped, and in which parent–child bonding can be developed or strengthened (Iwaniec, 1999a). If the maternal emotional tie to a baby requires attention, it can be addressed by teaching the mother how she can be more sensitive and proactive during feeding, bathing, changing, and responding promptly to the child's signals of distress in a manner which is soothing, warm, and anxiety-reducing. Nugent (1996) suggests the following techniques to increase secure attachment between children and mothers. Mothers are asked to hold infants while feeding in a gently comfortable way, talk to them while being fed, establish eye contact, and smile at the baby. They are advised not to give the bottle until the baby establishes eye contact, and when it does they should immediately offer bottle or breast, smile, and talk lovingly and reassuringly at the same time, making sure that the baby is held comfortably and closely. Mothers should stroke the baby's head and cheek, and let the baby grasp their fingers. When the baby is resistant and stiff, the mother is asked to hold it gently and close to her body, talking to it in a soft and warm way. Mothers are advised to use a rocking chair while holding the baby for a little while each day, and, if possible, three to four times a day. Mothers are asked to use a 'snuggle' carrier to increase physical closeness. When changing, bathing, or attending to a child, the mother is asked to show pleasure and reassurance by patting, kissing, smiling, and talking in a warm way. The tone of voice and manner of handling contribute to the building of trust and should have a soothing effect.

Older toddlers who are insecurely attached tend to show fear, apprehension, and tension when in their mothers' company. Equally, if the child's attachment to the father is insecure, he or she will show emotional distance and avoidance when in the father's company. Observation of parent–child interaction in such cases clearly demonstrates parental coldness, distance, and unresponsiveness to the child's emotional needs. To reduce mutually avoidant behaviour, and to increase emotional togetherness, carefully planned mutual interactions (increasing slowly in time as progress is made) should be introduced (e.g. play or other activities). Parents are shown how to interact and relate to their children, and how to create an atmosphere which is warm, encouraging, and free from anxiety (Iwaniec, Herbert, & McNeish, 1985b; Iwaniec, 1995, 1999a).

Parents (both mothers and fathers) are advised and then guided to begin having physical contact by sitting a child on the lap, holding it in a gentle way that is comfortable to the child a few times a day (lasting three to five minutes each time), while reading a story, describing pictures in the book or simply holding a child while watching children's programmes on the television. Again, the way a child is spoken to and held and emotional expression during these brief sessions of deliberate interactions are of great importance. A child who feels apprehensive in the parent's company will be stiff, unresponsive, and reluctant to participate, and will feel uneasy when sitting on the parent's lap. It takes time before the child begins to feel at ease and comfortable in the close physical proximity with the parent, and parent with the child. Repetition of these activities, conducted in a warm caring fashion over time, can bring children and parents closer together, and build trust in the child that its parents are loving and caring, and provide safety and security (Iwaniec, 1995, 1999a).

The author used the above techniques with considerable success when working with emotionally ill-treated children. It is important to proceed at the child's and parent's speed to produce any required change. In rejective or very poor relationships it may take a long time to bring about significant change. Perseverance and determination with the therapist assisting are key elements to successful outcomes, as can be illustrated by the Jex case.

Jex was born prematurely and spent two months in an intensive-care unit. The mother seldom visited him; she lived far away and was not well herself (including post-natal depression). Jex was a very difficult baby: for example, feeding, sleeping, and general responsiveness to care posed especial problems. The mother found it very difficult to enjoy her son and feel that he belonged to her. As time went on, her good intentions to love him disappeared as Jex's behaviour became more demanding, attention-seeking, and unrewarding. Instead of growing closer together they grew further and further apart, and when Jex was three-and-a-half years old they were mutually antagonistic. Jex was visibly and openly rejected by his mother. Maternal perceptions that it was Jex who rejected her love and attention were exacerbated by the fact that her first child (a year older) was a very easy and placid girl, and gave the mother much pleasure and satisfaction in parenting.

Apart from various methods used with the mother to restructure the way she felt, thought about, and perceived Jex and her role as a mother (cognitive work), several attachment-building techniques were used to build their relationship. One of them was what I called 'story-reading'. Early sessions of sitting Jex on his mother's lap and getting her to hold him tenderly and gently close to her were extremely difficult for the mother and anxiety-provoking for Jex. He sat stiffly at the edge of his mother's knee, and her hand almost never embraced his body. After six weeks, Jex began to take an interest in the book-pictures and began to respond to his mother's reading by asking questions. He sat more comfortably, and would move and become less tense. The mother also became less anxious, showed more warmth, and did not see the 'story-reading sessions' as an ordeal. After ten weeks we had a breakthrough. One day the mother rang me crying. I thought that something dreadful had happened but she reassured me that everything was fine, and the reason why she was so moved and emotional was because Jex put his arms around her neck and put his head on her shoulder while she was reading to him. As it was Jex's first loving gesture towards his mother she became overwhelmed by emotions and by the hard-earned message Jex was giving to his mother. 'I feel loved, wanted, comfortable, and at ease when I am with you – you have changed, so have I.' I knew that from that time on the progress would be fast and positive – and I was right.

IMPROVING CHILDREN'S ATTACHMENT BEHAVIOUR TO PARENTS WITH MENTAL-HEALTH PROBLEMS

Interventions targeting family-attachment relationships have the dual aim of providing a corrective emotional experience for the carer in the context of the parents' relationship with the therapist, as well as restructuring the parent–child relationship and, ultimately, providing a secure attachment for the child. As the mother comes to perceive herself as more positive and worthwhile, her beliefs about her role with others, including her role as a mother and her relationship with her child, become more adaptive, leading to more functional relationships with others and with her children (Fraiberg, Adelson, & Shapiro, 1975; Iwaniec, 1995).

Cicchetti, Toth, and Rogosch (1999) designed an intervention to enhance attachment relationships of parents with mental-health problems. They chose to target the intervention at the mothers who were presenting with significant symptoms of depression, often associated with a parenting style characterised by unavailability, lack of sensitivity, and rejection (De Wolff & Ijzendoorn, 1997) typical in psychological maltreatment. Mothers with toddlers were selected for assistance, as carers at a low ebb of depression often report feeling overwhelmed during this stage in their child's development. Intervention at this point in the child's development may be of particular help to parents with mental-health difficulties as they often report feeling overwhelmed by the competing demands of managing a household and the inquisitive, active, and independent needs of their toddler (Cicchetti & Aber, 1986). Furthermore, mothers with depression may have a tendency to feel rejected by the child's eagerness and interest to explore his environment, and perceive this as a lack of interest in the relationship with the mother. This, in turn, would appear to suggest a downward spiral, increasing the intensity and severity of the carer's symptoms of low mood and attachment difficulties with the child (Cicchetti *et al.*, 1999).

The study involved 108 parent–toddler dyads. Twenty-seven mothers with depression received the attachment intervention. They were compared to a group of 45 mothers and their toddlers (where the mothers had no current or past mental-health difficulties) and 36 mothers (with the diagnosis of depression) and their children who did not receive any therapeutic input at all. At the end of the intervention, the children whose parents participated in treatment demonstrated positive attachment behaviour, similar to children of parents who did not report any psychological difficulties. These included using the mother as a secure base, and seeking comfort and affection from the mother when recovering from upsetting events, to whereas attachment problems remained pronounced in the group of children whose parents reported depression and who did not receive any intervention.

The extremely promising results reported by the study suggest that attachment difficulties and problems in parent–child interaction are malleable and subject to change, particularly, although unexpectedly, in the toddler years. The strategies listed in Table 13.1 are based on the work of Cicchetti

Table 13.1   Attachment interventions

General Points:

- As parents' perceptions, attitudes, and beliefs regarding their infant and their relationship are more readily available and accessible in the presence of the infant, both parents *and* toddler attend every session.
- Allow the parent to lead the session, by initiating the activity with the child, agenda, or topic for discussion with the therapist.
- Create opportunities for interaction between:

  - parent and child
  - parent and therapist
  - child and therapist.

Child-Focused:

- Notice and comment on the child's growth and development.
- Alert the parent to the infant's accomplishments and needs.
- Highlight the activities where the child appears to be enjoying himself. For example, 'Notice how Ben smiles and relaxes when you hold him close to your chest.'

Table 13.1   (Continued)

- Reflect on the child's experiences and feelings as they interact with the parent.
- Encourage the parent to consider the child's experiences with the parent. For example, 'How do you think Ben is feeling when you try to feed him?' 'If Ben could talk what do you think he would say?'

Parent-Focused:

- Highlight the carer's strengths and parenting ability.
- Be alert to and respond to the carer's statements and interactions with their toddler.
- Reflect on the parents' thoughts and feelings about their child.
- Reflect on the parents' thoughts and feelings about parenthood and changes in role, activities, and responsibilities as the child develops.
- Reflect on and link the carer's perceptions and beliefs of parenting and attitudes towards her child to her own experience of parenting in childhood.
- Listen for evidence of the carer's experience of parenting.
- Allow the parent to discuss their childhood experiences of parenting, unresolved loss and/or rejection, separation, and abuse.
- Listen and link these conflicts, emotions and experiences to the mother's current perceptions of and relationship with their child.
- Link the parents' experience to the impact they currently have on the child.
- Drawing on the mother's experience, highlight the consequences of early childhood experiences and significance of these experiences to childcare, well-being, and development.
- Identify and explore additional options and therapeutic support for the parent or infant (e.g. in cases of developmental delay) if necessary.

Source: Based on Cicchetti *et al.* (1999) and Fraiberg *et al.* (1975)

et al. (1999) and Fraiberg *et al.* (1975) to promote attachment, and can be adapted and integrated into an intervention to enhance positive parent–child interaction and functional family relationships.

CHILD–PARENT PSYCHOTHERAPY

This therapy aims to resolve basic conflictual relationships between mother and her infant. Cramer *et al.* (1990) state that the symptoms presented by the infant are reactions to maternal impingement. It is argued that the mother in turn responds to the symptomatic behaviour with defences against anxiety, guilt, and depressive feelings. This psychotherapeutic approach takes a stand that the mother is capable of changing her mental representations of her infant (as well as herself as a mother). By assuming that her feelings and parenting style are based on the relationships she had with her parents (Leiberman, 1991; Fraiberg, 1980), the notion of inter-generational repetition is at the core of child–parent psychotherapy. Through the confused perceptions of motherhood based on the memories of being parented as a child and current difficulties with the baby, insights are thought to be facilitated by the re-enactment or repetition of the mother's early relationships which reflect in her current relationship with her infant. These inter-generational relationships are also explored through enactments in the transference with the therapist. The aim of the therapy is to enhance the mother's insight, and changes in maternal sensitivity and responsiveness to her child are believed to result from the mother's ability to differentiate her child from herself. It is argued that the mother becomes more able to perceive her infant as an individual in its own right and be able to respond more appropriately to the child's needs.

The relationship difficulties between mother and child, therefore, act as a catalyst for the psychotherapeutic work. However, the infant is not included directly in the therapy, and serves only as a reference point to facilitate change in the mother towards her child. The primary work is between the mother and the therapist. In this therapy the infant's spontaneous activity and play, his expression of need, his feelings, and the experiences in relation to his mother are exclusively focused upon maternal representations of him or her.

WATCH, WAIT, AND WONDER

Cohen (1996) describes a psychodynamic model which focuses on behav-ioural and representational levels of the infant–parent relationship. The child is perceived as an 'initiator' in this type of therapeutic intervention, and takes a lead in mutual intervention. This therapy is designed for the child to build secure attachment to its mother and for the mother to explore her own internal working models of herself in relation to an infant and her infant in relation to her. This therapeutic approach is believed to be revised through play, discussion, and understanding arising from new mother–child experiences gained in therapy.

There are two parts to the Watch, Wait, and Wonder (WWW) session. In the first part the therapist asks the mother to get down on the floor with the child and to respond to the child's initiation of interaction and to follow his/her lead. It is believed that such a therapeutic process enhances an observational reflective stance in the parent, and promotes greater sensi-tivity and responsiveness. The therapist observes mother–child interaction but does not interfere or disrupt what is going on. In part two of a session the therapist and the mother discuss the mother's own observations, thoughts, and feelings about the child's responsiveness and behaviour during the session. The mother is encouraged to understand why the child reacted in a particular way, what it meant to the child in terms of building trust, and problems which emerged in the process are discussed. This model of intervention is used with older children (four to nine years) and their parents, although attention is paid to protect the child from what is being said in front of him. The WWW therapy does not take into consideration maternal experiences of being parented as a child, and what influence such experiences could have upon the current mother–child relationship. This is a particularly useful model when dealing with emotionally neglected children, whose mothers paid little attention to their children's emotional needs and who are unable to observe and read a child's signals and cues. It is believed that the therapist can increase the depth of parental insight by exploring new experiences arising from mother–child play and mutual interaction.

VIDEO-RECORDING AND FEEDBACK

A variety of techniques using video can be used to increase parents' awareness and understanding of what is happening and how to correct inappropriate parental responses to their children. This is of particular importance and usefulness when working with emotionally abusive parents, who do not themselves hear what they are saying to a child and do not realise how negative their interaction is. Examples of aversive and positive parental responses to the child are videoed and then played back to parents, so they can hear and see themselves in action. They are asked to pay particular attention to their tone of voice, eye contact, facial expressions, and general body language when they speak to a child. They are asked to observe their child's anxious reaction to them and their apprehension when in the parent's company. The consequences of parental harsh and hostile behaviour (short- and long-term) are discussed, pointing to the effect on the child (e.g. low self-esteem, lack of security, low self-confidence, and the possibility of developing emotional problems). Parents are asked to imagine how they would feel and react if they were treated in the same way as they were treating their child. They are asked to 'put their feet into their child's shoes' (figuratively speaking). By asking parents to observe and reflect on their hostile behaviour it is hoped that they will be able to get in touch with their own and the child's feelings, which in turn will help them to recognise and empathise with pain and hurt inflicted by them on the child.

The second part of the session involves a therapist playing with the child (which is videoed, demonstrating appropriate tone of voice, encouragement, praise, connection, and loving physical touch). After a brief discussion the parents are asked to play with the child again, using a warmer approach and trying to put into practice newly learned behaviour when interacting with the child (Iwaniec & Hill, 2000).

RECALLING EARLY-CHILDHOOD MEMORIES

In order to identify better with the child's plight it is useful to ask parents to try to remember one or two of the most pleasant experiences from their own childhood, and one or two of the most painful. The counsellor tries to link those hurtful (and often still quite vivid) parental memories to the current situation involving their child, pointing to the anxiety- and fear-provoking effects of their behaviour on the child. Again, pleasurable memories are linked to future desirable and hopeful parental behaviour towards their child.

Parents tend to remember past unpleasantnesses; examples might include a violent father, deep embarrassments of being shamed and unfairly criticised in front of other people, loneliness and lack of affection, inability to please their parents, being blamed for all ills in the family, being treated differently to their siblings, not being heard or listened to, and so on.

Pleasurable memories of parents tend to cover a wide range; among them might be being taken by parents to the cinema, picnicking, outings, special occasions where they were given attention and felt important or appreciated, feelings of being protected, being played with and read stories to at night, and comforted when feeling frightened or ill. What becomes apparent is that those pleasurable experiences were rare, and that the parents felt unloved and unsupported when they were growing up. For some the negative experiences became a norm of child-rearing (as they did not know any better); for others, however, those experiences were seen as correct and appropriate as models for child-rearing. The statement that 'it did not do me much harm, I survived – why should not my child do so as well?' is commonly heard. In most cases, however, a child-rearing deficit is common, which in turn distorts the formation of affectionate and caring relationships between parents and children. Counselling can raise insight awareness and empathy, which can lay foundations for further work, using a variety of approaches and methods.

PARENT–CHILD INTERACTION THERAPY

An additional treatment, gaining increased attention and support from both practitioners and researchers alike to address child maltreatment is parent–child interaction therapy (PCIT) (Eyberg & Calzada, 1998). Rooted in attachment theory and social-learning principles, the primary aim of the treatment is to restructure the parent–child relationship, provide a good secure attachment for the child, disrupt maladaptive cycles of parenting, and improve parent–child interactions. The intervention involves a two-stage approach to treatment. Parents are taught skills that foster positive, nurturing, interaction patterns, namely: praise, reflection, imitations, description, and enthusiasm (PRIDE) in highly structured, step-by-step 'live-coached' play sessions, and activities between the carer and the child. Once noticeable improvements in the quality of the parent–child relationship are observed, the parent is subsequently taught positive discipline strategies (e.g. direct and clear commands, positive feedback, and time-out procedures that are developmentally appropriate for the child in the context of play sessions and activities).

The carer receives prompts and comments from the therapist who observes the interaction through a one-way mirror or observation room via an ear-mounted receiver/transmitter system. Parental behaviours are coded and charted during each session. Parents are provided with immediate feedback and progress on skill development and achievement. The parent is assigned daily homework activities, lasting 5 to 10 minutes, to reinforce the training material. Skills are subsequently generalised for use in more unstructured situations likely to occur within and outside the home. Although the treatment is not time-limited, and emphasises mastery and skill development, intense therapeutic contact with the family generally lasts for 12 to 20 weeks, with a series of booster sessions 1 month, 3 months, 6 months, and 1 year post-intervention (Eyberg & Calzada, 1998; Herschell, Calzada, Eyberg, & McNeil, 2002).

Although originally designed for families with younger children with behavioural problems, PCIT has been adapted for families with young people in their early teens and demonstrates promising results for families where maltreatment has occurred. In a review of the extant literature on PCIT and child physical abuse, Runyon, Deblinger, Ryan, and Thakkar-Kolar (2004) found PCIT significantly improved positive parent–child interactions, the children's behaviour problems and perceptions of parenting stress were reduced, as were significant risk-factors in the etiology of emotional abuse. Chaffin *et al*. (2004), in a study of 110 families known to social services for physical abuse, compared the efficacy of PCIT to a standard community-based parenting intervention for re-referrals to child-protection agencies and improvement in family relationships. Two years post-intervention, the authors reported that 19% of parents who received training in PCIT were re-referred to child-protection services compared with 49% of parents assigned to the standard community group, with the likelihood of re-referral linked to a reduction in aversive parent–child interactions emphasised by PCIT. Although there is a paucity of research directly examining the efficacy of PCIT emotional abuse and neglect, adopting the techniques to strengthen the bond between the parent and child, with the ultimate aim of improving attachment relationships, can clearly help families where psychological maltreatment has occurred.

WORKING WITH FOSTER-PARENTS – COUNSELLING REGARDING ATTACHMENT

Behaviour

Some of the frequent questions asked by foster-parents are related to difficulties in understanding why a child who has been badly treated by parents still misses them, wants to go back home, and appears to be suffering from separation anxiety. Why does he cry at night missing his mother, and why is he counting the days to the next access visit? A mother, they say, who more often than not left him hungry, unattended, dirty, and smelly, who was drunk most of the time, who screamed and called him nasty names, and who never had a good word to say about him. Some are puzzled as to why the child behaves in a dismissive way, ignoring attention, kindness, praise, and acceptance; they ask how long apprehension and emotional distance are going to last, and how they can help a child who hurts so much.

At such times it is necessary to explain the power of attachment and genetic predisposition which determines and maintains attachment relationships. Counselling and discussion help to look at attachment in a way that is easy to follow. This is an example of how one may deal with it.

Explaining to Foster-Parents

The fundamental need of all people is to form a strong emotional bond to someone as a protective measure. The need to attach is inborn (genetic), in order to achieve proximity for ensuring protection from danger. Attachment is built over time, and the quality of attachment is based on experiences which are either positive or negative. If experiences are positive (the child feels safe, comfortable, and is attended to when in distress), the child will form a secure attachment to the primary caregivers. If, on the other hand, those early caring experiences are negative (not being attended to when in distress, hungry, wet, cold, ill, or frightened), the child will acquire insecure attachment behaviour.

When a child comes to you, he or she brings memories and images of caring experiences (which were often painful, anxiety-provoking, and neglectful). Such children expect the same treatment from their foster-parent, as they are the only experiences they know, and therefore protect themselves from being hurt by being detached or distrustful, or reacting in a disruptive, attention-seeking way.

Why it Takes a Long Time to Change a Child's Attachment Style

Let us look at an example. If you memorise something (for example, a poem), you cannot wipe it out on demand. If you do not think about it for a while you begin to forget words, then lines, and eventually the whole poem. You will only have a general memory left, that you used to know a poem about this particular subject, but memory has faded away.

Imagine notes you have made on a piece of paper. You tried to rub them off, but you can still see a mark. It will take a long time to fade away. It might never be possible to get rid of it completely. It takes time to build trust when a child has been let down so many times before. Trust and a sense of security are built over time, and cannot come on demand. Repetition of positive, reliable experiences will build new ways of seeing people, trusting them, and seeking their protection when in danger or in need of help and reassurance. Foster-parents can speed up this process and help children placed in their care by:

1. Being patient and understanding as to why children behave in a difficult-to-manage way.
2. Showing emotional support – standing by them, and demonstrating predictable reactions to their behaviour.
3. Reasoning with the child – explaining why they do not like some of his/her behaviour, and which behaviour is liked.
4. Accepting that they are starved of attention and affection and therefore show attention-seeking and attention-needing behaviour.
5. Talking to foster-children about their parents if they want to, and not avoiding doing so. Not criticising the parent(s), or talking them down, as this will only intensify anger and despair. Talking about the parents as people who have difficulties and are unable to give as much love and good care as they should give.
6. Gradually getting a child physically closer; that is, sitting on laps or nearby; putting an arm around the child; asking simple questions – what he or she has done at the nursery school, what the child would like to do during the weekend, what programme he or she would like to watch on the television, etc.
7. If a child looks sad, withdrawn, irritable, or angry, acknowledging that he/she is not happy and that the child's distress is understood. Asking if help can be given by listening and talking about being upset.
8. Trying to engage the child in some activity, giving a task to distract the child from sad or disturbing thoughts.
9. Always giving praise when the child behaves well, or responds to requests, or shows willingness to do what he or she was told to do. It is important to do so as such children feel worthless, undeserving of being loved and wanted, and suffer from low self-esteem.

10. Not feeling hurt or angry when the child rejects attention – this is a perfectly normal and justifiable reaction under the circumstances. The child may be asked if it wants to have a quiet time to overcome a flow of sad and angry feelings.

11. At times it may be necessary to ask the child to go to his/her room to cool off and come back when he/she wants and when feeling better. When a child returns do not preach; just put your arm around the child and give a gentle hug.

12. Reading a story to a child at night, giving a kiss, hug, and big reassuring smile, as nights can be particularly difficult for children. Lying in bed brings back a lot of memories and often distorted thoughts which can be very distressing and self-blaming.

13. Bringing to the child's life worthwhile and constructive routines, rules, and boundaries. These rules and routines should be explained, making them clear and simple to a child so he or she can understand what is expected and why.

14. Not feeling guilty about giving a distressed child more attention (even if it behaves in a difficult way) and less to other children in the family. The other children (if there are any) can be told that this child needs help from all the family, not only from grown-ups, and that everyone must try to help by being kind and understanding to the child who is going through a difficult patch.

15. Trying to make the child feel wanted, loved, appreciated, enjoyed, and valued as a member of the family, respecting the child's background and attachment to its natural parents.

SUMMARY

Children who are emotionally abused are insecurely attached to their parents, and their relationship with their parents is very poor. They see people they come across as not trustworthy, and expect to be treated by everybody in a hostile and pain-inducing way. Such children show disturbed behaviour as this is the only way they can attract attention to their unhappiness, confusion, and feelings of insecurity. Quite often they are aggressive, disruptive, attention-seeking, and destructive when they are with other children in the nursery or school, and cause concern when placed with alternative carers. This chapter discussed how insecurely attached children and their parents or foster-parents can be helped. A few tested techniques for effectiveness have been outlined as examples for increasing parental awareness and know-how in building secure attachments and warm, caring relationships with the child needing help.

CHAPTER 14

DIRECT WORK WITH EMOTIONALLY ABUSED AND NEGLECTED CHILDREN AND YOUNG PEOPLE

CONTENTS

INTRODUCTION

Some children and young people require individual work to help them to resolve some of the deeply sited emotional disturbances or deficits in their social behaviour. Quite often such help needs to be provided by skilled practitioners specialising in therapeutic work with children and can be done in conjunction with the family social workers. Play therapies of different theoretical persuasions are useful methods to help emotionally troubled children, and some of them are going to be discussed in this chapter. Older children in foster-care or placed for adoption may need more sophisticated psychotherapy to reduce emotional conflict and set up a healing process. An illustration called 'jug of loving water' will be provided as an example of a wide range of similar therapeutic techniques available these days. Building resilience in children and helping them to cope and survive adversities in their lives is an important element of direct work with them. Choosing appropriate services, and putting the children in touch with suitable peers, adults' organisation, and hobbies will be discussed, and some practical suggestions will be provided.

As emotionally abused and neglected children lack self-confidence and are repressed in their social interactions (which often leads to bullying), social skills and assertiveness training will be presented briefly as an idea for further reading on the subject, as these are invaluable ways of helping shy, apprehensive young people of low self-esteem to build social contacts and to stand up for themselves in difficult situations. A case study is provided to illustrate some of the methods and techniques that can be used with such children.

PLAY THERAPY

Play is an important part of child development. Through play children learn skills which help them to negotiate their environment and develop language, motor, cognitive, and social skills, as well as acquire an understanding of themselves, others, and the world around them. Depending on their age and developmental level, children engage in play activities by themselves, observing and repeating the actions of others, or with other playmates. Through the activity of play a child can act out and test adult roles and expectations, learn social rules and consequences of behaviour, mastery, and achievement (as well as turn-taking and relationship skills).

All children play. Play is a natural, accessible, and safe method or tool for self-expression and exploration in childhood. For many children, as their verbal, cognitive, and reflective skills are insufficiently developed to communicate their feelings and experiences, play is a method where a practitioner can observe and have access to or at least an understanding of a child's thoughts, feelings, and attitudes and the impact of their experiences.

Theories of the importance of play in childhood go a long way back. One of the first persons to advocate studying the play of children in order to understand and educate them was Jean-Jacques Rousseau (1712–78). There have been several theories put forward to explain the meaning and utility of play in childhood; these generally emphasise its function as a means of preparation for the future, as a natural process of learning, and as a means of release from tension and of excess physical energies. In many ways play, for the child, is life itself. The child uses it in order to develop personality and ability to get on with other children. Play has been used to enhance understanding of children and as therapy to help them. Anna Freud (1895–1982) used play to uncover unconscious conflicts. This involved the interpretation of the symbolic meanings of drawings, paintings, games, and other forms of imagination play. Another system of infant analysis was formulated by Melanie Klein (1882–1960). In fact there have been several offshoots of psychoanalytical play therapy, e.g. Jungian sandplay, which is a non-verbal, non-rational form of therapy, enabling a child to regress into the unconscious where integration and healing can occur. Virginia Mae Axline developed a non-directive form of play therapy to solve some problems and develop more mature behaviour.

Play therapy is a dynamic therapeutic process of interaction. Through play activities with a therapist the child explores and communicates issues and experiences, feelings, and emotions, past and present. The therapist uses the therapeutic relationship and interaction with the child, established through play activities, to understand these behaviours, address the child's attachment needs, and provide a compensatory attachment experience which will ultimately modify self-perceptions and expectations of carers, damaged through the experience of maltreatment, according to the British Association of Play Therapists (BAPT).

The characteristic feature in working with children who have in some way been emotionally damaged is for the children to work through their feelings initially using a non-directive approach. Children who have been emotionally abused will go through certain stages during the therapeutic process. It needs to be remembered that these stages are not prescriptive and do not apply to every child.

The first stage is when the children's feelings of anxiety and anger are dormant and diffuse. This stage affects everything and can be shown in ways such as purposeless attacks on the play equipment and sometimes a marked show of fear.

Gradually as the child experiences the worker's acceptance and containment within a safe environment, the second stage emerges as anger directed at certain people (including the worker) and through symbolic play. This can be a difficult stage for a worker and the child, with the child needing to know that the worker accepts the child's feelings and is consistent in his/her acceptance. When this happens, confidence and self-esteem begins to grow.

As the third stage approaches, the child shows a range of feelings including fear and anger mixed together; for instance, loving a teddy bear one minute and smashing it on the floor the next. These feelings start with great intensity and gradually become expressed in milder ways. Finally, by the fourth stage the child has sorted and separated its feelings about people and situations, in line with how things are in reality. These stages can be dealt with using non-directive play therapy and incorporating reflective listening. In certain cases after the initial assessment period a more direct approach can be used.

However, sessions and activities with the child can either be heavily structured (and led by the therapist), or unstructured, with activities, conversations, and approach to materials led and directed by the child, depending on the theoretical and practical approach of the practitioner. In *directed play therapy* the therapist chooses the activity, devises the rules and tasks which engage both therapist and child. In *non-directed play therapy* the child selects the activity from a host of available toys, games, or activities, determines the rules and play activities, with certain basic limits devised by the therapist (Axline, 1969, 1971). The playroom setting, appointment time, and available materials remain the same each week to foster a sense of security and stability for the child. To facilitate exploration, additional play activities or materials are offered or made available over time, depending on the type of play therapy adopted by the clinician. Attempts and achievements at new play activities are recognised and praised to promote self-confidence, competence, and self-worth (Axline, 1971; Chan & Leff, 1988; Ryan, Wilson, & Fisher, 1995).

The therapist focuses on specific features of child–caregiver communication and contact to facilitate change in dysfunctional models of relationships and promote psychological health. These include face-to-face interactions; the arousal of interest, responsiveness, and dependability; vocalisations, mirroring and reflecting experiences; creating of active interest in play activities, with turn-taking; and encouragement of an atmosphere of acceptance, understanding, and consistency in order to respond to children's physical and emotional states. Older children, and those whose cognitive understanding is sufficiently advanced, are encouraged to use play as a method of exploration and expression of interpersonal difficulties.

Abused or neglected children typically suffer a delay in social and imaginative play, as well as aggressive and destructive interaction, passivity and withdrawal, self-criticism, hyper-vigilance and anxiety, and in cases where sexual abuse is thought to have occurred, sexual behaviour (White & Allers, 1994; Howard, 1986). For children and adolescents who have been subjected to maltreatment, therapists try to link the child's feelings, play, and behaviour to the abusive experience, and to support the child to reflect on the purpose of play activities and behaviours.

Research suggests that play therapy is an effective intervention for a host of childhood difficulties, with particular benefits for children in care (White & Allers, 1994). Significant improvements have been observed in self-esteem and reductions in behavioural problems for children aged 3 to 10 who were witnesses to domestic violence over a number of years (Kot, 1995). Additional benefits have been shown for children with speech and language difficulties, conduct problems, poor moods, and post-traumatic stress disorder (Ray, Bratton, Rhine, & Jones, 2001) as well as for children with a parent identified with substance-abuse problems (Springer, Phillips, Phillips, Cannady, & Kerst-Harris, 1992). Although play therapy is typically used as an individual method of treatment for the child, it can easily be integrated into a treatment package to address family relationships. Play therapy can also be adapted to involve parents, with the therapist functioning as a model not only for the child, but also for the parent. A therapist may invite the parent to interact with the child in the playroom or directly encourage the parent to observe the child's activity in the playroom, intervening when the parent lapses back to traditional and dysfunctional methods of caregiving.

Play therapists can design a structured programme where they model eye contact, voice tone, volume, and clarity, and distraction techniques to manage the child's behaviour. Parents observe the therapist with the child during the initial appointments, and are then subsequently invited to interact with the child in successive sessions. The parent practises skills and techniques modelled by the therapist, who provides feedback, reinforcing evident parental strengths and highlighting how the carer's behaviour affects the infant. For older children, play activities and materials for the child may be centred on language and interpersonal development, and parents may be guided to promote child development and adaptive behaviour.

After each session, parents and therapist can discuss the session. This can be a good point to give information to parents, to give tips on childcare, or provide practical support that could supplement the intervention. It can also be a good time to assess parents' motivation to maintain therapeutic contact and to be involved in treatment, and the opportunity can be taken to discuss any concerns, worries, or anticipated difficulties parents may have with the programme. By reviewing the session with parents, the therapist can develop a plan of needs and issues to be addressed in successive sessions (which may need to be modified depending on difficulties or advances the family makes).

Parents can also review video-recordings of the play session. They are invited to review and comment on their behaviour with the child, with particular attention to the tone of their voices, eye contact, facial expression, and body language. The impact of their behaviour on the child can be discussed, and honest feedback and additional modelling can be provided to supplement the session. Parents can be given handouts illustrating activities rehearsed in the playroom, and are encouraged to practise techniques between sessions. With emphasis on mastery and skill development, sessions generally continue until the carer routinely interacts with the child at an appropriate level previously defined and agreed with the carer in the treatment plan.

Iwaniec, Herbert, and McNeish (1985b) designed a treatment package which integrated play-therapy techniques for parents whose children have been diagnosed with non-organic failure to thrive; this yielded promising results for families where severe emotional abuse occurred. In addition to involving parents in play sessions with the child, parents were required to schedule 10 minutes of daily play-time with their child, practising these techniques, increasing to 30 minutes over a 4-week period. After sustained, intensive, and appropriate mother–child contact was established, mothers were encouraged to take the child everywhere for a 2-week period, practising responses and activities learned with the play therapist. Frequent home visits and telephone calls to monitor the programme were made to support and reinforce parents during this time.

Clinical contact with the family was subsequently reduced to one session per fortnight for a further six months. Some mothers (who initially found the contact with their children somewhat distasteful), after seeing their children smile, seek their presence, and respond to their efforts, appeared to increase their enjoyment of the children, or at least lessened their aversion, and appeared to reduce the children's apparent fears and anxiety responses. Interventions addressing the quality of parent–child interactions can lead to a number of benefits. Mothers learn to understand, adapt to, and anticipate their children's needs. As a result, infants increase attempts to interact with caregivers, promoting confidence in the carers' ability to parent and engage with their children. Parenting becomes more effective, and interactions between parent and child become mutually rewarding, satisfying, and benefiting to both parents and children (Iwaniec et al., 1985a; Wolfe, 1987).

PROMOTING RESILIENCE

Children who experience emotional abuse and neglect can often be degraded, criticised, ignored, unappreciated, or forgotten, and are generally uncared for. Despite living in such adverse situations, or with parents whose parenting style significantly increases the child's vulnerability to negative outcomes, a number of children appear to show amazing resilience. They reach developmental milestones within normal limits, achieve academic goals, develop and maintain positive relationships, and report good psychological health and well-being despite the negative effect and disdain which characterised the relationship with their carers (Fonagy et al., 1994; Garmezy & Rutter, 1983). Although how and why certain variables interact to promote resilience is poorly understood (Kirby & Fraser, 1997), a number of key factors have been linked to more adaptive outcomes, despite vulnerability and risks of difficulties associated with abuse. These can be divided into two separate areas: internal child-based characteristics and strengths; and external environmental or social forces. Both internal and external factors can operate across the child's experience and development, or may have more specific and focused psychological and developmental effects

(Rutter, 2002). Child-based factors can include a number of dispositional attributes, including an easy temperament, emotional and practical coping skills, social and relationship skills, cognitive ability, and an ability to reflect and draw upon an interpretation of the abuse that is adaptive and does not blame the child. External or environmental factors may include availability and access to support systems or agencies; a safe, organised, and predictable environment; and support services which may monitor, advocate, and promote a more adaptive emotional and social environment for the child.

A resilience-based approach to helping children is both positive and pragmatic. Practitioners advocating a resilience-based approach assume that change is possible, even in the most difficult and adverse situations. By capitalising on the strengths and resources naturally occurring in the child's social ecology, workers can build on and enhance a protective network for the child and support adaptive coping skills and strategies (Gilligan, 1997, 2001). The level of professional support and intervention required to promote resilience will vary depending on individual circumstances and the attributes of the child. Intervention strategies focus on reducing vulnerability, and on reducing and limiting the number of stressors and risk-factors in the child's environment. Treatment programmes will also highlight protective resources and will mobilise support systems. 'Resilience strings', whereby benefits and advantages of support in one area instigate a positive cycle of change for the child, are identified and enhanced.

Although not necessarily rooted in a specific theoretical orientation, themes common to attachment theory characterise many of resilience-based interventions. Relationships that are adaptive, supportive, protective, and fun are seen as key factors to promote resilience. Clinical and care-based decisions and suggestions for support will focus on advancing and supplementing the relationship network for the child. Interests and hobbies are also encouraged. Experiencing alternative role models should serve to challenge the child's perception that they are unloved, uninteresting, and unwanted. Engaging in a range of school-based activities or hobbies, and developing competence and skills in these areas, will allow the child to develop a positive self-image, identity, and feelings of self-worth (Daniel & Wassell, 2002; Friedman & Chase-Lansdale, 2002; Gilligan, 1997).

Daniel & Wassell (2002) and Gilligan (2001) highlighted a number of areas and strategies to promote resilience. Again, these could be adapted and integrated into a treatment programme to address the needs of the emotionally abused and neglected child. The therapist can choose or recommend a number of strategies which are generally quite accessible and inexpensive ways to promote resilience (and ultimately the psychological well-being of the child).

Secure Base

Health experiences of relationships and attachment security are believed to protect children against the effects of adversity (including psychological maltreatment), and to foster adaptive psychosocial functioning in later life (Shonkoff & Phillips, 2000). Yet the likelihood of positive trajectories appears primarily related to relationships that are both stable and continuous (Jackson & Thomas, 1999). A stable relationship is predictable for the child, defined by clear boundaries, where the child can develop a sense that others are responsive, safe, and reliable. A continuous relationship allows the child to develop a sense of familiarity within a network of relationships with the same carers. In continuous relationships a child can develop a sense of itself, a personal and cultural identity, and attain developmental skills. Unfortunately for many children who have experienced psychological abuse, their experience of parenting is neither stable nor predictable. Parents may be physically or psychologically unavailable to care for them. In some cases children may be removed from the family home for their own safety and well-being. They may also experience a number of carers in multiple placements. To promote psychological health and well-being, professionals who co-ordinate the care arrangements of the child need to build a supportive network that is consistent, well co-ordinated, and protective.

Helpful strategies include:

- Parents and/or carers may need support and guidance on how best to respond to the child's attachment style. The carer could benefit from informal sessions which teach:

  o how to reassure the child and respond to its needs;
  o how to tolerate the child's urge to reject a close emotional bond;
  o how to manage the child's ambivalence and apparent lack of interest in the carer.

- Carers should be encouraged to capitalise on opportunities for positive experiences with the child. Praise, encouragement, and organising special time for the child should be nurtured in order to communicate to the child that it is cared for, interesting, accepted, and important.
- Carers should develop his or her relationship with the child. This may include celebrating birthdays and holidays (e.g. Christmas). For children in care one such occasion may be the day the child came to live with the foster-parents.
- Promotion of routines and structures within the family home. Children will benefit from predictability and consistency of an organised and well-managed household. At the same time the carer should be encouraged to be flexible in order to allow the child to explore and develop other interests outside the family home.

- Separations should be anticipated. If, for what ever reason, the child should be separated from the carer, the child should know in advance and be given as much detail and choice about alternative care arrangements.
- The child should be helped to identify important and adaptive relationships in its life. These may include members of the child's extended family, cousins, or siblings. Contact should be promoted, and fun and pleasant activities scheduled for children with these people (e.g. shopping trips, visits to the park, zoo, or cinema, and walks in the country).

Education

School can provide an opportunity for maltreated children to gain the social and practical support they need. The predictability of the school routine can provide a secure base for the child which is both containing and a source of comfort. School also provides opportunities to develop positive relationships and to develop skills and abilities in specific subject areas and extra-curricular activities that enhance self-efficacy and self-esteem. Good educational attainment is also linked to an increased number of economic prospects and opportunities for financial security and independence (Kendall-Tackett & Eckenrode, 1996). For some children school will function both as a respite and distraction from the adversity experienced within the family home. For others, school may be a particularly stressful and emotionally painful experience. Difficulties (such as failing schoolwork or difficult peer relationships) may consolidate and perpetuate any negative self-perceptions, and place some children at risk of maladaptive outcomes (Cicchetti & Toth, 1995a).

Helpful strategies include:

- It may be necessary to provide some extra academic support for children who have experienced emotional abuse and neglect. Many of these children will not have been sufficiently stimulated in their home environment. They will lag behind their peers in basic skills and might benefit from extra tuition.
- Some children may also need extra support to approach tasks and may gain from guidance on how to concentrate and execute their work. Designating a specific area that is free from distraction should help concentration and allow the child to do its homework without interruption.
- Breaking down school-based tasks into simple chunks may be helpful for the child to learn and assimilate. This strategy could also be applied to academic tasks and activities.
- Promoting the child's involvement in extra-curricular activities such as school trips, sports teams, or after-school clubs will be helpful ways to make friends, develop social competences, and enhance the child's self-esteem and self-efficacy.

- Carers and parents could become more involved in school as a way of promoting interest in education and learning about the skills which teachers use to motivate and teach children.
- Practitioners, carers, and teachers could collaborate and meet regularly to monitor and review the child's academic progress and social inclusion. This will highlight potential obstacles and identify future therapeutic needs.

Peer Relationships and Friendships

Through their interaction with their peers, children develop language ability, empathic understanding of others' point of view, co-operation, and social skills (Carr, 2002). As with adults, peer relationships are also important sources of social support. Having friendships protects the individual against the stress of living in an adverse environment, and provides comfort and fun as well as a resource for information on how to manage stressful situations (Hartup, 1992; Thompson, 1995). Relationships and friendships also give the individual a sense that he or she is liked, valued, and worthwhile.

Children who have been subjected to psychological maltreatment often present with marked deficits in their play and peer relationships. These children often lack positive role models and experience of positive relationships, and are often ill-equipped to manage a peer-group environment. They are often seen to be unpopular, anxious, and attention-seeking (Iwaniec, 1983). Some children who have been subjected to abuse are also argumentative, yet seem to be open to repeated victimisation by bullies (Olweus, 1993). The emotionally abused or neglected child may subsequently be rejected by its peers, consolidating the view that it is unwanted and disliked. Not only is the repeated experience of rejection stressful in itself, but the child will have fewer opportunities for social activities, peer support, and corrective experiences (Daniel & Wassell, 2002), thus increasing the child's vulnerability to negative outcomes.

Helpful strategies include:

- Role play, modelling, and activities in session can be used to increase the child's repertoire and knowledge about peer relationships and skill.
- If the child has a talent or hobby, encourage him/her to join a group where it can meet other children with whom it shares common interests.
- The child may have an idiosyncratic and possibly maladaptive concept of friends and friendships. It would be worth challenging this perspective, possibly with cognitive techniques, and promoting the perspective that other children can be supportive. Suggesting to the child that he/she too can be good friends by listening or helping a friend with a difficulty may provide the child with increased opportunities for pro-social interaction with peers.

- Some children may be dependent on their parents for contact with peers and playmates. In situations where parents are socially isolated, play and friendship opportunities for children will be limited. Parents may benefit from practical support to widen their social circle and develop connections in their community. This would hopefully provide the family with some secondary benefit and provide the child with new friends and social opportunities.

Social Skills

As previously mentioned, children who have been subjected to maltreatment can be withdrawn, nervous about interacting with their peers, and find it difficult to express and assert their needs. Other children are often overtly aggressive and have learned that externalising their feelings, being disruptive, or hurting others attracts attention and intervention (Iwaniec, 1983). Without basic social skills, children will often have extreme difficulty establishing positive and meaningful relationships with pro-social peers. As a consequence children will fail to benefit from the social and instrumental support described above.

Helpful strategies include:

- Teach the child problem-solving and skills to manage conflict with others.
- Encourage the child to reflect on the actions and behaviour of others and to understand the consequences of its own behaviour.
- Encourage the child to recognise, accept, and show appreciation of help and support.
- Encourage carers to model pro-social behaviour, caring, and comfort.
- Involve the child in groups or community-based activities that promote responsibility and empathy (e.g. sponsored walks and mentoring younger children).
- Teach the child about what is acceptable and unacceptable behaviour. Provide the child with clear boundaries and guidelines about behaviour. Provide it with a plan or range of options on how to deal with other children or adults who involve it in a maladaptive cycle of interaction.
- Teach parents to highlight situations where the child demonstrates pro-social behaviour. For example, 'You were very kind when you...'

Interests, Activities, and Hobbies

Some of the benefits and advantages that education provides for the child are also true of interests, activities, and hobbies. Leisure pursuits and involvement in community groups and organisations can provide a child with pleasant experiences which will enhance self-efficacy and self-esteem.

Children who have been subjected to adversity or have experienced extreme events can often feel separated from mainstream society, or at least different from others. Hobbies and activities provide them with an opportunity to feel part of the 'mainstream' (Smith & Carlson, 1997). Developing skills and interests in a range of activities not only can diffuse the impact of adversity, but will also provide the child with a sense of competence and problem-solving (Quinton, Pickles, Maughan, & Rutter, 1993). By engaging in hobbies and activities the child can challenge him/herself, learn the consequences of its actions and develop a sense that its choices and decisions are of merit. This sense of self-determination should increase the child's sense of control and that many things in life can be predictable which, in turn, should promote a positive mood and emotional stability (Iso-Ahola, 1997).

Activities and interests can serve as a fun and non-emotive topic and opportunity for the parent and child to interact and develop their relationship. A hobby or activity can also provide the child with a new social network and opportunity to make friends with like-minded peers. Interests and hobbies may be creative (such as drama, music, and dance), sport-related (such as football, netball, swimming, etc.), or may involve community groups such as Brownies, Scouts, or Church groups. These interests, distractions, and activities can prove to be lifelines for children who have been exposed to, or are living with, adversity (Doyle, 2001).

SOCIAL-SKILLS TRAINING

Children who have been subjected to abuse or neglect generally have difficulties establishing functional and adaptive peer relationships and often demonstrate marked deficits in their social skills (Walker, Bonner, & Kaufman, 1988). Specific difficulties common to abused children include a lack of awareness or appreciation of the needs and feelings of others; an inability to understand the interests and perspectives of others; and a misunderstanding of social rules, roles, and expectations (Barahal, Waterman, & Martin, 1981; Goldstein, 1999). Children who have been abused most likely will have an external locus of control, which may make them more vulnerable to the opinions and comments of their peers (Walker *et al.*, 1988). In the absence of positive role models or experiences of adaptive relationship, it is not surprising that children who have been victimised by abuse find it difficult to establish and maintain positive relationships with others.

Strategies to teach children and adolescents social skills can involve a variety of methods and techniques. Social-skills training will generally involve an awareness of and attention to cognitive, behavioural, and environmental contexts which influence the child's behaviour. Demonstrating pro-social behaviour, role-playing, modelling, rehearsal, and feedback, either in a session or from a video-recording, are inexpensive techniques that are easy to use with children across the age range. Involving more socially competent peers as mentors or involving older children or teachers to model adaptive relationships and socialisation skills can extend the intervention beyond a clinic-based setting and be extremely helpful for the child. Group training sessions on social skills have yielded particular success with adolescents, who may also benefit from the opportunity to make friends and establish contacts with other group members (Bierman & Furman, 1984). Adolescent groups may benefit more from instruction and information components of the intervention, which provides them with a rationale for the approach, and can instil hope and encouragement that their difficulties can be addressed. This, in turn, should motivate young people to try out the techniques in social situations which they may otherwise have avoided.

Younger children may benefit more from more operant or concrete approaches. The child's life could be actively reinforced by a number of adults to demonstrate pro-social behaviour (including teachers, carers, and care staff). Alternatively, the child may benefit from a more structured programme where it is taught co-operation, communication, listening skills, and techniques to support peers. Beidel, Turner, and Morris (2000) designed an interesting intervention, focusing on improving the social skills of children with presentations of social phobia, which yielded extremely positive results that could equally be adapted for children victimised by psychological maltreatment. The authors included a parent-education package, and involved the children in weekly social-skills training and individual practice sessions. The practice sessions lasted 60 minutes and comprised preset activities and exercises devised in line with each child's individual social difficulties and problems. The social-skills sessions were conducted in small groups of 4 to 6 children and focused on conversational techniques and friendship skills. Modelling, rehearsal, and feedback were used to teach and reinforce pro-social behaviour. An interesting and novel component of the treatment package was the inclusion of additional sessions to practise social skills with peers. Children attended pizza parties, skating, and bowling activities, which gave them the opportunity to exercise their newly acquired social skills in environments and situations where benefits would be clearly demonstrated.

ASSERTIVENESS TRAINING

Many emotionally maltreated children, especially adolescents, show acute lack of assertive behaviour when interacting with peers. They are often victims of being bullied or used to the advantage of others. Because of lack of confidence and low self-esteem such children find it difficult to stand up for themselves without being aggressive or, more often, defenceless.

Assertive behaviour can perhaps be best described as the appropriate expression of feelings in social interactions. As a rule unassertive people and children lack the confidence both to express anger and disapproval, as well as affection and warmth. Such individuals often fail to express their real feelings because they are afraid of the consequences. For example, children who are bullied and are threatened with being beaten unless they give money or do what the bullies want them to do, will not assert themselves because of fear of challenging and being firm with demanding peers. Bullies easily identify and pick on a weak, shy, and frightened child, and can make his/her life extremely difficult.

Feelings only have meanings to others when they are expressed, and non-verbal expression (body language) is just as important as what is said. It is important to express feelings *at the time* when they are felt. Training young people in an assertive way how to behave when someone has done them a wrong, or is unreasonably demanding or threatening, is important for self-protection and self-respect. As a youngster learns to make a stand, when he knows he is in the right, not only will his own self-respect increase, but others will also respect him more. As the person becomes more assertive and insists that he is treated fairly and not taken advantage of, he will become less anxious in social situations. The training sessions include instruction, role-playing, rehearsals, video-recordings and mutual reviews of recorded performances, and preparation for real situations. The training includes: how to make requests; how to refuse persuasive requests; what to say; what not to say; the manner of speaking; and body language. For example:

- giving non-verbal assertive cues such as a high head position, eye contact, frowning, moving forward;
- stating the facts, e.g. 'I was here first – go and find another place'; 'I have no money to give you, and have no intention of giving you any';
- asking a rhetorical question such as 'Do you mind?'; 'You had better get out of my way – am I in your way?'

If this fails then an explicit demand is required and possibly a threat, e.g. 'I am going to report your behaviour if you carry on like that.'

Refusing Persuasive Requests

People often try to persuade us to do things we do not want to do, or we cannot do. The first thing we must be able to do is to have an opinion and attitudes of our own, and be able to express these openly. Avoid pretending to agree for the sake of 'keeping the peace' to 'buy friendships' or avoid confrontation: this does not work in the long run. Second, you are advised in training to listen to the parents', teachers', or peers' opinions and to respect them in the same way as a child wishes others to respect him/her. Finally, it must be made perfectly clear what the feelings are about – persuasive or threatening messages. There are many different ways we can say 'no'. It is important to be as clear and unambiguous as possible, and once we have said 'no' we must stick to it, because otherwise 'the door will be open' for further manipulation, pressure, and demands.

The following are some examples of assertive statements:

- Please do not do that again.
- Please do stop screaming and shouting at me.
- No, I am not going to do that.
- I like it when you talk to me peacefully.
- I like you.
- I am not satisfied.
- Will you kindly stop talking when I am listening to music?

Shy, apprehensive adolescents, lacking in confidence (especially those exposed to emotional denigration) require some training in how to stand up for themselves. Equally, those who react in an aggressive manner in interaction with other people benefit from social skills and assertiveness training.

THE JUG OF LOVING WATER

Children who are removed from parental care because of abuse bring with them an enormous number of emotional problems which have to be addressed by therapeutic means. Quite often little therapeutic work is done once the child is placed in a safe foster-home, assuming that good quality of care, routines, and structures in everyday life are good enough for the child's recovery. While it may be enough for some, it most definitely is not enough for those who are emotionally disturbed and have suffered emotional abuse and neglect for some time. The healing of pain and rebuilding of shattered self-esteem, confidence, and self-worth will not take place until specific help is provided addressing the child's confused thoughts and feelings and deep-seated betrayal of trust generally in people and specifically in its parents.

Play therapy, whether directive or non-directive, is a good means to help small children to overcome feelings of hurt, mistrust, anger, and confusion. However, older children will require a more sophisticated therapeutic input to help them come to terms with early experiences and to begin functioning in a more 'at peace' way. Such children will need to be guided to identify distorted feelings and to get in touch with them in order to facilitate an understanding of why they feel and behave in a way destructive to them and difficult for those who are trying to help and assist them.

Many years ago the author attended a course run by one of the adoption societies, where a very interesting therapeutic technique was demonstrated called a 'jug of loving water'. I have since used this technique very often with emotionally troubled children in foster-care. The results were always positive, although at times difficult for some children to cope with. The repetition of 'jug-of-loving-water' sessions is necessary to achieve the desired outcome for the child. For some it is a slow process as they find it difficult to cope with emerging messages and associated feelings, but for others it is much quicker and less painful. The basic principle is to go at the child's pace, and be able to read and judge how far the child is able to go at a particular time. If a child gets too distressed the process should be stopped, saying, 'We'll do a bit more next week, let's do something else now.'

The therapist needs to get familiar with the story below and use it in the appropriate way for a child. It can be read or told using different words.

Jug of Loving Water

Imagine for a moment that everyone coming to this world brings along a jug of loving water. As we grow the jug full of loving water grows as well. The people that we become and how we see ourselves are determined by what goes into this jug. Small babies cry because they are hungry, cold, or uncomfortable. A caring person responds to the baby's needs, such as for food, and the baby feels nurtured, safe, and at ease. Along with a full tummy, or being comforted, goes a sense of having a 'jug full of loving water' – the baby feels wanted, is being noticed, and feels that it has worth (which is the beginning of self-esteem), and that the world is a good place to be.

As the child grows, and if its parents continue to put good feelings into its jug by the way they interact with him/her, the level of good feeling that he/she has about itself is high: he or she feels confident, good, competent. Sometimes the parents slosh the child's jug and spill a little by being angry, critical, or inaccessible. Perhaps an accident, an illness, or a disappointment slops out some of the good feelings. But if the child is lucky enough to have nurturing, giving parents, the level of good feelings in the jug remains high. Before long the child learns that life is basically a good and friendly place. It likes itself and other people. Soon it begins to dip into its own jug and ladle good feelings into the jugs of those around the child, tentatively at first, and then more freely as he/she discovers that the response to his sharing brings him or her additional good feelings. As long as things go well and the child is surrounded by people who are happy and generous, the outpouring and receiving of good feelings become the life pattern, and all is well.

If, however, the child is born into a family that does not meet his/her needs or convey to him/her a sense of personal worth, the level in its jug remains low. The closer the jug of water is to empty, the more tightly the child clutches it, being afraid that someone will slosh out some of the precious, life-sustaining contents. If this child lives in a family where everyone is 'low jug', the terrible scarcity of loving water prevents any ladling of good feelings from one person to another. It becomes impossible for the child to share anything of itself with others. Unless something happens to help this child learn how to give and to receive, it is likely that the state of scarcity will make it impossible for the child to share with peers, a marriage partner, or children of his own when he grows up.

Feeling threatened, such children often try to raise their own levels of good feelings by constantly demanding that others give to them. This tends to make those around them even more guarded. Some children go so far as to construct a 'cover' for the top of the jug to prevent any loss of precious water. Unfortunately, this cover also prevents any good feelings from getting in; they just hit the lid, roll off, and are lost.

When an older fostered-out child first enters a family, the level of good feeling about itself is dangerously low – either because home offered him/her little or because the pain of the move has upset the child's emotional balance. As a result the child will demand more and accept less from others in his new family; some who feel angry will also watch carefully for the chance to strike out at other family members, causing everyone else to feel 'low jug'.

However the new child reacts, he/she enters a family with a set of new parents who are usually feeling strong and giving. These parents are eager to dish out their good feelings generously. What do they run into but an older child whose jug is impossibly low, who is unable to co-operate in the family giving, who demands excessively, or who is not even able to accept the good feelings ladled his way.

If the parents can keep their own spirits high they can usually give themselves time – time to reassure the demanding child that his/her needs will be met, time to help the closed-up child to relax, time to go back to the early infant-like days, and start to make up for the lack of earlier affection. When this happens things usually go well and the placement most often works out.

But it is vital that the foster-parents find other ways to replenish their own jug while they are filling the child's, until he/she is able to begin to give back to them. The amount of love, energy, and wisdom ladled out by the foster-parents must not be allowed to so deplete them that they run dry – for then the placement becomes so costly that it has little chance to succeed. Foster-parents may have to choose when and how they will give to their new child, to avoid becoming so drained that they start to dislike the youngster and see him as a threat and disappointment. And it is also important for the foster-parents to find ways to help the child give to himself/herself – to fill its own jug and to enhance its own sense of self-esteem.

Therapeutic Session

Fill a jug of water up to the top and name it as a child's jug. Fill two to three more jugs with water to represent a child's parents and foster-parents. Get a little ladle and some cling film.

Tell the child the story described above (use your own words as you do not need to follow it word by word). Ask the child to demonstrate, e.g. spilling loving water when parents are angry, ill, or when drunk; ladling loving water to others and to the child; when things go wrong in the family, the loving water in the jug is low (half a jug). The child may need to be placed with foster-parents. The child tries to protect water from disappearing completely by putting cling film on the top of the jug. By doing so the water neither gets out nor gets in. It means that feelings are very low and the child is very unhappy. Take the child through the journey of uncovering the top of the jug. Bit by bit more water is allowed to come in and some is even ladled to the foster-parents and other people in the family.

At each stage encourage a child to link spilling and pouring of the water from and into a jug with the child's experiences, and together reflect on how it feels to have the jug full of loving water, half-empty and almost empty.

Being sad, unhappy, confused, and hurting inside you put the cover on top (the cling film) to prevent more water being spilled out, but by doing this nothing comes in, and everyone is unhappy and hurt. What do you need to do to let good feelings in? If you get more loving water into your jug you will feel better, you will see that you are being loved and wanted, so you can ladle some of your loving water to others.

If the child is stuck or unable to talk about his/her experiences, prompt a bit to keep uncovering good and bad feelings and bringing them up to the surface. Help the child to name these feelings and suggest what to do to get lots of loving water and keep it there.

CASE STUDY

William (eight years old) was fostered out as a result of lifelong maternal ill-treatment of him. He presented as a very troubled child both at school and at home. Because of his aggressive and disruptive behaviour he was suspended from school on several occasions from the age of six years. William's history was one of rejection by his mother, exposure to violence between his parents, drug-addictive behaviour by his mother, and then alcohol abuse by his stepfather. He was rejected by his mother at birth, and for the first three months she would not do anything for him. He was cared for by his father. Although she was forced to look after him, their relationship was extremely poor, and William's attachment to his mother became very insecure.

As maternal behaviour became more emotionally and physically abusive William became more attention-seeking, destructive, and aggressive to others. He never cried when he was physically punished, but cried when he was threatened with abandonment and told that he was not loved or wanted. William lived in constant fear of being pushed away by his mother, who reacted to him in an irritable and hostile way when she was short of drugs, and then in a dismissive way when she was under the influence of substances. He learned by observation that, in order to solve a problem or to show dissatisfaction, he had to be violent, physically and verbally, just as his parents had done all the time.

At reception into care he presented as a very troubled child. He attacked other children in the foster-home, slapped them across the face, kicked and threw things about, and was petrified to be left in the bedroom (the light had to be left on all the time). He kept asking whether all the doors were locked and whether he was safe. He followed his foster-parents everywhere, telling them that he loved them and asking whether they loved him. If there was not immediate reassurance he would get extremely distressed.

William needed help to become more secure and trustful, less anxious, more wanted and appreciated, less fearful, and less attention-seeking. He needed to rebuild his perceptions that people where he lived were caring, friendly, and trustworthy; that his routines and rules were predictable; that he would be helped when in difficulties; and, above all, that he would be safe.

In order to organise appropriate help for William, more information was needed to choose suitable therapeutic methods (e.g. why was he petrified of being in the room by himself? Why was he checking whether the doors were locked? Why could he tolerate rooms downstairs, but not upstairs?). Apart from regular information we needed to tease out some of the hidden fears, confusions, and paralysing anxiety. 'Viewing the house' interviewing technique was used to find out why certain rooms horrified him. Sometimes I used this technique as 'I want to buy this house, and can you show me around the house and describe each room to me – telling me which ones are "good feeling" rooms and which ones are "bad and scary rooms", which ones I should avoid and why?'

Viewing My House

Children can reveal much about themselves by drawing pictures or making models of houses. Most of their positive or negative experiences come from their homes and from knowledge of the people who live in them. Children might be asked to tell *how* they feel when they are in different rooms; *what* happens when they are there; *why* they are there; *what* makes them feel happy or content, and what does not; *who* is in that room/those rooms with them, or, if they are alone in the room/rooms.

Step 1   Draw a house or build one with Lego or bricks.
Step 2   Draw or make individual rooms that resemble those in the child's house.
Step 3   Ask the child to take you to the room he/she likes best.
Step 4   Ask the child what he/she likes about that room, and what happens there to make him/her feel happy or content.
Step 5   Ask the child to take you to the room he/she does not like.

Step 6   Ask the child what happens there that makes him/her feel bad or uncomfortable.

Step 7   Observe the child's behaviour and reactions.

Step 8   Ask the child if there are other rooms/places which he/she does not like.

Step 9   Ask again what makes him/her feel bad when he/she is there. Establish if there is another person there with the child.

Step 10   Observe the child's reactions, and the non-verbal communication. If there is apprehension or a sudden change of mood, prompt gently in order to get the child to elaborate on a description of events.

Step 11   Assuming that the child has indicated some form of maltreatment, work out what kind of further questions you need to ask.

The second assessment tool to facilitate teasing out William's confused feelings about his mother's emotional unavailability and painful relationship, was story compilation called 'Memories' (see Chapter 10, p. 219, for description of the technique).

Both assessment tools revealed acute emotional ill-treatment of William by his mother (e.g. being locked in rooms upstairs without food, water, or toys, even for a whole weekend; being told that if he made a noise the witch would come to take him away, etc.). It also revealed that he tried hard to please his mother, but she would not take any notice of him. When he told her that he loved her she would say, 'Get lost' or 'But I do not love you', etc. 'The jug of loving water' was used twice a week for two months to help him understand and come to terms with his mother's rejection of him, and to help him to accept and learn to trust his foster-parents. Structured play and activity sessions were used, involving foster-parents and their children, to build mutually rewarding memories and experiences. Night stories and special evening times were introduced to reduce his anxiety and fear about safety and security at night, and to create a feeling of ease when in his bedroom. Additionally, he started to attend an after-school club which he enjoyed and which helped him to develop positive interactions with his peers.

After eight months his foster-parents stated that 'William is a perfectly normal boy, as any other child of his age. He is considerate, helpful, and loving, but still requires reassurance that he is loved as well.'

SUMMARY

Emotionally abused and neglected children need individual help on a one-to-one basis, especially those who have been exposed to multiple forms of ill-treatment over a long time. Play therapy, of different types, is a very useful method to help children who are in care and who present attachment problems.

The skilled therapist may detect themes in the child's play, preoccupations which point to conflicts or areas of tension in the family, at school, or in some aspects of the child's life (e.g. abuse, neglect, or rejection) which are blocking or distorting development. The use of conversation and imaginative assessment tools (as illustrated in William's case) help the practitioner to diagnose and then choose appropriate helping methods. Quite often the child's problems are so tied up with parental attitudes and treatment of the child that parents have to be involved even in the play, to teach them interaction skills, both physical and verbal.

This chapter provided examples of direct work with children and adolescence, including: building resilience at all ages; social skills and assertiveness training for teenagers, and an example of psycho-therapy ('the jug of loving water') for emotionally disturbed children. A case study was provided to illustrate some of the methods described in the chapter which can be used in practice.

CHAPTER 15

HELPING PARENTS AND FAMILIES

CONTENTS

INTRODUCTION

Very often parents need help in their own right in order to improve the quality of their lives and that of their children. Some of the methods discussed in this chapter are meant to point out how to help parents individually to examine and reflect on their own problems and work out strategies to change for the better. Personal counselling aims to help people to help themselves, and by achieving personal growth it is believed that understanding of their children's growing needs and parental responsibilities will be enhanced as well. Personal counselling is frequently linked to parental psychoeducation, where parents receive developmental counselling/education regarding a wide range of children's developmental needs and how things can go wrong for the child if parents do not facilitate meeting developmental tasks. Psychoeducation can be provided on an individual or group work basis, so group work with emotionally abusive parents will be briefly discussed, pointing to its advantages.

Marital/couple problems are frequent fixtures of emotionally maltreating parents, so 'couple work' will be briefly discussed, describing ways of helping to resolve marital issues between couples. Family therapy, with special emphasis on systemic work, will be elaborated on, drawing the reader's attention to the plight of a scapegoated child within the family.

COUNSELLING

The main task of counselling is to help parents reflect on the problems they are experiencing and to direct them to a better understanding of themselves and their behaviour. The counsellor's aim is to direct the client to personality and behavioural change; such change arises from the client–counsellor relationship, built on trust and frank discussions. Thus, counselling involves rigorous exploration of presenting problems, clarifying conflicting issues and confused assumptions, and searching for alternative ways of describing and understanding problems and dealing with them. Counselling aims to help people to help themselves. The emphasis is put on self-help, similar to the problem-solving approach, calling on the inner resources of the person who is in difficulties. In order to facilitate the required changes the counsellor should be warm, non-judgmental, empathetic, and respectful to the person involved. The process of reaching a person should not be rushed, and assumptions should not be made. Counselling can promote personal growth and more mature ways of acting and reacting, thinking first and responding, for example, to a child in a more thought-through way. The therapeutic process here enhances the socialisation and education of parents.

There are many types of counselling. One of them is the Rogerian 'client-centred' approach. The goal of Rogerian intervention is to work with the person in a non-intrusive manner in order to remove the incongruity the person has developed between the experiencing inner self and the self that person presents to others; by addressing these issues it is hoped to increase positive self-regard and self-direction. Rogerian theory is based on the notion that a person is essentially good, rational, realistic, social, and forward-looking, but some people may need help with their basic impulse to grow. The assumption is that people have within themselves not only the ability to solve problems, but also the growth impulse to better themselves, which can make their behaviour more mature, responsible, and satisfying. The therapeutic process with emotionally abusive parents aims to facilitate education, and is seen as a freeing of growth capacities, which enables them to develop empathy, understanding, and control of their behaviour towards their children. Reflective counselling with parents who were abused as children, and who abuse their own children, can play an important role in bringing feelings and memories of those events to the surface, and linking them to their children's feelings of being abused.

The aim is to raise empathy, awareness, and change of behaviour towards their children. It needs to be remembered, however, that some abusive parents (who have little insight, limited intellectual abilities, and lead highly dysfunctional lives) are unlikely to benefit from counselling. They may need more practical and structured help in order to produce some change. For many emotionally abusive parents, counselling is advisable for several reasons:

1. It lays the foundation for further work, use of services, and commitment to co-operate with family support-workers.
2. It provides an opportunity for the parents to be heard, to describe how they see themselves, and to indicate problems with which they feel entrapped.
3. It reassures parents that their pain and difficulties in relating to the child have been addressed.
4. It makes them feel cared for and listened to.
5. It builds up trust and a good working relationship.
6. It provides the worker with a better understanding of the capacities and inner resources of parents.
7. It helps to identify strengths as well as limitations.
8. It helps to make realistic decisions regarding care plans and needs.
9. It helps to make decisions about the children's future, and in which direction intervention should go.

Emotionally abusive parents are often themselves emotionally deprived of support, help, or direction, and they have no one to turn to for help; they might be reluctant to approach child-welfare agencies for fear of losing their children. Counselling often helps to reduce that fear and might 'open a door' to more sincere anxiety-free sharing of true feelings and difficulties.

Counselling can also be used in work with small groups, where a situation or a case is described and group members (with their counsellor) look for explanations and possible remedies. They are encouraged to view the situation through the eyes and hearts of the children. They are urged to recall memories of their own childhood – those which were pleasant and those which were painful, frightening, and anxiety-provoking – and their feelings of helplessness and confusion. They are asked to link their childhood experiences to those of their children in order to make them aware of their children's pain and suffering, hoping that increased insight of their children's plight will change their behaviour.

FAMILY THERAPY

Introduction

Family-therapy approaches offer parents and children the opportunity to address the core issue of dysfunction in emotional abuse and neglect, namely family relationships. By exploring family processes, improving communication skills and family interactions, as well as increasing emotional and practical support among family members, advocates of family therapy suggest that the overall functioning of the family unit *in tandem* with the psychological well-being of individual members will be significantly advanced. Several theoretical approaches have developed over the years which fall under the broad umbrella of family therapy. Although they may vary on a variety of issues (e.g. who should be involved or invited to participate in the intervention; strategies to initiate therapeutic change and progress; the relative influence of cognitions and community values, systems, and beliefs), all are firmly rooted in family-systems theory which provides an important and driving conceptual base. A helpful summary of the main and most popular models is provided in Table 15.1 (adapted from Walsh, 1982).

Family-systems theory emphasises the interactive and reciprocal effects of relationships, behaviour, and family process on children, parents, and the family unit. Each member of the family is considered to hold an equally important, separate, yet connected role in the system which is rooted in the beliefs and attitudes of the family (reinforced in the context of relationships within the family and the interactions within the broader community in which the family lives) in a process termed 'circular causality'. Family-systems theory assumes that individual roles, relationships, behaviour, and patterns of communication have meaning and have a function as the family tries to maintain a state of stability and 'homeostasis' through phases of transition and change in its own natural life cycle. Advocates of family therapy assume that these ideas and experiences are often rooted in the childhood history, experience, and family of origin of the parent, and are maintained and perpetuated across generations, affecting the coping resources, expressions of emotion, and support and parenting style that currently exists in the nuclear family unit (Von Bertalanffy, 1968; Nichols & Schwartz, 1991).

When individual members of the family present with difficulties or when problems exist in the family unit, dysfunction is not assumed to be a result of one specific issue or person, but is considered to be a product or symptom of an interaction of maladaptive processes and relationships within the family. Difficulties in family relationships that may compromise the psychological health and well-being of individual family members may evolve when boundaries are unclear and those family members are enmeshed in each other's lives, are over protective, and over involved. Conversely, problems can also occur when boundaries are rigid and inflexible and family members have considerable difficulties negotiating and/or resolving challenges and disagreements. Additional problems may result where family members label and channel their difficulties on to one member, i.e. a scapegoat, thus drawing attention away from core issues of dysfunction (Minuchin, Montalvo, Guerney, Rosman, & Schumer, 1967; Ranney & Cottone, 1991). These relationship styles are typical of families where emotional abuse occurs.

However, authors who advocate family-therapy approaches in relation to child abuse acknowledge limitations to the concept of circular interactions and, by extension, the assumption that maltreatment occurs due to reciprocal

Table 15.1 Major models of family therapy

Model of family therapy	View of normal family functioning	View of dysfunction, symptoms	Goals of therapy

Structural	1. Boundaries clear and firm
	2. Hierarchy with strong parental subsystem
	3. Flexibility of system for:
	  a. Autonomy and interdependence
	  b. Individual growth and system maintenance
	  c. Continuity and adaptive restructuring in response to changing internal (developmental) and external (environmental) demands
		Symptoms result from current family structural imbalance:
		  a. Malfunctioning hierarchical
		  b. Maladaptive reaction to changing requirements (development, environmental)
			Reorganise family structure:
			  a. Shift members' relative positions to disrupt malfunctioning pattern and strengthen parental hierarchy
			  b. Create clear, flexible boundaries
			  c. Mobilise more adaptive alternative patterns

Strategic	1. Flexibility
	2. Large behavioural repertoire for:
	  a. Problem resolution
	  b. Life cycle passage
	3. Clear rules governing hierarchy
		1. Multiple origins of problems: symptoms maintained by family's:
		  a. Unsuccessful problem-solving attempts
		  b. Inability to adjust to life cycle transitions
		  c. Malfunctioning hierarchy; triangle of coalition across hierarchy
		2. Symptom is a communicative act embedded in interaction pattern
			1. Resolve presenting problem only; specific behaviourally defined objectives
			2. Interrupt rigid feedback cycle; change symptom-maintaining sequence to new outcomes

Table 15.1 (Continued)

Model of family therapy	View of normal family functioning	View of dysfunction, symptoms	Goals of therapy
Behavioural-social change	1. Maladaptive behaviour is not reinforced 2. Adaptive behaviour is rewarded 3. Exchange of benefits outweighs costs 4. Long-term reciprocity	Maladaptive, symptomatic behaviour reinforced by a. Family attention and reward b. Deficient reward exchanges (for example, coercion) c. Communication deficit	Concrete, observable behavioural goals; change contingencies of social reinforcement (interpersonal consequences of behaviour): a. Rewards for adaptive behaviour b. No rewards for maladaptive behaviour

Psychodynamic	1. Parental personalities and relationships well differentiated
	2. Relationship perceptions based on current realities, not projections from past
	3. Relational equitability
	4. Family task requisites
	  a. Parental coalition
	  b. Generation boundaries
	  c. Sex-lined parental roles
		Symptoms due to family projection process stemming from unresolved conflicts and losses in family origin	1. Insight and resolution of family of origin conflict and losses
			2. Family projection processes
			3. Relationship reconstruction and reunion
			4. Individual and family growth

Family system therapy	1. Differentiation of self
	2. Intellectual/emotional balance
		Functioning impaired by relationship with family of origin:
		a. Poor differentiation
		b. Anxiety (reactivity)
		c. Family projection process
		d. Triangulation
			1. Differentiation
			2. Cognitive functioning
			3. Emotional reactivity
			4. Modification of relationships in family system:
			  a. Detriangulation
			  b. Repair of cut-offs

Source: Adapted from Walsh (1982).

and circular interactions between parents and children. While recognising the influence and interaction of parental history (where it is likely they were also vulnerable and subjected to maltreatment as children) and child variables (such as temperament) in an abusive interaction, a linear perspective is taken. The child is clearly and unequivocally identified as the victim, due to the unequal power relationship that exists within the family hierarchy. Therefore blame, responsibility, and lack of protection clearly lie with the parent as perpetrator (Cottone, 1988).

The key aims of family therapy for families at risk of maltreatment are restructuring the interaction patterns, re-establishing a healthy balance between individual members and the family system, and challenging and amending maladaptive beliefs and attitudes maintaining dysfunctional patterns of interaction.

Essential Components

Family-therapy sessions generally last from 60 to 90 minutes. They are usually scheduled at 3- to 6-week intervals to allow the family to generate their own solutions, practise relationship skills, and produce more adaptive ways of managing their difficulties. Before each appointment the family-therapy team meets to produce a hypothesis for the session. They discuss issues that could be raised and schedule times for breaks. The session is led by 1 or 2 therapists, working together, while members of the team observe the interaction through a one-way mirror or observation room. The lead therapists receive live supervision from the 'reflecting team' via ear-mounted receivers. Midway through the session, the lead therapist takes a break and meets with other members of the team. At some point after a break, the family receives feedback and reflections of the team. Comments are positive, with particular attention to progress and change, and refer to the family belief-system and culture. The lead therapist may give feedback directly, or the 'reflecting team' may choose to have a conversation about the family, sitting in the same seats and positions which the family assumed during the therapeutic session. Case discussion and possibilities for the future occur after the family has left.

Family relationships and communication styles are the practical focus of the intervention. Family therapists pay particular attention to the phrases, level of physical contact, and communication style of both parents and children. Family-systems theory assumes these behaviours reflect beliefs, attitudes, roles, and rules which dominate within the family culture and are maintained and supported by the system and by each member to varying degrees. The therapist is mindful of family culture and attitudes, and rules regarding those beliefs. The practitioner suggests or presents small amendments to the behaviour of the system and offers alternative perspectives, 'realities', or interpretations for family members in order to foster new beliefs and behaviours as well as to enable more adaptive interaction and communication patterns for the family.

Balance, structure, boundaries, autonomy, and connectedness of family members are also important features and additional foci of interventions. *Triangles*, or groupings of family members (where one member plays a specific role to support others), are also highlighted and discussed. At one point, certain roles may have been adaptive in the life cycle of the family, but over time they may become maladaptive and could be the source of greater problems for the family system (Jackson, 1957; Minuchin, 1974; Minuchin, Rosman, & Baker, 1978).

Techniques

Family therapists use a variety of techniques to facilitate change and to promote more aptive methods to address their problems. Again, depending on the orientation of the clinician, the presenting problems and the resources of the family (both practical and emotional), family therapists will use or adapt some of the following methods and techniques to mobilise the family and promote more adaptive relationships.

Identifying Roles, Rules, Family Histories, and Belief-Systems

The *genogram* (see Figures 15.1 and 15.2) is a technique often used during the initial sessions in family therapy, and provides a diagram and pictorial representation of the family history and structure. Names, dates, marriages, deaths, separations, and divorces are documented. Other relevant facts are noted and important stories or events are often discussed by the family. Genograms provide a wealth of information about the experiences, strengths, and difficulties which can characterise the family history and belief-system. Relating this information to the therapist can function as an early indicator of family relationships and communication style as the family unit executes an accessible and non-threatening task.

Another way to explore the history of the family and to gain therapeutic insight into family connections, histories, and power struggles includes a *family floor plan*. Ask families to draw the plan of their home, indicating space and territory that each family member normally occupies. Triangles and sub-systems operating within the family may become apparent in this exercise. Poignant and meaningful issues relating to the experiences and history of the family may be raised as members reflect on and explain who (and why) is occupying particular areas in the home. Parents may also choose to complete the task for their family of origin. As they begin to explore their own family

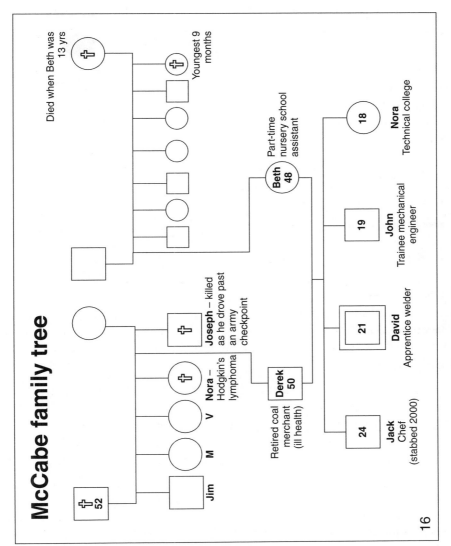

Figure 15.1 Diagram of genogram

16

Symbols

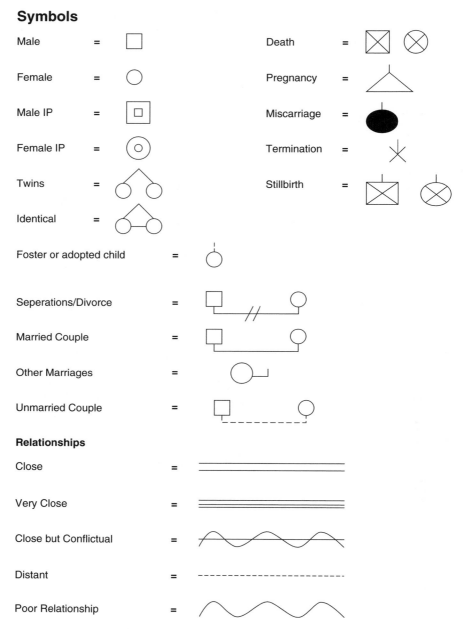

Figure 15.2 Genogram symbols and relationships

Note: IP stands for identified person/problem, which means the family identifies a person with problems that need help in sorting out.

history, they may identify the roots of the abuse and come to realise that they are carrying on patterns learned as children. Discussing their own experiences will also highlight to their spouses that they too may have been victimised. This realisation may help parents to feel less guilty, but will also hopefully increase their feelings of empathy for their own child and prevent further abuse.

Family photos can also yield invaluable information about the family. Responses of both parents and children to pictures, events, and periods within their family circle can be an invaluable resource of information regarding relationships, roles, and family rules. Alternatively, family members could be asked to bring significant photos with them and discuss their choice and reasons for bringing the photos to the session.

Not only do these very simple techniques function as a means of getting to know the family, but they can identify very significant information which maintains the family in a cycle of dysfunction. By raising these issues and reflecting on these concepts in session, the therapist brings implicit beliefs and attitudes out into the open. This, in turn, should hopefully promote the family's interest and curiosity in their relationship patterns and the influence they have on each other. This should also function as a strong force of change.

Challenging Dysfunctional Family Beliefs, 'Truths', and Attitudes

Reframing, or rather offering a more positive connotation of a situation or behaviour, is a common activity used by most family therapists. Basically, the therapist offers an alternative interpretation of the behaviour or event, which should challenge the meaning of the event for the family. Providing the family with an 'alternative reality' may serve as a catalyst and allow members to question what appears to be accepted 'truths'. Considering alternative interpretations should hopefully promote change in how family members perceive and ultimately interact with each other.

Reframing and offering a positive perspective can be somewhat problematic where abuse has occurred. This may be further complicated in situations where the parent denies the abuse or when the parents assert that the child initiated or provoked the maltreatment. In these circumstances, it may be more helpful to focus and praise families for engaging in the therapeutic process, attending sessions and discussing distressing topics and situations as a reflection of their love and affection for each other despite their difficulties. If parents continue to deny their responsibility for the abuse, reframing questions and reflections may go some way to aiding the family in generating an explanation or 'shared script' of the events that is appropriate and acceptable to all family members. It will be important for children to understand that they did not deserve or were not responsible for the maltreatment.

Building Relationship and Communication Skills

Emotional abuse and neglect are characterised by a set of dysfunctional patterns of communication and interaction which have a detrimental affect on the child. Addressing the relationship styles of the parent and child, therefore, is fundamental in promoting healthy family functioning and well-being. Throughout the intervention the therapist will teach, model, and/or encourage the following:

- listening skills – teaching each family member to allow others to speak without interruption;
- turn-taking – giving each family member an allotted time to express themselves;
- reflecting feelings – summarising the feelings of a family member to let them know you have heard what they have said;
- brainstorming – asking all family members to give their opinion or perspective on a particular issue.

The therapist may also use *circular questioning* as a means to build relationship skills. In these situations a family member is asked to take the perspective of another family member on a particular issue and event. This can be an extremely helpful method to increase the parent's awareness and understanding of the feelings and perspective of their children.

In situations when family members have difficulty communicating their feelings and making requests, or may have restrained emotions and feelings towards another family member, partner, or parent who no longer lives in the family home, the *empty chair* technique may be of some use. Often used in marital work, a spouse may express his/her feelings to the partner (absent, but represented by the empty chair), then play the role of the spouse and continue a typical conversation. This technique may be particularly helpful when there has been loss or separation after bereavement in the family, or a parent has been removed for the health and safety of the children.

Acknowledging and increasing the awareness of cycles of maladaptive behaviour will be of benefit to the family to help them anticipate and prevent difficulties. During the course of the session, a member of the family therapy team records notes, circumstances, and events relating to family stories. From *tracking* the sequence of events, a therapist will look for a pattern of events and behaviours which led to a maladaptive outcome for the system. This cycle or sequence of behaviour may be discussed and relayed to the family at an appropriate time in the session.

In circumstances where family relationships are characterised by a considerable level of conflict, the therapist may also teach the family to express their feelings or opinions in a fair, non-violent way. Teaching the family problem-solving techniques may also be of help to prevent difficult interactions and stressful situations. These skills and techniques could be practised in the context of a *family meeting*. The therapist may encourage the family to schedule meetings at regular and specific times, where they meet and share concerns and difficulties and review how they are getting on with each other. Family meetings should include all family members and be subject to rules agreed in the therapeutic session. Individuals who cannot or choose not to attend agree to abide by any decisions made. Reverting back to traditional patterns of interaction, identified during the assessment process (such as criticism or nagging), is not allowed. Providing a structure and time whereby the family make a concerted effort to interact with each other in a positive way should result in more adaptive patterns of communication, which will hopefully generalise to characterise family relationships.

Suggesting *pleasant activities, trips*, and *special days* is important for family therapy. Couples and families frequently engage in routines. Although helpful in terms of organising and managing the family tasks, routines can also imply boredom or reflect that the family is stuck in patterns of interaction from which they are unable to deviate. Family members may feel unappreciated, taken for granted, and apathetic about the time the family spends together (which may seem predictable and uninteresting). Suggesting day trips and activities, within the financial means of the family, yet outside their normal routine, may provide new and exciting challenges. Engaging in new activities may also lead to new roles within the system as new talents and abilities come to the fore. Organising and allocating time and activities may be particularly important for the parental couple. Specific times in the evening or days could be set aside whereby the couple spends time away from the children. Apart from renewing or re-establishing their roles as partners in a couple, rather than mother or father, the couple could use this time to express how much they care about each other.

Challenging Family Structure, Balance, and Hierarchies

Roles, hierarchies, balance of power, and decision-making can be significant sources of dysfunction and difficulty. Seating arrangements or use of space within the therapeutic room can prove interesting and highlight how each member views himself or herself in relation to the family unit. The Sculpting technique (e.g. asking clients to change their seating arrangements) can displace alliances within the system and provide an opportunity to challenge 'triangles' and relationships which are currently maladaptive. This technique may be expanded on by asking a family member to reorganise the group and position individuals in a preferred arrangement. Family members could be encouraged to role-play or re-enact a situation which would lead to the preferred organisation of the family. This may encourage flexibility and change for the whole system.

Improving the Well-Being and Health of the System

It is believed that the system can have a profound affect on an individual, and so may an individual on the entire family system. It may be that, through the course of the intervention a family may report significantly more difficulties; for example, children may present with toileting problems or sleep difficulties, and parents may report depressed moods or anxieties. For cases involving emotional abuse, parents may wish to discuss aspects of their own childhood which might include experiences of maltreatment. Individual family members may benefit from individual counselling or therapeutic support. Providing additional and separate sessions for one family member may produce a sufficient level of change to impact the whole system. This will depend on the issues involved and is discussed in detail in sections specifically referring to individual work with either parents or children.

Again, similar to other methods of intervention, research studies evaluating the efficacy of family-therapy techniques for emotional abuse and neglect are uncommon. However, the literature investigating the benefits of family therapy for conduct and behavioural problems is certainly established, and suggests improved family communication and lower rates of clinical referral (see Alexander, Hotzworth-Monroe, & Jameson, 1994 for a review). As family relationships and communication are at the core of emotional abuse and neglect, it can be assumed that family therapy will also be of considerable benefit to children subjected to psychological maltreatment. In some of the rare studies which have explored the value of family therapy to parents and children where such maltreatment has occurred, significant improvement in the quality of parent–child interaction and parental sensitivity and responsiveness to the child's needs are observed. After the intervention, children of these families are also considered more assertive and competent at expressing their needs and requests (Brunk *et al.*, 1987; Meezan & O'Keefe, 1998). Although further work is needed before accurate conclusions can be made, integrating family therapy-based techniques should enhance any intervention to remediate the affects of emotional abuse and neglect.

PSYCHOEDUCATION

Many parents who engage in maladaptive interaction patterns with their children often lack appropriate caregiving skills and suitable knowledge about child development and effective parenting (Carter, Osofsky, & Hann, 1991). Parents who maltreat their children also often have inappropriate and inaccurate expectations of their child's behaviour during its early years, and often overestimate its developmental skills and abilities (Iwaniec *et al.*, 1988). Some parents are unable to accept that the child may not yet be ready to complete a task, and may perceive the youngster as lazy and disobedient.

When children are continuously faced with tasks for which they are cognitively or developmentally unequipped, they can become anxious, confused, and nervous, which leads to emotional and behavioural problems as well as a sense of ineffectiveness. The parent, in turn, can often become frustrated and critical, when the child fails to achieve expectations, or may become aggressive and forceful rather than remain patient and guide the child to learn appropriate behaviour when it is ready (Miller, 1988). In some families, parents view the child's failure and emotional reaction or outburst as an intentional act to annoy or provoke them (Larrance & Twentyman, 1983). Even at an early age, a cycle of emotionally abusive parenting can occur; parents may feel dissatisfied with the child, may criticise it, deprive the child of affection or treats, or tell the child off for being stupid, incapable, and good for nothing. Some parents may resort to smacking and aggression as a method to punish the child and justify their actions as a means to teach the child a lesson and promote learning when, in fact, it will have the opposite affect.

Providing information and giving knowledge to the parent about what would normally be expected (given the child's age, gender, ability, and developmental stage) and offering methods to promote 'optimal' development and progress are just as important (if not more so) than suggesting ways to cope with and manage difficult or problematic behaviour. Equally important will be to focus on health, hygiene, and safety issues for the child. Home visits to understand the natural environment of the family may be helpful in order to identify family need but also to provide information and techniques that should encourage healthy development and well-being, and prevent accidents which would be attributed to neglect. The responsibilities of parenting and appropriate discipline strategies will also be important topics to address. The primary aim of this type of intervention is to educate parents, and it accepts that bringing up children is difficult and requires skill, but, like all skills, with help and support it can be learned.

Abusive and neglectful parenting will invariably have a significant impact on the child. In early childhood these children may present a host of developmental problems which cause additional difficulties to the parent–child relationship. Tantrums, biting, bed-wetting, and toilet-training problems, for example, may be reactions to or even communications of a child's discomfort and distress. Given the carer's lack of appropriate knowledge and parenting skills which gave rise to the maltreatment, it is likely that these additional difficulties may serve to further increase the parents' dislike of and lack of interest in the child. These problems may increase the likelihood of aversive interactions, further escalating the child's vulnerability. Depending on the issues defined at assessment, isolating and identifying these problems may provide the first step in building positive relationships between parent and child. To equip parents with basic knowledge suggestions as to how to manage these common childhood difficulties will increase positive and practical coping skills, reduce stress, and may dissipate intense negative emotions otherwise directed at the child. As a consequence, the family will be less likely to revert to maladaptive interchanges and an overall improvement child and family functioning hopefully will result (Taylor & Beauchamp, 1988).

Parents often compare their child(ren) with those of friends or neighbours, so it is essential to educate them about individual differences in speed of development and how to encourage a child to learn different skills. Sometimes simple reassurance that there is nothing wrong with the child, or that a type of behaviour is normal for a particular developmental stage, is enough to change parental perception of (and consequently attitudes to) the child. In the case of emotional and physical neglect, where a child's development might be delayed due to lack of stimulation, attention, and proper care, parents need to be guided and instructed on what to do and why. This is often the case with toddlers, when temper tantrums and oppositional behaviour are interpreted as intentional, naughty, and wicked, and not as expressions of inner frustration when striving to master a skill. Bowel and bladder control are other examples of often unrealistic expectations and faulty perception on the part of parents. To illustrate this problem, let us look at Alan's case.

> Alan was two-and-a-half years old. He looked withdrawn, and he was unwilling to engage in any activities. He suffered from colds and recurring chest infections. The health visitor noted that he was panic-stricken when asked to go to the bathroom, and he cried when he was taken there. His mother complained that he wet and soiled himself out of sheer laziness, and said that her next-door neighbour's daughter (the same age as Alan) had been clean and dry for some time, as had the son of her mother's best friend, who was one month younger than he was. Mother–child interaction was tense, and her attitudes toward Alan were visibly negative.

> When designing parent-training interventions in cases similar to Alan's, it is useful to have a pictorial demonstration or graph, illustrating life tasks or skills and the chronological age at which those tasks or skills should be acquired. Parents need to be told what the time-span is, and how it may differ between children, depending on individual circumstances and capabilities. An example of bowel and bladder control is shown on a developmental ladder in Figure 15.3.

Parents who maltreat their children are often exposed to multiple stressors and live in chaotic environments. Financial worries, domestic and community violence, substance abuse, inadequate housing, and limited employment and training opportunities are common factors in the lives of families where maltreatment occurs. As well as providing information about child development, education sessions could include information and contacts about resources within the family's local community which could offer

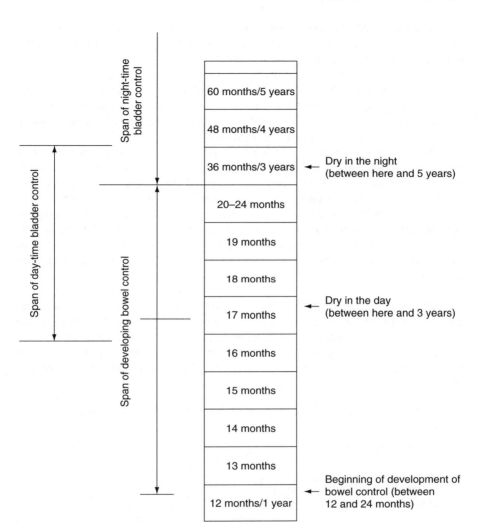

Figure 15.3   Developmental ladder (bowel and bladder control)
Source: Iwaniec (1995)

additional practical and emotional support. When designing education programmes, specific interventions to account for these issues may need to be developed and tailored to the parents referred. When delivering this intervention, practitioners will also need to be flexible and account for the needs of the family. For example, teenaged parents may be struggling with issues of personal identity and separateness; parents with little income may be having to manage competing demands and pressures to run a household;

and parents with minimal education may not have the experience of accessing groups or self-help materials to manage children; all may find the concept of parent education particularly difficult.

It will also be important to try and involve fathers in any intervention. Unlike other family-oriented programmes, which view both mothers and fathers as having the same parenting strengths, weaknesses, skills, and abilities, parent-training recognises the different knowledge and experiences which parents of each gender provide. Intervention will need to incorporate this issue and demonstrate how they both offer extremely valuable, yet different, roles and skills. Palm (1997) suggests it may be beneficial to include fathers in any intervention, identifying safe topics for fathers to discuss and address in information sessions, high-lighting strengths that fathers bring to the parenting role, listening and attending to the unique stories which fathers will bring to the informa-tion sessions, and acknowledging the strengths that a man can bring to the parenting role.

Parent-training could be presented as a number of sessions in a clinic setting, possibly with other families, increasing potential options for social support or during activities with the family, such as home visits. For practitioners designing an educational programme for parents where maltreatment has occurred, it may be helpful to consider the following points.

- Keep the child's needs as the focus and at the centre of the intervention.
- Focus on topics of:

  o Child development;
  o Health;
  o Safety;
  o Hygiene;
  o Discipline.

- Provide information and tips for parents on how to interact, play with, and encourage their child.
- Help parents to develop age-appropriate expectations for their child; this may include charts, pictures, or booklets, documenting expected child-based skills and abilities for each chronological age. For parents with younger children, this could be presented for each chronological month.
- Give information that will provide practical support to families. This may include budgeting, assistance with transport, or childcare arrangements.
- Give information that may provide access to emotional support for families. This may include a list of voluntary groups or charity-based organisations that may of assist-ance to the family.
- Vary frequency and intensity of parent-training sessions, depending on the parents' need.
- Provide information relevant to the family's strengths and weaknesses.

GROUP WORK WITH EMOTIONALLY ABUSIVE AND NEGLECTFUL PARENTS

One of the recognised characteristics of emotionally maltreating parents and carers is social isolation and little social support. As parenting skills are not that well established, especially for first-time parents, and these days there is less support from extended families, it is useful and beneficial to find a source of mutual help and problem-solving. Such support can be provided by group work, either informally (run as a social gathering) or formally (based on a programme of intervention). If mothers appear to be less psychologically available to their children (because of feeling depressed, tired, or not being aware of their children's emotional needs) a formal programme of group work may give them an opportunity to talk about their own problems as well as those associated with childcare. Many mothers of emotionally ill-treated children suffer from low self-esteem and lack of confidence, as they feel they are being blamed for their children's unhappiness, emotionally disturbed behaviour, and poor relationships within the family. While some knowingly distance themselves emotionally from the child, the majority do so unwittingly, believing that what they do is correct and appropriate.

Parents' or mothers' groups may be particularly beneficial as they provide opportunities to meet other parents who are faced with similar problems regarding their children, and who may well experience similar stresses in other areas of their lives. There are many advantages for meeting in a group. These might include the provision of a forum for peer support, opportunities to exchange personal experiences (e.g. tips and ideas on what works or does not work when parenting children), having time out of the house, the possibility of building friendships, and exchanges of telephone numbers so that contact can be maintained outside group meetings. Such meetings also demonstrate that group members are not unique and there are other families coping with similar problems. In addition, members of such groups have chances to learn from formal and informal discussions, to participate in role play and problem-solving, and to get involved in group exercises.

However, the running of effective parent-training groups is not free from problems. First, they are time-consuming to organise (to prepare their content and to provide the necessary teaching material). Particular difficulties arise when trying to set up timetables for group work which will be convenient for everyone concerned (working fathers, for instance, may often find regular attendance inconvenient or even out of the question). Group work, in comparison with individual work, is more cost-effective, but has also some limitations, particularly when rejecting and neglecting parents are involved. They feel ashamed, embarrassed, and therefore reluctant to share their experiences with completely strange people, so a combination of group work and individual work would seem to be an appropriate combination in these circumstances. Parents can be prepared before group work for 'learning in public' and talking about their negative feelings and difficulties experienced with children; the fact that the group leader already knows them helps to break the ice. It is also helpful to involve such parents in group planning; they need to 'own' a stake in that group work and to feel that they have contributed to its creation. Levels of attendance and commitment to participate and to learn depend on early involvement of prospective group members in work-planning (Iwaniec, 1995; 1997).

Planning Group Work

Good preparation will determine the success of group work. There are some general rules that need to be taken into consideration when planning this work. It is necessary to:

1. negotiate and discuss specific issues that parents would like to explore;
2. discuss and learn from the prospective group members;
3. list points and work out the logical order, always starting from general, impersonal, unthreatening ones to more complex, challenging, and personal issues and feelings;
4. find at least one co-worker;
5. find a group work consultant (it does *not* have to be a line manager);
6. find a private and quiet place for group work;
7. make provision for children while parents/mothers have their session;
8. plan each session before group work starts;
9. prepare and organise teaching materials, videos, audio-tapes, materials for play sessions, and other aids; and
10. work out an evaluation system.

David and Frank Johnson, authors of the book *Joining Together*, have made several suggestions for successful group work which can be adapted to a particular set and range of problems. For example, when planning and setting up a group for emotionally abusive and neglectful mothers, the following principles should be observed (cited in Herbert, 1989).

1. *Definition of terms and concepts*: Group members need to be provided with terms and definitions of those terms (such as reinforcement, stimulation, interaction, discipline, attachment, trust-building, maltreatment, neglect, abuse, modelling, rehearsal, and so on) to help to achieve full participation from all members. Group leaders should describe each concept, giving examples or providing alternative words (for instance, interaction means 'what you do with the child and how you are doing it', involving playing, reading, talking, supervising, instructing, and everyday activity).

2. *Negotiation and/or establishment of goals*: Goals and objectives should be made clear and agreed for each session (for instance, self-control training would include short instruction, role play, modelling, brainstorming, discussion, clarification, and giving instruction for homework). Viewing of videos dealing with a topic, or getting a handout to prepare members for the session can be helpful and appreciated, as everybody concerned is given an equal opportunity to participate in the discussions and the exercises. Each session should allow time to review homework tasks for each member of the group.

3. *Encouragement of free and fair discussion*: In order to learn and to feel a part of the group, each member should be encouraged to freely, openly, and fairly express feelings and ideas, attitudes, and beliefs. Each group should have a few basic rules about what is allowed and what is not (like scape-goating, bullying, and excessive criticism of any one member).

4. *Integration of the material*: Constant connections should be made where appropriate between topics covered early on and current themes (for example, links between stress-management techniques, problem-solving, self-control, and child-discipline). Parent-training groups should try out practical ideas, such as communicating with children who are apprehensive and fearful of their parents by means of role play or homework tasks. Discussions or instructions alone are unlikely to be helpful without preliminary sessions to encourage familiarity with methods and applications in practice.

5. *Encouragement of the application of discussion material*: Group members should be actively and constantly encouraged and reminded to link what they have learned to their own lives, circumstances, and needs. They should also be prompted to report back to the group the 'feedback' they received from trying different methods and techniques at home.

6. *Evaluation of the quality of the discussions*: Group members should be asked to examine critically their performance as a body and as individuals, and their contributions to the success or failure of the efficacy of the group.

Effective Group Intervention

It is extremely important to select an appropriate place for group work. The room should be bright, with comfortable seating, and should be warm. Seats should be arranged in a circle, so that group members can see and hear each other. Video-equipment, flip-charts, cassette-players, and other teaching aids should be checked and prepared beforehand, so that no time is wasted and no embarrassing pauses occur during the times allotted for sessions.

It must be remembered that emotionally abusive parents are very defensive and are reluctant to talk about themselves, so the group leaders should start from neutral topics such as child development and child needs, and a dispassionate look at the behavioural problems of children. An early exploration of parental feelings towards children, and an examination of the ways in which parents attempt to manage the behaviour of their children, can be intimidating and consequently may arrest full participation (and learning processes). Once group members get to know each other and begin to feel more comfortable in each other's company, explorations of feelings and airing of personal difficulties and dilemmas can begin. Group leaders should facilitate (but not dominate) group life; they should keep an eye on the group dynamics, they must make sure that every member has an opportunity to speak, and they need to restrain those members who try to dominate or 'hog' the discussion. Group leaders should ensure that sessions are conducted according to plan in structured ways, and that they periodically sum up the discussions, set and explain homework, and give group members opportunities to ask questions, clarify confusing issues, and tailor acquired knowledge to personal needs and circumstances.

DEALING WITH MARITAL PROBLEMS

Interventions with parents to address the marital relationship can be a fundamental component of the treatment process to address emotional abuse and neglect. It is not uncommon (in cases where child maltreatment is identified) to discover that parents are unhappy or angry, and resent each other. The couple may report high levels of indifference, dissatisfaction, and disappointment with their partner, dysfunctional communication strategies, and ineffective methods of conflict-management which often lead to episodes of overt verbal and physical aggression to manage disagreements, disputes, and family issues (Edelson, 1999).

Marital conflict can fluctuate between violence, hostility, aggressive fights, and quarrels to 'silent days' and an atmosphere of tension (where communication does not occur, yet feelings of underlying hostility remain ever palpable). Children growing up in a home characterised by marital discord (and, in severe cases, domestic violence) live in permanent fear, insecurity, and exposure to and threats of active scenes of violence. Children can be caught in the middle of marital conflict. They are often used as bargaining tools or 'pawns' in power struggles between the couple. They are the focus in child-rearing disagreements or may be used to justify parental behaviour, which the other partner finds upsetting. Being the subject of disagreement between both partners may unfairly lead the child to blame itself and take responsibility for initiating parental arguments and distress. Unfortunately, as parents may be preoccupied with relationship difficulties with their partner, carers will have less emotional energy to attend to their children's needs and provide them with adequate care and support. Although emotional maltreatment of children, in these circumstances, may not be intentional, it is unavoidable.

Marital discord significantly increases the likelihood of child maltreatment (Cummings, 1997). Difficult emotions experienced by a parent after an aversive exchange with his or her partner can sometimes be communicated to a child. Conflictual interchanges, either physical or verbal, can be maintained with the child, increasing its vulnerability to maltreatment. Research studies have illustrated how marital discord is strongly associated with children's behavioural problems, in particular aggressive outbursts and misbehaviour (e.g. Reid & Crisafulli, 1990). It may be that the child demonstrates increased levels of externalising behaviour to cope with the emotional difficulties and tension evident within the family system or has learned that aggressive methods of social interaction, modelled by parents, are valid and appropriate methods of communication and conflict resolution. In either case, when indeed the child presents these behaviours in the family home, they appear to precipitate additional episodes of conflict for the couple (Jaffe *et al.*, 1990). This maintains the family in a vicious cycle and downward spiral of aggression, fear, tension, and anxiety which are damaging to parental and family relationships and cause immense physiological and psychological distress to the child (Hetherington, 1999). In such cases, intervention strategies to address the marital relationship are imperative to improve family interchanges and remedy the effects of emotional abuse and neglect for the child.

Marital or couples therapy is generally offered once a week in sessions generally lasting 60 to 90 minutes. The sessions may be led by 1 or 2 therapists working 'co-jointly' with the couple. The number of sessions offered to the couple depends on the severity of their problems, the theoretical orientation of the therapist, and preferred technique. A contract is usually drawn up to oblige the couple to work towards set goals in order to improve their relationship. The counsellor serves as a mediator during negotiations and discussions. Each partner states his or her expectations, desired outcomes, and willingness to meet the other halfway. Compromises need to be negotiated to make the therapeutic process work in a balanced and fair manner.

Marital work with couples tends to draw on an eclectic mix of systems, psychodynamic and CBT approaches, and techniques. Therapists with leanings towards systems theories of psychopathology may focus on relationship styles rooted in family-of-origin experiences which influence the couple, whereas therapists favouring social-learning theory and techniques may concentrate on each partner's current understanding, approach, and view of the relationship. Regardless of the theoretical orientation and perspective of the counsellor, the therapist attempts to assist the couple to cultivate mutually acceptable problem-solving strategies and communication skills to provide each partner with positive or at least less dysfunctional methods of interaction. Regardless of the theoretical orientation of the therapist, the counsellor views the *couple* as the 'client', rather than considering each partner separately. The therapist promotes fair, impartial, and equal relationships with both partners, remaining neutral and supportive to them throughout therapeutic contact. Both partners attend each session, although each partner may be invited to attend independently in the assessment phase.

During the course of therapeutic contact, couples are encouraged to address communication problems, affairs, mismatched expectations, power struggles, divisions, and loss of love and affection. Particular attention is paid to areas of common ground, as a basis to appreciate the strengths of the couple's relationship. The therapist is also attentive to the couple's arguments and issues of disagreement. Alternative ways of communication and active listening are taught, and possible explanations and interpretations for each partner's behaviour are offered. The importance of communication, openness, and voicing dissatisfaction when difficulties present themselves are emphasised to avoid communication breakdown. The art of compromise and use of positive reinforcement techniques are advocated to promote positive interchanges between the couple. As couples with entrenched and dysfunctional interaction patterns demonstrate high arousal and become overwhelmed, tense, and agitated when attempting to address challenging issues, techniques to tolerate stress-provoking situations are modelled and practised in session. These can include relaxation training, distraction and visualisation techniques, constructive self-talk, and increased awareness as to when to discontinue discussions with partners. Practical activities (such as sharing tasks and responsibilities and scheduling pleasant activities for the family) and (for couples without children) establishing what each partner likes and wants, will benefit and supplement therapeutic contact (Fennell & Weinhold, 2003).

Couples are invited to practise skills modelled and raised in the session to address a non-emotive issue. The therapist provides feedback and reinforces the couple's strengths and progress in positive communication. Once the couple feel competent to address non-emotive issues, they are encouraged to address problems which generally lead to communication difficulties, conflict, and lapses into dysfunctional patterns of interaction. When addressing difficult issues, the therapist can encourage the couple to draw on the strategies promoted throughout the intervention process, reinforcing adaptive strategies, consolidating relationship skills and supplementing the repertoire of the couple to manage challenges and relationship difficulties. A skilful relationship counsellor can help some couples to find the way out of a self-destroying maze. In the long run, such help will also assist the children trapped, like their parents, in the downwards spiral of misery and hurt.

SUMMARY

A few examples have been provided on how emotionally abusive parents can be helped directly to relate in a more positive way to their children and to better understand their children's developmental needs. Methods such as personal counselling and psychoeducation address those issues. Additionally, marital or couple therapy is often needed, as in many families where emotional abuse is a feature of children's lives it may also be a feature in the lives of the parents.

Marital work with violent and uncommitted partners or those who abuse alcohol or drugs is used either to get the couple to solve the problems in their relationship or to help them to separate if reconciliation is impossible and not wanted.

Family therapy is used to review family functioning by every member of the family and when a particular child is scapegoated by the parents and (at times) siblings as well. Different types of family therapy were discussed with specific focus on the systemic model.

SECTION 4

THE BURDEN OF PROOF: LEGAL AND SOCIAL WORK DIFFICULTIES IN DEALING WITH EMOTIONAL-ABUSE AND NEGLECT CASES

CHAPTER 16

THE BURDEN OF PROOF: LEGAL AND SOCIAL WORK DIFFICULTIES IN DEALING WITH EMOTIONAL-ABUSE AND NEGLECT CASES

CONTENTS

INTRODUCTION

Despite a growing body of research pointing to the negative effects of emotional abuse and neglect, cases are often not comprehensively assessed and seldom investigated with the same rigour as other forms of maltreatment. For an emotional-abuse case to reach court means that serious concerns about the child's welfare have been identified, and in many instances the case has been known to social services and a selective level of intervention in terms of family support has not been effective. A number of factors makes it difficult to determine threshold criteria for such abuse. For a behaviour to be legally or administratively categorised as abusive the behaviour must exceed a level of severity and chronicity that is perceived to put a child at risk of injury. However, it is difficult to establish and substantiate injury in cases of emotional abuse and neglect because of unclear physical and psychological indicators. In practice it is not easy to demonstrate that presenting problems in a child's behaviour and development are the results of psychological aggression and hostility, or emotional dismissal of the child by the parents or carers. Therefore, few cases of sole emotional abuse reach the threshold for significant harm (Straus & Field, 2003). Establishing psychological injury with reasonable confidence when assessing the case is problematic, as training of professionals relating to identification and assessment of child abuse is largely focused on physical and sexual abuse and neglect, and only superficially on emotional abuse. In addition, as emotional abuse alone has rarely led to coercive intervention, there are few established judicial precedents to guide court actions in such cases (Hart *et al.*, 2002). Without an expert witness (knowledgeable of emotional abuse) carrying out an independent assessment and advising the court of the effects of such abuse on the child, care orders are seldom made.

There is little doubt that making judgements as to where to draw the line between what is just harsh and unsympathetic parenting style and what is persistently hostile and seriously restrictive parental behaviour (which paralyses child development and leads to various emotional disturbances and a profound sense of helplessness) are rather difficult but not impossible. It is, at times, difficult to be absolutely sure that various disturbances are merely the result of emotional abuse and that another form of abuse is not taking place as well, or that other factors are not contributing to the child's disturbed emotional state and poor developmental attainment. Equally, it needs to be remembered that children vary in their reactions and developmental outcomes when experiencing adversities in their daily lives. Some show amazing resilience and survival capacity while others experiencing similar treatment succumb to ill effects. Each child, therefore, has to be dealt with individually in terms of vulnerability and resilience in his/her special family circumstances.

However, research has indicated that use of psychological aggression can be a more normative parenting tactic than is generally perceived in western culture. For example, a total of 90% of a national representative sample of Americans reported using at least 1 or more forms of psychological aggression during the previous 12 months (Straus & Field, 2003). Such low frequency of incidence (and probably intensity and duration) is seldom classified as emotional abuse, but rather as less optimal parenting. For the behaviour to be judged damaging, and therefore requiring legal action, it must show a clear and current danger to the child's developmental potentials (Garbarino *et al.*, 1997). However, a lack of clarity remains as to how frequent or severe the maltreatment must be in order to harm the child, although good knowledge about child development (and understanding of the dynamics of emotional abuse) should help in decision-making.

The threshold for significant harm in cases of emotional maltreatment appears to rest in a loosely defined point between labelling all forms of emotional aggression as abusive (which clearly it is not) and arguing that children are resilient to most forms of emotionally aggressive parental behaviour, which again is not true. While some children are untouched by parental hostility, others, who show more vulnerability, are affected by such parental action. It very much depends on the child's psychological make-up, and on the continuity of maltreatment and the intensity, severity, age of the child and duration, and availability of outside support systems which may aid as survival and escape. As Garbarino *et al.* (1997) note, the point at which a clear and present danger to a child's welfare arises can be set far too high.

When assessing threshold criteria it is important to examine the potential relative impact of factors such as sub-type, onset, frequency, severity, chronicity, and stage of development on the way in which the child cognitively processes experiences of being abused (Belsky, 1991; Manly *et al.*, 2001). It is also important to consider factors such as the nature of the relationship of the child to the abuser and the culture in which the acts occur (Hart *et al.*, 2002). Children who have reasonably open and frequent interaction with abusive parents may believe that parental behaviour is correct, although painful.

In comparison with other forms of maltreatment, few cases of emotional abuse and neglect reach the criteria for significant harm. Emotional abuse tends to be more likely to be judged to reach the threshold of significant harm in cases of persistent and severe emotional neglect, rejection, or abandonment, and in cases in which the child is mis-socialised, encouraged into prostitution, exposed to drugs and alcohol or family violence, and subjected to cruel or sadistic parental behaviours. Cases of emotional maltreatment that are combined with other forms of abuse (such as physical abuse, physical neglect, and sexual abuse) are also more likely to reach the threshold for significant harm. When such a case has been judged to have reached the criteria for significant harm the case proceeds to the public law courts where an application for a care order is made and a care plan drawn up to protect the child from subsequent harm. Children who have been judged to be at risk of significant harm, or to have suffered significant harm, require urgent intervention and generally require removal from the abusive environment.

This chapter will discuss various reasons why cases of sole emotional abuse seldom reach the courts, and why very few care orders are granted based on emotional abuse alone. Decision-making regarding the futures of these children by legal and social work professionals will be explored, and shortcomings of assessments (which often overlook repetitive and chronic parental behaviour leading to emotional harm) will be elaborated upon. The role of well-informed experts in advising the courts about the effects of emotional abuse on children and the necessity for multidisciplinary training will be briefly discussed.

LEGAL AND SOCIAL WORK DECISIONS IN CASES OF EMOTIONAL ABUSE

General statistics in relation to emotional abuse and neglect show that registration and application to the court to obtain an order have increased in the last decade. However, granting of a care order in cases of sole emotional abuse remains infrequent because of the absence of legal criteria to guide decision-making in setting up reliable and fair limits for meeting significant-harm requirements.

Legal decision-makers struggle to make sense of emotional abuse because it requires them to make judgements about parental behaviour and the existence and quality of parent–child interaction and relationships rather than basing their decision on well-documented and observed acts of harm to a child over a long period of time. To be considered as suitable to bring before the court, an application has to fit the definition and accompanying guidance of the Children Act 1989 (in England and Wales, and equivalents in Scotland and Northern Ireland), which states that, in order to consider emotional abuse as harmful, allowing court intervention, there must be proof that there is 'an actual or likely severe adverse effect on the emotional and behavioural development of a child caused by persistent or severe emotional ill-treatment or rejection' (DoH, 1991).

The above definition requires not only well-informed interpretation of the parental behaviour and the effect on the developing child, but also good understanding as to what are the likely long-term consequences if the ill-treatment or abuse continues. As what may or may not happen in the future is uncertain, the legal and social work professions shy away from making assumptions that emotionally inappropriate parental behaviour may cause a child serious harm which can linger to the next generation of parenting. Legal judgements are made on facts and certainties and not on assumptions; therefore, decisions in such cases are difficult to make. Additionally, the very private and highly nebulous, intangible qualities of emotional abuse make it a difficult concept to define, interpret, and judge in a useful, operational, and legal sense. Equally, problematic parental behaviour in this area of child maltreatment is often hard to judge because it is largely a relative judgement and a socially subjective one. The value-laden nature of judgments goes against any uniformly accepted framework.

By contrast to physical and sexual abuse (which are event-driven), and incidents of abuse (which are relatively easy to identify and prove as abusive), emotional maltreatment and neglect are based on repetitive, chronic, accumulative acts of parental behaviour which do not always show serious ill effects reaching significant harm at the time of investigation (although they may show serious cause for concern). Ayre (1998) stated that the child-protection system is activated only when it is believed that the threshold of significant harm has been crossed and the child-protection service can make a case against parents in the courts. Hesitations and apprehensions regarding processing such cases through the courts do not apply only to the legal profession, but also to social workers and others who, one way or another, deal with child-abuse cases. Dingwall, Eckelaar, and Murray (1983) postulated that child-protection workers showed a tendency to view emotional abuse as something that is not quite good, but not serious enough to warrant legal proceedings simply because parents love their children, and they were reluctant to look for evidence to prove maltreatment. Only when parents refused to participate in problem-resolution did they reframe their attitudes and opinion. Such optimism and beliefs proved to be dangerous to many children and exposed them to unnecessary pain and emotional hardship.

Iwaniec and Hill (2000) found that often no action was taken when cases of emotional abuse and neglect were referred, both in terms of further assessment of needs and investigation for protection purposes. Such decision and practices are based on conflicting principles arising from the philosophy of the Children Act (1989) which is seen, on the one hand, 'as no Order Act, but on the other, that the welfare of the child is paramount' and that 'delays in decision-making should be avoided'. Additionally, working in partnership with parents is advocated and parental responsibilities are included in the legal framework.

APPLICATIONS TO THE COURT

Applications for a care order in cases of sole emotional abuse are infrequent due to the difficulties in proving that significant harm criteria have been reached and that such harm resulted from emotional maltreatment, and not for other reasons. These cases, however, should not be more challenging to take through the courts than any other cases of different types of problems and concerns about child welfare and safety if they are serious enough to take action. The courts are looking for evidence that parental behaviour and quality of childcare are not just of poor quality, but put a child at risk of serious long-term emotional damage. A child who shows considerable developmental delays and emotional problems because of parental rejection, violent behaviour within the family, persistent verbal hostility, threats, unrealistic expectations, emotional tormenting, or crippling overprotection (to mention just a few), has no less serious problems than those presented by a child who has been physically abused by his parents. What is important in such cases is an identification of harm that a child is currently suffering, or likely to suffer, if parental behaviour is not going to change. Equally, it is important to assess parental capacity to change within the child's developmental time-span.

Children cannot wait indefinitely for their parents to give up chronic alcohol abuse resulting in violence and neglect (or drug misuse and constant aggravation), or to overcome mental-health problems, to be able to facilitate emotional nurturing, and so on. Children have to acquire skills and competencies of different kinds to be prepared for independent living and to develop interpersonal relationship skills to learn how to relate and interact with other people. They need to be provided with the behavioural model which will give them examples of what is good and appropriate and what is a sensitive and responsible lifestyle.

Emotionally abusive parents not only do not facilitate appropriate developmental attainments, but they seriously disturb developmental processes and trigger off and maintain emotional problems of equally serious consequences (e.g. bizarre eating patterns, anorexia nervosa, encopresis, enuresis, stealing, running away, elective mutism, attempted suicide, and self-harming behaviour, among other problems). While physical abuse can kill or cripple a child for life, it is true to say that emotional abuse can and does also incapacitate emotionally for life. For example, children who are exposed to crippling overprotection, or who have been persistently denigrated and ridiculed in a hostile way (creating overwhelming self-doubt and low self-esteem) may not be able to function independently and confidently as adults, to believe in themselves, to make appropriate decisions nor to provide nurturing and sensitive care for their own children as adults. 'One cannot pour from an empty jug'; in other words, one cannot expect emotionally maltreated children to become nurturing parents. These parents need constructive, basic training on parenting and better understanding of how their careless and abusive behaviour affects the child. Unless these children are helped during the formative years of their lives, the likelihood is that the harm they experienced as children will continue to reflect on their functioning as parents.

There is plenty of evidence presented in the literature, and in the previous chapters of this book, to review the way we deal with emotional-abuse cases. Some cases will need to go to court in order to protect children from daily emotional pain, fear, anxiety, and subsequent harm, while others can be dealt with in the community. It will be necessary to demonstrate to the court that evidence of emotional abuse gathered over time, and coming from various sources, constitutes a legitimate reason to seek an order. It is also necessary to inform the court as to what preventive family-support measures have been tried in order to help the parents, the parents' ability and motivation to make use of help provided to them, and the level of their emotional capacity to take and to give.

Expert assessments may be of help in complicated cases and of assistance to the courts in decision-making.

CHILDREN'S RIGHTS AND THE PARENTS' RIGHTS AS LEGAL REQUIREMENTS

The child-centred approach to assessment and intervention made an enormous contribution to enhancing the rights of children in all areas of child welfare and protection. Knowledge about children's rights has increased and practices in how to implement and protect these rights have improved in recent years (Kilkenny *et al.*, 2005). Less is known, however, about the European Convention of Human Rights in relation to the rights of parents and, in particular, in cases of enforced accommodation and care order application. It is important to observe the principles of human rights as the Convention dictates when dealing with removal of children from parental care, either through accommodation or care order application.

The way accommodation is used is, at times, in sharp contrast to what the Children Act 1989 intended, as found by a number of studies (Brandon *et al.*, 1999; Donaldson, 2003; Hunt *et al.*, 1999). In some instances parents are not clearly informed or given written notification as to what is happening and how long the child will be looked after, what the parents should do to get their children back, and what services/help are going to be given to assist them in a process of change. It was also found that parents were threatened with taking the case to court if they did not agree to voluntary reception into care. At times parental fear and vulnerability are used instead of informed consent and clear information when trying to safeguard the child and protect it from possible harm. Such situations are very difficult for social workers, as they are often trapped in a no-win situation. However, it needs to be remembered that parents have rights too, and they deserve to be treated with respect, according to the requirements of the European Convention on Human Rights. The Convention was incorporated into domestic legislation in October 2000 as a further challenge to social work and legal practices.

The Human Rights Act 1998 has been described 'as probably the most important piece of constitutional legislation this century' (Donaldson, 2003). It has been said that the effect of the Act is to 'bring rights home' (p. 9). The rights referred to are those set out in the European Convention on Human Rights and Fundamental Freedoms (ECHR). The Human Rights Act (1998) incorporates the Convention into law of the United Kingdom and allows those rights set out in the ECHR to be enforceable in domestic courts. There are two articles relevant to this book arising from the ECHR: Article 6, Right to a Fair Trial, and Article 8, Right to Family Life.

The importance of ECHR compliance in the conduct of activities aimed at protecting the child is of growing concern to the courts (Donaldson,

2003). This is reflected in the judgements from the European Court of Human Rights. It is also increasingly of concern in domestic courts as is apparent in two judgements that will be discussed in relation to Articles 6 and 8.

Article 6 of the ECHR deals with the determination of an individual's civil rights and obligations and sets out the entitlement to a fair trial and public hearing within a reasonable time by an independent and impartial tribunal established by law. J. Munby in *Re* C (care proceedings: disclosure of local authority's decision-making process) (2002) EWHC 1379 (Fam) outlined concerns about how parents' rights under the European Convention on Human Rights could be compromised. Of particular concern to the court were a number of crucial decision-making 'professional meetings' at which the mother was not in attendance and not represented, nor was there an agenda of what was to be discussed or minutes of what was discussed. In a far-reaching judgment Munby pointed out that rights under Article 6 (Right to a Fair Trial) were 'absolute' and were not confined to the 'purely judicial' process; unfair treatment at any part of the litigation process could involve a breach not only of Article 8 (Right to Family Life) but also of Article 6. As has been mentioned there was evidence that the decision that the child should be accommodated was not always one that parents were involved in, and once the child became looked after it could be more difficult for the parent to have the child returned to their care.

A recent judgement from the Court of Appeal in Northern Ireland has focused attention on the parents' Article 8 rights when social services are taking action to protect a child. The case in question was the removal of a newborn baby at birth, where there was a history of alcohol misuse by both parents and three children from the family were already in care. The judgement from the Court of Appeal contained this important observation:

> In all the great volume of written material generated by the Trust in this case we have been unable to find a single reference to Article 8. If the Trust had addressed the issue of the mother's Convention rights (as it certainly should have done) there would surely have been some mention of this in the papers. We are driven to the conclusion that the Trust did not consider the question of the appellant's Article 8 rights at any stage. Quite apart from that consideration, however, we consider that it is a virtually impossible task to ensure protection of these rights without explicit recognition that these rights were engaged. ([2005] NICA 8 KER F5204 p. 35)

The case before the Court of Appeal was found by the judges to be one where the mother's Convention rights were infringed because there was no explicit recognition of her right to family life in the action taken by the Trust to protect a child believed to be at risk. The actions taken by the Trust were all under the supervision of the court.

The judgement from the Court of Appeal is particularly pertinent to the focus of this discussion as it also commented on the issue of permanence and the balance to be achieved with other factors when making decisions about a child's future care:

> It is not surprising that research into the subject discloses that it is desirable that permanent arrangements be made for a child as soon as possible. Uncertainty as to his future, even for a very young child, can be deeply unsettling. Changes to daily routine will have an impact and a child needs to feel secure as to who his carers are. It is not difficult to imagine how disturbing it must be for a child to be taken from a caring environment and placed with someone who is unfamiliar to him. It is therefore entirely proper that this factor should have weighed heavily with the Trust and with the Judge in deciding what is best for him. But, as we have said this factor must not be isolated from other matters that should be taken into account in this difficult decision. It is important to recognise that the long term welfare of a child can be affected by the knowledge that he has been taken from his natural parents, particularly if he discovers it was against their will. ([2005] NICA 8 KER F5204 p. 36)

GATHERING INFORMATION

As emotional abuse or neglect are not event-led, information about incidents, observation of parental behaviour, attitudes and actions towards the child, as well as their interaction and quality of relationships, need to be systematically recorded. Equally, information regarding the child's behaviour, reactions, developmental outcomes, emotional disturbances, and other concerns coming from professionals, various family members, or neighbours have to be noted. Such information is essential for proving that a child has been exposed to harmful parental or other carers' behaviour or actions for a considerable time, and that such parental behaviour has had disturbing effects on a child's development, growth, self-esteem, attachment, educational attainments, ability to form interpersonal relationships (particularly with peers), and so on. The list is endless. The chronology must be compiled before the case goes to court by social workers and guardians, to evidence significant harm or likely significant harm.

The usefulness of chronologies has been noted by many researchers, lawyers and judges (e.g. Hunt *et al.*, 1999; Donaldson, 2003; Allweis, 2000; Iwaniec *et al.*, 2004). Judge Allweis (2000) emphasised the importance of taking an overview of the case, rather than concentrating on isolated events or problems, when dealing with cases of neglect or emotional abuse. In the paper to the Rochdale Area Child Protection Committee, Judge Allweis noted that the failure of senior managers to take a dispassionate view of family functioning (to see the wood from the trees) caused delays in dealing with such cases. Commenting on the judicial experience in dealing with emotional abuse and neglect he also noted that once the evidence was collated and presented in a chronologically explicit way, the evidence of neglect or emotional abuse was often overwhelming, so that the only real issue was not what had happened, but what should happen in terms of the care plan. Judicial guidance on gathering and organising information from, at times, many case files, relating to the harm of the child due to emotional abuse, can also assist practitioners.

Donaldson, in her study of *The Changing Face of Care* (2003), draws our attention to the importance of chronology in cases of care order applications and, when the chronology of harmful incidents, actions, and behaviour was provided by the children's guardian, it assisted the court in decision-making and speeding up the proceedings. She also reported that in most cases where children were accommodated, social services failed to compile a chronology of events, in spite of the fact that reports were prepared for child-protection case conferences and Looked After Children (LAC) reviews. The absence of a chronology in cases of children being looked after (through the provision of accommodation) was a cause for concern, as it was difficult to disentangle (from often badly recorded bulk files) what was evidence, and what were opinions, assumptions, and perceptions, at times of dubious value. In comparison, the cases involving children who were the subject of care proceedings were always accompanied by a chronology. This is an important point from the 'good practice' point of view, as is an ability to provide good-quality, relevant information when it becomes necessary (and often at short notice). Good organisation of gathered data is essential when transfer of a case to another social worker takes place, and for decision-making purposes.

DECISION-MAKING

When and how to intervene in cases of emotional abuse is not only a problem for social workers, but also for the legal profession. Social workers often believe that legal decision-making in such cases favours the carer over the child. At the same time, social workers may appear to lawyers to allow the cases to drift for a long time – at times for years – because of the inability to substantiate the effect of emotional maltreatment on a child. If a case of emotional abuse or neglect eventually reaches court there may be overwhelming evidence of harm to the child and, as a result, the judiciary and, indeed, children's guardians, may be at a loss to understand why the case was not brought sooner so the harm could have been terminated earlier. This state of affairs is not surprising as social workers have to deal with conflicting issues (such as the rights of the child versus the rights of the parents, the European Convention on Human Rights, and the principle of minimal intervention). Additionally, attempting to prove, and reaching a decision, that emotional abuse has attained a level of significant harm can be something to avoid rather than confront, because of the burden of proof which courts require to make an order. The tension between the courts and social services is well-documented by researchers and practitioners (Masson, 2000; Donaldson, 2003; Hunt *et al.*, 1999) and described as 'uneasy'. Social workers often feel that they are badly treated by the legal profession, while lawyers feel that they are just doing their work as the adversarial system requires.

The view of social work within the court context, and the ease with which court professionals can dismiss the social work contribution, is another factor that requires attention if appropriate referral of emotional abuse is to be realised. The difficulty for the social worker of presenting cases of emotional abuse and neglect in the context of an adversarial legal system cannot be underestimated. The adversarial system works on the principle that the best solution will result from vigorous challenging and arguments, and the rules provide both sides with a fair opportunity to persuade the court. The court is there to ensure that it is a fair fight, and that each party gets a fair hearing.

INDEPENDENT ASSESSMENT OF EXPERT WITNESS

In order for the judge or magistrate to make a decision as to the best solution for the child, he or she will need to have an expert opinion about the child's development, interpretation of the child's disturbed behaviour, parental capacity to change, personality profile, or any state of mental health or disability which might stand in the way of positive parenting. In emotional-abuse cases assessment of attachment of children to parents and parental bonding to children will be of interest and importance as it will help development of a focused care plan addressing emotional deficit in trust and relationship-building of a child. Expert witnesses are appointed by the court and their duties are to the court rather than to individual parties. Experts are independent and unconnected with the cases they are assessing and on which they are advising. Finding well-informed and reliable experts who can quickly do the work is difficult. Assessment by expert witnesses was identified as a major contributing factor to unnecessary delay in Larkin, McSherry, and Iwaniec's (2005) study. Delay, attributable to a slow process of appointing expert witnesses and of negotiating costs with legal aid, has been highlighted by many researchers (Donaldson, 2003; Hunt *et al.*, 1999; McSherry *et al.*, 2004). A particular shortage of parenting and mental-health experts leads to extra costs, as such people have to be brought from distant places. In order to shorten waiting-time in gathering different experts' reports, and to reduce the cost, a joint letter of instruction from the social services and parents is often issued to share the services of one expert. It has been found that letters of instruction to the experts are not always well thought-through (e.g. seeking information which is not of prime importance to the case, so time is spent investigating issues of dubious value). At times instructions to the expert are far too wide and lengthy, requesting not the opinion of an expert but a full-blown investigation, and a care plan for the child. To prepare such a report is both costly and time-consuming, so care should be taken when instructing an expert to do an independent assessment. An appropriate or carefully thought-through letter of instruction can reduce delays and costs. However, engagement of expert witnesses is essential in complicated cases to protect the child and the liberty and rights of parents. An impartial, well-informed assessment is crucial in emotional-abuse cases in order to help the judge arrive at a fair evidence-based decision.

ISSUES FOR SOCIAL WORKERS AND LAWYERS WORKING TOGETHER

For the reasons stated above the application to court of an emotional-abuse and neglect case tends to be made only after other options have been tried and failed. However, social workers are anxious to avoid court proceedings. It can be argued that while a reduction in the number of cases coming before the court (of all types of abuse) might have been a result of legislative change, it appears that children who have been exposed to emotionally harmful parenting might have benefited by their cases being brought before the court sooner (as demonstrated by the case study in Chapter 12, p. 279). If Liza's case had been brought to court a few years earlier the likelihood is that she would not have developed anorexia; would have been free, by now, of bed-wetting; would not have self-harmed; and would not present as an extremely emotionally disturbed teenager. Factors that potentially exacerbate difficulties in decision-making in chronic and acute emotional abuse have been discussed throughout this book, and various reasons why this is the case have been debated; these concerned social services processes – the organisation of information in case files, accessing appropriate assessments, engagement of families suspicious of social services' intervention – and balancing positives and negatives in the functioning of families.

As was stated earlier, social workers find the court environment anxiety-provoking, alien, and discomfiting, so they reluctantly make an application in cases of neglect and emotional abuse, not only because court work is difficult to them in a general sense, but also because emotional abuse (in its own right) is difficult to prove at the best of times, but in particular by an inexperienced person. Additionally, skills required for successful navigation through the legal process appears to be complicated by the frequent turnover of staff in the family- and childcare teams. Quite often very junior and inexperienced staff members are asked to present in court a case (which may be of poor quality due to lack of confidence and experience) and which, in turn, may impede the credence given by the judge or magistrate. The lack of confidence of social workers in their own expertise and that of their legal department is demonstrated by being wary of challenging a guardian, or presenting a care plan without the backing of an expert (Donaldson, 2003; Iwaniec *et al.*, 2004). Shortage of resources further complicates application of cases to court.

These problems are not unique to British social workers or to the legal profession. The study carried out by Sheehan (2001) in Australia, of magistrates' decision-making in child protection, found that welfare practitioners were the dominant suppliers of case information to the court. However, magistrates tended to express doubts about State intervention in family life; they also questioned how information on family life was gathered and whether child-protection workers were competent in what they were doing; as a result they were reluctant to rely on the evidence provided by welfare workers. In addition, as the application was brought by the welfare agency, welfare workers were viewed as the 'prosecutors' in an adversarial system. Magistrates (not unreasonably) argued that the welfare staff could not be both objective witnesses and 'prosecutors' at the same time.

Donaldson, in her study *The Changing Face of Care* (2003), found that when the case entered the legal process, social workers found themselves operating in a different, unfamiliar system with different aims and objectives. It is argued that the lack of certainty expressed in statements made by social workers disappoints the law's demand for decisiveness and finality (King & Piper, 1990). Lawyers may complain that they are not given clear answers regarding children's outcomes, but it is not always clear in the cases of emotional abuse as to what these outcomes may be. Some children are more resilient than others, and it is not always apparent at the time of investigation what protective factors may emerge in the course of children's lives. Predictions, however, can be made which are based on empirical evidence accumulated from other similar cases. It is important, therefore, to be familiar with research in the area of concern. It has been argued that clashes between social work professionals and lawyers have a lot to do with differences in ideological values rather than disputes over the likely outcomes. The demands of the legal process and the court's need for clear evidence in order to determine what should happen to a child may not be the most important issues in the minds of social workers, who may desire to keep the case away from court in the first place. On the other hand, better preparation of social workers for the demands of the legal process might well act as a counterbalance to the view that court applications should be avoided at all costs. Such change of attitudes may also improve the management of cases as they come before the court.

There is good evidence that written judgements are particularly important as they may produce valuable practice guidance from members of the judiciary experienced in dealing with emotional abuse and neglect cases (Allweis, 2000). Of course, it is not argued that every case will lend itself to such far-reaching judgement; however, a clear pronouncement on the evidence that was, and was not, persuasive might assist in the preparation of other cases for court. It is, therefore, argued that better use should be made of judgements and case law through training for social workers, and that such judgements should be appropriately interpreted. It is also argued that social workers, during their training, should routinely observe contested cases and direction hearings in order to demystify the court process and help them to learn court skills.

While social workers need to learn more about legal processes and adapt to court behaviour, lawyers have to become more familiar with and better informed about problems of human development and the psychopathology of family and community functioning. Mutual training would benefit both parties.

TRAINING

The expectations expressed by the Children Act of creating a unified and well-informed jurisdiction to manage the court cases effectively and expertly have not been fully achieved. Concerns have been raised that the levels of training and expertise across all professional groups need to improve. Inconsistencies in court requirements for specialist expertise of counsel and accreditation of solicitors were identified by McSherry et al. (2004). They noted that the lack of requirements for accreditation was a common problem that contributed to protracted proceedings, with some solicitors being unfamiliar with the tasks and issues with which they were expected to deal, and trying to learn while the case was progressing. It was also noted in McSherry et al.'s project that, despite the complex child-protection work being dealt with by the courts, some individuals were operating in the courts without sufficient training or knowledge to provide competent service to the courts or children and families involved. Many of those interviewed felt that compulsory training for all, including the judiciary, would be beneficial, and refresher and up-dating courses or seminars would keep professionals up-to-date with rapidly changing family law.

Many studies pointed to the fact that many social workers have not sufficient experience to prepare and deal with the cases in the court. As court work takes up a sizeable proportion of a social worker's workload, in-depth training about the litigation would be beneficial and would help social workers to approach court work with a higher level of confidence (Hunt et al., 1999; Donaldson, 2003; McSherry et al., 2004).

Joint short courses (or, at least, seminars on emotional abuse and neglect) are of particular importance to all who have to make decisions about these children's future and work out suitable care plans. It is now widely recognised that provision of interdisciplinary training would benefit identifying, assessing for seriousness, and processing emotional maltreatment cases through the courts, as well as learning from each other about the professional and legal constraints within which each professional must operate. For example, social workers often complain that they are being criticised in court for issues outside their control that can lead to delay or less adequate quality of the report (such as insufficient resources, supervision, and lack of experience). Equally, social workers have to learn that legal professions have to conduct their work within the legal framework and adhere their conduct to 'the letter of the law'. There is no doubt that awareness of each professional's roles and responsibilities within court work has increased substantially, and there are some excellent examples of interdisciplinary promotion of learning together (Allweis, 1999), but we have a long way to go to feel comfortable 'in each other's company' in the courtroom, where the welfare of the child should be the major concern of us all.

A Way Forward – Joining Hands Together to Help Children

As very few cases of emotional abuse (which went through the court process) have been published by the judges, there is an obvious lack of knowledge of how the cases were judged and what factors and information helped to make a final decision. It would be helpful if ways were found to bring the judicial decision-making processes into the public domain, so others can learn how they are formulated, and what is needed to make such process easier. The best way to achieve better understanding of how emotional abuse is seen and understood is to have joint training of all those who are charged to deal with these cases at different times, starting from identification, through assessment and attempts to help these families, and then making application to the court and court proceedings. There is no better way than to have a case-study approach to learning, as each professional will present the case and identify problems within his or her professional orientation and work remit, which can then be questioned, clarified, and justified. Mutual discussion can lead to better informed decision-making in relation to the child and parents. Such joint training could enhance confidence of all concerned as it would increase knowledge about consequences of serious emotional abuse, would provide opportunities for professionals outside the legal system to become familiar with legal language, and such fora may help in interpreting labels and definitions in a helpful and operational way. Training of this kind would need to have an expert on emotional abuse, so the debate about emotional abuse and neglect would be well-informed and accurate.

The problem of multidisciplinary training is a difficult one as it requires time away from the courtroom or hospital where judges and doctors have to be dealing with the very cases about which we are worried. However, such training is essential if cases of emotional abuse and neglect are to be dealt with effectively and appropriately. Unfortunately, the training that child-protection workers, judges, police, prosecutors, doctors, teachers, health visitors, and others associated with childcare receive on the topic of child maltreatment focuses almost exclusively on recognising, evidencing, and proving physical and sexual abuse or acute (easy to see) physical neglect. Until recently (since the effect of domestic violence was recognised as harmful to children) the documentation of children's mental injuries related to emotional maltreatment has, sadly, never been an essential element of professional training for those with legal responsibilities to intervene in cases of serious harm to children. It is generally felt that the legal profession has to make an effort to familiarise itself with the manifestations and conse-quences of emotional abuse, while child-protection workers and others dealing with children must learn that courts need evidence of abuse and clear statements based on facts, and how such abuse harmed, or is likely to harm, a child.

The picture of judges' involvement in training or attending conferences varies across the United Kingdom, and there is an upward trend of interest and participation. For example, the senior family judge from Manchester County Court frequently gives talks at training events and conferences about substantive issues (e.g. neglect or emotional abuse), and how such cases should be prepared for the court.

SUMMARY

The difficulties for social workers in presenting a case of emotional abuse within the legal process have been noted. From judicial perspectives, drawing on experience of hearing cases of emotional abuse or neglect over many years, it is argued that obvious signs of emotional maltreatment are often overlooked or ignored by social services. The reason for the lack of decisive action, culminating in an application to court, can include agencies failing to consider an overview of the case and not co-operating to make crucial decisions that will benefit the child. The difficulties for social workers in bringing a case of emotional abuse or neglect to the court have been discussed, pointing to the conflicting requirements of the Children Act (1989), and chronic shortage of human and material resources. Poor under-standing of the mechanisms triggering and maintaining emotional prob-lems, and inadequate knowledge of normal child development and developmental psychopathology are briefly discussed, pointing to the reasons why significant harm is not always recognised. It is hoped that greater awareness will stimulate the development of strategies to counteract impediments to making early enough decisions.

A chronology summarising key features and events in the case history has been noted to be of benefit, not only to social work practitioners in their decision-making, but also to the court after proceedings have been commenced. Equally, comprehensive assessments (including expert opinion on emotional abuse and psychological or psychiatric viewpoints concerning parental functioning) are important to decision-making both in and out of the court. It is hoped that the new Framework for the Assessment of Children in Need and Their Families will facilitate a broad, integrated approach to assessment. In addition, the Protocol for Judicial Case Management in Public Law Children Act Cases recognises the problems facing seriously understaffed social services' departments, focuses on the need to make better use of available resources, identifies the need for social work chronology of significant dates and events in the child's life, and provides an invaluable social services assessment and care-planning aide-memoire.

It has been noted that social workers would benefit from training in court skills to give them confidence when dealing with complex legal issues. The court, on the other hand, critical on occasions of the actions of social workers, also needs to develop a greater understanding of the problems.

REFERENCES

Aber, J.L., & Cicchetti, D. (1984). The socio-emotional development of maltreated children: An empirical and theoretical analysis. In H. Fitzgerald, B. Lester, & M. Yogman (Eds.), *Theory and research in behavioural pediatrics* (Vol. **2**, pp. 147–199). New York: Plenum Press.

Achenbach, T.M., Howell, C.T., Aoki, M.F., & Rauh, V.A. (1993). Nine year outcome of the Vermont Intervention program for low birth weight infants. *Pediatrics*, **91** (1), 45–55.

Acton, R.G., & During, S.M. (1992). Preliminary results of aggression management training for aggressive parents. *Journal of Interpersonal Violence*, **7**, 410–417.

Agnew, R. (1992). Foundation for a general strain theory of crime and delinquency. *Criminology*, **30**, 47–88.

Ahmed, Y., Whitney, I., & Smith, P. K. (1991). A survey service for schools on bully/victim problems. In P.K. Smith & D.A. Thompson (Eds.), *Practical approaches to bullying*. London: David Fulton.

Ainsworth, M.D.S. (1980). Attachment and child abuse. In G. Gerbner, C.J. Ross, & E. Zigler (Eds.), *Child abuse: An agenda for action* (pp. 35–47). New York: Oxford University Press.

Ainsworth, M.D.S. (1982). Early caregiving and later patterns of attachment. In M.H. Klaus & M.O. Robertson (Eds.), *Birth, interaction and attachment, exploring the foundations for modern perinatal care*. Skillman, NJ: Johnson and Johnson Baby Products Pediatric Round Table Series.

Ainsworth, M.D.S. (1989). Attachments beyond the infancy. *American Psychologist*, **44**, 709–716.

Ainsworth, M.D.S., Blehar, M.C., Waters, E., & Wall, S. (1978). *Patterns of attachment: A psychological study of the strange situation*. Hillsdale, NJ: Lawrence Erlbaum.

Alexander, J.F., Holtzworth-Monroe, A., & Jameson, P. (1994). Research on the process and outcome of marriage and family therapy. In A.E. Bergin & S.L. Garfield (Eds.), *Handbook of psychotherapy and behaviour change* (4th ed.). New York: John Wiley & Sons.

Alexander, P.A. (1992). Application of attachment theory to the study of child sexual abuse. *Journal of Consulting and Clinical Psychology*, **60**, 185–195.

Alison, L. (2000). What are the risks to children of parental substance misuse? In F. Harbin & M. Murphy (Eds.), *Substance misuse and child care: How to understand, assist and intervene when drugs affect parenting*. Lyme Regis: Russell House Publishing.

Allweis, M. (2000). Neglect and Assessment – A Judicial Perspective. Paper given at Rochdale Area Child Protection Committee (ACPC) conference, 13 October 2000.

American Professional Society on the Abuse of Children (APSAC, 1995). *Guidelines for the Psychosocial Evaluation of Suspected Psychological Maltreatment in Children and Adolescents*. Chicago, IL: APSAC.

Ammerman, R.T. (1992). Sexually abused children with multiple disabilities: Each is unique, as are their needs. *NRCCSA News*, **1** (4), 13–14.

Ammerman, R.T., & Baladerian, N.J. (1993). *Maltreatment of children with disabilities*. National Committee to Prevent Child Abuse. Chicago, IL: APSAC.

Ammerman, R.T., & Patz, R.J. (1996). Determinants of child abuse potential: Contribution of parent and child factors. *Journal of Clinical Child Psychology*, **25** (3), 300–307.

Ammerman, R.T., Kolko, D.J., Kirisci, L., Blackman, T.C., & Dawes, M.A. (1999). Child abuse potential in parents with histories of substance use disorders. *Child Abuse and Neglect*, **23** (12), 1225–1238.

Arias, I. (2004). The legacy of child maltreatment: Long-term health consequences for women. *Journal of Women's Health*, **13** (5), 468–473.

Axford, N., Little, M., Madge, F., & Morpeth, L. (2001). *Children supported and unsupported in the community: Analysis of the descriptive data and implications for policy and practice*. Dartington: Dartington Social Research Unit.

Axline, V.M. (1969). *Play therapy*. New York: Ballantine Books.

Axline, V.M. (1971). *Dibs: In search of self*. Harmondsworth: Penguin.

Ayre, P. (1998). Significant harm: Making professional judgments. *Child Abuse Review*, **7**, 330–342.

Azar, S., & Wolfe, D. (1998). Child physical abuse and neglect. In E.J. Mash & R.A. Barkley (Eds.), *Treatment of childhood disorders* (2nd ed., pp. 501–544). New York: Guilford Press.

Azar, S.T., & Siegel, B.R. (1990). Behavioural treatment of child abuse: A developmental perspective. *Behaviour Modification*, **14**, 279–300.

Azar, S.T., Robinson, D.R., Hekimian, E., & Twentyman, C.T. (1984). Unrealistic expectations and problem-solving ability in maltreating and comparison mothers. *Journal of Consulting and Clinical Psychology*, **52**, 687–691.

Baldry, A.C. (2003). Bullying in schools and exposure to domestic violence. *Child Abuse and Neglect*, **27** (7), 713–732.

Bandura, A. (1977). *Social learning theory*. Englewood Cliffs, New York, NY: Prentice-Hall.

Barahal, R.M., Waterman, J., & Martin, H.P. (1981). The social cognitive development of abused children. *Journal of Consulting and Clinical Psychology*, **49**, 508–516.

Barnett, B., & Parker, G. (1998). The parentified child: Early competence or childhood deprivation? *Child Psychology and Psychiatry Review*, **3** (4), 146–155.

Barter, C. (2003). *Abuse of children in residential care*. NSPCC Information Briefing, October 2003, London.

Beck, A.T. (1976). *Cognitive therapy and the emotional disorders*. New York: New American Library.

Beck, A.T., & Weishaar, M. (1989). Cognitive therapy. In H. Arkowitz, L.E. Beutler, A. Freeman, & K. Simon (Eds.), *Handbook of cognitive therapy*. Dordrecht: Kluwer Academic.

Beck, G. (1995). Bullying among young offenders in custody. In N.K. Clarke & G.M. Stephenson (Eds.), *Criminal behaviour: Perceptions, attributions and rationality*. Issues in Criminological and Legal Psychology No. 22. Leicester: The British Psychological Society.

Behl, L.E., Conyngham, H.A., & May, P.F. (2003). Trends in child maltreatment literature. *Child Abuse and Neglect*, **27** (2), 215–229.

Beidel, D.C., Turner, S.M., & Morris, T.L. (2000). Behavioural treatment of childhood social phobia. *Journal Consulting and Clinical Psychology*, **68**, 1072–1080.

Belsky, J. (1980). Child maltreatment: An ecological integration. *American Psychologist*, **35**, 320–335.

Belsky, J. (1984). The determinants of parenting: A process model. *Child Development*, **55**, 83–96.

Belsky, J. (1991). Psychological maltreatment: Definitional limitations and unstated assumptions. *Developmental Psychopathology*, **3**, 31–36.

Belsky, J. (1993). Etiology of child maltreatment: A developmental-ecological analysis. *Psychological Bulletin*, **14**, 413–434.

Belsky, J. (1999). Interactional and contextual determinants of attachment security. In J. Cassidy & P. Shaver (Eds.), *Handbook on attachment, theory, research and clinical applications*. New York: Guilford Press.

Belsky, J., & Cassidy, L. (1994). Attachment theory and evidence. In M. Rutter & D. Hay (Eds.), *Development through life* (pp. 373–402). London: Blackwell Science.

Belsky, J., & Stratton, P. (2002). An ecological analysis of the etiology of child maltreatment. In K. Browne, H. Hanks, P. Stratton, & C. Hamilton (Eds.), *Early prediction and prevention of child abuse: A handbook*. Chichester: John Wiley & Sons.

Belsky, J., & Vondra, J. (1989). Lessons from child abuse: The determinants of parenting. In D. Cicchetti & V. Carlson (Eds.), *Child maltreatment: Theory and research on the causes and consequences of child abuse and neglect*. Cambridge and New York: Cambridge University Press.

Benbenishty, R., Zeira, A., & Astor, R.A. (2002). Children's reports of emotional, physical and sexual maltreatment by educational staff in Israel. *Child Abuse and Neglect*, **26** (8), 763–782.

Benedict, M.I., White, R.B., Wulff, L.M., & Hall, B.J. (1990). Reported maltreatment of children with multiple disabilities. *Child Abuse and Neglect*, **14**, 207–217.

Bierman, K.L., & Furman, W. (1984). The effects of social skills training and peer involvement on the social adjustment of preadolescents. *Child Development*, **55**, 151–162.

Bifulco, A., Brown, G.W., & Harris, T. (1987). Childhood loss of parent, lack of adequate parental care and adult depression: A replication. *Journal of Affective Disorder*, **12**, 115–128.

Binggeli, N.J., Hart, S.N., & Brassard, M.R. (2001). *Psychological maltreatment: A study guide*. Thousand Oaks, CA: Sage.

Bithoney, W.G., & Newberger, E.H. (1987). Child and family attributes of failure to thrive. *Journal of Developmental and Behavioural Pediatrics*, **8** (1), 32–36.

Black, D.A., Smith Slep, A.M., & Heyman, R.E. (2001). Risk factors for child psychological abuse. *Aggression and Violent Behavior*, **6** (2/3), 189–201.

Blakemore, S.J. (2005, February). Life before three, play or hot-housing? *RSA Journal*, pp. 36–39.

Blizzard, R.M., & Bulatovic, A. (1993). Psychological short stature: A syndrome with many variables. *Baillière's Clinical Endocrinology and Metabolism*, **6** (3), 637–712.

Bowlby, J. (1958). The nature of the child's tie to his mother. *International Journal of Psychoanalysis*, **39**, 350–373.

Bowlby, J. (1969). *Attachment and loss: Attachment*. New York: Basic Books.

Bowlby, J. (1973). *Attachment and loss: Vol. 2. Separation, anxiety and anger*. Harmondsworth: Penguin.

Bowlby, J. (1984). *Attachment and loss: Vol. 1. Attachment* (2nd ed.). Harmondsworth: Penguin.

Bowlby, J. (1988). *A secure base. Clinical application of attachment theory*. London: Routledge.

Brandon, M., Thoburn, J., Lewis, A., & Way, A. (1999). *Safeguarding children with the Children Act 1989*. London: Stationery Office.

Brassard, M.R., Germain, R., & Hart, S.N. (1987). *Psychological maltreatment of children and youth*. New York: Pergamon Press.

Bream, V., & Buchanan, A. (2003). Distress among children whose separated or divorced parents cannot agree arrangements for them. *British Journal of Social Work*, **33**, 227–238.

Brennan, K.A., Shaver, P.R., & Tobey, A.E. (1991). Attachment styles, gender and parental problem drinking. *Journal of Social and Personal Relationships*, **8**, 451–466.

Briere, J., & Runtz, M. (1990). Differential adult symptomatology associated with three types of child abuse histories. *Child Abuse and Neglect*, **14**, 357–364.

Briggs, F., & Hawkins, R.M.F. (1996). *Child protection: A guide for teachers and child care professionals*. St Leonards, NSW: Allen & Unwin.

British Crime Survey (2003). *Domestic violence: The hideout, what's going on at home*. London: The Home Office. www.thehideout.org.uk

Bronfenbrenner, U. (1979). *The ecology of human development*. Cambridge, MA: Harvard University Press.

Bronfenbrenner, U. (1993). *Parenting – An ecological perspective* (pp. vii–xii). Hillsdale, New York, and London: Erlbaum Associates.

Brown, J., Cohen, P., Johnson, J.G., & Smailes, E.M. (1999). Childhood abuse and neglect: Specificity of effects on adolescent and young adult depression and suicidality. *Journal of the American Academy of Child and Adolescent Psychiatry*, **38**, 1490–1496.

Brunk, M., Henggeler, S.W., & Whelan, J.P. (1987). Comparison of multisystemic therapy and parent training in the brief treatment of child abuse and neglect. *Journal of Consulting and Clinical Psychology*, **55**, 171–178.

Bullock, R., & Little, M. (2002). The contribution of children's' services to the protection of children. In K.D. Browne, H. Hanks, P. Stratton, & C. Hamilton, *Early prediction and prevention of child abuse: A handbook*. Chichester: John Wiley & Sons.

Burgess, R., & Richardson, R. (1984). Coercive interpersonal contingencies as a detriment of child maltreatment. In R.F. Dangel & R.A. Polster (Eds.), *Parent training: Foundations of research and practice*. New York: Guilford Press.

Burnett, B.T. (1993). The psychological abuse of latency age children: A survey. *Child Abuse and Neglect*, **17**, 441–454.

Burrell, B., Thompson, B., & Sexton, D. (1994). Predicting child abuse potential across family types. *Child Abuse and Neglect*, **18** (12), 1039–1049.

Butler, I., Scanlan, L., Robinson, M., Douglas, G., & Murch, M. (2003). *Divorcing children: Children's experience of their parents' divorce*. London: Jessica Kingsley.

Butler-Sloss, E. (2001, May). Contact and domestic violence. *Family Law*, pp. 355–358.

Byrne, B. (1999). Ireland. In P.K. Smith, Y. Morita, J. Junger-Tas, D. Olweus, R. Catalano, & P. Slee (Eds.), *The nature of school bullying: A cross-national perspective*. London: Routledge.

Byrne, E.A., Cunningham, C.C., & Sloper, P. (1988). *Families and their children with Down's Syndrome: One feature in common*. London: Routledge.

Camras, L.A., & Rappaport, S. (1993). Conflict behaviours of maltreated and non-maltreated children. *Child Abuse and Neglect*, **17**, 455–464.

Carlson, E., & Sroufe, L.A. (1995). Contribution of attachment theory to developmental psychopathology. In D. Cicchetti & D.J. Cohen (Eds.), *Developmental psychopathology: Vol. 1. Theory and methods* (pp. 581–617). New York: John Wiley & Sons.

Carlson, V., Cicchetti, D., Barnett, D., & Braunwald, K. (1989). Finding order in disorganization: Lessons from research on maltreated infants' attachments to their caregivers. In D. Cicchetti & V. Carlson (Eds.), *Child maltreatment: Theory and research on the causes and consequences of child abuse and neglect* (pp. 494–528). Cambridge: Cambridge University Press.

Carr, A. (2002). *The handbook of child and adolescent clinical psychology.* London: Routledge.

Carter, S.L., Osofsky, J.D., & Hann, D.M. (1991). Speaking for the baby: A therapeutic intervention with adolescent mothers and their infants. *Infant Mental Health Journal, 12* (4), 291–301.

Cassidy, J. (1988). Child-mother attachment and the self at age six. *Child Development, 57*, 331–337.

Cassidy, L., & Berlin, I.J. (1994). The insecure-ambivalent pattern of attachment: Theory and research. *Child Development, 65*, 971–991.

Cawson *et al.* (2001) cited in Evans (2002), pp. 5–6.

Cawson, P., Wattam, C., Brooker, S., & Kelly, G. (2000). *Child maltreatment in the United Kingdom: A study of the prevalence of child abuse and neglect.* London: NSPCC.

Chaffin, M. *et al.* (2004). Parent-child interaction therapy with physically abusive parents: Efficacy for reducing future abuse reports. *Journal of Consulting and Clinical Psychology, 72* (3).

Chaffin, M., Kelleher, K., & Hollenberg, J. (1996). Onset of physical abuse and neglect: Psychiatric substance abuse and social risk factors from prospective community samples. *Child Abuse and Neglect, 20*, 191–203.

Chan, J.M., & Leff, P.T. (1988). Play and the abused child: Implications for pediatric care. *Children's Health Care, 16*, 169–176.

Christian, C.W. (1999). Child abuse and neglect. In J.A. Silver, B.J. Amster, & T. Haecker, (Eds.), *Young children and foster care* (pp. 195–212). Baltimore, MD: Paul H. Brookes Publishing Co.

Cicchetti, D., & Aber, J.L. (1986). Early precursors to later depression: An organizational perspective. In L. Lipsitt & C. Rovee-Collier (Eds.), *Advances in infancy* (Vol. **4**, pp. 81–137). Norwood, NJ: Ablex.

Cicchetti, D., & Rizley, R. (1981). Developmental perspectives on the etiology, intergenerational transmission and sequelae of child maltreatment. *New Directions in Child Development, 11*, 96–647.

Cicchetti, D., & Toth, S.L. (1995a). Developmental psychopathology and disorders of affect. In D. Cicchetti & D. Cohen (Eds.), *Developmental psychopathology: Vol. 2. Risk, disorder, and adaptation* (pp. 369–420). New York: John Wiley & Sons.

Cicchetti, D., & Toth, S.L. (1995b). A development psychopathology perspective on child abuse and neglect. *Journal of American Academy of Child and Adolescent Psychiatry, 34* (5), 541–565.

Cicchetti, D., Rogosch, F., Lynch, M., & Holt, K. (1993). Resilience in maltreated children: Processes leading to adaptive outcome. *Developmental Psychopathology, 5*, 629–647.

Cicchetti, D., Toth, S.L., & Bush, M. (1988). Developmental psychopathology and incompetence in childhood: Suggestions for intervention. In B. Lahey & A. Kazdin (Eds.), *Advances in clinical child psychology* (Vol. **11**, pp. 1–71). New York: Plenum.

Cicchetti, D., Toth, S.L., & Rogosch, F.A. (1999). The efficacy of toddler-parent psychotherapy to increase attachment security in offspring of depressed mothers. *Attachment and Human Development, 1*, 34–66.

Clarke, A., & Clarke, A. (2000). *The prediction of individual development.* London: Jessica Kingsley.

Clarke, A.M., & Clarke, D.B. (2000). *Early experiences and the life path*. London: Jessica Kingsley.

Claussen, A., & Crittenden, A. (1991). Physical and psychological maltreatments: Relations among types of maltreatment. *Child Abuse and Neglect*, **15**, 5–18.

Cleaver, H., Unell, I., & Aldgate, J. (1999). *Children's needs: Parenting capacity*. London: Department of Health.

Clees, T.J., & Gast, D.L. (1994). Social safety skills instruction for individuals with disabilities: A sequential model. *Education and Treatment of Children*, **17**, 163–184.

Cohen, D. (1996). Family violence from a communication perspective. In D. Cohen & S. Lloyd (Eds.), *Family violence from a communication perspective*. Beverley Hills, CA: Sage.

Cohen, S., & Warren, R.D. (1987). Preliminary survey of family abuse of children served by United Cerebral Palsy centers. *Developmental Medicine and Child Neurology*, **29**, 12–18.

Colton, M. (2002). Factors associated with abuse in residential child care institutions. *Children and Society*, **16**, 33–44.

Compass, B.E., Hinden, B.R., & Gerhardt, C.A. (1995). Adolescent development: Pathways and processes of risk and resilience. *Annual Review of Psychology*, **45**, 265–293.

Connell, A., & Farrington, D.P. (1996). Bullying among incarcerated young offenders: Developing an interview schedule and some preliminary results. *Journal of Adolescence*, **19** (1), 75–93.

Corcoran, G. (2000). Family interventions with child physical abuse and neglect: A critical review. *Children and Youth Services Review*, **22**, 563–591.

Cotroneo, N. (1986). Families and abuse: A contextual approach. In M.A. Karpel (Ed.), *Family Resources* (pp. 413–437). New York: Guilford Press.

Cottone, R.R. (1988). Epistemological and ontological issues in counselling: Implications of social systems theory. *Counselling Psychology Quarterly*, **1**, 357–365.

Cousins, W., Monteith, M., Larkin, E., & Percy, A. (2003). *The care careers of younger looked after children: Findings from the Multiple Placements Project*. Institute of Child Care Research, Queen's University Belfast.

Cramer, B. *et al.* (1990). Outcome evaluation in brief mother-infant psychotherapy: A preliminary report. *Infant Mental Health Journal*, **2**, 278–300.

Crittenden, P.M. (1988). Family and dyadic patterns of functioning in maltreating families. In K. Browne, C. Davies, P. Stratton, & C. Hamilton (Eds.), *Early prediction and prevention of child abuse: A handbook*. Chichester: John Wiley & Sons.

Crittenden, P.M. (1992). Quality of attachment in the pre-school years. *Development and Psychopathology*, **4** (1), 28–33.

Crittenden, P.M., & Ainsworth, M.D.S. (1989). *Child maltreatment and attachment*. In D. Cicchetti & V. Carlson (Eds.), *Handbook of child maltreatment: Clinical and theoretical perspectives* (pp. 432–463). New York: Cambridge University Press.

Crittenden, P.M., Claussen, A.H., & Sugarman, D.B. (1994). Physical and psychological maltreatment in middle childhood and adolescence. *Development and Psychopathology*, **6**, 145–164.

Cross, S.B., Kaye, E., & Ratnofsky, A.C. (1993). *A report on the maltreatment of children with disabilities*. Washington, DC: National Center on Child Abuse and Neglect.

Cullingford, C., & Morrison, J. (1996). Who excludes whom?: The personal experience of exclusion. In E. Blyth & J. Milner (Eds.), *Exclusion from school: Inter-professional issues for policy and practice*. London: Routledge.

Cummings, E.M. (1998). Children exposed to marital conflict and violence: Conceptual and theoretical directions. In G.W. Holden, R. Geffner, & E.N. Jouriles (Eds.), *Children exposed to marital violence: Theory, research, and applied issues* (pp. 55–93). Washington, DC: American Psychological Association.

Cunningham, C.C., & Sloper, P. (1977). Parents of Down's Syndrome babies: Their early needs. *Child: Care, Health and Development*, **3**, 325–347.

Dahl, R. (2003). Beyond the raging hormones: The tinderbox in the teenage brain. *Cerebrum*, **5** (3).

Dallam, S.J. (2001). The long-term medical consequences of childhood maltreatment. In K. Franey, R. Geffner, & R. Falconer (Eds.), *The cost of child maltreatment: Who pays? We all do*. San Diego, CA: Family Violence and Sexual Assault Institute.

Daniel, B., & Wassell, S. (2002). *The school years: Assessing and promoting resilience in vulnerable children* (Vol. **2**). London: Jessica Kingsley.

Daniel, B., Wassell, S., & Gilligan, R. (1999). *Child development for child care protection workers*. London: Jessica Kingsley.

De Pear, S., & Garner, P. (1996). Tales from the exclusion zone: The views of teachers and pupils. In E. Blyth & J. Milner (Eds.), *Exclusion from school: Inter-professional issues for policy and practice*. London: Routledge.

De Wolff, M.S., & Van Ijzendoorn, M.H. (1997). Sensitivity and attachment. *Child Development*, **68**, 571–591.

Department of Health (2000). *Quality protects: Disabled children numbers and categories and families*. London: Department of Health.

Department of Health, Department for Education and Employment, Home Office (2000). *Framework for the assessment of children in need and their families*. London: Stationery Office.

Department of Health, Education and Science (1991). *Working together under the Children Act 1989*. London: HMSO.

Department of Health, Home Office and Department for Education and Employment (1999). *Working together to safeguard children: A guide to interagency working to safeguard and promote the welfare of children*. London: Stationery Office.

DeRobertis, E.M. (2004). The impact of long-term psychological maltreatment by one's maternal figure: A study of the victim's perspective. *Journal of Emotional Abuse*, **4** (2), 27–51.

Dexter, P., & Towl, G. (1995). An investigation into suicidal behaviours in prison. In N.K. Clarke & G.M. Stephenson (Eds.), *Criminal behaviour: Perceptions, attributions and rationality*. Issues in Criminological and Legal Psychology No. 22. Leicester: The British Psychological Society.

Diaz, R., Neal, C., & Vachio, A. (1991). Maternal teaching in the home of proximal development: A comparison of low and high risk dyads. *Merrill-Palmer Quarterly*, **37**, 83–107.

Dilalla, D.D., & Crittenden, P.M. (1990). Dimensions of maltreated children's home behaviour: A factor analytic approach. *Infant Behaviour and Development*, **13**, 439–460.

Dingwall, R., Eckelaar, J., & Murray, T. (1983). *The protection of children: State intervention and family life*. Oxford: Blackwell.

Disability Discrimination Act 1995. (1995). London: Stationery Office.

Dodge, K.A. *et al.* (2003). Peer rejection and social information-processing factors in the development of aggressive behavior problems in children. *Child Development*, **74** (2), 374–393.

Donaldson, T. (2003). *The changing face of care under the Children (NI) Order 1995: A prospective study of decision-making and care outcomes for looked-after children.* Unpublished PhD thesis, Queen's University Belfast.

Donaldson, T., & Iwaniec, D. (in press*).* The face of the Children's Order. *British Journal of Social Work.*

Doyle, C. (1997). Emotional abuse of children: Issues for intervention. *Child Abuse Review*, **6**, 208–227.

Doyle, C. (1998). *Emotional abuse of children: Issues for intervention.* Unpublished PhD thesis, University of Leicester, England.

Doyle, C. (2001). Surviving and coping with emotional abuse in childhood. *Clinical Child Psychology and Psychiatry*, **6** (3), 387–402.

Doyle, C. (2003). Child emotional abuse: The role of educational professionals. *Educational and Child Psychology*, **20** (1), 8–21.

Drotar, D., & Sturm, L. (1988). Prediction of intellectual development in young children with histories of non-organic failure to thrive. *Journal of Pediatric Psychology*, **13** (2), 218–296.

Duncan, R.D. (1999). Maltreatment by parents and peers: The relationship between child abuse, bully victimization, and psychological distress. *Child Maltreatment*, **4** (1), 45–55.

Dykman, R.A., Ackerman, P.T., Loizou, P.C., & Casey, P.H. (2000). An event-related study of older children with an early history of failure to thrive. *Developmental Neuropsychology*, **18** (2), 187–212.

Dyson, G.P., Power, K.G., & Wozniak, E. (1997). Problems with using official records from young offender institutions as indices of bullying. *International Journal of Offender Therapy and Comparative Criminology*, **41** (2), 121–138.

D'Zurilla, T.J., & Goldfried, M.R. (1971). Problem-solving and behaviour modification. *Journal of Abnormal Psychology*, **78**, 107–126.

D'Zurilla, T.J., & Nezu, A.M. (1990). Development and preliminary evaluation of the social problem solving inventory. *Psychological Assessment: A Journal of Consulting and Clinical Psychology*, **2**, 156–193.

Easterbrooks, A., & Goldberg, W. (1990). Security of toddler-parent attachment: Relation to children's sociopersonality functioning during kindergarden. In M.T. Greenberg, D. Cicchetti, & M.T. Cummings (Eds.), *Attachment in the pre-school years* (pp. 221–244). Chicago, IL: University of Chicago Press.

Edelson, J. (1999). Children's witnessing of adult domestic violence. *Journal of Interpersonal Violence*, **14** (8), 526–534.

Egeland, B., & Erickson, M. (1987). Psychologically unavailable caregiving. In M.R. Brassard, R. Germain, & S.N. Hart (Eds.), *Psychological maltreatment of children and youth* (pp. 110–120). New York: Pergamon Press.

Egeland, B., Kalkoske, M., Gottesman, N., & Erickson, M.F. (1990). Preschool behaviour problems: Stability and factors accounting for change. *Journal of Child Psychology and Psychiatry*, **31** (6), 891–910.

Egeland, B., Sroufe, L.A., & Erickson, M. (1983). The developmental consequences of different patterns of maltreatment. *Child Abuse and Neglect*, **7**, 459–469.

Ellis, A. (1973). *Humanistic psychotherapy: The rational emotive approach.* New York: The Julian Press.

Emery, R.E., & Laumann-Billings, L. (2002). Child abuse. In M. Rutter & E. Taylor (Eds.), *Child and adolescent psychiatry* (4th ed.). Oxford: Blackwell Science.

English, D.J. (1998). The extent and consequences of child maltreatment. *The Future of Children*, **8** (1), 39–53.

Erickson, M.F., & Egeland, R. (2002). Child neglect. In J. Myers, L. Berliner, J. Briere, C. Hendrix, C. Jenny, & T. Reid (Eds.), *The APSAC handbook on child maltreatment*. London: Sage.

Erickson, M.F., Egeland, R., & Pianta, R. (1989). The effect of maltreatment on the development of young children. In D. Cicchetti & V. Carlson (Eds.), *Child maltreatment: Theory and research on the causes and consequences of child abuse and neglect* (pp. 647–684). New York: Cambridge University Press.

Erikson, E.H. (1963). *Childhood and society*. New York: W. W. Norton.

Eslea, M., Stepanova, E., & Cameron-Young, B. (2002). *Aggressive classroom management: Do teachers bully pupils?* Paper presented at International Society for Research on Aggression, World Meeting.

Espelage, D.L., & Asidao, C.S. (2001). Conversations with middle school students about bullying and victimisation: Should we be concerned? *Journal of Emotional Abuse*, **2** (2/3), 49–62.

Evans, H. (2002). *Emotional Abuse*. NSPCC Information Briefings. www.nspcc.org.uk/inform

Eyberg, S.M., & Calzada, E. (1998). *Parent-child interaction therapy: Procedures manual*. Unpublished manuscript, University of Florida.

Fantuzzo, J.W., & Mohr, W.K. (1999). Prevalence and effects of child exposure to domestic violence. *The Future of Children*, **9** (3), 21–32.

Farber, E.A., & Egeland, B. (1987). Invulnerability among abused and neglected children. In E.J. Anthony & B. Cohler (Eds.), *The invulnerable child*. New York: Guilford Press.

Farmer, E., & Owen, M. (1995). *Child protection practice: Private risks and public remedies – decision making intervention and outcome in child protection work*. London: HMSO.

Feldman, M., & Werner, S.E. (2002). Collateral effects of behavioural parent training on families of children with developmental disabilities and behaviour disorders. *Behavioural Interventions*, **17**, 75–83.

Fennell, D., & Weinhold, B. (2003). *Counseling families: An introduction to marriage and family therapy*. Denve, Co: Eove Publishing.

Fleming, A.K. (1939). Some childhood memories of Rudyard Kipling. *Chambers Journal* (March and July), 168–172, 506–511.

Fonagy, P., Steele, H., & Steele, M. (1991). Maternal representation of attachment during pregnancy predict the organization of infant-mother attachment at one year of age. *Child Development*, **62**, 891–905.

Fonagy, P., Steele, M., Steele, H., Higgit, A., & Target, M. (1994). The Emanuel Miller memorial lecture 1992. The theory and practice of resilience. *Journal of Child Psychology and Psychiatry*, **35**, 231–257.

Forehand, R., & Long, N. (1996). *Parenting the strong-willed child*. Chicago IL: Contemporary Books.

Foster, S.L., & Robin, A.L. (1989). *Negotiating parent-adolescent conflict: A behavioural-family systems approach*. New York: Guilford Press.

Fraiberg, S. (1980). *Clinical studies in infant mental health*. New York: Basic Books.

Fraiberg, S., Adelson, E., & Shapiro, V. (1975). Ghosts in the nursery: A psychoanalytic approach to the impaired infant-mother relationships. *Journal of the American Academy of Child and Adolescent Psychiatry*, **14**, 397–421.

Friedman, R.J., & Chase-Lansdale, P.L. (2002). Chronic adversities. In M. Rutter & E. Taylor (Eds.), *Child and adolescent psychiatry* (4th ed., pp. 261–276). Oxford: Blackwell Science.

Friedrich, W.N., & Boriskin, J.A. (1978). Primary prevention of child abuse: Focus on the special child. *Hospital and Community Psychiatry*, **29**, 248–256.

Frodi, A., & Lamb, M. (1980). Child abusers' responses to infant smiles and cries. *Child Development*, **51**, 238–241.

Froelich, J., Doepfner, M., & Lehmkuhl, G. (2002). Effects of combined cognitive behavioural treatment with parent management training in ADHD. *Behavioural and Cognitive Psychotherapy*, **30**, 111–115.

Frude, N. (2003). A framework for assessing the physical abuse of children. In M.C. Calder & S. Hackett (Eds.), *Assessment in child care: Using and developing framework for practice*. Lyme Regis: Russell House Publishing.

Gagné, M.-H. (1995). *A conceptual and empirical review on psychological violence against children*. Les Cahiers d'Analyse du GRAVE (Vol. 2 [1]). Montréal: Groupe de recherche et d'action sur la victimisation des enfants.

Garbarino, F., Guttmann, E., & Seeley, J.W. (1986). *The psychologically battered child*. San Francisco: Jossey-Bass.

Garbarino, J., Eckenrode, J., & Bolger, K. (1997). The elusive crime of psychological maltreatment. In J. Garbarino & J. Eckenrode (Eds.), *Understanding abusive families: An ecological approach to theory and practice*. San Francisco: Jossey-Bass.

Garmezy, N., & Rutter, M. (1983). *Stress, coping, and development in children*. New York: McGraw-Hill.

George, C., & Main, M. (1979). Social interactions of young abused children: Approach, avoidance and aggression. *Child Development*, **50**, 306–318.

George, C., Kaplan, N., & Main, M. (1985). *Adult attachment interview*. Unpublished manuscript, University of California at Berkeley.

Gibbs, I., & Sinclair, I. (1999). Treatment and treatment outcomes in children's homes. *Children and Family Social Work*, **4**, 1–8.

Gilligan, R. (1997). Beyond permanence? The importance of resilience in child placement practice and planning. *Adoption and Fostering*, **21** (1), 12–18.

Gilligan, R. (2001). *Promoting resilience. A resource guide on working with children in the care system*. London: British Agencies for Adoption and Fostering.

Glaser, D. (2002). Emotional abuse and neglect (psychological maltreatment): A conceptual framework. *Child Abuse and Neglect*, **26**, 697–714.

Glaser, D., & Prior, P. (2000). Predicting emotional abuse and neglect. In K. Browne, H. Hanks, P. Stratton, & C. Hamilton (Eds.), *Early prediction and prevention of child abuse: A handbook*. Chichester: John Wiley & Sons.

Glaser, D., & Prior, V. (1997). Is the term child protection applicable to emotional abuse? *Child Abuse Review*, **6** (5), 315–329.

Glaser, D., & Prior, V. (2002). Predicting emotional abuse and neglect. In K. Browne, H. Hanks, P. Stratton, & C. Hamilton (Eds.), *Early prediction and prevention of child abuse: A handbook*. Chichester: John Wiley & Sons.

Glaser, D., Prior, V., & Lynch, M.A. (2001). *Emotional abuse and emotional neglect: Antecedents, operational definitions and consequences*. York: BASPCAN.

Goddard, C.R. (1996). *Child abuse and child protection: A guide for health, education and welfare workers*. Melbourne: Churchill Livingstone.

Gohlke, B.C., Khadilkar, V.V., Skuse, D., & Stanhope, R. (1998). Recognition of children with psychosocial short stature: A spectrum of presentation. *Journal of Pediatric Endocrinology and Metabolism*, **11**, 509–517.

Goldson, E. (1987). Failure to thrive; an old problem revisited. *Progress in Child Health*, **7**, 83–99.

Goldstein, A.P. (1999). *The prepare curriculum: Teaching prosocial competencies*. Champaign, IL: Research Press.

Good, T.L., & Brophy, J.E. (1987). *Looking in classrooms* (4th ed.). New York: Harper & Row.

Gortmaker, S.L., Walker, D.K., Weitzman, M., & Sobal, A.M. (1990). Chronic conditions, socioeconomic risks and behaviour problems in children and adolescents. *Pediatrics*, **85**, 267–276.

Gough, D. (2002). To or for whom: A social policy perspective on child abuse and child protection. In K.D. Brown, H. Hanks, P. Stratton, & C. Hamilton (Eds.), *Early prediction and prevention of child abuse: A handbook*. Chichester: John Wiley & Sons.

Goulet, C., Bell, L., St-Cyr Tribble, D., Paul, D., & Lang, A. (1998). A concept analysis of parent-infant attachment. *Journal of Advanced Nursing*, **28**, 1071–1081.

Gracia, E. (1995). Visible but unreported: A case for the 'not serious enough' cases of child maltreatment. *Child Abuse and Neglect*, **19**, 1083–1093.

Graham-Bermann, S.A. (2002). Child abuse in the context of domestic violence. In J. Myers, L. Berliner, J. Briere, C. Hendrix, C. Jenny, & T. Reid (Eds.), *The APSAC handbook on child maltreatment*. London: Sage.

Greenough, W.T., Black, J.E., & Wallace, C.S. (1987). Experience and brain development. *Child Development*, **58**, 539–559.

Griffin, J., & Tyrell, J. (2002). *Psychotherapy and the human givens* (2nd ed.). Chalvington: HG Publishing.

Gross, A.B., & Keller, H.R. (1992). Long-term consequences of childhood physical and psychological maltreatment. *Aggressive Behaviour*, **18** (3), 27–58.

Grossman, D. (1995). *On killing*. Boston, MA: Little, Brown.

Haider, A.J. (2003). Tackling domestic violence within the Asian community. Conference Proceedings, September 2003, Cardiff.

Haj-Yahia, M.M. (2001). The incidence of witnessing interpersonal violence and some of its psychological consequences among Arab adolescent. *Child Abuse and Neglect*, **25**, 885–907.

Hansen, D.J., Pallotta, G.M., Tishelman, A.C., Conaway, L.P., & MacMillan, V.M. (1989). Parental problem-solving skills and child behaviour problems: A comparison of physically abusive, neglectful, clinic and community families. *Journal of Family Violence*, **4**, 353–368.

Harris, N., Eden, K., & Blair, A. (2000). *Challenges to school exclusion: Exclusion, appeals and the law*. London: Routledge.

Hart, S.N., Binggeli, N.J., & Brassard, M.R. (1998). Evidence for the effects of psychological maltreatment. *Journal of Emotional Abuse*, **1** (1), 27–58.

Hart, S.N., Brassard, M.R., Binggeli, N.J., & Davidson, H.A. (2002). Psychological maltreatment. In J. Myers, L. Berliner, J. Briere, C. Hendrix, C. Jenny, & T. Reid (Eds.), *The APSAC handbook on child maltreatment*. London: Sage.

Hart, S.N., Brassard, M.R., & Germain, R.B. (1987). Psychological maltreatment in education and schooling. In M. Brassard, R. Germain, & S.N. Hart (Eds.), *Psychological maltreatment of children and youth*. New York: Pergamon Press.

Hart, S.N., Brassard, M.R., & Karlson, H.C. (1996). *Psychological maltreatment*. In J. Briere, L. Berliner, J.A. Bulkley, C. Jenny, & T. Reid (Eds.), *The APSAC handbook on child maltreatment* (2nd ed.). Thousand Oaks, CA: Sage.

Hart, S.N., Germain, R.B., & Brassard, M.R. (1987). The challenge: To better understand and combat psychological maltreatment of children and youth. In M.R. Brassard, R. Germain, & S.N. Hart (Eds.), *Psychological maltreatment of children and youth*. New York: Pergamon Press.

Harter, S., & Marold, D.B. (1994). The directionality of the link between self-esteem and affect: Beyond causal modelling. In D. Cicchetti & S.L. Toth (Eds.), *Rochester symposium on developmental psychopathology: Vol. 5. Disorders and dysfunctions of the self* (pp. 333–369). Rochester, NY: University of Rochester Press.

Hartup, W.W. (1992). Friendships and their developmental significance. In H. McGurk (Ed.), *Childhood social development: Contemporary perspectives*. Hove: Erlbaum.

Hawthorne, J., Jesspo, J., Pryor, J., & Richards, M. (2003). Supporting children through family change: A review of services. *Foundations* No. 323. York: Joseph Rowntree Foundation.

Hazan, C., & Shaver, P.R. (1987). Attachment as an organizational framework for research on close relationships. *Psychological Inquiry*, **5**, 1–22.

Hemenway, D., Solnick. S., & Carter, J. (1994). Child-rearing violence. *Child Abuse and Neglect*, **18** (12), 1011–1020.

Hepburn, A. (2000). Power lines: Derrida, discursive psychology and the management of accusations of teacher bullying. *British Journal of Social Psychology*, **39**, 605–628.

Herbert, M. (1974). *Emotional problems of development in children*. London: Academic Press.

Herbert, M. (1987). *Behavioural treatment of children with problems: A practice manual*. London: Academic Press.

Herbert, M. (1988). *Working with children and their families*. London: British Psychological Society and Routledge.

Herbert, M. (1989). *Working with children and their families*. Chicago, IL: Lyceum Books.

Herbert, M. (1998a). *Clinical child psychology: Social learning, development and behaviour* (2nd ed.). Chichester: John Wiley & Sons.

Herbert, M. (1998b). *Conduct disorders of childhood and adolescence* (2nd ed.). Chichester: John Wiley & Sons.

Herschell, A.D., Calzada, E.J., Eyberg, S.M., & McNeil, C.B. (2002). Parent-child interaction therapy: New directions in research. *Cognitive and Behavioral Practice*, **9**, 9–16.

Hetherington, E.M., & Stanley-Hagan, M. (1999). The adjustment of children with divorced parents: A risk and resiliency perspective. *Journal of Child Psychology and Psychiatry*, **40** (1), 129–140.

Hetherington, E.M. (1999). Should we stay together for the sake of the children? In E.M. Hetherington (Ed.), *Coping with divorce, single parenting and remarriage: A risk and resilience perspective* (pp. 93–116). Mahwah, N.J.: Erlbaum.

Higgins, D.J., & McCabe, M.P. (2001). Multiple forms of child abuse and neglect: Adult retrospective reports. *Aggression and Violent Behaviour*, 6, 547–578.

Hildyard, K., & Wolfe, D.A. (2002). Child neglect: Developmental issues and outcomes. *Child Abuse and Neglect*, **26**, 679–695.

Himelein, M.J., & McElrath, A.V. (1996). Resilient child sexual abuse survivors: Cognitive coping and illusion. *Child Abuse and Neglect*, **20**, 747–758.

Hobbs, G., Hobbs, C., & Wynne, J. (1999). Abuse of children in foster and residential care. *Child Abuse and Neglect*, **23**, 1239–1252.

Hoglund, C.L., & Nicholas, K.B. (1995). Shame, guilt, and anger in college students exposed to abusive family environments. *Journal of Family Violence*, **10** (2), 141–157.

Hollburn-Cobb, C. (1996). Adolescent-parents' attachment and family problem-solving styles. *Process*, **35** (1), 57–82.

Hollingworth, J. (1987). Community support: Children and disability. *Australian Child and Family Welfare*, **12** (4), 19–21.

Holzworth-Munroe, A., Smutzler, N., & Sandin, E. (1997). A brief review of the research on husband violence: Part II The psychological effects of husband violence on battered women and their children. *Aggression and Violent Behavior*, **2** (2), 179–213.

Howard League for Penal Reform (2001). *Children in prison: Provision and practice at Castington*. London: Howard League for Penal Reform.

Howard League for Penal Reform (2002). *Children in prison – barred rights: An independent submission to the United Nations Committee on the Rights of the Child*. London: Howard League for Penal Reform.

Howard League for Penal Reform (2003). *Solitary confinement for children in prison is unlawful*, 17 July 2003. http://web.ukonline.co.uk/howard.league/press/ 170703.html

Howard League for Penal Reform (2004). Solitary confinement breaches the UN convention on the rights of the child. *Howard League Magazine*, **22** (1), 7.

Howard, A.C. (1986). Developmental play ages of physically abused and non-abused children. *American Journal of Occupational Therapy*, **40**, 691–695.

Hughes, H.M., & Graham-Bermann, S.A. (1998). Children of battered women: Impact of emotional abuse and adjustment. *Journal of Emotional Abuse*, **1** (2), 23–50.

Hughes, J.R., & Gottlieb, L.N. (2004). The effects of the Webster-Stratton parenting program on maltreating families: Fostering strengths. *Child Abuse and Neglect*, **28**, 1081–1097.

Hunt, J., Macleod, A., & Thomas, C. (1999). The last resort: Child protection, the courts and the 1989 Children Act. *Studies in Evaluating the Children Act 1989*. London: HMSO.

Hyman, I., & Zelikoff, W. (1987). Educator-induced post-traumatic stress disorder. *Communique* (a newsletter of the National Association of School Psychologists). London.

Hyman, I.A., & Snook, P.A. (1999). *Dangerous schools: What we can do about the physical and emotional abuse of our children*. San Francisco: Jossey-Bass.

Hyman, I.A., Zelikoff, W., & Clarke, J. (1988). Psychological and physical abuse in schools: A paradigm for understanding post-traumatic stress disorder in children and youth. *Journal of Traumatic Stress*, **1** (2), 243–267.

Ingram, R.E., Overbey, T., & Fortier, M. (2001). Individual differences in dysfunctional automatic thinking and parental bonding: Specificity of maternal care. *Personality and Individual Differences*, **30**, 401–412.

Ireland, T., & Widom, S.C. (1994). Childhood victimization and risk for alcohol and drug arrests. *International Journal of the Addictions*, **29**, 235–274.

Isabella, R., Belsky, J., & Von Eye, A. (1989). Origins of infant-mother attachment: An examination of interactional synchrony during the infant's first year. *Developmental Psychology*, **25**, 12–21.

Isabella, R.A. (1994). Origins of maternal role satisfaction and its influences upon maternal interactive behaviour and infant-mother attachment. *Infant Behaviour and Development*, **17**, 381–388.

Iso-Ahola, S.E. (1997). A psychological analysis of leisure and health. In J.T. Haworth (Ed.), *Work, leisure and well-being* (pp. 131–144). London: Routledge.

Iwaniec, D. (1983). *Social and psychological factors in the aetiology and management of children who fail to thrive*. PhD thesis, University of Leicester, Faculty of Science.

Iwaniec, D. (1995). *The emotionally abused and neglected child: Identification, assessment and intervention*. Chichester: John Wiley & Sons.

Iwaniec, D. (1997). Evaluating parent training for emotionally abusive and neglectful parents; comparing individual versus individual and group intervention. *Research on Social Work Practice*, **7** (3), 329–349.

Iwaniec, D. (1999a). Child abuse – parenting, identification and treatment. In D. Messer & F. Jones (Eds.), *Psychology for social carers*. London: Jessica Kingsley.

Iwaniec, D. (1999b). Lessons from 20-year follow-up study on children who failed to thrive. *Child Care in Practice*, **5** (2), 128–139.

Iwaniec, D. (2000). From childhood to adulthood: A 20-year follow-up study of children who failed-to-thrive. In D. Iwaniec & M. Hill (Eds.), *Child welfare policy and practice: Current issues emerging from child care research*. London: Jessica Kingsley.

Iwaniec, D. (2003). Identifying and dealing with emotional abuse and neglect. *Child Care in Practice*, **9** (1), 49–61.

Iwaniec, D., (2004). *Children who fail to thrive: A practice guide*. Chichester: John Wiley & Sons.

Iwaniec, D., Donaldson, T., & Allweis, M. (2004). The plight of neglected children: Social work and judicial decision-making, and management of neglect cases. *Child and Family Law Quarterly*, **6** (4), 423–436.

Iwaniec, D., & Herbert, M. (1999). Multi-dimensional approach to helping families who emotionally abuse their children. *Children and Society*, **13**, 365–379.

Iwaniec, D., Herbert, M., & McNeish, A.S. (1985a). Social work with failure-to-thrive children and their families, Part I: Psychosocial factors. *British Journal of Social Work*, **15**, 243–259.

Iwaniec, D., Herbert, M., & McNeish, A.S. (1985b). Social work with failure-to-thrive children and their families. Part II: Behavioural social work intervention. *British Journal of Social Work*, **15** (4), 375–389.

Iwaniec, D., Herbert, M., & Sluckin, A. (1988). Helping emotionally abused children who fail-to-thrive. In K. Browne, C. Davies, P. Stratton, & C. Hamilton (Eds.), *Early prediction and prevention of child abuse: A handbook*. Chichester: John Wiley & Sons.

Iwaniec, D., Herbert, M., & Sluckin, A. (2002). Helping emotionally abused and neglected children and abusive carers. In K. Browne, H. Hanks, P. Stratton, & C. Hamilton (Eds.), *Early prediction and prevention of child abuse: A handbook*. Chichester: John Wiley & Sons.

Iwaniec, D., & Hill, M. (Eds.) (2000). *Child welfare policy and practice: Current issues in child care research*. London: Jessica Kingsley.

Iwaniec, D., & Sneddon, H. (2001). Attachment style in adults who failed to thrive as children: Outcomes of a 20-year follow-up study of factors influencing maintenance or change in attachment style. *British Journal of Social Work*, **31**, 179–195.

Iwaniec, D., & Sneddon, H. (2002). The quality of parenting of individuals who had failed to thrive as children. *British Journal of Social Work*, **32** (3), 283–298.

Jackson, D. (1957). The question of family homeostasis. *Psychiatric Quarterly* (Suppl.), **31**, 79–90.

Jackson, S., & Thomas, N. (1999). *On the move again? What works in maintaining stability for looked after children*. Ilford: Barnardos.

Jacobson, S. (2002). Parents sue over humiliation. http://www.vachss.com/help_text/archive/parents_sue.html

Jaffe, P., Wolfe, D., & Wilson, S.K. (1990). *Children of battered women*. Newbury Park, CA: Sage.

James, M. (1994). Domestic violence as a form of child Abuse: Identification and prevention. Issues in Child Abuse Prevention Number 2. http://www.aifs.org.au/nch/issues2.html

Janowski, A. (1999). Poland. In P.K. Smith, Y. Morita, J. Junger-Tas, D. Olweus, R. Catalano, & P. Slee (Eds.), *The nature of school bullying: A cross-national perspective*. London: Routledge.

Jaudes, P.K., & Diamond, L.J. (1985). The handicapped child and child abuse. *Child Abuse and Neglect*, **9**, 341–347.

Jellen, L.K., McCarroll, J.E., & Thayer, L.E. (2001). Child emotional maltreatment: A 2-year study of US Army cases. *Child Abuse and Neglect*, **25** (5), 623–639.

Jenkins, J., & Keating, D. (1999). *Risk and resilience in six- and ten-year-old children*. Hull: Applied Research Branch, Strategic Policy, Human Resources Development Canada (HRDC).

John, P. (1996). Damaged goods?: An interpretation of excluded pupils' perceptions of schooling. In E. Blyth & J. Milner (Eds.), *Exclusion from school: Inter-professional issues for policy and practice*. London: Routledge.

Johnson, J.G., Cohen, P., Brown, J., Smailes, E.M., & Bernstein, D.P. (1999). Childhood maltreatment increases risk for personality disorders during early adulthood. *Archives of General Psychiatry*, **56**, 600–606.

Jones, D., Peterson, D.M., Goldberg, P.F., Goldberg, M., & Smith, J. (1995). *Risky situations: Vulnerable children*. Minneapolis, MN: PACER Center.

Jonson-Reid, M., Drake, B., Kim, J., Porterfield, S., & Han, L. (2004). A prospective analysis of the relationship between reported maltreatment and special education eligibility among poor children. *Child Maltreatment*, **9**, 382–394.

Kafka, F. (1919). *'Letters to his father' in the diaries 1910–1923*, complete and unabridged. London: Secker & Warburg Octopus.

Kairys, S.W., Johnson, C.F., & the Committee on Child Abuse and Neglect (2002). The psychological maltreatment of children – Technical report. *Pediatrics*, **109** (4), 1–3. http://www.pediatrics.org/cgi/content/full/109/4/e68

Kaufman, J. (1991). Depressive disorders in maltreated children. *Journal of the American Academy of Child and Adolescent Psychiatry*, **30**, 257–265.

Kaufman, J., & Cicchetti, D. (1989). Effects of maltreatment on school-age children's socioemotional development: Assessments in a day-care setting. *Developmental Psychology*, **25**, 516–524.

Kaufman, K.L., Johnson, C.F., Cohn, D., & McCleery, J. (1992). Child maltreatment prevention in the health care and social service system. In D.J. Willis, E.W. Holden, & M. Rosenberg (Eds.), *Prevention of child maltreatment: Developmental and ecological perspectives* (pp. 1–16). New York: John Wiley & Sons.

Kavanagh, C. (1982). Emotional abuse and mental injury: A critique of the concept and recommendation for practice. *Journal of American Academy of Child and Adolescent Psychiatry*, **21**, 171–177.

Keen, J., & Alison, L.H. (2001). Drug misusing parents: Key points for health professionals. *Archives of Disease in Childhood*, **85**, 296–299.

Keiley, M.K., Howe, T.R., Dodge, K.A., Bates, J.E., & Petit, G.S. (2001). The timing of child physical maltreatment: A cross-domain growth analysis of impact on adolescent externalizing and internalizing problems. *Development and Psychopathology*, **13**, 912–981.

Kelley, S.J. (2002). Child maltreatment in the context of substance abuse. In J.E. Myers, L. Berliner, J. Briere, C. Hendrix, C. Jenny, & T. Reid (Eds.), *The APSAC handbook on child maltreatment*. London: Sage.

Kelly, B., Thornberry, T., & Smith, C. (1997). *In the wake of childhood maltreatment*. Washington, DC: National Institute of Justice.

Kendall-Tackett, K.A., & Eckenrode, J. (1996). The effects of neglect on academic achievement and disciplinary problems: A developmental perspective. *Child Abuse and Neglect*, **20**, 161–169.

Kendrick, A. (1998a). *Abuse of children in residential and foster care: A brief review*. Scottish Institute for Residential Child Care. http://www.sircc.strath.ac.uk/research/kendrick.html

Kendrick, A. (1998b). *Bullying and peer abuse in residential child care: A brief review*. Scottish Institute of Residential Child Care. http://www.sircc.strath.ac.uk/research/kendrick1.html

Kendrick, A. (1998c). *'Who do we trust?' The abuse of children living away from home in the United Kingdom*. Paper presented to 12th International Congress on Child Abuse and Neglect; Protecting Children: Innovation and Inspiration, ISPCAN – International Society for Prevention of Child Abuse and Neglect, Auckland, 6–9 September 1998.

Kennedy, M. (1989). The abuse of deaf children. *Child Abuse Review*, **3**, 3–7.

Kennedy, M. (1990). The deaf child who is sexually abused-is there a need for a dual specialist? *Child Abuse Review*, **4**, 3–6.

Kent, A., & Waller, G. (2000). Childhood emotional abuse and eating psychopathology. *Clinical Psychology Review*, **20** (7), 887–903.

Kent, A., Waller, G., & Dagnan, D. (1999). A greater role of emotional than physical or sexual abuse in predicting disordered eating attitudes: The role of mediating variables. *International Journal of Eating Disorders*, **25**, 159–167.

Kerig, P.K., & Fedorowicz, A.E. (1999). Assessing maltreatment of children of battered women: Methodological and ethical consideration. *Child Maltreatment*, **4** (2), 103–115.

Kernic, M.A., Wolf, M.E., Holt, V.L., McKnight, B., Huebner, C.E., & Rivara, F.P. (2003). Behavioral problems among children whose mothers are abused by an intimate partner. *Child Abuse and Neglect*, **27**, 1231–1246.

Kilkenny, U. *et al.* (2005). *Children's rights in Northern Ireland and the UN Convention on the Rights of the Child*. Northern Ireland Commissioner for Children and Young People (p. 245). http://www.niccy.org/

Kilpatrick, R. (2003). *Exclusion from school – exclusion from society: Reversing the trend?* Paper presented at QUB Institute of Child Care Research Seminar Series, 12/12/2003.

Kinard, E.M. (1995). Mother and teacher assessment of behaviour problems in abused children. *Journal of the American Academy of Child and Adolescent Psychiatry*, **34**, 1043–1053.

King, M., & Piper, C. (1990). *How the law thinks about children*. Aldershot, Brookfield USA, Hong Kong, Singapore, and Sydney: Gower.

Kipling, R. (1990). *House of desolation*. London: Penguin.

Kipling, R. (1995). *Baa baa, black sheep*. Short story, republished, London: Penguin Group.

Kirby, L.D., & Fraser, M.W. (1997). Risk and resilience in childhood. In L.D. Kirby & M.W. Fraser (Eds.), *Risk and resilience in childhood: An ecological perspective* (pp. 10–33). Washington, DC: NASW Press.

Klaus, M.H., & Kennell, J.H. (1982). *Parent-infant bonding* (2nd ed.). St Louis: The C.V. Mosby Company.

Klosinski, G. (1993). Psychological maltreatment in the context of separation and divorce. *Child Abuse and Neglect*, **17**, 557–563.

Knutson, J.F. (1995). Psychological characteristics of maltreated children: Putative risk factors and consequences. *Annual Review of Psychology*, **46**, 401–431.

Koestner, R., Zuroff, D.C., & Powers, T.A. (1991). The family origins of adolescent self-criticism and its continuity into adulthood. *Journal of Abnormal Psychology*, **100**, 191–197.

Kolko, D.J. (1998). Integration of research and treatment. In J.R. Lutzker (Ed.), *Handbook of child abuse research and treatment: Issues in clinical child psychology*. New York: Plenum.

Kolko, D.J., & Swenson, C.C. (2002). *Assessing and treating physically abused children and their families. A cognitive-behavioural approach*. London: Sage.

Koluchowa, J. (1991). Severely deprived twins after 22 years observation. *Studia Psychologica*, **33**, 23–28.

Kot, S. (1995). *Intensive play therapy with child witnesses of domestic violence*. Unpublished dissertation. Denton, TX: University of North Texas.

Kragthorpe, C. et al. (1997). *Let's prevent abuse: A prevention handbook for people working with young families*. Minneapolis, MN: PACER Center.

Krugman, R.D., & Krugman, M.K. (1984). Emotional abuse in the classroom: The pediatrician's role in diagnosis and treatment. *American Journal of Diseases of Children*, **134**, 284–286.

Kumpulainen, K., Rasanen, E., & Henttonen, I. (1999). Children involved in bullying: Psychological disturbance and the persistence of the involvement. *Child Abuse and Neglect*, **23** (12), 1253–1262.

Kurtz, P.D., Gaudin, J.M., Wodarski, J.S., & Howing, P.T. (1993). Maltreatment and the school-aged child: School performance consequences. *Child Abuse and Neglect*, **17** (5), 581–589.

Laing, R.D. (1976). *The facts of life*. Prolog and Penguin Books.

Larkin, E. (2003). *A longitudinal study of parent-infant bonding*. Unpublished PhD dissertation. The Queen's University of Belfast.

Larkin, E., McSherry, D., & Iwaniec, D. (2005). Room for improvement? Views of key professionals involved in Care Order proceedings. *Child and Family Law Quarterly*, **17** (2), 231–245.

Larrance, D.T., & Twentyman, C.T. (1983). Maternal attributions and child abuse. *Journal of Abnormal Psychology*, **92**, 449–457.

Latimer, W.W. (1998). Adolescent substance abuse: Identifying bio psychosocial risk and protective factors associated with resiliency. In D.L. Wong, *Nursing care of infants and children* (4th ed.). St Louis: Mosby.

Lernihan, U. (2003). *A Study of kinship foster carers in Northern Ireland in relation to: (1) Selected characteristics in the wider context of traditional foster carers; (2) The attitude of kinship foster carers to the involvement of social services in their lives*. PhD thesis, Queen's University Belfast.

Lesnik-Oberstein, M., Koers, A.J., & Cohen, L. (1995). Parental hostility and its sources in psychologically abusive mothers: A test of the three factor theory. *Child Abuse and Neglect*, **19**, 33–49.

Lieberman, A.F. (1991). Attachment theory and infant-parent psychotherapy: Some conceptual, clinical and research issues. In D. Cicchetti & S. Toth (Eds.), *Models and integrations* (Vol. 3, pp. 261–288). Rochester Symposium on Developmental Psychopathology. Hillsdale, NJ: Lawrence Erlbaum.

Lieberman, A.F. (1999). Negative maternal attributions: Effects on toddler's sense of self. *Psychoanalytic Inquiry*, **19**, 737–756.

Little, L. (2004). Victimisation of children with disabilities. In K.A. Kendall-Tackett (Ed.), *Health consequences of abuse in the family* (pp. 95–109).

Little, M., & Mount, K. (1999). *Prevention and early intervention with children in need.* Aldershot: Ashgate.

Lynch, M.A., & Browne, K.D. (1997). The growing awareness of emotional maltreatment. *Child Abuse Review*, **6**, 313–314.

Lyon, J. (1996). Introduction: Adolescents who offend. *Journal of Adolescence*, **19**, 1–4.

Lyons-Ruth, K., Alpen, L., & Repacholi, B. (1993). Disorganised infant attachment classification and maternal psychosocial problems as predictors of hostile-aggressive behaviour in the pre-school classroom. *Child Development*, **64**, 572–585.

MacCarthy, D., & Booth, E. (1970). Parental rejection and stunting of growth. *Journal of Psychosomatic Research*, **14** (3), 259–265.

MacDonald, R., & Marsh, J. (2003). *Missing school: Educational engagement and youth transitions in poor neighbourhoods.* Paper presented at Uncertain Transitions: Youth in Comparative Perspective Symposium, University of Edinburgh, June 2003.

Maclean, M. (2004). Together and apart: Children and parents experiencing separation and divorce. *Foundations* No. 314. York: Joseph Rowntree Foundation.

MacMillan, A.B. (1984). Failure to thrive: An historical perspective. In *Failure to Thrive Symposium* (pp. 4–31). Ontario Centre for the Prevention of Child Abuse. Toronto: Ontario Ministry of Community and Social Services.

Madge, N. (1997). *Abuse and survival: A fact file.* London: The Princes Trust – Action.

Main, M. (1990). Cross-cultural studies of attachment organization: Recent studies, changing methodologies and the concept of conditional strategies. *Human Development*, **33**, 48–61.

Main, M., & George, C. (1985). Responses of abused and disadvantaged toddlers to distress in age mates: A study in the day care setting. *Developmental Psychology*, **21**, 407–412.

Main, M., & Goldwyn, R. (1984). Predicting rejection of her infant from mother's representation of her own experience: Implications for the abused-abusing intergenerational cycle. *Child Abuse and Neglect*, **8**, 203–217.

Main, M., & Solomon, J. (1986). Discovery of an insecure, disorganised/disoriented attachment pattern: Procedures, findings and implications for the classification of behaviour. In M. Yogman & T.B. Brazelton (Eds.), *Effective development in infancy* (pp. 95–124). Norwood, NY: Ablex.

Malinosky-Rummell, R., & Hansen, D.J. (1993). Long-term consequences of childhood physical abuse. *Psychological Bulletin*, **114** (1), 68–79.

Malo, C., Moreau, J., Chamberland, C., Leveille, S., & Roy, C. (2004). Psychological abuse of children and adults: Parental cognition, emotions and behaviours associated with the risk of psychological maltreatment of preschoolers. *Journal of Emotional Abuse*, **4** (2), 1–26.

Manion, I.G., & Wilson, S. (1995). *An examination of the association between histories of maltreatment and adolescent risk behaviours.* Catalogue No. H72-21/139-1995E. Ottawa: National Clearinghouse on Family Violence, Health Canada.

Manly, J.T., Kim, J.E., Rogosch, F.A., & Cicchetti, D. (2001). Dimensions of child maltreatment and children's adjustment: Contributions of developmental timing and subtype. *Development and Psychopathology*, **13**, 759–782.

Marchant, R. (1991). Myths and facts about sexual abuse and children with disabilities. *Child Abuse Review [old series]*, **5** (2), 22–24.

Marchant, R., & Cross, M. (1993). *Places of safety: Institutions, disabled children and abuse.* In ABCD Reader. London: NSPCC.

Marchant, R., & Page, M. (1993). *Bridging the gap: Child protection work with children with multiple disabilities.* London: NSPCC.

Masson, J. (2000). Thinking about contact – a social or a legal problem? *Child and Family Law Quarterly*, **12** (1), 15–30.

Matas, L., Arend, R.A., & Sroufe, L.A. (1978). Continuity of adaptation in the second year: The relationship between quality of attachment and later competence. *Child Development*, **49**, 547–556.

Mayseless, O., Bartholomew, K., Henderson, A., & Trinke, S. (2004). 'I was more her Mom than she was mine': Role reversal in a community sample. *Family Relations*, **53** (1), 78–86.

McGee, R.A., & Wolfe, D.A. (1991). Psychological maltreatment: Toward an operational definition. In D. Cicchetti (Ed.), *Development and psychopathology* (Vol. 3, pp. 3–18). Cambridge: Cambridge University Press.

McGee, R.A., Wolfe, D.A., & Wilson, A. (1997). Multiple maltreatment experiences and adolescent behaviour problems: Adolescents' perspectives. *Development and Psychopathology*, **9**, 131–149.

McGuigan, W.M., & Platt, C.C. (2001). The predictive impact of domestic violence on three types of child maltreatment. *Child Abuse and Neglect*, **25**, 869–883.

McNeal, C., & Amato, P.R. (1998). Parents' marital violence: Long-term consequences for children. *Journal of Family Issues*, **19** (2), 123–139.

McSherry, D., Iwaniec, D., & Larkin, E. (2004). *Counting the costs: The Children (NI) Order 1995, social work and the courts.* Institute of Child Care Research, Queen's University Belfast.

Meezan, W., & O'Keefe, M. (1998). Multi-family group therapy: Impact on family functioning and child behavior. *Families in Society*, **79**, 32–44.

Mercer, R.T. (1990). *Parents at Risk.* New York: Springer.

Messer, D.J. (1999). Communication, bonding, attachment and separation. In D. Messer & F. Jones (Eds.), *Psychology and social care.* London and Philadelphia: Jessica Kingsley.

Miller, S.A. (1988). Parents' beliefs about children's cognitive development. *Child Development*, **59**, 259–285.

Miller, W.R., & Rollnick, S. (1991). *Motivational interviewing: Preparing people to change addictive behaviour.* New York: Guilford Press.

Miller, W.R., & Rollnick, S. (2002). *Motivational interviewing: Preparing people for change* (2nd ed.). New York: Guilford Press.

Milne, R., & Bull, R. (1996). Interviewing children with mild learning disability with the cognitive interview. In N.K. Clark & G.M. Stephenson (Eds.), *Investigative and forensic decision making.* Leicester: British Psychological Society.

Milner, J.S., & Chilamkurti, C. (1991). Physical child abuse perpetrator characteristics: A review of the literature. *Journal of Interpersonal Violence*, **6**, 345–366.

Minuchin, S. (1974). *Families and family therapy.* Cambridge, MA: Harvard University Press.

Minuchin, S., Montalvo, B., Guerney, B.G., Rosman, B.L., & Schumer, F. (1967). *Families of the slums*. New York: Basic Books.

Minuchin, S., Rosman, B.L., & Baker, L. (1978). *Psychosomatic families: Anorexia nervosa in context*. Cambridge, MA: Harvard University Press.

Mitchell, G. (2005). Emotional abuse and neglect: An overview. Part I. *Representing Children*, **17** (3), 189–196.

Mitchell, L.M., & Buchele-Ash, A. (2000). Abuse and neglect of individuals with disabilities: Building protective supports through public policy. *Journal of Disability Policy Studies*, **10** (2), 225–243.

Montague, A. (1978). *Touching: The human significance of the skin* (pp. 77–79). New York: Harper & Row.

Moran, P.B., Vuchinich, S., & Hall, N.K. (2004). Associations between types of maltreatment and substance use during adolescence. *Child Abuse and Neglect*, **28**, 565–574.

Morimoto, Y., & Sharma, A. (2004). Long-term outcomes of verbal aggression: The role of protective factors. *Journal of Emotional Abuse*, **4** (2), 71–99.

Morrison, J.A., Frank, S.J., & Holland, C.C. (1999). Emotional development and disorder in young children in the child welfare system. In J.A. Silver, B.J. Amster, & T. Haecker (Eds.), *Young children and foster care* (pp. 33–67). Baltimore, MD: Paul H. Brookes Publishing Co.

Mullen, P.E., Martin, J.L., Anderson, J.C., Romans, S.E., & Herbison, G.P. (1996). The long-term impact of the physical, emotional, and sexual abuse of children: A community study. *Child Abuse and Neglect*, **20**, 7–21.

Murphy, G. (1994). Understanding challenging behaviour. In E. Emerson (Ed.), *Severe learning disabilities and challenging behaviours: Designing high quality services*. London: Chapman & Hall.

Nabuzoka, D., & Smith, P. (1993). Sociometric status and social behaviour of children with and without learning difficulties. *Journal of Child Psychology and Psychiatry*, **34** (8), 1435–1448.

Nagel, B., & Leiper, R. (1999). A national survey of psychotherapy with people with learning disabilities. *Clinical Psychology Forum*, **129**, 8–14.

National Clearing House on Child Abuse and Neglect Information (2001). *The risk and prevention of maltreatment of children with disabilities*. www.calib.com/nccanch/pubs/prevenres/focus.cfm

Navarre, E.L. (1987). Psychological maltreatment: The core component of child abuse. In M.R. Brassard, R. Germain & S.N. Hart (Eds.), *Psychological maltreatment of children and youth* (pp. 45–58). New York: Pergamon Press.

Newport, P. (1991). *Linking child abuse with disability*. London: Barnardos.

Ney, P., Fung, T., & Wickett, A.R. (1994). The worst combinations of child abuse and neglect. *Child Abuse and Neglect*, **18** (9), 705–714.

Nichols, M.P., & Schwartz, R.C. (1991). *Family therapy: Concepts and methods* (2nd ed.). Needham Heights, MA: Allyn & Bacon.

Novaco, R.W. (1975). *Anger control: The development and evaluation of an experimental treatment*. Lexington, MA: D.C. Heath & Co., Lexington Books.

Novaco, R.W. (1979). The cognitive regulation of anger and stress. In P. Kendall & S. Hollan (Eds.), *Cognitive-behavioural interventions: Theory, research, and procedures*. New York: Academic Press.

Novaco, R.W. (1985). Anger and its therapeutic regulation. In M.A. Chesney & R.H. Rosenman (Eds.), *Anger and hostility in cardiovascular and behavioural disorders*. New York: Hemisphere.

NSPCC (2003). *It doesn't happen to disabled children*. London: NSPCC.

Nugent, O. (1996). Issues of bonding and attachment. *Child Care in Practice*, **2** (4), 24–28.

O'Hagan, K. (1995). Emotional and psychological abuse: Problems of definition. *Child Abuse and Neglect*, **19** (4), 449–461.

Oates, R.K. (1996). *The spectrum of child abuse: Assessment, treatment, and prevention*. New York: Brunner/Mazel.

Oates, R.K., & Yu, J.S. (1971). Children with non-organic failure to thrive: A community problem. *Australian Medical Journal*, **2** (4), 199–203.

O'Connor, T. (2003). Early experiences and psychological development: Conceptual questions, empirical illustrations, and implication for intervention. *Development and Psychopathology*, **15**, 671–690.

O'Donnell, I., & Edgar, K. (1998). Routine victimisation in prisons. *The Howard Journal*, **37** (3), 266–279.

O'Hagan, K.P. (1995). Emotional and psychological abuse: Problems of definition. *Child Abuse and Neglect*, **19** (4), 449–461.

Olds, D.L. *et al.* (1999). Prenatal and infancy home visitation by nurses: Recent findings. *The Future of Children*, **9** (1), 44–65.

Ollendick, T.H., & Cerny, J.A. (1981). *Clinical behaviour therapy with children*. New York: Plenum.

Olweus, D. (1993). *Bullying at school: What we know and what we can do*. Oxford: Blackwell.

Olweus, D. (1999). Norway. In P.K. Smith, Y. Morita, J. Junger-Tas, D. Olweus, R. Catalano, & P. Slee (Eds.), *The nature of school bullying: A cross-national perspective*. London: Routledge.

Oppenheimer, L. (1990). *The self-concept: European perspectives on its development, aspects, and applications*. New York, NY, USA: Springer-Verlag Publishing.

Osofsky, J.D. (1999). The impact of violence on children. *The Future of Children*, **9** (3), 33–49.

Packman, J., & Hall, C. (1999). *From care to accommodation*. London: Stationery Office.

Palm, G.F. (1997). Promoting generative fathering through parent and family education. In A.J. Hawkins & D.C. Dollahite (Eds.), *Generative fathering: Beyond deficit perspectives* (pp. 167–182). Newbury Park, CA: Sage.

Patrick, M., Hobson, R.P., Cesde, D., Howard, R., & Vaughan, B. (1994). Personality disorder and the representation of early social experience. *Development and Psychopathology*, **6**, 375–388.

Patterson, G.R. (1982). *Coercive family process*. Eugene, OR: Castalia.

Patterson, G.R., & Forgarchm, M.S. (1987). *Parents and adolescents living together, Part 1: The basics*. Eugene, OR: Castalia.

Patton, R.G., & Gardner, L.I. (1962). Influence of family environment on growth: The syndrome of maternal deprivation. *Paediatrics*, **30**, 957–962.

Paulson, J.S. (1983). Covert and overt forms of maltreatment in the preschools. *Child Abuse and Neglect*, **7**, 45–54.

Pemmaraju Rao, R. (2001). Children of alcoholics: Caged, silenced songbirds. http://www.vachss.com/help_text/styles/archive-print.php

Percy-Smith, B., & Matthews, H. (2001). Tyrannical spaces: Young people, bullying and urban neighbourhoods. *Local Environment*, **6** (1), 49–63.

Perry, B.D. (2001a). *Bonding and attachment in maltreated children: Consequences of emotional neglect in childhood*. Child Trauma Academy, Parent and Caregiver Education Series, **1** (4). http://www.childtrauma.org/CTAMATERIALS/Attach_ca.asp

Perry, B.D. (2001b). The neurodevelopmental impact of violence in childhood. In D. Schetky & E. Benedek (Eds.), *Textbook of child and adolescent forensic psychiatry.* Washington, DC: American Psychiatric Press.

Perry, B.D. (2004). The impact of abuse and neglect on the development brain. *Retrieved,* **31** (3), 79–100 from http://teacher.scholastic.com/professional/bruceperry/abuseneglect.htm

Perry, M.A., & Doran, L.D. (1983). Developmental and behavioural characteristics of the physically abused child. *Journal of Clinical Child Psychology,* **12**, 32–34.

Powell, G.F., Brasel, J.A., & Blizzard, R.M. (1967). Emotional deprivation and growth retardation simulating idiopathic hypopituitarism: I. Clinical evaluation of the syndrome. *New England Journal of Medicine,* **276** (23), 1271–1278.

Prochaska, J., & DiClemente, C. (1982). Transtheoretical therapy: Toward a more integrative model of change. *Psychotherapy: Theory, Research, and Practice,* **19**, 176–288.

Prugh, D., & Harlow, R. (1962). *Marked deprivation in infants and young children in deprivation of maternal care.* Public Health Papers No. 14. Geneva: World Health Organisation.

Quinton, D., Pickles, A., Maughan, B., & Rutter, M. (1993). Partners, peers, and pathways: Assortative pairing and continuities in conduct disorder. *Development and Psychopathology,* **5** (4), 760–783.

Ranney, E.C., & Cottone, R.R. (1991). Emotional abuse in the family: The need for awareness and treatment. *Journal of Mental Health Counselling,* **13**, 435–448.

Ray, D., Bratton, S., Rhine, T., & Jones, L. (2001). The effectiveness of play therapy: Responding to the critics. *International Journal of Play Therapy,* **10** (1), 85–108.

Reid, J.B. (1986). Social interactional patterns in families of abused and non-abused children. In C. Lahn-Waxler, E.M. Cummings, & R. Lanotte (Eds.), *Altruism and aggression: Biological and social origins.* Cambridge: Cambridge University Press.

Reid, W.J., & Crisafulli, A. (1990). Marital discord and child behavior problems: A meta-analysis. *Journal of Abnormal Child Psychology,* **18**, 105–117.

Rich, D.J., Gingersich, K.J., & Rosen, I.A. (1997). Childhood emotional abuse and associated psychopathology in college students. *Journal of College Student Psychotherapy,* **11**, 13–28.

Robin, A.L., Kent, R.N., O'Leary, K.D., Foster, S., & Prinz, R.J. (1977). An approach to teaching parents and adolescents problem-solving skills: A preliminary report. *Behaviour Therapy,* **8**, 639–643.

Rodgers, B., & Pryor, J. (1998). Divorce and separation: The outcomes for children. *Foundations* No. 6108. York: Joseph Rowntree Foundation.

Rodgers, C.S., Lang, A.J., Laffaye, C., Satz, L.E., Dresselhaus, T.R., & Stein, M.B. (2004). The impact of individual forms of childhood maltreatment on health behaviour. *Child Abuse and Neglect,* **28**, 575–586.

Rogow, S. (2002). Silent victims: Emotional abuse and neglect of children with disabilities. *International Journal of Special Education,* **17**, 11–14.

Rohner, R.P. (1986). *The warmth dimension: Foundations of parental acceptance – rejection theory.* Beverly Hill, CA: Sage.

Rohner, R.P., & Brothers, S.A. (1999). Perceived parental rejection, psychological maladjustment and borderline personality disorder. *Journal of Emotional Abuse,* **1** (4), 81–95.

Rollnick, S., & Miller, W.R. (1995). What is motivational interviewing. *Behavioural and Cognitive Psychotherapy,* **23**, 325–334.

Rorty, M., Yager, J., & Rossotto, M.A. (1994). Childhood sexual, physical, and psychological abuse in bulimia nervosa. *American Journal of Psychiatry*, **151**, 1122–1126.

Runyon, M.K., Deblinger, E., Ryan, E.E., & Thakkar-Kolar, R. (2004). An overview of child physical abuse: Developing an integrated parent-child cognitive-behavioral treatment approach. *Trauma, Violence, and Abuse*, **5** (1), 65–85.

Rutter, M. (1979). Maternal deprivation, 1972–78: New findings, new concepts, new approaches. *Child Development*, **50**, 283–305.

Rutter, M. (1985). Resilience in the face of adversity: Protective factors and resistance to psychiatric disorder. *British Journal of Psychiatry*, **147**, 598–611.

Rutter, M. (1986). The developmental psychopathology of depression: Issues and perspectives. In M. Rutter, C.E. Izard, & P.B. Read (Eds.), *Depression in young people: Developmental and clinical perspectives*. New York: Guilford Press.

Rutter, M. (1987). Parental mental disorder as a psychiatric risk factor. In R. Hales & A. Frances (Eds.), *American Psychiatric Association Annual Review* (Vol. 6). New York: Academic Press.

Rutter, M. (1990a). Psychological resilience and protective mechanisms. In J. Rolf *et al.*, *Risk and protective factors in the development of psychopathology*. New York: Cambridge University Press.

Rutter, M. (1990b). Psychosocial resilience and protective mechanisms. *American Orthopsychiatric Association*, **6** (4), 316–331.

Rutter, M. (1995a). Psychosocial adversity: Risk, resilience and recovery. *South African Journal of Child and Adolescent Psychiatry*, **7** (2), 75–88.

Rutter, M. (1995b). Clinical implications of attachment concepts: Retrospect and prospect. *Journal of Child Psychology and Psychiatry*, **36** (4), 549–571.

Rutter, M. (1999). Resilience concepts and findings: Implications for family therapy. *Journal for Family Therapy*, **21**, 119–144.

Rutter, M. (2000). Resilience reconsidered: Conceptual considerations, empirical findings, and policy implications. In J.T. Shonkoff & S.J. Meisels (Eds.), *Handbook of early childhood intervention* (2nd ed., pp. 651–682). New York: Cambridge University Press.

Rutter, M. (2002). Resilience reconsidered: Conceptual considerations, empirical findings, and policy implications. In J.P. Shonkoff & S.J. Meisels, *Handbook of early childhood intervention* (2nd ed.). Cambridge: Cambridge University Press.

Rutter, M., & the English and Romanian Adoptees Study Team (1998). Developmental catch-up, and deficit following adoption after severe global previation. *Journal of Child Psychology and Psychiatry*, **39** (4), 465–476.

Ryan, V., Wilson, K., & Fisher, T. (1995). Developing partnerships in therapeutic work with children. *Journal of Social Work Practice*, **9** (2), 131–140.

Rycus, J.S., & Hughes, R.C. (1998). *Field guide to child welfare: Vol. 3. Child development and child welfare*. Washington, DC: Child Welfare League of America.

Santelli, B., Turnbull, A., Marquis, J., & Lerner, E. (1997). Parent-to-parent programs: A resource for parents and professionals. *Journal of Early Intervention*, **21** (1), 73–83.

Saunders, M., Mazzucchelli, T.G., & Studman, L. (2004). Stepping Stones Triple P: The theoretical basis and development of an evidence-based positive parenting program for families with a child with disability. *Journal of Intellectual and Developmental Disability*, **29**, 265–283.

Schaffer, H.R. (1977). *Studies in mother-infant interaction*. London: Academic Press.

Schinke, S.P., Schilling, R.F., Kirham, M.A., Gilschrist, L.D., Barth, R.P., & Blythe, B.J. (1986). Stress management skills for parents. *Journal of Child and Adolescent Psychotherapy*, **3**, 293–298.

Schmidt Neven, R. (1996). *Emotional milestones from birth to adulthood: A psychodynamic approach*. London: Jessica Kingsley Publishers.

Schorr, M. (2002). Belittling, shaming child causes lasting damage. http://www.vachss.com/help/archive/belittling.html

Scott, S. (2002). Parent training programmes. In M. Rutter & E. Taylor (Eds.), *Child and adolescent psychiatry* (4th ed.). Oxford: Blackwell.

Seagull, E.A.W., & Scheurer, S.L. (1986). Neglected and abused children of mentally retarded parents. *Child Abuse and Neglect*, **10**, 493–500.

Sedlak, A.J. (1997). Risk factors for the occurrence of child abuse and neglect. *Journal of Aggression, Maltreatment and Trauma*, **1**, 149–187.

Serketich, W.J., & Dumas, J.E. (1996). The effectiveness of behavioural parent training to modify anti-social behaviour in children: A meta-analysis. *Behaviour Therapy*, **27**, 171–186.

Sheehan, R. (2001). *Magistrate's decision-making in child protection cases*. London: Ashgate.

Sheldon, B. (1995). *Cognitive behavioural therapy, research, practice and philosophy*. London: Routledge.

Shengold, L. (1989). *Soul murder: The effects of childhood abuse and deprivation*. London: Yale University Press.

Shields, A., Cicchetti, D., & Ryan, R. (1994). The development of emotional and behavioural self regulation and social competence among maltreated school-age children. *Development and Psychopathology*, **6**, 57–75.

Shonkoff, J.P., & Phillips, D.A. (2000). *From neurons to neighborhoods: The science of early childhood development*. Washington, DC: National Academy Press.

Shumba, A. (2002). The nature, extent and effects of emotional abuse on primary school pupils by teachers in Zimbabwe. *Child Abuse and Neglect*, **26** (8), 783–791.

Shure, M.B., & Spivack, G. (1971). *Solving interpersonal problems: A program for four year old nursery school children*. Training script. Philadelphia, PA: Hahnemann Medical College Department of Mental Health Science.

Silver, H.K., & Finkelstein, M. (1967). Deprivation-dwarfism. *Journal of Pediatrics*, **70** (3), 317–324.

Sinclair, I., & Gibbs, I. (1998). *Children's homes: A study in diversity*. Chichester: John Wiley & Sons.

Skuse, D. (1984). Extreme deprivation in childhood: Theoretical issues and a comparative review. *Journal of Child Psychology and Psychiatry*, **25**, 543–572.

Skuse, D., Albanese, A., Stanhope, R., Gilmore, J., & Voss, L. (1996). A new stress-related syndrome of growth failure and hyperphagia in children associated with reversibility of growth-hormone insufficiency. *Lancet*, **348** (9024), 353–358.

Skuse, D., Gilmour, J., Tian, C.S., & Hindmarsh, P. (1994b). Psychosocial assessment of children with short stature: A preliminary report. *Acta Paediatrica Supplement*, **406**, 11–16.

Skuse, D., Pickles, A., Wolke, D., & Reilly, S. (1994a). Postnatal growth and mental development: Evidence for a Sensitive Period. *Journal of Child Psychology and Psychiatry*, **35** (3), 521–546.

Skuse, D., Wolke, D., & Reilly, S. (1992). Failure to thrive: Clinical and developmental aspects. In H. Remschmidt & M.H. Schmidt (Eds.), *Developmental psychopathology*. Lewiston, NY: Hogrefe & Huber.

Skuse, D.H. (1989). Emotional abuse and neglect. *British Medical Journal*, **298**, 1692–1695.

Sloper, P., & Turner, S. (1993). Risk and resistance factors in the adaptation of parents of children with severe physical disability. *Journal of Child Psychology and Psychiatry*, **34**, 167–188.

Sluckin, A. (2000). 'Selective Mutism'. In James Law & Alison Parkinson, with Rashmin Pamhne (Eds.), *Communication difficulty in childhood*. Oxford: Ratcliffe Medical Press.

Sluckin, W., Herbert, M., & Sluckin, A. (1983). *Maternal bonding*. Oxford: Blackwell.

Smith, C., & Carlson, B. (1997). Stress, coping and resilience in children and youth. *Social Science Review*, **71**, 231–256.

Smith, P.K. (1999). England and Wales. In P.K. Smith, Y. Morita, J. Junger-Tas, D. Olweus, R. Catalano, & P. Slee (Eds.), *The nature of school bullying: A cross-national perspective*. London: Routledge.

Smith, P.K., Morita, Y., Junger-Tas, J., Olweus, D., Catalano, R., & Slee, P. (Eds.) (1999). *The nature of school bullying: A cross-national perspective*. London: Routledge.

Smith, P.K., & Sharp, S. (Eds.) (1994). *School bullying: Insights and perspectives*. London: Routledge.

Sobsey, D. (1994). *Violence and abuse in the lives of people with disabilities: The end of silent acceptance?* Baltimore, MD: London: Paul H. Brookes Publishing Co.

Sobsey, D. (2002). Exceptionality, education and maltreatment. *Exceptionality*, **10**, 29–46.

Sobsey, D., Randall, W., & Parrila, R.K. (1997). Gender differences in abused children with and without disabilities. *Child Abuse and Neglect*, **21**, 707–719.

Solomon, C.R., & Serres, F. (1999). Effects of parental verbal aggression on children's self-esteem and school marks. *Child Abuse and Neglect*, **23**, 339–351.

Somer, E., & Braunstein, A. (1999). Are children exposed to interparental violence being psychologically maltreated? *Aggression and Violent Behaviour*, **4** (4), 449–456.

Spillane-Grieco, E. (2000). From parent verbal abuse to teenage physical aggression? *Child and Adolescents Social Work Journal*, **17**, 411–430.

Spinner, M.R., & Siegel, L. (1987). Non-organic failure to thrive. *Journal of Preventive Psychiatry*, **3** (3), 279–297.

Spitz, R.A. (1945). Hospitalism: An inquiry into the genesis of psychiatric conditions in early childhood. *Psychoanalytic Study of the Child*, **1**, 53–74.

Spitz, R.A. (1946). Hospitalism: A follow-up report. *Psychoanalytical Study of the Child*, **2**, 113–117.

Springer, J.F., Phillips, J., Phillips, L., Cannady, L., & Kerst-Harris, E. (1992). CODA: A creative therapy program for children in families affected by abuse of alcohol or other drugs. *Journal of Community Psychology*, **3**, 55–74.

Sroufe, L.A. (1979). The coherence of individual development: Early care, attachment, and subsequent developmental issues. *American Psychologist*, **34**, 834–841.

Sroufe, L.A. (1983). Infant caregiver attachment and patterns of adaptation in preschool: The roots of maladaption and competence. In M. Perlmutter (Ed.), *Minnesota symposium on child psychology. Vol. 16. Development and policy concerning children with special needs* (pp. 41–83). Hillsdale, New York: Lawrence Erlbaum Associates.

Steinberg, M.A., Hylton, J.R., & Wheeler C.E. (1998). *Responding to maltreatment of children with disabilities: A trainer's guide.* Washington, DC: US Department of Health and Human Services, National Center on Child Abuse and Neglect.

Steinhauer, P.D. (1983). Assessing for parenting capacity. *American Journal of Orthopsychiatry*, **53**, 468–481.

Stern, S.B., & Azar, S.T. (1998). Integrating cognitive strategies into behavioural treatment for abusive parents and families with aggressive adolescents. *Clinical Child Psychology and Psychiatry*, **3**, 387–403.

Sternberg, K.J. *et al.* (1993). Effects of domestic violence on children's behavior problems and depression. *Developmental Psychology*, **29** (1), 44–52.

Stevenson, J. (1999). The treatment of the long-term sequelae of child abuse. *Journal of Child Psychology and Psychiatry Allied Disciplines*, **40**, 89–111.

Straus, M.A., & Field, C.J. (2003). Psychological aggression by American parents: National data on prevalence, chronicity, and severity. *Journal of Marriage and Family*, **65**, 795–808.

Suligman, M.E.P. (1975). *Helplessness.* San Francisco: Freeman.

Sullivan, P.M., & Knutson, J.F. (1998). The association between child maltreatment and disabilities in a hospital-based epidemiological study. *Child Abuse and Neglect*, **22**, 271–288.

Sullivan, P.M., & Knutson, J.F. (2000). Maltreatment and disabilities: A population-based epidemiological study. *Child Abuse and Neglect*, **24**, 1257–1274.

Sullivan, P.M., Knutson, J.F., Scanlan, J.M., & Cork, P.M. (1997). Maltreatment of children with disabilities: Family risk factors and prevention implications. *Journal of Child Centred Practice*, **4**, 33–46.

Suomi, S.J. (1995). Influence of attachment theory on ethological studies of bio-behavioural development in non-human primates. In S. Goldberg, R. Muir, & J. Kerr (Eds.), *Attachment theory: Historical, developmental, and clinical significance* (pp. 185–202). Hillsdale, NJ: Analytic Press.

Sutton, C. (1999). *Helping families with troubled children: A preventive approach.* Chichester: John Wiley & Sons.

Sutton, C. (2000). *Child and adolescent behaviour problems: A multidisciplinary approach to assessment and intervention.* Leicester: The British Psychological Society.

Swearer, S.M., & Doll, B. (2001). Bullying in schools: An ecological framework. *Journal of Emotional Abuse*, **2** (2/3), 7–23.

Talbot, N.B., Sobel, E.H., Burke, B.S., Lindeman, E., & Kaufman, S.B. (1947). Dwarfism in healthy children: Its possible relation to emotional, nutritional and endocrine disturbances. *New England Journal of Medicine*, **263**, 783–793.

Taylor, K.D., & Beauchamp, C. (1988). Hospital-based primary prevention strategy in child abuse: A multi-level needs assessment. *Child Abuse and Neglect*, **12** (3), 343–354.

Thoburn, J., Wilding, J., & Watson, J. (2000). *Family support in cases of emotional maltreatment and neglect.* London: Stationery Office.

Thomas, A., & Chess, S. (1977). *Temperament and development.* New York: Brunner/Mazel.

Thomas, A., Chess, S., & Birch, H.G. (1970). The origin of personality. *Scientific American*, **223**, 102–109.

Thompson, R.A. (1995). *Preventing child maltreatment through social support.* Thousand Oaks, CA: Sage.

Thompson, R.A. (1999). Early attachment and later development. In J. Cassidy & P.R. Shaver (Eds.), *Handbook of attachment: Theory, research, and clinical applications* (pp. 265–286). New York: Guilford Press.

Thornberry, R.P., Ireland, T.O., & Smith, C.A. (2001). The importance of timing: The varying impact of childhood and adolescent maltreatment on multiple problem outcomes. *Development and Psychopathology*, **13**, 957–979.

Tomison, A.M. (1996a). Child maltreatment and disability. National Child Protection Clearing House Issues Paper no. 7, AIFS, Melbourne.

Tomison, A.M. (1996b). Child maltreatment and substance abuse. Discussion Paper 2. National Child Protection Clearinghouse. http://www.aifs.org.au/nch/discussion2.html

Tomison, A.M. (2000). Exploring family violence: Links between child maltreatment and domestic violence. *Issues in Child Abuse Prevention, National Child Protection Clearinghouse Issues Paper*, **13**. Australian Institute of Family Studies.

Tomison, A.M., & Tucci, J. (1997). Emotional abuse: The hidden form of maltreatment. *Issues in Child Abuse Prevention, No. 8*. Melbourne: National Child Protection Clearinghouse. http://www.aifs.org.au/nch/issues8.html

Toth, S.L., Manly, J.T., & Cicchetti, D. (1992). Child maltreatment and vulnerability to depression. *Development and Psychopathology*, **4**, 97–112.

Tricket, P.K., & Susman, E.J. (1988). Parental perceptions of child-rearing practices in physically abusive and non-abusive families. *Development Psychology*, **24**, 270–276.

Trinder, L., Beek, M., & Connolly, J. (2002). Children's and parents' experience of contact after divorce. *Foundations* No. 092. York: Joseph Rowntree Foundation.

Trocme, N.M., MacLaurin, B.J., Fallon, B.A., Dakiuk, J.F., Tourigny, M., & Billingsley, D.A. (2001). Canadian Incidence Study of Reported Child Abuse and Neglect: Methodology. *Canadian Journal of Public Health*, **92** (4), 259–263.

Trowell, J. (1983). Emotional abuse of children. *Health Visitor*, **56** (7), 252–255.

Troy, M., & Sroufe, L.A. (1987). Victimisation among pre-schoolers: Role of attachment relationship history. *Journal of the American Academy of Child and Adolescent Psychiatry*, **26**, 166–172.

US Department of Health and Human Services. (1999). *Blending perspectives and building common ground: A report to Congress on substance abuse and child protection*. Washington, DC: US Government Printing Office.

Vachss, A. (1994, August 28). You carry the cure in your own heart. *Parade Magazine*.

Van Bakel, H., & Riksen-Walraven, M. (2002). Parenting and development of one-year-olds: Links with parental, contextual and child characteristics. *Child Development*, **73** (1), 256–273.

Van Ijzendoorn, M.H., Juffer, F., & Duyvesteyn, M.G.C. (1995). Breaking the inter-generational cycle of insecure attachment: A review of the effects of attachment-based interventions on maternal sensitivity and infant security. *Journal of Child Psychology and Allied Disciplines*, **36**, 225–248.

Varia, R., Abidin, R.R., & Dass, P. (1996). Perceptions of abuse: Effects on adult psychological and social adjustment. *Child Abuse and Neglect*, **20**, 511–526.

Varnham, S. (2001). Conduct unbecoming: The dilemma of a school's responsibility in respect of teacher misconduct towards pupils. *Education and the Law*, **13** (2), 109–125.

Verdugo, M.A., Bermejo, B.G., & Fuertes, J. (1995). The maltreatment of intellectually handicapped children and adolescents. *Child Abuse and Neglect*, **19**, 205–215.

Vetere, A. (1993). Using family therapy in services for people with learning disabilities. In J. Carpenter & A. Treacher (Eds.), *Using family therapy in the 90s*. Oxford: Blackwell.

Vig, S., & Kaminer, R. (2002). Maltreatment and developmental disabilities in children. *Journal of Maltreatment and Developmental Disabilities in Children*, **14**, 371–386.

Von Bertalanffy, L. 1968. *General system theory: Foundations, developments, applications.* New York: Braziller.

Waitman, A., & Conboy-Hill, S. (1992). *Psychotherapy and mental handicap.* London: Sage.

Walker, C., Bonner, B., & Kaufman, K. (1988). *The physically and sexually abused child: Evaluation and treatment.* New York: Pergamon Press.

Walsh, N. (1982). *Normal family process.* New York: Guilford Press.

Webster-Stratton, C. (1991). Annotation: Strategies for helping families with conduct disordered children. *Journal of Child Psychology and Psychiatry*, **32**, 1047–1062.

Webster-Stratton, C. (1998). Parent-training with low-income families: Promoting parental engagement through a collaborative approach. In J.R. Lutzker (Ed.), *Handbook of child abuse research and treatment.* New York: Plenum.

Webster-Stratton, C., & Herbert, M. (1994). *Troubled families: Problem children.* Chichester: John Wiley & Sons.

Westcott, H., & Clement, M. (1992). *NSPCC experience of child abuse in residential care and educational placements: Results of a survey,* London: NSPCC.

Westcott, H.L. (1993). *Abuse of children and adults with disabilities.* London: NSPCC.

Westcott, H.L., & Jones, D.P.H. (1999). The abuse of disabled children. *Journal of Child Psychology and Psychiatry*, **40** (4), 497–506.

White, J., & Allers, C.T. (1994). Play therapy with abused children: A review of the literature. *Journal of Counselling and Development*, **72** (4), 390.

Whiting, L. (1976). Defining emotional neglect. *Children Today*, **5**, 2–5.

Whitney, I., Smith, P.K., & Thompson, D. (1994). Bullying and children with special education needs. In P.K. Smith & S. Sharp (Eds.), *School bullying: Insights and perspectives.* London: Routledge.

Whitten, C.F. (1976). Failure to thrive. Can treatment be effectively investigated? *American Journal of Diseases of Children*, **130** (1), 15.

Widdowson, E.M. (1951). Mental contentment and physical growth. *Lancet*, **260**, 1316–1318.

Widom, C.S. (1999a). Post-traumatic stress disorder in abused and neglected children grown up. *American Journal of Psychiatry*, **156**, 1223–1229.

Widom, C.S. (1999b). Childhood victimization and the development of personality disorders: Commentary. *Archives of General Psychiatry*, **56** (7).

Widom, C.S., & White, H.R (1997). Problem behaviours in abused and neglected children grown up: Prevalence and co-occurrence of substance abuse, crime and violence. *Criminal Behaviour and Mental Health*, **7**, 287–310.

Williams, K., Chambers, M., Logan, S., & Robinson, D. (1996). Association of common health symptoms with bullying in primary school children. *British Medical Journal*, **313**, 17–19.

Willner, P. (2005). The effectiveness of psychotherapeutic interventions for people with learning disabilities: A critical overview. *Journal of Intellectual Disability Research*, **49** (1), 73–85.

Wolcott, D. (1997). *Children with disabilities: Risk factors for maltreatment.* A dissertation presented to the College of Education, University of Denver, Colorado, USA.

Wolfe, D. (1987). *Child abuse: Implications for child development and psychopathology.* Newbury Park, CA: Sage.

Wolfe, D.A. (1988). Child abuse and neglect. In E.J. Mash & L.G. Terdal (Eds.), *Behavioural assessment of childhood disorders* (pp. 627–669). New York: Guilford Press.

Wolfe, D.A. (1991). *Preventing physical and emotional abuse of children*. New York: Guilford Press.

Wolfe, D.A., Edwards, B., Manion, I., & Koverola, C. (1988). Early intervention for parents at risk for child abuse and neglect: A preliminary report. *Journal of Consulting and Clinical Psychology, 56,* 40–47.

Wolfe, D.A., & Wekerle, C. (1993). Treatment strategies for child physical abuse and neglect – a critical progress report. *Clinical Psychology Review,* **13** (6), 473–500.

Wolock, I., & Magura, S. (1996). Parental substance abuse as a predictor of child maltreatment re-reports. *Child Abuse and Neglect,* **20** (12), 1183–1193.

World Health Organisation (1999). *Report of the consultation on child abuse prevention.* WHO, Geneva, 29–31 March 1999, Geneva: WHO.

Youngblade, L.M., & Belsky, J. (1990), Social and emotional consequences of child maltreatment. In R.T. Ammerman & M. Hersen (Eds.), *Children at risk: An evaluation of factors contributing to child abuse and neglect*. New York: Plenum.

INDEX